*automotive
air conditioning*

automotive air conditioning

Boyce H. Dwiggins

DELMAR PUBLISHERS
COPYRIGHT ©1978
BY LITTON EDUCATIONAL PUBLISHING, INC.

15 14 13 12 11 10 9 8 7 6 5 4

LIBRARY OF CONGRESS CATALOG CARD NUMBER: 76-14093

ISBN 0-8273-1007-2

Printed in the United States of America
Published Simultaneously in Canada by
Delmar Publishers, A Division of
Van Nostrand Reinhold, Ltd.

DELMAR PUBLISHERS • ALBANY, NEW YORK 12205

A DIVISION OF LITTON EDUCATIONAL PUBLISHING, INC.

PREFACE

In 1967 when the first edition of *Automotive Air Conditioning* was published, the air-conditioning industry predicted that "In the next few years, one-half of all domestic cars will be equipped with factory-installed air conditioners." Today, the industry prediction is eighty percent. The growth in popularity of mobile air conditioning far exceeds all early predictions.

The information given in this text is a balanced introduction to automotive air conditioning. The student will develop a basic understanding of the theory, diagnostic practices, and service procedures essential to air conditioning. At the same time, the student will develop habits of sound practice and good judgment in the performance of all air-conditioning procedures. The instructional units can be regarded as entry level for those who apply immediately the basic skills developed in the class and shop. The units are preparatory for those who plan continued study in advanced phases of refrigeration and air conditioning, including systems not related to automotive applications.

The text contains three basic sections. Section 1 is arranged in the natural order of dependence of one principle, law, or set of conditions upon another. The material within a unit follows an organized pattern which helps the student to see relationships. Section 2 guides the student in the performance of system diagnostic procedures. Section 3 presents step-by-step instructions for the application of specific service procedures. It is suggested that each topic in this section be considered as an assignment that is to be carried out by the student.

A Glossary is provided to aid in identifying component parts and phrases relevant to air conditioning.

An Instructor's Guide provides solutions to all of the objective questions and problems. Suggested answers are given wherever there may be variations in the responses given by the students. Lesson plans are provided for each unit of the text.

Boyce H Dwiggins organized one of the first courses in vocational education for Automotive Air Conditioning. This course has run continuously since 1965. He was in charge of automotive classes as a county-level administrator and was a consultant for the writing of educational specifications for a five-shop automotive complex in an area vocational center.

The author has served as an examiner, administering the "Automotive Excellence" test for the International Garage Owner's Association for the certification of auto mechanics. He was invited to serve with a committee of the National Institute for Automotive Service Excellence to write the certification test for automotive air conditioning.

Mr. Dwiggins holds patents on teaching devices and copyrights on teaching material in the field of refrigeration. He has conducted workshops for air-conditioning and automotive teachers throughout the eastern United States.

Mr. Dwiggins was founder and president of Instructional Motivation Systems, Inc., and is now in charge of the Air-conditioning, Refrigeration, Heating, and

Ventilation Learning Systems Department of Technovate, Inc. Technovate is engaged in the development and manufacture of learning systems used in public, federal, and private schools throughout the free world.

Automotive Air Conditioning is one of a series of texts developed for automotive instruction. Other texts in the series are:

Automotive Oscilloscope
Automotive Steering Systems
Automotive Service and Repair Tools
Automotive Starting and Charging Systems
Automotive Science
Interpreting Automotive Systems
Practical Problems in Mathematics for Automotive Technicians

A current catalog including prices of all Delmar educational publications is available upon request. Please write to:

Catalog Department
Delmar Publishers
50 Wolf Road
Albany, New York 12205

Or call Toll Free: (800) 354-9815

CONTENTS

SECTION 3 SERVICE PROCEDURES

SECTION 1
BASIC THEORY

UNIT 1 INTRODUCTION

Refrigeration and air conditioning are not discoveries of the twentieth century. Simple forms of refrigeration and air conditioning were in use twelve thousand years ago. Although these early systems were crude by today's standards, they served the same purpose as modern units.

Many aspects of modern life were made possible only after sophisticated air-conditioning systems were developed. Numerous vital components associated with the United States space program could not have been manufactured without the use of air conditioning. For example, many precision mechanical and electrical parts must be manufactured and assembled under very strict tolerances. These tolerances require the control of temperature and humidity within a range of a few degrees.

Fig. 1-1 Electronic components assembled in temperature/humidity controlled space

Automotive air conditioning was available in 1940, but it did not become popular until 1960. Since that time, interest in air conditioning has increased yearly. Air conditioning is now one of the most popular selections in the entire list of automotive accessories.

In 1962, slightly more than eleven percent of all cars sold were equipped with air conditioners. This percentage accounted for 756,781 units, including both factory-installed systems and those added after the purchase of the automobile. Just five years later, in 1967, the total number of installed air-conditioning units rose to 3,546,255. At the present time, nearly eighty percent of all automobiles sold are equipped with air-conditioning units. It is expected that the usage of these units will remain at approximately eighty percent. This means that eighty cars out of every one hundred cars on the road will be equipped with factory-installed or add-on air conditioning. When air conditioning was first used in automobiles, it was considered a luxury. Its usefulness soon made air conditioning a necessity.

At this point, the definition of air conditioning should be reviewed before tracing its history and its application to the automobile. Air conditioning is the process by which air is cooled, cleaned, and circulated. In addition, the quantity and quality of the conditioned air are controlled. This means that the temperature, humidity, and volume of air are controlled in any given situation. Under ideal conditions, air conditioning can be expected to accomplish all of these tasks at the same time. The student should recognize that the air-conditioning process includes the process of refrigeration (cooling by removing heat).

HISTORICAL DEVELOPMENT OF AIR CONDITIONING

Refrigeration, as we know it today, is less than seventy-five years old. Some of its principles, however, were known as long as ten thousand years before Christ.

The Egyptians developed a method for removing the heat from the Pharaoh's palace. The walls of the palace were constructed of huge stone blocks, each weighing over a thousand tons. Every night, three thousand slaves dismantled the walls and moved the stones to the Sahara Desert. Since the temperature in the desert is cool during the night, the stones gave up the heat they had absorbed during the day. Before daybreak the slaves moved the stones back to the palace site and reassembled the walls, figure 1-2. As a result of this crude form of refrigeration, it is thought that the Pharaoh enjoyed temperatures of about 80°F inside the palace while the temperature outside soared to about 130°F. Three thousand men worked all night to do a job that modern refrigeration easily handles. Although the work effort is less today, the same principle of refrigeration is applied to present systems as

Fig. 1-2. Moving stones of Pharaoh's palace back in place.

was applied in the Pharaoh's time. That is, heat is removed from one space and is transferred to another space.

Shortly after the beginning of the twentieth century, T.C. Northcott of Luray, Virginia became the first man known to history to have a home with central heating and air conditioning. A heating and ventilating engineer, Northcott built his house on a hill above the famous Caverns of Luray. Because of his work, he knew that air filtered through limestone was free of dust and pollen. This fact was important because both Northcott and his family suffered from hay fever.

Some distance behind his house he drilled a five-foot shaft through the ceiling of the cavern. He installed a forty-two-inch fan in the shaft to pull eight thousand cubic feet of air per minute through the shaft. He then constructed a shed over the shaft and from this built a duct system to the house. The duct was divided into two chambers, one above the other. The upper chamber carried air from the cavern and was heated by the sun. This chamber provided air to warm the house on cool days. The lower chamber carried cool air from the cavern; this air was used to cool the house on warm days.

The humidity (moisture content) of the air from the cavern was controlled in a chamber in Northcott's basement where air from both ducts was mixed. The warmer air contained a greater amount of moisture than the cooler air. Northcott was able to direct conditioned air from the mixing chamber of the air system to any or all of the rooms in his house through a network of smaller ducts. In the winter, the air was heated by steam coils located in the base of each of the branch ducts.

Each year more than 350,000 people visit the Caverns of Luray where the temperature is a constant 54°F (12.22°C) and the air is always free of dust and pollen. Visitors are impressed by the fact that in this residence, the ingenuity of one inventor provided central heating and air conditioning long before these conveniences were available on a large scale.

Domestic Refrigeration

Domestic refrigeration systems appeared first in 1910, even though ice has been made artificially since 1820. In 1896, the Sears, Roebuck and Company catalog offered several *refrigerators* for sale, figure 1-3, page 4. The refrigeration, however, was provided by ice. The "ice box" shown held twenty-five pounds of ice and was useful only for the short-term storage of foods. Incidentally, the selling price for this refrigerator was $5.65.

The first manually operated refrigerator was produced by J.L. Larsen in 1913. The Kelvinator Company produced the first automatic refrigerator in 1918. The acceptance of this new refrigerator was slow. By 1920 only about two hundred units had been sold.

In 1926, the first hermetic (sealed) refrigerator was introduced by General Electric. The following year Electrolux introduced an automatic absorption unit. A four-cubic foot refrigerator was introduced by Sears, Roebuck and Company in 1931. The refrigerator cabinet, figure 1-4, page 5, and the refrigeration unit were shipped separately and required assembly. The cost of this refrigerator was $137.50. In terms of the price per square foot, the 1931 refrigerator is comparable to the modern refrigerator.

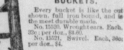

Fig. 1-3 Early "refrigerator" was actually an icebox (1896)

Fig. 1-4 Early refrigerator (1931)

Air Conditioning

The first automotive air-conditioning unit appeared on the market in 1927. True air conditioning was not to appear in cars for another thirteen years. However, air conditioning was advertised as an option in some cars in 1927. At this time, air conditioning meant only that the car could be equipped with a heater, a ventilation system, and a means of filtering the air.

In 1940, Packard offered the first method of cooling a car by means of refrigeration. Actually, Packard's first units were commercial air conditioners adapted for automotive use. Two years earlier a few passenger buses had been air conditioned by the same method.

Accurate records were not kept in the early days of automotive air conditioning. However, it is known that before World War II there were between 3,000 and 4,000 units installed in Packards. Defense priorities for materials and manufacturing prevented the improvement of automotive air conditioning until the early 1950s. At that time, the demand for air-conditioned vehicles began in the Southwest.

Many large firms were able to report increased sales after air conditioning was installed in the cars of their salespeople. Many commercial vehicles are now air conditioned, including buses and taxicabs. Truckers realize larger profits because drivers who have air-conditioned cabs average more mileage than those who do not.

In 1967, all of the state police cars on the Florida Turnpike were air conditioned. Since then, law enforcement agencies across the nation have added air conditioning to their vehicles.

Yesterday and Today

From this brief history it can be seen that although forms of air conditioning and refrigeration were in use thousands of years ago, the period of rapid growth for the refrigeration industry has occurred in the past half century.

Atomic submarines are able to remain submerged indefinitely due, in part, to air conditioning. Modern medicine and delicate machine components are perfected in scientifically controlled atmospheres. Computer centers are able to function properly because they are kept within a specific range of temperature and humidity levels.

The Industry

Automobile air conditioning today is no longer a luxury — it is a necessity. Millions of Americans enjoy the benefits it produces. Businesspeople are able to drive to appointments in comfort and arrive fresh and alert. People with allergies are able to travel without the fear of coming into contact with excessive dust and airborne pollen. Because of the extensive use of the automobile in America, automobile air conditioning is playing an important role in promoting the comfort, health, and safety of travelers throughout the land. Today eighty percent of all cars produced are equipped with air conditioners.

There has been a rapid increase in the number of cars, trucks, and recreational vehicles (RVs) equipped with air-conditioning systems during the past twenty-five years.

It is easy to understand how automotive air conditioning has become the industry's most sought after product. In the South and Southwest, specialty auto repair shops base their entire trade on selling, installing, and servicing automotive air conditioners throughout the year.

The Service Technician

How does all this affect the student of automotive air conditioning? As the popularity of air conditioning in vehicles increases, it is obvious that the need for installation, maintenance, and service technicians will also increase. Many shops that just a few years ago added air-conditioning service as a sideline, now find it to be their primary business.

The air-conditioning technician must have a working knowledge and understanding of the operation and function of the circuits and controls of the automotive air conditioner and a good knowledge of the equipment, special tools, techniques, and tricks of the trade.

Air conditioning has made it possible for the space age to become part of the twentieth century. What was fiction at the turn of the century is commonplace today. The service technician's contribution to the industry may help make today's fiction commonplace by the twenty-first century.

REVIEW

Select the appropriate answer from the choices given for the following questions.

1. How did moving the stones of the Pharaoh's palace into the desert help to keep the palace cool?

    a. The palace was given a chance to air out.
    b. The stones gave up heat in the desert during the day.
    c. The stones gave up heat in the desert during the night.
    d. The stones could be easily rotated for reassembly.

2. The first advertised air conditioning for a car was

    a. in 1940, by Packard.
    b. in 1927, consisting of a heater, a ventilation system, and a filter.
    c. in 1926, by General Electric.
    d. after the war, in the 1950s.

3. What is the greatest technical accomplishment to date, which was made possible, in part, by air conditioning?

    a. The space program
    b. Modern medicine
    c. Atomic submarines
    d. All of the choices are perhaps equally as great.

4. What percentage of the total domestic car production will be equipped with air conditioning this year?

    a. In excess of 80%   c. About 70%
    b. Between 70% and 80%   d. About 90%

5. The first hermetic (sealed) refrigerator, the type still used today, was introduced by

    a. J.L. Larsen in 1913.   c. General Electric in 1926.
    b. the Kelvinator Company in 1918.   d. Electrolux in 1927.

UNIT 2 BODY COMFORT

The normal temperature of the adult human body is 98.6°F (37°C). This temperature is sometimes called subsurface or deep-tissue temperature as opposed to surface or skin temperature. An understanding of the process by which the body maintains its temperature is helpful to the student because it explains how air conditioning helps keep the body comfortable.

THE BODY PRODUCES HEAT

All food taken into the body contains heat in the form of calories. The large or great calorie is used to express the heat value of food. The large calorie is the amount of heat required to raise one kilogram of water one degree Celsius. In addition, 252 calories equal one British thermal unit. One British thermal unit (Btu) equals the amount of heat needed to raise the temperature of one pound of water one degree Fahrenheit. One calorie of heat is required to raise the temperature of one gram of water one degree Celsius.

As calories are taken into the body, they are converted into energy and stored for future use. The conversion process generates heat. All body movements use up the stored energy and in doing so, add to the heat generated by the conversion process.

The body consistently produces more heat than it requires. Therefore, for body comfort, all of the excess heat produced must be given off by the body.

THE BODY REJECTS HEAT

The constant removal of body heat takes place through three natural processes which all occur at the same time. These processes are:

- convection
- radiation
- evaporation

1 LB. WATER   2 LB. WATER

RAISED 1° F
REQUIRES 1 BTU

RAISED 1° F
REQUIRES 2 BTU

Fig. 2-1 Effect of weight on BTU

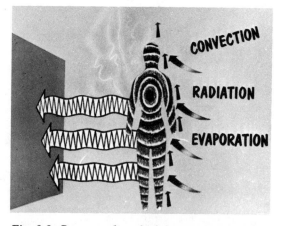

Fig. 2-2 Processes by which heat is removed from the body.

Convection

The convection process of removing heat is based on two phenomena:

Heat flows from a hot surface to a surface containing less heat. For example, heat flows from the body to the air surrounding the body when the air temperature is less than the skin temperature.

Heat rises. This is evident by watching the smoke from a burning cigarette, or the steam from boiling water.

When these two phenomena are applied to the body process of removing heat, the following occurs:

- The body gives off heat to the surrounding air (which has a lower temperature).
- The surrounding air becomes warmer and moves upward.
- As the warmer air moves upward, air containing less heat takes its place. The convection cycle is then completed.

Radiation

Radiation is the process which moves heat from a heat source to an object by means of heat rays, figure 2-4. This principle is based on the phenomenon that heat moves from a hot surface to a surface containing less heat. Radiation takes place independently of convection. The process of radiation does not require air movement to complete the heat transfer. This process is not affected by air temperature although it is affected by the temperature of the surrounding surfaces.

The body quickly experiences the effects of sun radiation when it moves from a shady to a sunny area.

Evaporation

Evaporation is the process by which moisture becomes a vapor, figure 2-5, page 10. As moisture vaporizes from a warm surface, it removes heat and thus cools the surface. This process takes place constantly on the surface of the body. Moisture is given off through the pores of the skin. As the moisture evaporates, it removes heat from the body.

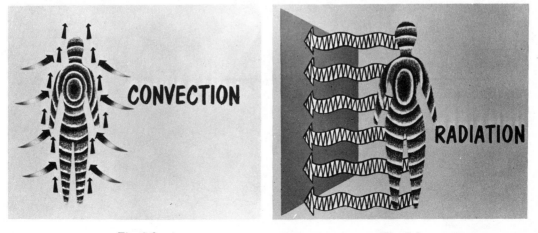

Fig. 2-3   Fig. 2-4

Perspiration appearing as drops of moisture on the body indicates that the body is producing more heat than can be removed by convection, radiation, and normal evaporation.

CONDITIONS THAT AFFECT BODY HEAT

The three main factors that affect body heat are temperature, humidity, and air movement, figure 2-6.

Temperature

Cool air increases the rate of convection; warm air slows it down.

Fig. 2-5

Cool air lowers the temperature of the surrounding surfaces. Therefore, the rate of radiation increases. Since warm air raises the surrounding surface temperature, the radiation rate decreases. In general, cool air increases the rate of evaporation and warm air slows it down. The evaporation rate also depends upon the amount of moisture already in the air and the amount of air movement.

Humidity

Moisture in the air is measured in terms of humidity. For example, 50 percent relative humidity means that the air contains half the amount of moisture that it is capable of holding at a given temperature.

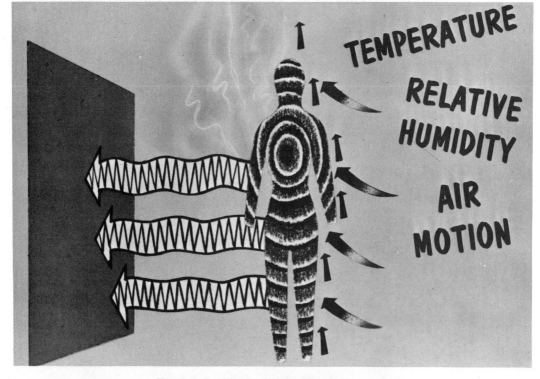

Fig. 2-6 Conditions which affect body comfort

A low relative humidity permits heat to be taken away from the body by evaporation. Because low humidity means the air is relatively *dry*, it can readily absorb moisture. A high relative humidity has the opposite effect. The evaporation process slows down in humid conditions; thus, the speed at which heat can be removed by evaporation decreases. An acceptable comfort range for the human body is 72° to 80°F (22.2°C to 26.6°C) at 45% to 50% relative humidity.

Air Movement

Another factor which affects the ability of the body to give off heat is the movement of air around the body. As the air movement increases:

- The evaporation process of removing body heat speeds up because moisture in the air near the body is carried away at a faster rate.

- The convection process increases because the layer of warm air surrounding the body is carried away more rapidly.

- The radiation process increases because the heat on the surrounding surfaces is removed at a faster rate. As a result, heat radiates from the body at a faster rate.

As the air movement decreases, the processes of evaporation, convection, and radiation decrease.

REVIEW

Select the appropriate answer from the choices given for the following questions.

1. What is the normal body temperature?

    a. 96.7°F (35.9°C)　　　　　　　　　c. 96.8°F (36.0°C)
    b. 97.6°F (36.4°C)　　　　　　　　　d. 98.6°F (37.0°C)

2. How many calories are there in one Btu?

    a. 525　　　　　　　　　　　　　　　c. 252
    b. 522　　　　　　　　　　　　　　　d. 225

3. What is the relative humidity when the air holds one-fourth of all the moisture it can hold?

    a. 25%　　　　　　　　　　　　　　　c. 75%
    b. 50%　　　　　　　　　　　　　　　d. 100%

4. The temperature and humidity comfort range for the human body is

    a. 72°F – 80°F (22.2°C – 26.6°C) at 45% – 50% humidity.
    b. 72°F – 80°F (22.2°C – 26.6°C) at 50% – 55% humidity.
    c. 68°F – 70°F (20.0°C – 21.1°C) at 45% – 50% humidity.
    d. 68°F – 70°F (20.0°C – 21.1°C) at 50% – 55% humidity.

5. The human body gives off heat by

   a. evaporation.
   b. convection.

   c. radiation.
   d. All of these are correct answers.

6. Why do humans perspire?

7. The body receives heat in two ways. Describe one way.

8. A group of people in an enclosed room causes the temperature of the room to increase. Explain why this happens.

9. Describe the process of heat transfer by radiation.

10. What effect does cool air have on the process of heat transfer by convection?

UNIT 3 MATTER

The effects of heat energy within an air-conditioning system must be understood by the technician. Thus, the topics which follow deal with matter, heat, pressure, and the principles of refrigeration. These physical laws are basic to an understanding of air-conditioning systems.

Matter is defined as anything that occupies space and has weight. All things are composed of matter and are found in one of

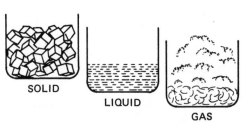

Fig. 3-1 Three basic states of matter

three forms: solid, liquid, or gas, figure 3-1. As an example, consider one of the more common substances, water. Water in its natural form is liquid. If enough of its natural heat is removed, it turns to ice, a solid. If heat is added to water and its temperature is raised enough, it boils and vaporizes, changing to gas (steam).

Although various procedures can be applied to matter to cause it to change from one state to another, most objects and things are usually thought of in their natural state.

For example, water, as a liquid, flows and cannot take a shape of its own. Therefore, water assumes the shape of the container in which it is placed. In a container, water exerts an outward and downward force. The greatest force of the water is toward the bottom, lessening toward the top of the container.

As another example, steam or gas dissipates into the surrounding air if it is not contained. When placed in a sealed or enclosed container, gas exerts pressure in all directions with equal force.

When water occurs in the solid state as ice, it holds a certain shape and size. Ice exerts force in a downward direction only.

THE STRUCTURE OF MATTER

All matter, regardless of its state, is composed of small parts (particles) called molecules. Each molecule of matter is actually the smallest particle of a material which retains all the properties of the original material. For example, if a grain of salt is divided in two, and each subsequent particle is divided again (and the process is continued until the grain is divided as finely as possible), the smallest stable particle having all the properties of salt is a molecule of salt. The word *stable* means that a molecule is satisfied to remain as it is.

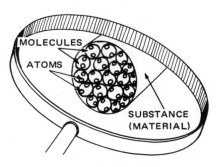

Fig. 3-2 The structure of matter

Although the molecule may seem to be the smallest possible division, each molecule is in itself made up of even smaller particles of matter. These particles are known as *atoms*. When compared with the molecule, the atoms within a molecule are not always stable. Instead, atoms tend to join with atoms of other substances to form new and different molecules and substances.

The speed freedom (or position) and the number of molecules determines: the state of the material, the temperature of the material, and the effect the material has on other parts or mechanisms of which it may be a part.

ARRANGEMENT AND MOVEMENT OF MOLECULES

A given material consists of millions and millions of molecules which are all alike. Different materials have different molecules. The characteristics and properties of different materials depend on the nature and arrangement of the molecules. In turn, the behavior of each molecule largely depends on the material (substance) of which the molecule is composed, figure 3-3.

Regardless of the state of a material, the molecules within the material are continuously moving. This movement is called *kinetic* energy because it is an energy of motion. The addition of heat energy to a material increases the kinetic energy of the molecules of the material. In solids, the motion of the molecules is in the form of vibration. That is, the particles never move far from a fixed position. In figure 3-4, note how the addition of heat energy affects the motion of the molecules of water in each of its three states.

NATURAL GAS MOLECULE
(METHANE)

WATER MOLECULE

FOUR HYDROGEN ATOMS COMBINED WITH
ONE CARBON ATOM

TWO HYDROGEN ATOMS COMBINED WITH
ONE OXYGEN ATOM

Fig. 3-3 Molecules

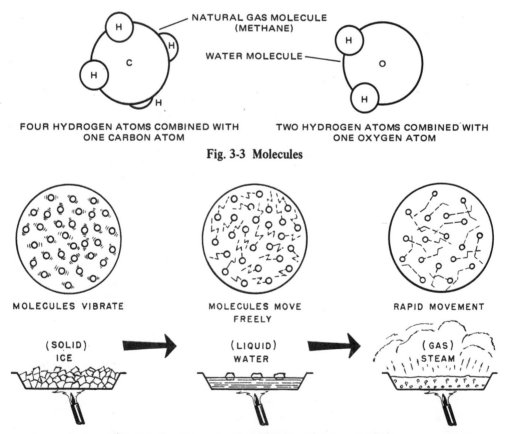

MOLECULES VIBRATE

MOLECULES MOVE
FREELY

RAPID MOVEMENT

(SOLID)
ICE

(LIQUID)
WATER

(GAS)
STEAM

Fig. 3-4 Freedom of molecules in basic states of matter

When heat energy is added to or removed from a material, a change in the state of the material occurs. Heat, then, is the factor that governs the movement of the molecules making up the substance. The removal of heat causes the molecular action to slow down: liquids solidify and gases become liquids. The addition of heat causes the molecular action to speed up: liquids boil and solids become liquids.

REVIEW

Select the appropriate answer from the choices given for the following questions.

1. What are examples of the three states of matter?

    a. Steel, water, and air
    b. Ice, water, and steam
    c. Rock, ocean, and cloud
    d. All of these choices are examples of the three states of matter

2. A solid exerts pressure in

    a. all directions equally.
    b. one direction (down).
    c. two directions (out and down).
    d. three directions (up, out, and down).

3. Atoms tend to join with other atoms of a different substance to form

    a. stronger atoms.
    b. a different substance.
    c. a stable molecule.
    d. All of these choices are correct answers.

4. Energy in motion is known as

    a. static energy.
    b. kinetic energy.
    c. fixed energy.
    d. free energy.

Briefly answer each of the following questions.

5. The three states of matter are __?__, __?__, and __?__.

6. When heat is removed from a fluid, a change in state from a __?__ to a __?__ is caused.

7. In which direction does matter in the gaseous state exert pressure?

8. Steam is water in the __?__ state.

9. How can water be changed from a liquid to steam?

10. How does the movement of the molecules differ between water and steam?

UNIT 4 HEAT

As stated in Unit 2, heat can be transmitted in one of three ways: by conduction, convection, or radiation.

The term *conduction* means that heat is being transferred through a solid. For example, when food is frying in a pan, heat from the burner is conducted through the pan and to the food.

Convection means that heat transfer is taking place as a result of the circulation of a fluid. The automobile cooling system is a good example of convection cooling. The coolant (a mixture of water and antifreeze) in the cooling system removes the heat created by the engine by carrying it from the engine block to the radiator. The heat is then dissipated into the surrounding air.

Radiation is the term used when heat is transmitted through a medium and the medium does not become hot. An example of this situation is the way in which people acquire sunburns at the beach. That is, part of the heat from the sun is transmitted to the skin through the air.

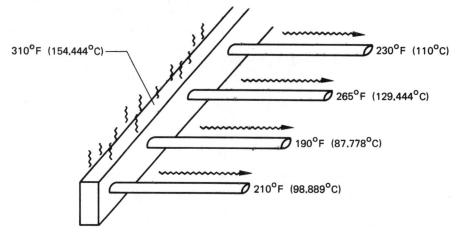

Fig. 4-1 Metals differ in conductivity

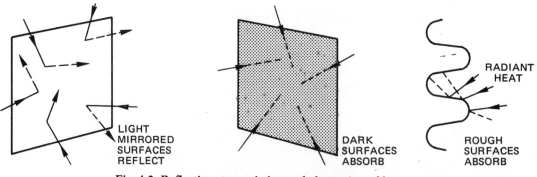

Fig. 4-2 Reflection, transmission and absorption of heat rays

SENSIBLE HEAT

Sensible heat is any heat that can be felt and can be measured on a thermometer. One example of sensible heat is the heat in the surrounding air. The temperature of this air is called the *ambient temperature.* When this temperature drops ten or fifteen degrees, one feels cool. An increase in the temperature causes one to feel warmer.

MEASUREMENT OF HEAT

Heat energy is measured in terms of the calorie. There are large and small calories. The *gram calorie,* the smallest measure of heat energy, is known as the *small calorie.* This discussion of measurements is concerned with the *kilogram calorie,* also known as the *large calorie.* One kilogram calorie (1 kg-cal) is required to raise the temperature of one gram (1 g) of water from 14.5°C to 15.5°C.

In refrigeration and air conditioning, heat energy is expressed in British thermal units (Btu). There are 252 calories (0.252 kg-cal) in one Btu. To raise the temperature of one pound (0.4536 kg) of water 1°F (0.556°C), 1 Btu (0.252 kg-cal) is required.

Water is liquid between the temperatures of 32°F (0°C) and 212°F (100°C). This is a range of 180°F (100°C) and is called the *subcooled liquid range* for water. For each Btu (0.252 kg-cal) of heat added to one pound (0.4536 kg) of water in this range, the temperature of the water increases 1°F (0.556°C).

Thus, if 180 Btu (45.36 kg-cal) of heat energy are added to one pound (0.4536 kg) of water at 32°F (0°C), the temperature of the water is increased to 212°F (100°C).

To obtain the final value of the water temperature, divide the Btu (or kg-cal) being added to the water by the number of pounds (or kilograms) of the water. This value is then added to the original temperature (°F or °C) to obtain the new temperature.

Btu ÷ pounds (lb.) = H (heat)
H + original temperature = new temperature

Thus, by adding 180 Btu (45.36 kg-cal) to one pound (0.4536 kg) of water at 32°F (0°C), the result is:

English
180 Btu ÷ 1 lb. = 180°F
180°F + 32°F = 212°F

Metric
45.36 kg-cal ÷ 0.4536 kg = 100°C
100°C + 0°C = 100°C

Now, if 180 Btu (45.36 kg-cal) of heat energy are added to ten pounds (4.536 kg) of water at 32°F (0°C), the temperature of the water is raised to only 50°F (10°C), as follows:

English
180 Btu ÷ 10 lb. = 18°F
18°F + 32°F = 50°F

Metric
45.36 kg-cal ÷ 4.536 kg = 10°C
10°C + 0°C = 10°C

Although the same amount of heat energy is added to both water samples and the temperature of both samples is increased, there is ten times as much water in the second sample. Therefore, the temperature of this sample is increased only one-tenth as much as the original sample. To raise the temperature of ten pounds (4.536 kg) of water from 32°F (0°C) to 212°F (100°C), the addition of 1,800 Btu (453.6 kg-cal) of heat energy is required:

English
1,800 Btu ÷ 10 lb. = 180°F
180°F + 32°F = 212°F

Metric
453.6 kg-cal ÷ 4.536 kg = 100°C
100°C + 0°C = 100°C

LATENT HEAT

Latent heat is the term applied to the heat required to cause a change of state of matter. This heat cannot be recorded on a thermometer, nor can it be felt. The British thermal unit (Btu) is used as the standard measure for latent heat.

It was shown previously that a change of state occurs when a solid changes to a liquid or a liquid changes to a gas or vice versa. Water at atmospheric pressure between 32°F (0°C) and 212°F (100°C) is called *subcooled liquid*. Water at 212°F (100°C) is called *saturated liquid*. That is, water at 212°F (100°C) contains all of the heat it can hold and still remain a liquid. Any additional heat will cause the water to vaporize.

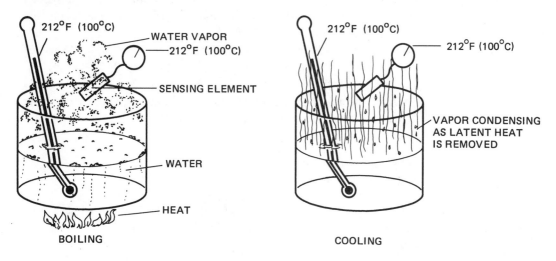

Fig. 4-3 Effect of latent heat

To change the state of one pound (0.4536 kg) of water at 212°F (100°C) to one pound (0.4536 kg) of steam at 212°F (100°C) requires an amount of heat equal to 970 Btu (244.44 kg-cal). This heat is called the *latent heat of vaporization*. Remember that this latent heat cannot be measured on a thermometer and does not cause a change in the temperature of the water.

In addition, steam at 212°F (100°C) gives up 970 Btu (244.44 kg-cal) of heat per pound (0.4536 kg) as it condenses into water at 212°F (100°C). The heat released in this process is called the *latent heat of condensation*.

The additional removal of heat at the rate of 1 Btu (0.252 kg-cal) per pound (0.4536 kg) lowers the temperature of the water. This temperature decrease can be measured on the thermometer until 32°F (0°C) is reached. (A later section of this unit covers the use of thermometers to make heat measurements.)

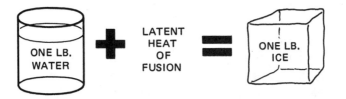

Fig. 4-4 Change from liquid to solid state

At 32°F (0°C), all of the heat that can be removed from the water without causing a change of state is removed. The heat that must be removed so that one pound (0.4536 kg) of water at 32°F (0°C) can be changed to one pound (0.4536 kg) of ice is 144 Btu (35.288 kg-cal). This value of heat energy is called the *latent heat of fusion.*

This principle governing the addition and removal of heat energy is the basis for refrigeration and air conditioning. A refrigerant is selected for its ability to absorb and to give up large quantities of heat rapidly.

Figure 4-5 illustrates the relative values of the latent heat of fusion and the latent heat of vaporization for water.

SPECIFIC HEAT

Every element or compound has its own heat characteristics. Every substance has a different capacity for accepting and emitting heat.

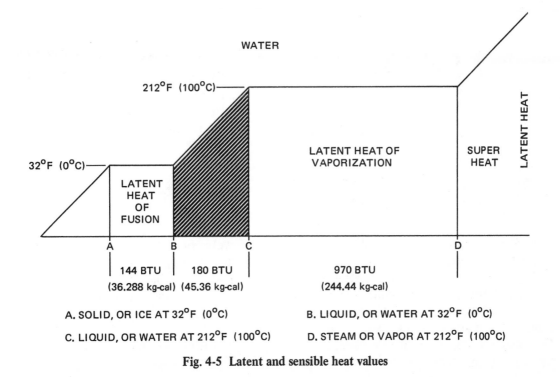

Fig. 4-5 Latent and sensible heat values

The capacity to accept (absorb) or emit (expel) heat is known as the *specific heat* or *thermal heat* of a substance. Specific heat is defined as the amount of heat that must be absorbed by a material if it is to undergo a temperature change of 1°F (0.556°C).

The following experiment can be performed with three small balls, each made of a different substance such as copper, steel, and glass. Heat the balls in a container of hot oil until they all reach the same temperature. Now, place each of the three balls on a slab of paraffin and observe what happens. Each ball sinks to a different depth in the paraffin. The depth to which each ball sinks depends on the amount of heat emitted. This experiment illustrates that different materials, at the same temperature, absorb and emit different amounts of heat.

A scale is used to show the relationship of the abilities of various substances to absorb or emit heat. Water (H_2O) is used as a standard to which other substances are compared. The value of water is given as 1 or 1.000. When compared to water, most substances require less heat per unit of weight to cause an increase in their temperature. Two exceptions to this statement are ammonia (NH_3) with a specific heat of 1.100 and hydrogen (H) with a specific heat of 3.410.

For example, since the specific heat of glass is 0.194, it requires less than 1/5 the number of Btu to raise its temperature as required for an equal amount of water. The specific heat of copper (Cu) is 0.093. This means that just under 1/11th the value in Btu is required to raise the temperature of copper as required for an equal amount of water.

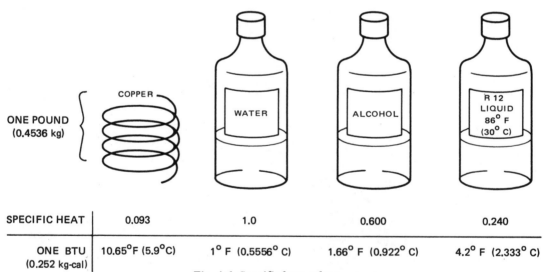

	COPPER	WATER	ALCOHOL	R 12 LIQUID 86° F (30° C)
ONE POUND (0.4536 kg)				
SPECIFIC HEAT	0.093	1.0	0.600	0.240
ONE BTU (0.252 kg-cal)	10.65°F (5.9°C)	1° F (0.5556° C)	1.66° F (0.922° C)	4.2° F (2.333° C)

Fig. 4-6 Specific heat values

When a comparison is made between glass and water or copper and water, it can be seen that only 0.194 and 0.093 times as much heat energy is required to change the temperature of these materials 1°F (0.625°C). This is true because materials vary in their ability to absorb, emit, and exchange heat. Thus, if equal amounts of copper, steel, glass, or any other substance are heated through equal changes of temperature, each material will absorb a different amount of heat.

Since it is known that the specific heat of water is 1.000, and that one Btu (0.252 kg-cal) is required to raise the water temperature 1°F (0.625°C) per pound (0.4536 kg),

SPECIFIC HEAT VALUES OF SELECTED SOLIDS, LIQUIDS, AND GASES	
Air 0.240	Nitrogen 0.240
Alcohol 0.600	Oxygen 0.220
Aluminum 0.230	Rubber 0.481
Brass 0.086	Silver 0.055
Carbon dioxide 0.200	Steel 0.118
Carbon tetrachloride 0.200	Sulphuric acid 0.336
Gasoline 0.700	Tin 0.045
Lead 0.031	Water, sea 0.940

Table 4-1

there is a simple way of determining how many degrees (F or C) per unit of weight other materials can be raised.

$$\frac{1,000}{\text{SPECIFIC GRAVITY}} \div \frac{\text{WEIGHT}}{\text{HEAT ENERGY}} = \text{TEMPERATURE CHANGE}$$

For example, the specific heat of aluminum (A1) is 0.230. By applying the previous formula, it is found that one Btu (0.252 kg-cal) raises the temperature of one pound (0.4536 kg) of aluminum 4.35°F (2.42°C).

English

$$\frac{1.00}{0.230} \quad \text{x} \quad \frac{1 \text{ lb.}}{1 \text{ Btu}} \quad =$$

4.34783 ÷ 1 = 4.34783°F
(round off to 4.35°F)

Metric

$$\frac{1.00}{0.230} \quad \text{x} \quad \frac{0.4536 \text{ kg}}{0.252 \text{ kg-cal}} \quad =$$

4.34783 ÷ 1.8 = 2.41545°C
(round off to 2.42°C)

Values for other materials can be determined in the same manner. Thus, for lead with a specific heat of 0.031, one Btu (0.252 kg-cal) raises the temperature of one pound (0.4536 kg) of lead 32.25°F (17.92°C):

English

$$\frac{1.00}{0.031} \quad \text{x} \quad \frac{1 \text{ lb.}}{1 \text{ Btu}} \quad =$$

32.2581 ÷ 1 = 32.2581°F
(round off to 32.26°F)

Metric

$$\frac{1.00}{0.031} \quad \text{x} \quad \frac{0.4536 \text{ kg}}{0.252 \text{ kg-cal}} \quad =$$

32.2581 ÷ 1.8 = 17.9211°C
(round off to 17.92°C)

A certain type of specific heat is called a *heat load*. When dealing with automobiles, the heat load is an important factor in the efficiency of air-conditioning systems. Items to be considered in determining the heat load include the color of the automobile, the amount of glass area, and the number of passengers.

When determining the refrigeration requirements for a particular application, the specific heats of all materials involved must be considered in the heat load. For example, in a refrigerated truck body, the specific heat of the product being cooled is an important factor, as is the amount of insulation and the type of material in the body. The number of times the doors are opened and closed as well as the length of time the product is to be refrigerated are also important factors.

COLD — THE ABSENCE OF HEAT

What is meant by the term cold? Cold is the absence of heat. If cold is to be understood, then the student must first understand what heat is. Heat is energy and is present in all things. Heat cannot be contained. The molecular structure of all things is changed into one of three forms by heat.

Heat is molecular movement. For example, Unit 3 showed that water is liquid between 32°F (0°C) and 212°F (100°C). If heat is added to water at 212°F (100°C), its molecular movement is increased. As a result, water vaporizes and turns to steam. When heat is removed from water at 32°F (0°C), its molecular movement is decreased. The water then solidifies and turns to ice.

All matter generates heat which is called specific heat. The body generates heat that must be overcome if one is to feel cool. The food stored in the refrigerator generates heat that must be overcome if the food is to be kept at a safe temperature as required for short term or long term storage. Any matter that is to be cooled must first have its specific heat removed or overcome.

If it is now asked, "What is cold?", it appears that the answer is that cold is the absence of all heat. If this is true, at what point is all the heat removed from matter? Ice, at 32°F (0°C), is said to be cold. But solid carbon dioxide (CO_2), or dry ice, is even colder at its normal temperature of –109.3°F (–165.8°C). Dry ice is so cold that if it is touched, one has the sensation of being burned. However, it cannot be said that dry ice is cold either because it still contains a large amount of heat as measured in Btu.

Absolute cold, then, is the absence of all heat. Complete absence of heat does not occur until the temperature of –459.67°F (–273.16°C) is reached. All temperature above this value contains heat. For example, –459°F still contains 0.67°F of heat; –273°C still contains 0.16°C of heat.

Absolute cold, like other absolutes, has not yet been achieved by scientists. A Dutch physicist, Wander de Haas, working at the University of Leiden (Holland), achieved a temperature of 0.0044°C above absolute zero. In 1957, Dr. Arthur Spohr, working at the U.S. Naval Research Laboratory, achieved a temperature of less than one-millionth of a degree Kelvin (K) above absolute zero (0.000001 K). The Kelvin scale, used in physics, uses 0 K for absolute cold, 273 K as the freezing point for water, and 373 K as its boiling point.

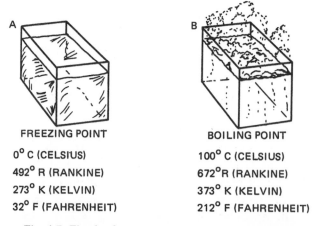

FREEZING POINT

0° C (CELSIUS)
492° R (RANKINE)
273° K (KELVIN)
32° F (FAHRENHEIT)

BOILING POINT

100° C (CELSIUS)
672°R (RANKINE)
373° K (KELVIN)
212° F (FAHRENHEIT)

Fig. 4-7 Fixed reference points on temperature scales

In summary then, cold is the absence of heat energy. According to current scientific theory, absolute zero is the point at which all molecular movement stops. Since molecular movement causes heat energy, it follows that if there is no movement there is no heat.

THERMOMETERS

Long ago, it was recognized that it was desirable to have a device to measure the temperature of matter to determine how much heat the object or matter contained. Such a device became known as a *thermometer.*

About 1585, Galileo Galilei constructed a crude water thermometer. Although this thermometer was very inaccurate, the principles stated by Galileo in the construction of his device helped other scientists to design more accurate instruments.

Over a hundred years later, in 1714, Gabriel D. Fahrenheit constructed a thermometer using a column of mercury. From the time of Galileo and until Fahrenheit's experiments, temperature measuring devices used tubes of alcohol and other substances as indicators.

Fahrenheit realized that even though many thermometers had been made, none of these devices had been constructed to a standard scale. Recognizing the need for a standard scale, Fahrenheit decided that a zero should be placed on the tube to indicate the absence of heat. He then reasoned that all values above zero were relative and contained so many units of heat.

Fahrenheit then decided that it was necessary to take his tube of mercury to be calibrated to the coldest location that could be found in the world. After talking with sailors, he decided that Iceland was the ideal place to make his measurements.

Once in Iceland, he waited until he was told that "This is the coldest day we have seen." He then made a mark on his glass tube to indicate zero, the absence of heat. He waited until it became warmer and noted that as the ice melted, his mercury column expanded 32/1000th of its original volume. This measurement was repeated several times and each time the same expansion of the mercury column occurred. Fahrenheit designated this point as 32°.

He also noted that normal body temperature was 98.6° and that when water boiled his column of mercury expanded to 212/1000th of its original volume.

Fahrenheit's thermometer was accepted as the standard and was the most widely used device for many years. There are, however, three other scales in use today.

While Fahrenheit was working on his thermometer, Anders Celsius, a Swedish astronomer, proposed the centigrade thermometer. On this thermometer he designated the temperature of melting ice as 0° and the boiling point of water as 100°. This scale, now known as the Celsius scale, is used in metric measurement.

In 1848, at the age of 24, W.T. Kelvin (Lord Kelvin) proposed the absolute scale of temperature, which still bears his name. The Kelvin scale is used in scientific work. A comparison of the various temperature scales is given in figure 4-8, page 24.

The Rankine scale thermometer is named after its inventor W.J.M. Rankine, a Scottish engineer. On the Rankine scale, the freezing point of water is 492°R and its boiling point is 672°R.

Kelvin temperature equivalents are obtained by adding 273° to the Celsius temperature; the Celsius equivalent is obtained by subtracting 273° from the Kelvin temperature.

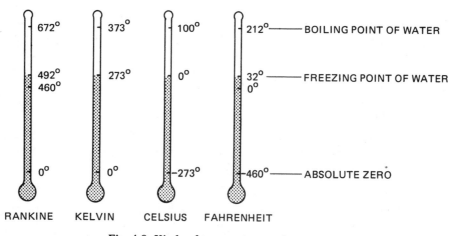

Fig. 4-8 Kinds of temperature scales

Rankine temperature equivalents are obtained by adding 460° to the Fahrenheit temperature; the Fahrenheit equivalent is obtained by subtracting 460° from the Rankine temperature.

Several types of thermometers are available to the service technician, figure 4-9. The most popular style is the stem/dial thermometer. This thermometer has an all metal stem and an easy-to-read dial.

In general, the accuracy of this type of thermometer is ±1% through the entire indicated temperature scale. Several ranges are available: 0°F to 220°F and -40°F to +160°F. The latter range is the most popular for use with air-conditioning systems. Both ranges can be used on either the high side of a refrigeration system, figure 4-10, or on the low side of the system, figure 4-11.

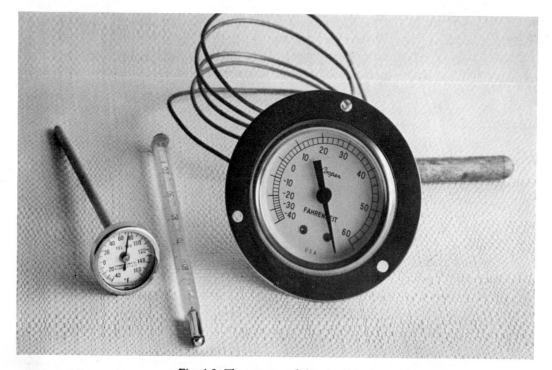

Fig. 4-9 Three types of thermometers

Fig. 4-10 Thermometer used to check condenser temperature

Fig. 4-11 Thermometer used to check evaporator temperature

TEMPERATURE CONVERSION

Most of the servicing work on air conditioners and refrigeration systems deals with temperature values on the Fahrenheit scale. However, the conversion to the metric system means that the student should be able to work with the Celsius scale as well. On many occasions, the student will be required to make conversions between the Fahrenheit and Celsius scales.

The conversions are quite simple.

For example, to change a Celsius reading to Fahrenheit:

- multiply the Celsius reading by 9/5
- Add 32°

Assume that it is necessary to convert a temperature of 115°C to the Fahrenheit equivalent.

First, multiply the value by 9/5:	115°C x 9/5	=	207°
Then add 32:	207° + 32°	=	239°F
Thus	115°C	=	239°F

As another example, consider the boiling point of water at 100°C or 212°F. Given the value of 100°C, it can be proved that the Fahrenheit equivalent is indeed 212°.

$$100°C \times 9.5 = 180°$$
$$180° + 32° = 212°F$$

To change a Fahrenheit reading to the Celsius equivalent, the Fahrenheit value is first reduced by 32° and then is multiplied by 5/9.

Thus, to change a Fahrenheit reading to Celsius:

- subtract 32°
- multiply by 5/9

By applying these steps the Celsius equivalent of a temperature of 221°F can be found.

$$221°F - 32° = 189°$$
$$189° \times 5/9 = 105°C$$

This formula can be proved just as in the previous case by converting the boiling point of water on the Fahrenheit scale, 212°F, to its Celsius equivalent.

$$212°F - 32° = 180°$$
$$180° \times 5/9 = 100°C$$

REVIEW

HEAT

Select the appropriate answer from the choices given.

1. What is the smallest measure of heat energy?
   a. Btu (0.252 kg-cal)
   b. Gram calorie
   c. Kilogram calorie
   d. One gram

2. What is the boiling point of water at sea level?

   a. 212°F (100°C)   c. 121°F (85°C)
   b. 198.6°F (92.55°C)   d. 189.6°F (123.11°C)

3. If 180 Btu (45.36 kg-cal) are added to eight pounds (3.6288 kg) of water at 35°F (1.667°C), what is the new temperature?

   a. 215°F (101.67°C)   c. 57.5°F (14.17°C)
   b. 145°F (62.78°C)   d. 75.5°F (24.17°C)

4. If ten Btu (2.52 kg-cal) are removed from one pound of water (0.4536 kg) at 35°F (1.667°C), what is the new temperature?

   a. 25°F (-3.89°C)   c. 45°F (7.22°C)
   b. 32°F (0°C)   d. 35°F (1.667°C)

5. What is absolute cold?

   a. -459.67°F (-273.16°C)   c. The absence of heat.
   b. Absolute zero.   d. All are correct answers.

Briefly answer each of the following questions.

6. Define sensible heat.

7. What is meant by the term ambient temperature?

8. What is latent heat?

9. Explain the process of heat transfer by convection.

10. If 160 Btu (40.32 kg-cal) of heat energy is added to five pounds (2.268 kg) of water at 77°F (25°C), what is the new temperature? Show the formula and figures used to arrive at the answer.

THERMOMETERS

Briefly answer each of the following questions. Show the formulas used for determining the temperature conversions and show all calculations.

11. Change 25°C to Fahrenheit.

12. Change 40°C to Fahrenheit.

13. Change 0°C to Fahrenheit.

14. Change 59°F to Celsius.

15. Change 113°F to Celsius.

16. Change 32°F to Celsius.

17. Name four temperature scales in use today.

18. Of the four scales now used, which one is most commonly used in air-conditioning work?

19. How did Fahrenheit determine that the freezing point of water was 32° on his scale?

20. What is normal body temperature on the Fahrenheit scale? On the Celsius scale?

UNIT 5   PRESSURE

To understand air conditioning one must understand pressure. The best example of the action of pressure and what it means is shown by the air (gas) envelope around the earth (see unit 3).   This gas consists primarily of oxygen, 21% by volume, and nitrogen, 78% by volume, figure 5-1. The remaining 1% consists of several other gases. This combination of gases is called the atmosphere.   It extends nearly six hundred miles above the earth and is held in place by the gravitational pull of the earth.

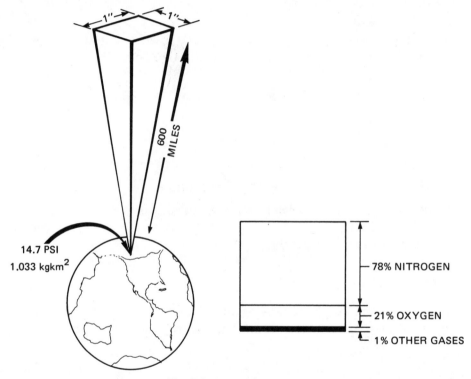

Fig. 5-1 Atmospheric pressure

ATMOSPHERIC PRESSURE

The six-hundred mile belt of gas surrounding the earth exerts a pressure that is measured in pounds per square inch, psi (English system) or kilograms per square centimeter, kg/cm^2 (metric system).   For a one square inch area (square centimeter), the pressure of the 600-mile column of gas is 14.69 psi ($1.0326 \; kg/cm^2$). This figure, rounded off to 14.7 psi ($1.033 \; kg/cm^2$), is known as the atmospheric pressure.

PRESSURE MEASUREMENT

Service manuals provided by manufacturers often refer to the normal pressure of an air-conditioning system as psi or psig. In some cases, this pressure is also referred to as psia. However, there is a considerable difference between the actual meanings of the three abbreviated terms.

The abbreviation for pounds per square inch is psi. This term refers to the amount of pressure per square inch and does not consider or compensate for atmospheric pressure. In general, the phrase, "The low-side gauge should read 28 psi," really means 28 psig (1.97 kg/cm²).

Pounds per square inch gauge, abbreviated psig, is the amount of pressure in pounds per square inch indicated on a gauge that is adjusted to atmospheric pressure at sea level. Zero pressure on a gauge so adjusted compensates for the atmospheric pressure at sea level of 14.696 psi, usually rounded off to 14.7 psi (1.033 kg/cm²).

Pounds per square inch absolute, abbreviated psia, refers to the amount of pressure measured from absolute zero. This value equals the gauge pressure plus 14.7 psi (1.033 kg/cm²). Thus, a gauge calibrated in psia reads 14.7 (1.033 kg/cm²) without being connected to a pressure source.

As an example, assume that two gauges are connected to the same test port of an air conditioner. One gauge is calibrated in psig and reads 28 pounds (1.97 kg/cm²) of pressure (zero reference). The other gauge is calibrated in psia and reads approximately 43 pounds (3.023 kg/cm²). That is, (28 psi + 14.7 psi = 42.7 psia) (1.97 kg/cm² + 1.033 kg/cm² = 3.002 kg/cm²).

TEMPERATURE AND PRESSURE

All pressures above atmospheric pressure are referred to as gauge pressures. All pressures below atmospheric pressure are said to be in the vacuum range.

Zero gauge pressure remains zero regardless of what the altitude is. Pressures above atmospheric pressure are recorded as pounds per square inch gauge or psig. Pressures below atmospheric pressure are recorded as inches of mercury or in. Hg (in. is the abbreviation for inch and Hg is the abbreviation or the chemical symbol for mercury).

At sea level (where the atmospheric pressure is equal to 14.7 psi or 1.033 kg/cm²), the boiling point of water is 212°F (100°C). At any point higher than sea level, the atmospheric pressure is lower and so is the boiling point of water. The point at which water boils decreases at the rate of 1.1°F (0.61°C) per thousand feet of altitude. To find the boiling point of water at any given altitude, multiply the altitude (in thousands of feet) by 1.1 for °F or by 0.61 for °C. The result of this operation is then subtracted from 212°F (100°C) to obtain the new boiling point.

For example, in an airplane flying at a height of 12,000 feet, water boils at about 198.8°F (92.66°C).

English			Metric		
12,000 ft. ÷ 1,000	=	12	12,000 ft. ÷ 1,000	=	12
12 x 1.1°	=	13.2°	12 x 0.61°	=	7.32°
212°F – 13.2°F	=	198.8°F	100°C – 7.32°C	=	92.68°C

In Colorado, water boils at a lower temperature than it does in the flatlands or at sea level.

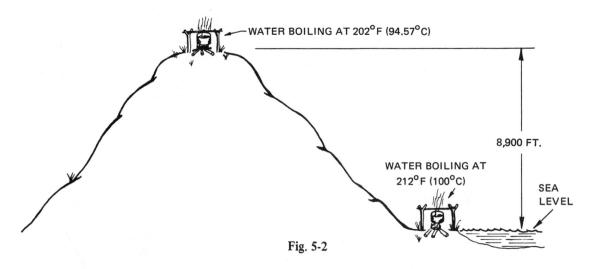

Fig. 5-2

At an elevation of 8,900 feet, the boiling point can be determined as follows:

English			Metric		
8,900 ft. ÷ 1,000	=	8.9	8,900 ft. ÷ 1,000	=	8.9
8.9 x 1.1°	=	9.79 or 9.8°	8.9 x 0.61	=	5.429°
212°F – 9.8°F	=	202.2°F	100°C – 5.43°C	=	94.57°C

Thus, the boiling point of water at this elevation is about 202°F (94.44°C).

It should be noted that the small error in the comparisons of temperatures (converting Fahrenheit to Celsius or Celsius to Fahrenheit) is due to the conversion factors of 1.1°F and 0.61°C per thousand feet. If both of these factors are extended to four or five decimal places, the error is reduced.

It should also be noted that water boils when it contains all the heat it can for a given condition. Thus, when water boils at a lower temperature, it contains less heat; when it boils at a higher temperature, it contains more heat.

If the boiling point of water is affected by a pressure drop, it is reasonable to assume that a pressure increase also affects the boiling point of water.

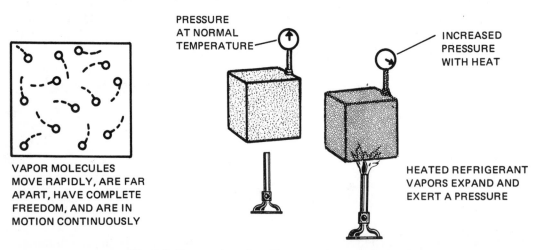

Fig. 5-3 Temperature rise affects movement and pressure

This principle is often put to use when food is prepared in a pressure cooker. The boiling point of the water is increased because the pressure is increased. As the water changes from a liquid to steam, a pressure is created because the vapor cannot escape from the sealed pot. As a result, the vapor is superheated to a higher temperature. The food cooks much faster because it is exposed to a greater temperature and pressure.

The automobile cooling system is another example where the temperature is increased by increasing pressure. Some system manufacturers have been able to increase the working pressure of a cooling system to sixteen pounds of pressure or more. With each increase of a pound of pressure, the boiling point of the water (or coolant) is increased about three degrees Fahrenheit.

A cooling system containing a pressure cap rated at 7 psi (0.49 kg/cm^2) causes an increase in the boiling point of the coolant. To find the new boiling point of the coolant (with the pressure cap in place), multiply the rating of the cap in pounds by 3°F (1.67°C). This number is then added to 212°F (100°C) to obtain the new boiling point.

$$7 \text{ psi} \times 3°F = 21°F$$
$$21°F + 212°F = 233°F$$

OR

$$7 \text{ psi} \times 1.67°C = 11.69°C$$
$$11.69°C + 100°C = 111.69°C$$

The boiling point of the coolant in a system containing a 12-pound cap can be found in the same manner.

$$12 \text{ psi} \times 3°F = 36°F$$
$$36°F + 212°F = 248°F$$

OR

$$12 \text{ psi} \times 1.67 = 20.04°C$$
$$20.04°C + 100°C = 120.04°C$$

Thus, the new boiling point is 248°F (120°C).

Assume that an apparatus is known to hold the temperature of a coolant to 260°F (126.67°C). It is desired to pressurize the system. The size of the pressure cap must be determined by subtracting the normal boiling point of water from the desired temperature. This result is then divided by 3°F (1.67°C) to obtain the required cap size in pounds. In this case, a 16-pound cap is required.

$$260°F - 212°F = 48°F$$
$$48°F \div 3°F = 16 \text{ psi}$$

OR

$$126.67°C - 100°C = 26.67°C$$
$$26.67°C \div 1.67 = 15.97 \text{ psi}$$

If water boils at a higher temperature when pressure is applied to it and at a lower temperature when the pressure is low, it is obvious that the temperature can be controlled to a greater degree of accuracy if the pressure is controlled.

REVIEW

Select the appropriate answer for the choices given.

1. What is the atmospheric pressure at sea level?

   a. 0 psia (0 kg/cm²)
   b. 14.7 psig (1.033 kg/cm²)
   c. Either a or b is correct.
   d. Neither a nor b are correct.

2. What is the chemical symbol for mercury?

   a. θ
   b. "
   c. ε
   d. Hg

3. How is the chemical symbol for mercury used in air-conditioning or refrigeration service?

   a. To indicate pressure
   b. To indicate vacuum
   c. For the boiling point of water
   d. For the condensing point of refrigerant

4. The new boiling point of water at an elevation of 8,500 feet is

   a. 202.7°F (203°F) (95°C).
   b. 201.25°F (201°F) (93.88°C).
   c. 221.3°F (221°F) (105°C).
   d. 221.75°F (222°F) (105.55°C).

5. What is the new boiling point of water at a pressure of 3 psig (1.47 kg/cm²)?

   a. 215°F (101.67°C)
   b. 218°F (103.33°C)
   c. 221°F (105.0°C)
   d. 224°F (106.66°C)

Briefly answer each of the following questions.

6. Define pressure.

7. What is the chief advantage of a pressurized cooling system in a car?

8. How does driving a car at high altitudes affect the water temperature in a pressurized cooling system?

9. Define the term psig.

10. To prevent water, as a coolant in the car cooling system, from boiling at an operating temperature of 257°F (125°C), what is the pressure rating of the pressure cap? Show the formula used in arriving at the answer.

UNIT 6 PRINCIPLES OF REFRIGERATION

AIR CONDITIONING

When one hears the term air conditioning, usually the first thing that comes to mind is cold fresh air. Actually, a true air-conditioning system automatically controls the temperature, humidity, purity, and circulation of the air. In automotive applications, air conditioning is any system that cools and dehumidifies the air inside the passenger compartment of an automobile or truck.

THE MECHANICAL REFRIGERATION SYSTEM

The mechanical refrigeration system installed in a modern vehicle uses a special refrigerant to absorb heat inside the evaporator. To do this, the refrigerant changes from a liquid to a vapor. Since the evaporator is located inside the passenger compartment, air blown over the fins of the evaporator is directed to the passengers for their comfort.

It is necessary to remove the heat absorbed by the refrigerant from the inside of the evaporator. One possible method of removing this heat is to expel the heat-laden refrigerant vapor to the outside air. However, this is an expensive procedure. The preferred method is to reclaim the refrigerant for reuse in the system. The heat alone is removed and expelled to the outside air.

The process of reclaiming the refrigerant begins at the compressor. The function of the compressor is to pressurize the heat-laden vapor until its pressure and temperature are much greater than that of the ouside air. The compressor also pumps the vapor to the condenser. At the condenser, the vapor gives up its heat and changes back to a liquid. The condenser is located outside the passenger compartment. Since the air passing over the condenser is much cooler than the vapor inside the condenser, the vapor gives up much of its heat and changes back to a liquid. The liquid refrigerant then passes from the condenser to the receiver/drier where it is stored until it is needed again by the evaporator.

This example of a mechanical refrigeration system demonstrates three basic laws of refrigeration which are the basis of all natural and mechanical refrigeration systems.

LAW I

To refrigerate is to remove heat. The absence of heat is cold. Heat is ever present.

Law I is illustrated by the refrigeration system of an automobile. Heat is removed from the passenger compartment of the automobile. In so doing, the temperature is lowered. The absence of heat is cold.

LAW II

Heat is ready to flow or pass to anything that has less heat. Nothing can stop the flow of heat; it can only be slowed down. Heat cannot be contained no matter how much insulation is used.

Law II is demonstrated by the special refrigerant in the evaporator. In this instance, heat is ready to flow to anything that contains less heat.

LAW III

If a change of state is to take place there must be a transfer of heat. If a liquid is to change to a gas, it must take on heat. The heat is carried off in a vapor. If a vapor is to change into a liquid it must give up heat. The heat is given up to a less hot surface or medium.

Law III is shown by the liquid refrigerant in the evaporator. That is, as the refrigerant takes on heat, it changes to a vapor. The heat is carried off to be expelled outside the car.

TON OF REFRIGERATION

For many years, refrigeration units were rated in horsepower (h.p.). The horsepower is a theoretical unit of energy. One horsepower is the amount of energy required to raise 33,000 pounds one foot in one minute.

These early refrigeration units had ratings of 1/4 h.p., 1/2 h.p., 3/4 h.p., and 1 h.p. Such a rating, however, was a very inaccurate method of describing the output of an air-conditioning unit since the horsepower value referred only to the compressor size.

Another term used to describe the capacity of an air-conditioning system is the ton. A *ton* of refrigeration is generally considered to be equivalent to one horsepower. An air-conditioning unit with a rating of 1/2 h.p. is also said to have half a ton of refrigeration.

The value of a ton of refrigeration in Btu/hr. can be determined if the latent heat of fusion for water is known. The amount of heat required to cause a change of state of one pound of ice at 32°F to one pound of water at 32°F is 144 Btu.

In applying this value, it must be remembered that a ton of matter (water) contains 2,000 pounds. Since 144 Btu are required to change one pound of solid water (ice) to a liquid, the equivalent value for one ton can be found by multiplying the amount of energy required to change one pound by 2,000 pounds.

$$144 \text{ Btu} \times 2,000 \text{ lb.} = 288,000 \text{ Btu}$$

This value is the amount of heat energy (in Btu) required to change the state of one ton of ice to one ton of liquid in twenty-four hours. To determine the Btu/hr. for a ton of refrigeration, divide 288,000 by 24.

$$144 \text{ Btu} \times 2,000 \text{ lb.} = 288,000 \text{ Btu}$$
$$288,000 \text{ Btu} \div 24 \text{ hr.} = 12,000 \text{ Btu/hr.}$$

One ton of refrigeration is thus equivalent to 12,000 Btu/hr. Most air-conditioning units now sold have a Btu rating. When a manufacturer lists an air-conditioning unit as a one-ton unit, the Btu rating must also be listed. For example, a 3/4-ton unit should have a rating of 9,000 Btu. This practice is followed to prevent units of lower capacity being sold as one-ton units.

$$144 \text{ Btu} \times 2,000 \text{ lb.} \quad = \quad 288,000 \text{ Btu}$$
$$288,000 \text{ Btu} \times 3/4 \text{ ton} = \quad 216,000 \text{ Btu}$$
$$216,000 \text{ Btu} \div 24 \text{ hr.} \quad = \quad 9,000 \text{ Btu/hr.}$$

Thus, each quarter ton of refrigeration is equivalent to 3,000 Btu.

What is the rating, ih tons, for an 11,000 Btu/hr. unit? Since the value of 11,000 Btu is close to that of a one-ton unit, the h.p. or ton rating of this unit is also established at one. The same reasoning also applies to a 13,000 Btu/hr. unit so that it too is called a one-ton unit.

In a similar fashion, assume that machine (A) is rated at 10,525 Btu/hr. and machine (B) is rated at 13,475 Btu/hr. Since both of these values are closer to 1 h.p. than they are to the next fractional horsepower (1/4 horsepower), they both are rated as 1 h.p. Actually, the two machines are almost a quarter of a horsepower apart in their ratings.

Machine A	10,525 Btu/hr.
Machine B	13,475 Btu/hr.
Difference	2,950 Btu/hr.

It is easy to see that there is a wide range in the Btu/hr. value of an air-conditioning unit rated at 1 ton. The consumer should be aware of this range when considering the purchase of refrigeration equipment of any size.

Automotive air conditioners are rated at well over a ton of refrigeration. Because of the tremendous heat load in the car, a unit rated at 8,000 to 10,000 Btu does a very poor job of keeping the average modern car cool.

For example, General Motors rates its factory-installed units at a full 1 3/4 tons, or about 21,000 Btu. This value is the same amount of cooling that is required to cool the average two-bedroom house. Of course, a house is well insulated and does not have as great a problem of heat loss by radiation as the automobile experiences.

REVIEW

Briefly answer each of the following questions.

1. What is a ton of refrigeration?
2. What is a horsepower of refrigeration?
3. Why are modern air-conditioning units rated in terms of Btu/hr. rather than by the ton or horsepower?
4. The Btu rating of a one-ton unit can range between what values?
5. What is the capacity of the air conditioner of the average car today?
6. The absence of _____ is cold.
7. Heat is ready to flow to anything that has less _____ .
8. As the liquid refrigerant takes on _____ it changes to a _____ .
9. Heat is dissipated in the outside air by the _____ .
10. As a refrigerant gives up its heat, it changes from a _____ to a _____ .

UNIT 7   REFRIGERANTS

The term *refrigerant* refers to the fluid used in a refrigeration system to produce cold by removing heat. For automotive refrigeration systems, Refrigerant 12 is used. It has the highest safety factor of any refrigerant available that is capable of withstanding high pressures and temperatures without deteriorating or decomposing.

Nature has not provided a perfect refrigerant. Thus it was necessary to devise a compound for automotive use. A fluorinated hydrocarbon known as carbon tetrachloride was selected since it met the requirements most closely with only a few minor changes.

Carbon tetrachloride (popularly known as carbon-tet), consists of one atom of carbon (C) and four atoms of chlorine (C1). The chemical symbol for this compound is CCl_4. To change carbon tetrachloride into a suitable refrigerant, two of the chlorine atoms are removed and two atoms of fluorine (F) are introduced in their place. The new compound, known as dichlorodifluoromethane, is Refrigerant 12. It has many applications in various types of refrigeration systems. The chemical symbol for Refrigerant 12 is CCl_2F_2. This means that one molecule of the refrigerant contains one atom of carbon, two atoms of chlorine, and two atoms of fluorine.

Refrigerant 12 is ideal because of its stability at high and low operating temperatures. It does not react with most metals, such as iron, aluminum, copper, or steel. Refrigerant 12 is soluble in oil and does not react with rubber. Thus, neither the refrigerant nor any rubber it contacts are harmed. Refrigerant 12 is nonflammable and nonexplosive in both gaseous and liquid forms. It is not harmful to animal or plant life. R12 also does not affect the taste, odor, or color of water or food.

Refrigerant 12 is odorless in concentrates of less than 20%. In greater concentrations, it can be detected by the faint odor of its original compound, carbon tetrachloride.

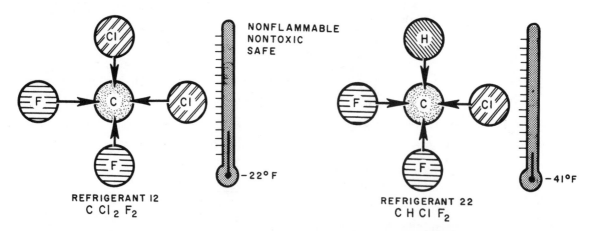

Fig. 7-1 Composition, boiling point, and properties of refrigerants

TEMPERATURE AND PRESSURE RELATIONSHIP OF REFRIGERANT 12

One of the characteristics of Refrigerant 12 which makes it a suitable refrigerant for automotive use is the fact that the temperature (on the Fahrenheit scale) and English system pressure values in the 20 to 80 psi range are very close.

Figure 7-2 shows that there is only a slight variation between the temperature and pressure values of the refrigerant in this range. These variations can be detected by sensitive thermometers and pressure gauges. In this range, the assumption is made that for every pound of pressure recorded, the temperature is the same. For example, figure 7-2 indicates that for a pressure of 23.1 psig, the temperature is 23°F. This value is the temperature of the refrigerant itself. It is not the temperature of the outside surface of the container or the air passing over it.

The objective in automotive air conditioning is to allow the evaporator to reach its coldest point without icing. Since ice forms at 32°F, the fins and cooling coils of the evaporator must not be allowed to reach a colder temperature. Because of the temperature rise through the walls of the cooling fins and coils, the temperature of the refrigerant may be several degrees cooler than that of the air passing through the evaporator.

For example, a pressure gauge reading of 28 psig means that the temperature of the refrigerant in the evaporator is about 30°F. Because of the temperature rise through the fins and coils, the air passing over the coil is about 34° or 35°F.

Temp. F	Press. psi	Temp. F	Press. psi	Temp. F	Press. psi	Temp. F	Press. psi	Temp. F	Press. psi
0	9.1	35	32.5	60	57.7	85	91.7	110	136.0
2	10.1	36	33.4	61	58.9	86	93.2	111	138.0
4	11.2	37	34.3	62	60.0	87	94.8	112	140.1
6	12.3	38	35.1	63	61.3	88	96.4	113	142.1
8	13.4	39	36.0	64	62.5	89	98.0	114	144.2
10	14.6	40	36.9	65	63.7	90	99.6	115	146.3
12	15.8	41	37.9	66	64.9	91	101.3	116	148.4
14	17.1	42	38.8	67	66.2	92	103.0	117	151.2
16	18.3	43	39.7	68	67.5	93	104.6	118	152.7
18	19.7	44	40.7	69	68.8	94	106.3	119	154.9
20	21.0	45	41.7	70	70.1	95	108.1	120	157.1
21	21.7	46	42.6	71	71.4	96	109.8	121	159.3
22	22.4	47	43.6	72	72.8	97	111.5	122	161.5
23	23.1	48	44.6	73	74.2	98	113.3	123	163.8
24	23.8	49	45.6	74	75.5	99	115.1	124	166.1
25	24.6	50	46.6	75	76.9	100	116.9	125	168.4
26	25.3	51	47.8	76	78.3	101	118.8	126	170.7
27	26.1	52	48.7	77	79.2	102	120.6	127	173.1
28	26.8	53	49.8	78	81.1	103	122.4	128	175.4
29	27.6	54	50.9	79	82.5	104	124.3	129	177.8
30	28.4	55	52.0	80	84.0	105	126.2	130	182.2
31	29.2	56	53.1	81	85.5	106	128.1	131	182.6
32	30.0	57	55.4	82	87.0	107	130.0	132	185.1
33	30.9	58	56.6	83	88.5	108	132.1	133	187.6
34	31.7	59	57.1	84	90.1	109	135.1	134	190.1

Fig. 7-2 Temperature-pressure chart (for Refrigerant 12)

HANDLING REFRIGERANT

Liquid refrigerant should be properly stored and used since it can cause blindness if it splashes into the eyes. In addition, if refrigerant is allowed to contact the skin, frostbite may result.

A refrigerant container should never be exposed to excessive heat or be allowed to come into contact with a heating device. The increase in refrigerant pressure inside the container as a result of heating can become great enough to cause the container to explode.

If refrigerant is allowed to come into contact with an open flame or heated metal, a poisonous gas is created. Anyone breathing this gas becomes violently ill. *Remember — refrigerant is not a toy*. It should be handled only by a trained refrigeration service technician.

The term *Freon* is commonly used to refer to Refrigerant 12. Freon and Freon 12 are registered trademarks of the E.I. duPont de Nemours and Company. These terms should be applied only to refrigerant manufactured or packaged by this company or by a processing plant licensed by duPont.

Refrigerant 12 is also packaged in the United States under several other brand names, such as Genatron 12, Isotron 12, and Ucon 12. An industry-accepted abbreviation for Refrigerant 12 is R12.

R12 is commonly packaged in 14-ounce cans which are called pound cans. This refrigerant is also available in 2-pound and 2 1/2-pound cans. These cans use a special adapter as a means of transferring the refrigerant to a system. No attempt should be made to remove the refrigerant by other means.

R12 is also available in 10- and 12-pound disposable cylinders, and in 25- and 145-pound deposit cylinders. It is also sold to manufacturers in 2,000-pound cylinders, tank trucks, and railroad tank cars.

The pound cans of refrigerant are the most popular because of their convenience and the ease of measuring the proper amount of refrigerant into a system. However, bulk packaging of refrigerant (in cylinders or tanks) generally is the least expensive method of buying refrigerant.

R12 drums and cylinders are painted white for easy identification. However, there is no standard system of refrigerant color codes. Some manufacturers may use different colors to designate the same refrigerant. Therefore, it is suggested that the contents of a cylinder be identified before the refrigerant is introduced into the system. Do not rely on the color of the container as a means of identification.

Refrigerant 12 is used in all modern automotive applications (some earlier units used Refrigerant 22).

Refrigerant 22, figure 7-1, has the same basic composition as R12, with one exception. For R22, a chlorine atom is removed and an atom of hydrogen is introduced in its place. Refrigerant 22 is known as monochlorodifluoromethane. The chemical symbol for R22 is $CHClF_2$. This is a popular refrigerant for window units and commercial air conditioning systems.

REVIEW

Refer to the Temperature-Pressure Chart in figure 7-2 to answer questions 1 through 6.

1. The refrigerant temperature for a gauge reading of 21 psi is _____ .

2. The refrigerant temperature for a gauge reading of 30 psi is _____ .

3. The refrigerant temperature for a gauge reading of 36 psi is _____ .

4. If the refrigerant temperature is 24°F, the gauge should read _____ .

5. If the refrigerant temperature is 50°F, the gauge should read _____ .

6. If the refrigerant temperature is 34°F, the gauge should read _____ .

For questions 7 through 10, cross out the incorrect word or words so that each sentence reads correctly.

7. Between (15) (20) (25) psig and (80) (85) (90) psig the temperature and pressure values of Refrigerant 12 are very close.

8. To prevent ice formation on the fins and coils of the evaporator, the temperature should never be allowed to go below (28°F) (30°F) (32°F).

9. Refrigerant in the (liquid) (gas) state, if allowed to strike the eye, can cause (damage) (blindness).

10. If Refrigerant 12 comes into contact with an (open flame) (heated metal), it (causes an explosion) (creates a poisonous gas).

UNIT 8 SPECIAL SAFETY PRECAUTIONS

Of the many refrigerants available for use in air-conditioning and refrigeration systems, Refrigerant 12 is the only one used in automotive air conditioning. Unit 7 briefly covered some of the hazards associated with the use of R12. Because it is important that the student be aware of these hazards, this unit will restate them. In addition, safety procedures will be outlined to assist the student in learning the correct methods of handling R12.

Recall that Refrigerant 12 is:

- odorless
- undetectable in small quantities
- colorless
- nonstaining

However, R12 is dangerous because of the damage it can do if it strikes the human eye or comes into contact with the skin. Since the evaporation temperature of R12 is -21.6°F (-29.9°C), suitable eye protection should be worn by anyone handling R12 to protect the eyes from splashing refrigerant. If R12 does enter the eye, freezing of the eye can occur with resultant blindness. The procedure outlined below is suggested if R12 enters the eyes.

1. Do not rub the eye.
2. Splash large quantities of cool water into the eye to increase the temperature.
3. Tape a sterile eye patch in place to prevent dirt from entering the eye.
4. Go immediately to a doctor or hospital for professional care.
5. *Do not attempt self-treatment.*

If liquid R12 strikes the skin, frostbite can occur. The same procedure outlined for emergency eye care can be used to combat the effects of R12 contact with the skin.

Refrigerant 12 is harmless unless it is released in a confined space. Under this condition, it may cause drowsiness. However, the automobile owner and the service technician need not be concerned about the safety of the automotive air conditioner because the capacity of the unit is too small to cause any difficulty. Refrigerant 12 must not be allowed to come into contact with an open flame or a very hot metal. The result of the exposure of R12 to a great deal of heat is the formation of a poisonous gas, phosgene. This gas can make a person very ill when inhaled. Phosgene gas inhaled in small amounts over a period of time can be cumulative, resulting in a toxic condition.

The following rules must be observed when handling R12 and other similar refrigerants.

1. Above 130°F (54.44°C), liquid refrigerant completely fills a container and hydrostatic pressure builds up rapidly with each degree of temperature rise. To provide

for some margin of safety, never heat a refrigerant cylinder above 125°F (51.66°C) or allow it to reach this temperature.

2. Never apply a direct flame to a refrigerant cylinder or container. Never place an electrical resistance heater near or in direct contact with a container of refrigerant.

3. Do not abuse a refrigerant cylinder or container. To avoid damage, use an approved valve wrench for opening and closing the valves. Secure all cylinders in an upright position for storing and withdrawing refrigerant.

4. *Do not handle refrigerant without suitable eye protection.*

5. *Do not discharge refrigerant into an enclosed area having an open flame.*

6. *When purging a system, discharge the refrigerant slowly.*

7. For an automotive refrigeration system, *do not introduce anything but pure Refrigerant 12 and approved refrigerant oil into the system.*

REVIEW

Briefly answer each of the following questions.

1. What can happen if Refrigerant 12 strikes the skin?

2. What can happen if Refrigerant 12 strikes the eye?

3. What is the most important safety measure to observe if liquid refrigerant strikes the eye?

4. What gas is given off by Refrigerant 12 when it comes in contact with an open flame?

5. Why should one not overheat the refrigerant container?

UNIT 9   THE REFRIGERATION CIRCUIT

This unit is concerned with the basic refrigeration circuit. The following description of the refrigeration part of the air-conditioning system is intended to familiarize the service technician with the general arrangement and function of the components in the system. A complete understanding of the overall operation of the system is necessary when working on air-conditioning units. Each component of the system will be examined in detail.

> CAUTION: It should be emphasized again that eye protection is recommended when servicing air-conditioning units.

Study the schematic diagram of the components of the refrigeration system, figure 9-1. The compressor (B) pumps heat-laden refrigerant vapor from the evaporator (A). The refrigerant is compressed at (B) and then is sent, under high pressure, to the condenser (C) as a superheated vapor.

Since this vapor is much hotter than the surrounding air, it gives up its heat to the outside air flowing through the condenser fins.

As the refrigerant vapor gives up its heat, it changes to a liquid. The condensed liquid refrigerant is filtered, dried, and temporarily stored, under pressure, in the receiver/drier (D) until it is needed by the evaporator.

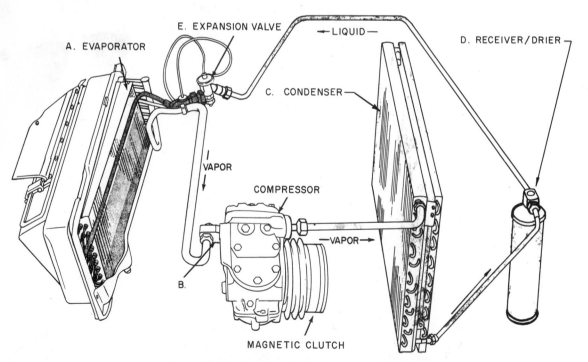

Fig. 9-1 Refrigeration system components (typical)

Liquid refrigerant is metered from the receiver/drier into the evaporator by the thermostatic expansion valve (E). This valve controls the flow of refrigerant in this part of the system. The pressure of the refrigerant is lowered by the expansion valve. As a result, the refrigerant begins to boil and change to a vapor. During this process, the refrigerant picks up heat from the warm air passing through the fins of the evaporator. Thus, the process repeats as this heat is transmitted first to the compressor, and then to the condenser for dissipation.

In the following discussion, the sizes of the system hoses are given, as is the state of the refrigerant in the hoses and in the components. Although the hose sizes may vary in different systems, the state of the refrigerant at various points in all systems is the same.

RECEIVER/DRIER

The discussion of the refrigeration system components begins with the receiver/drier assembly, figures 9-2 and 9-3. This device stores the refrigerant until it is needed. The receiver/drier (or drier) is a cylindrical metal can with two fittings and, in most cases, a sight glass. The drier is located in the high-pressure side of the air-conditioning system. In general, the drier contains 100% liquid refrigerant. The assembly can be divided into two parts: the receiver and the drier.

The receiver section of the tank is a storage compartment. This section holds the proper amount of extra refrigerant required by the system to insure proper operation. The receiver insures that a steady flow of liquid refrigerant can be supplied to the thermostatic expansion valve.

The drier section of the tank is simply a bag of desiccant, such as silica gel, that can absorb and hold a small quantity of moisture.

A screen is placed in the receiver/drier to catch and prevent the circulation of any debris that may be in the system. Although this screen

Fig. 9-2 Receiver/driers

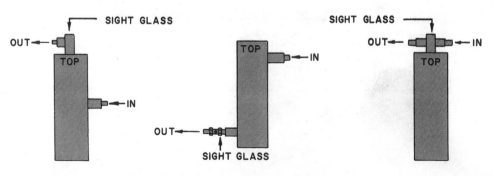

Fig. 9-3 Three types of receiver/drier assemblies

is not serviceable, there are two other filtering screens in the system that can be cleaned or replaced if necessary.

The refrigerant then moves from the receiver/drier through a rubber hose called the *liquid line* to the valve. The liquid line is usually 3/8-in. diameter hose; however, in certain cases, it may also be 1/4 in. or 1/2 in. in diameter. In addition to rubber, the line may be made of copper, steel, or aluminum. For most applications, rubber hose approved for this type of service is used. The refrigerant in the liquid line is high-pressure liquid, figure 9-4.

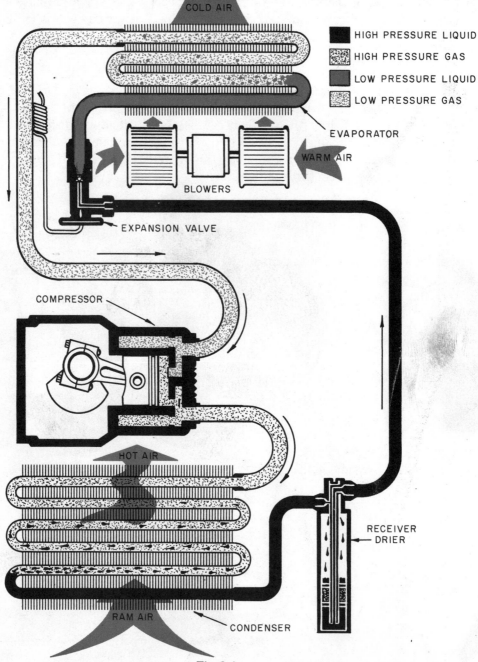

COLD AIR

HIGH PRESSURE LIQUID
HIGH PRESSURE GAS
LOW PRESSURE LIQUID
LOW PRESSURE GAS

EVAPORATOR

WARM AIR

BLOWERS

EXPANSION VALVE

COMPRESSOR

HOT AIR

RECEIVER DRIER

RAM AIR

CONDENSER

Fig. 9-4

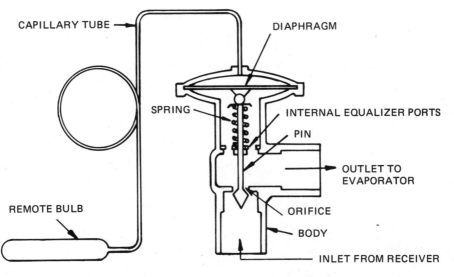

Fig. 9-5 Thermostatic expansion valve

THERMOSTATIC EXPANSION VALVE

The thermostatic expansion valve, or TXV, figure 9-5, is located at the inlet side of the evaporator. This valve is the controlling device for the system and separates the high side of the system from the low side. A small restriction, or orifice, in the valve allows only a small amount of liquid refrigerant to pass through the valve into the evaporator from the drier. The amount of refrigerant passing through the valve depends upon the evaporator temperature. The orifice is about 0.008 in. (0.0203 cm) in diameter. A pin can be raised and lowered in the orifice to change the size of the opening (up to the 0.008-in. diameter). It is evident that only a small amount of refrigerant can enter even when the valve is wide open.

The refrigerant inside the thermostatic expansion valve and immediately after it is 100% liquid. The liquid soon changes state however. As soon as the liquid pressure drops, the liquid refrigerant begins to boil. As it continues to boil, it must absorb heat. This heat is removed from the air passing over the coils and fins of the evaporator. As a result, the air feels cool. Remember, the heat is being removed from the air, cold air is not being created.

The thermostatic expansion valve meters the proper amount of refrigerant into the evaporator. Refrigerant that is properly metered into the evaporator is 100% liquid

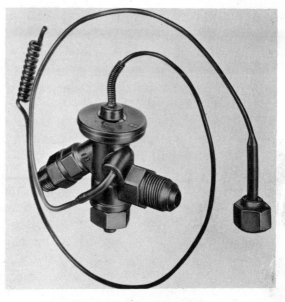

FLARE TYPE

Fig. 9-6 Externally equalized thermostatic expansion valve

just after the thermostatic expansion valve and 100% vapor (gas) at the outlet, or tail-pipe, of the evaporator. The expansion valve has a sensing element called a remote bulb or capillary bulb, figure 9-6. This bulb is attached to the evaporator tailpipe to sense outlet temperatures. In this manner, the expansion valve can regulate itself (see Unit 18).

EVAPORATOR

The evaporator, figure 9-7, is the part of the refrigeration system where the refrigerant vaporizes as it picks up heat. Heat-laden air is forced through and past the fins and tubes of the evaporator. Heat from the air is picked up by the boiling refrigerant and is carried in the system to the condenser.

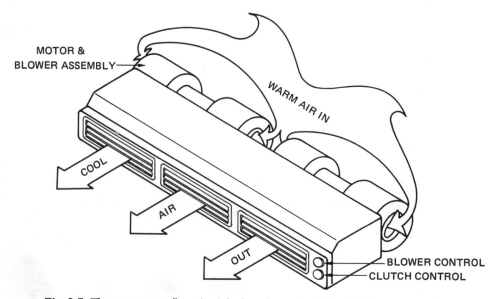

Fig. 9-7 The evaporator (heat is picked up from the air inside the evaporator)

Factors which are important in the design of an evaporator include the size and length of the tubing, the number of fins, and the amount of air passing through and past the fins. The heat load is also an important consideration. *Heat load* refers to the amount of heat, in Btu units, to be removed.

The evaporator may have two, three, or more rows of tubing as determined by the design to fit a specific housing and still be able to achieve the rated capacity in Btu. The refrigerant as it leaves the evaporator on its way to the compressor is low-pressure gas.

If too much refrigerant is metered, the unit floods. As a result, the unit does not cool because the pressure of the refrigerant is higher and it does not boil away as quickly. In addition, when the evaporator is filled with liquid refrigerant, the refrigerant cannot vaporize properly. This step is necessary if the refrigerant is to take on heat. A flooded evaporator allows an excess of liquid refrigerant to leave the evaporator, with the result that serious damage may be done to the next component, the compressor.

If too little refrigerant is metered into the evaporator, the system is said to be starved. Again, the unit does not cool because the refrigerant vaporizes or boils off too rapidly, long before it passes through the evaporator.

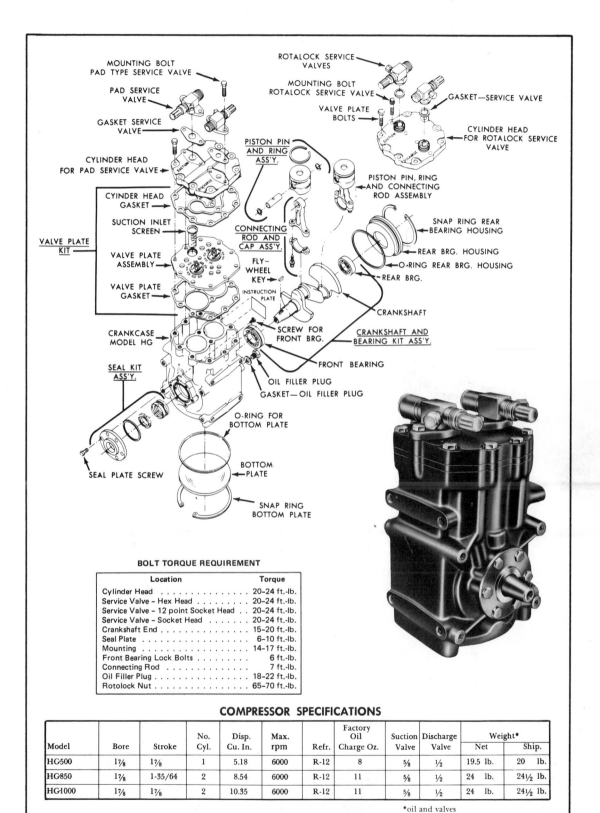

BOLT TORQUE REQUIREMENT

Location	Torque
Cylinder Head	20–24 ft.-lb.
Service Valve – Hex Head	20–24 ft.-lb.
Service Valve – 12 point Socket Head . .	20–24 ft.-lb.
Service Valve – Socket Head	20–24 ft.-lb.
Crankshaft End	15–20 ft.-lb.
Seal Plate	6–10 ft.-lb.
Mounting	14–17 ft.-lb.
Front Bearing Lock Bolts	6 ft.-lb.
Connecting Rod	7 ft.-lb.
Oil Filler Plug	18–22 ft.-lb.
Rotolock Nut	65–70 ft.-lb.

COMPRESSOR SPECIFICATIONS

Model	Bore	Stroke	No. Cyl.	Disp. Cu. In.	Max. rpm	Refr.	Factory Oil Charge Oz.	Suction Valve	Discharge Valve	Weight* Net	Weight* Ship.
HG500	1⅞	1⅞	1	5.18	6000	R-12	8	⅝	½	19.5 lb.	20 lb.
HG850	1⅞	1-35/64	2	8.54	6000	R-12	11	⅝	½	24 lb.	24½ lb.
HG1000	1⅞	1⅞	2	10.35	6000	R-12	11	⅝	½	24 lb.	24½ lb.

*oil and valves

**Fig. 9-8 Exploded view and parts assembly kit,
models HG500, HG850 & HG1000 automotive compressors**

COMPRESSOR

The compressor, figure 9-8, page 47, is a pump designed to raise the pressure of the refrigerant. When the refrigerant pressure is increased, it condenses more rapidly in the next component, the condenser.

The aftermarket or add-on air conditioners generally use a two-cylinder compressor manufactured by York, Tecumseh, or Sankyo. American Motors and some Ford Motor Company cars also use these compressors with factory-installed units. Chrysler Corporation uses two-cylinder compressors manufactured by the Air-Temp Division.

General Motors' factory-installed units used a Frigidaire five-cylinder compressor until 1961. In 1962, General Motors began using a Frigidaire six-cylinder compressor with three double-ended pistons. The six-cylinder compressor is also used in many late model Ford Motor Company cars.

A one-cylinder Tecumseh compressor is used in many aftermarket air-conditioner installations in compact cars.

Each piston of the compressor is equipped with a set of suction and discharge valves and valve plates. While one piston is on the intake stroke, the other is on the compression stroke, figure 9-9. The piston draws in refrigerant through the suction valve and forces it out through the discharge valve. When the piston is on the down-stroke, or intake stroke, the discharge valve is held closed by the action of the piston and the higher pressure above it. At the same time, the suction reed valve is opened to allow low-pressure gas to enter. When the piston is on the upstroke, or compression stroke, refrigerant is forced through the discharge valve and the suction valve is held closed by the same pressure.

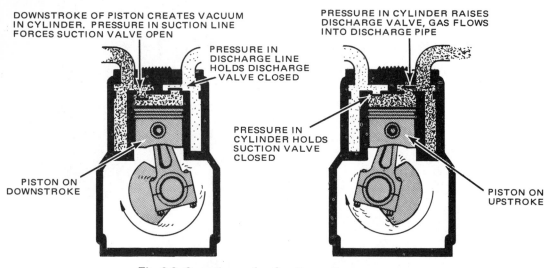

Fig. 9-9 Operating cycle of reciprocating compressor

The compressor separates the low side of the system from the high side. The refrigerant entering the compressor is low-pressure gas. When the refrigerant leaves the compressor, it is a high-pressure gas.

The compressor is equipped with service valves which are used to service the air-conditioning system. The manifold and gauge set is connected into the system at the service valve ports. All procedures such as evacuating and charging the system are carried out through the manifold and gauge set.

The hose leaving the compressor contains high-pressure gas. This hose is made of rubber and is usually 1/2 in. (12.7 mm) in diameter (although a 5/8-in. or 15.88 mm line may be used). Known as the hot-gas discharge line, it connects to an inlet on the condenser. This inlet is always on the top side of the condenser.

CONDENSER

The purpose of the condenser is the opposite of that of the evaporator. Refrigerant in the gaseous state liquefies or condenses in the condenser. To do so, the refrigerant must give up its heat in Btu. Ram air, or the air passing over the condenser, carries the heat away from the condenser and the gas condenses. The heat removed from the refrigerant (so that it can change to a liquid), is the same heat that was absorbed in the evaporator to change the refrigerant from a liquid to a gas.

The refrigerant is almost 100% gas when it enters the condenser. A very small amount of gas may liquefy in the hot-gas discharge line, but the amount is so small that it does not affect the operation of the system.

The refrigerant is not 100% liquid when it leaves the condenser. Since only a certain amount of heat can be handled by the condenser at a given time, a small percentage of the refrigerant leaves the condenser in a gaseous state. Again, this condition does not affect the system operation since the next component is the receiver/drier.

As indicated previously, the inlet of the condenser must be at the top of the unit, figure 9-10. With the inlet in this position, the condensing refrigerant can flow to the bottom of the condenser where it is forced, under pressure, to the drier through the liquid line.

The refrigerant in the condenser is a combination of liquid and gas under high pressure. Extreme care must be exercised when servicing this component of the system.

From the condenser, the refrigerant continues to the receiver/drier through the liquid line. At this point, the cycle starts over again. The liquid line from the condenser can be either a rubber or a metal line in a variety of sizes.

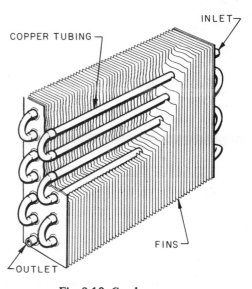

Fig. 9-10 Condenser

SUMMARY

The entire refrigeration cycle exhibits several processes as the refrigerant changes state in various sections of the system. When the pressure of the refrigerant drops in the evaporator, the refrigerant boils. While boiling, the refrigerant picks up heat. The compressor raises the temperature and pressure of the refrigerant so that it condenses in the condenser. At this point, the refrigerant gives up the same heat (in Btu) that it picked up in the evaporator.

The thermostatic expansion valve controls the flow of refrigerant into the evaporator and thereby separates the high side of the system from the low side. The compressor increases gas pressure and separates the low side of the system from the high side. This is the basic air-conditioning circuit from which all of the other automotive refrigeration circuits are patterned. A good understanding of the simple circuit makes an understanding of the other circuits much easier.

REVIEW

Briefly answer each of the following questions.

1. What is the purpose of the desiccant in the receiver/drier?
2. What happens if the receiver section of the drier is omitted?
3. What happens if the thermostatic expansion valve is omitted?
4. Which is the more serious problem: a flooded evaporator or a starved evaporator? Why?
5. Indicate the state of the refrigerant immediately as it enters the evaporator.
6. What is the state of the refrigerant as it leaves the evaporator?
7. What is the purpose of the compressor service valves?
8. What is the purpose of the compressor suction reed valve?
9. What is the purpose of the compressor discharge reed valve?
10. Why should eyes be protected from refrigerant?
11. Refer to figure 9-11 and indicate the state of the refrigerant (high-pressure liquid, high-pressure gas, low-pressure liquid, low-pressure gas) at the points indicated on the diagram.
12. Refer to figure 9-11 and name the component parts indicated.
13. The direction of the refrigerant flow is from (the drier to the expansion valve) (the expansion valve to the drier). Select the correct answer.
14. The expansion valve is located at the _____ of the evaporator.

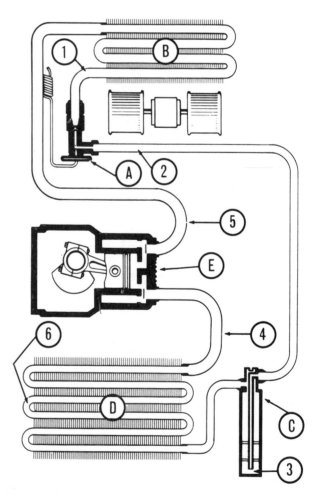

Fig. 9-11 The refrigeration system

UNIT 10   THE ELECTRICAL CIRCUIT

This unit is concerned with the basic refrigeration electrical circuit, figure 10-1. The circuit includes the rheostat or three-speed fan switch and the temperature control thermostat. Each component of the circuit is discussed, as is its purpose and placement in the air-conditioning circuit. The function of each component is described and troubleshooting and servicing notes are also given.

The refrigeration electrical circuit should be connected to a separate accessory circuit from the fuse block or the ignition switch of the automobile. Number 12 wire is to be used for this circuit which should have either a 20-ampere fuse or a circuit breaker as a protective device.

Blower Control

The blower control may be a rheostat or a two- or three-speed switch. The rheostat control permits the selection of a full range of blower speeds from fast to slow.

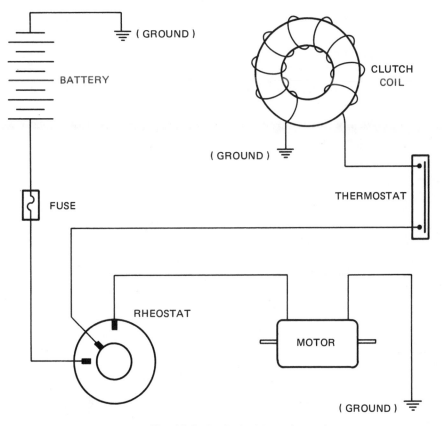

Fig. 10-1 Typical wiring schematic

The two- or three-speed switch limits blower speeds to steps such as high-low or high-medium-low.

When the blower control is energized at any speed on most units, current is fed to the thermostat. Once the unit is turned on, the blower speeds can be changed without affecting the current to the thermostat. When the control is turned off, the current to the thermostat is also turned off.

Thermostat

The thermostat is a control device that reacts to changing temperatures and causes electrical contacts to make and break. The thermostat has a capillary, or sensing tube, which extends into the evaporator core. This capillary serves as a monitor to sense the evaporator temperature.

Some refrigeration systems use a bimetallic thermostat for temperature control. This type of thermostat does not have a capillary tube, but relies on the temperature of the air passing over it to cause the points to make and break. However, this type of thermostat is not as accurate as the capillary tube thermostat. The bimetallic thermostat is becoming more popular because it requires less space for installation and is less expensive than the capillary thermostat.

Clutch

When the thermostat closes the electrical contacts, current flows to the clutch field and energizes the clutch. As a result, the compressor crankshaft begins to turn and the refrigeration cycle starts. When the temperature of the evaporator drops to a predetermined point, usually about 33°F (0.55°C), the contacts open and the clutch disengages. This period permits a defrost cycle in the evaporator and prevents the formation of ice.

When the clutch disengages, the blowers continue to operate at their predetermined speed. As the evaporator temperature rises, usually to about 45°F (7.22°C), or 12°F (6.67°C) above the cutout point, the contacts in the thermostat again close. The clutch is thus reengaged to continue the refrigeration cycle.

REVIEW

Briefly answer each of the following questions.

1. What effect is there on the clutch when the electrical contacts in the rheostat close?
2. How is the clutch affected when the electrical contacts in the thermostat open?
3. What is the normal temperature rise between the temperatures at which the thermostat cuts out and when it cuts in again?
4. Which type of thermostat is the better one?
5. What is the rheostat used for?

UNIT 11   REFRIGERATION OIL

The moving parts of a compressor assembly must be lubricated to prevent damage during operation. Oil is used on these moving parts and on the seals and gaskets as well. In addition, a small amount of oil is added to the refrigerant which circulates through the system. This refrigerant/oil combination maintains the thermostatic expansion valve in the proper operating condition.

The type of oil which must be used in an automotive air-conditioning system is a nonfoaming oil specifically designed for use in certain types of air conditioners. This special oil is known as *refrigeration oil* and is available in several grades and types, figure 11-1.

Refrigeration oil is clear to light yellow in color. Any impurities will cause the oil to range in color from brown to black. Another characteristic of re- frigeration oil is that it is practically odorless. Thus, a strong odor of oil in the system indicates that the oil is impure. Impure oil must be removed and re- placed with clean, fresh oil. The receiver/drier should also be replaced and a good pumpdown performed before the system is recharged.

Fig. 11-1 Refrigerant oil charge for adding oil to system

THE CLASSIFICATION OF REFRIGERATION OIL

The classification of refrigeration oil is based on three factors: viscosity, compatibility with refrigerants, and pour point.

Viscosity

The *viscosity rating* for a fluid is based on the time, in seconds, required for a measured quantity of the fluid to pass through a calibrated orifice when the temperature of the fluid is 100°F (37.8°C). The resistance to flow of any liquid is judged by the viscosity rating of the fluid. The higher the viscosity number, the thicker the liquid.

The fluorocarbon group of refrigerants (R12 is included in this group) requires oil with a viscosity of about 300 for air-conditioner service. Some air conditioners, however, can use an oil with a viscosity rating as high as 1,000.

The Saybolt Universal Viscosity (SUV) is defined as the time in seconds required for sixty cubic centimeters of oil, at 100°F (37.8°C), to flow through a standard Saybolt orifice.

Compatibility

Refrigeration oil must be compatible with the refrigerant used in the system. This means that the oil must be capable of existing (remaining an oil) when mixed with the refrigerant. In other words, the oil is not changed or separated by chemical interaction with the refrigerant.

The compatibility of a refrigeration oil with a refrigerant is determined by a test called a *floc test* F. This test is performed by placing a mixture containing 90% oil and 10% refrigerant in a sealed glass tube. The mixture is then slowly cooled until a waxy substance appears. The temperature at which this substance forms is recorded as the *floc point*.

Pour Point

The temperature at which an oil will just flow is its *pour point*. This temperature is recorded in degrees Fahrenheit. The pour point is a standard of the American Society for Testing Materials (ASTM).

SERVICING TIPS

The oil level of the compressor should be checked each time the air conditioner is serviced. Always check the manufacturer's recommendations before adding oil to the air-conditioning system. The procedures for adding oil to all compressors can be found under the heading of Service Procedures, Section 3, in this text.

When the oil is not being poured, the oil container must remain capped. Always be sure that the cap is in place and tightly secured. Oil absorbs moisture and moisture is damaging to the air conditioner.

SUMMARY

The properties of a good refrigeration oil are low wax content, good thermal and chemical stability, low viscosity, and a low pour point. A few simple rules are listed as follows for handling refrigeration oil:

DO

- Use only approved refrigeration oil.
- Make sure the cap is tight on the container when not in use.
- Replace oil if there is any doubt of its condition.
- Avoid contaminating the oil.

DO NOT

- Transfer oil from one container to another.
- Return used oil to the container.
- Leave the oil container uncapped.
- Use a grade of oil other than that recommended for the air conditioner.

REVIEW

Briefly answer each of the following questions.

1. What does viscosity mean?

2. What is the primary purpose of the refrigeration oil?

3. List three ways refrigeration oil can become contaminated.

4. Why is special refrigeration oil to be used in an air-conditioning system rather than motor oil?

5. Under what conditions should all oil be replaced in the air-conditioning system?

UNIT 12 MOISTURE

For all practical purposes, refrigerant can be considered to be moisture free. The moisture content of new refrigerant should not exceed ten parts of moisture per million parts of refrigerant (10 ppm).

If new refrigerant and refrigeration oil are used in a system, then any moisture found in the system must come from outside sources, such as a break in a line or from improperly fastened hoses or fittings on the installation.

Whenever a unit is removed from the system for repair or replacement air is introduced into the system. As a result, there is always a danger of moisture entering the unit since air contains moisture. Refrigerant absorbs moisture readily when exposed to it. To keep the system as moisture free as possible, all air conditioners use a receiver/drier which contains a bag of desiccant such as silica gel. Desiccants are able to absorb and hold a small quantity of moisture.

Any water introduced into the system in excess of the amount that the desiccant can handle is free in the system. Even one drop of free water cannot be controlled and causes irreparable damage to the internal parts of the air conditioner.

Moisture in greater concentrations than 20 ppm causes serious damage. To illustrate how small an amount 20 ppm is, one small drop of water in an air-conditioning system having a capacity of three pounds amounts to 40 ppm, or twice the amount that can be tolerated.

Refrigerant 12 reacts chemically with water to form hydrochloric acid. The heat generated in the system speeds up the acid forming process. The greater the concentration of water in the system, the more concentrated is the corrosive acid formed.

The hydrochloric acid corrodes all of the metallic parts of the system, particularly those made of steel. Iron, copper, and aluminum parts are damaged by the acid as well. The corrosive process creates oxides which are released into the refrigerant as particles of metal which form a sludge. Further damage is caused when oxides plug the screens in the thermostatic expansion valve, compressor inlet, and the drier itself.

One automotive air-conditioner manufacturer indicates that alcohol, or methanol, should be added to the system. This manufacturer states that a system freezeup can be avoided by adding 2 cm^3 of alcohol per pound of refrigerant. However, the addition of alcohol to the system can cause even greater damage since the drier seeks out alcohol even more than moisture in the system. Thus, the drier releases all of its moisture and absorbs the alcohol. This additional free moisture in the system can now cause more severe damage to the system components. Once a system is saturated with moisture, irreparable damage is done to the interior of the system. If the moisture condition is neglected long enough, pinholes caused by corrosion appear in the evaporator and condenser coils and in any metal tubing used in the system. Any affected parts must be replaced.

In addition, aluminum parts can become so corroded that the compressor is unserviceable. Valves and fittings can be damaged so severely that they are no longer usable.

Whenever there is evidence of moisture in a system, a thorough system cleanout is recommended. Such a cleanout should be followed by the installation of a new drier and a complete system pumpdown using a vacuum pump. Unit 13 covers the process of moisture removal in detail.

The air-conditioning technician can prevent the introduction of unwanted moisture and dirt into a system by following a few simple rules.

- When servicing the air conditioner, always install the drier last.
- When servicing the air-conditioner parts always cap the open ends of hoses and fittings immediately.
- Never work around water, outside in the rain, or in very humid locations.
- Do not allow new refrigerant or refrigeration oil to become contaminated.
- Always keep the refrigeration oil container capped.
- Develop clean habits; do not allow dirt to enter the system.
- Keep all service tools free of grease and dirt.
- Never fill a unit without first insuring that air and moisture are removed.

REVIEW

Briefly answer each of the following questions.

1. What is the maximum moisture content allowable in new refrigerant?
2. List three ways that moisture can enter the system.
3. What component part of the system attracts the most moisture?
4. What effect does the addition of alcohol have on the system as far as freezeup is concerned?
5. What undesirable effect does the addition of alcohol have on the refrigeration system?
6. What acid is formed by the chemical combination of refrigerant and water?
7. Name the materials that are damaged most severely by hydrochloric acid.
8. How can hydrochloric acid be eliminated?
9. How can one prevent the formation of hydrochloric acid?
10. The hydrochloric acid corrodes the metallic components of a system to produce oxides. How do these oxides affect the system?

UNIT 13   MOISTURE REMOVAL

Unit 12 indicated the problems which can arise due to excessive moisture in a refrigeration system. It was stated that after any repair work, the system must be pumped down to remove any moisture present. This unit shows how a refrigeration system is pumped down and explains how moisture is removed in a vacuum. Recall that a pressure below zero pounds gauge pressure is referred to in terms of inches of mercury (in. Hg).

The removal of moisture from a system can cause serious problems for the service technician who is not equipped with the proper tools. a vacuum pump is a must for air-conditioning service. Although other methods can be used, the vacuum pump is still the most efficient means of moisture removal. Figures 13-1 and 13-2 show typical vacuum pumps in common use.

Moisture is removed in the air-conditioning system by creating a vacuum. In a vacuum, the moisture in the system boils. The pumping action of the vacuum pump then pulls the moisture in the form of a vapor from the system. When the pressure is increased on the discharge side of the pump, the vapor again liquefies. This process usually occurs inside the pump.

Fig. 13-1   Standard vacuum pump

It is possible to use the air-conditioning compressor to evacuate the system. However, this procedure is not recommended because a minimum of thirty minutes is required to remove the moisture at a compressor speed of about 1,750 rpm. Recall that the compressor is lubricated by oil contained in the refrigerant. Since the compressor runs dry when it is operated as a vacuum pump, the compressor can be seriously damaged. When the pressure is increased inside the pump, the vapor again liquefies (usually inside the pump). Thus, if the automotive compressor is used to evacuate the system, the moisture-laden vapor is pulled out of the system and most of it is deposited

Fig. 13-2   Lightweight high-vacuum pump suitable for automotive air-conditioning service

inside the compressor. Nothing is gained in this procedure since the moisture is still inside the system.

The student should review Unit 5 for information relating to how a vacuum pump accomplishes moisture removal. Unit 5 covers temperature-pressure relationships and the boiling of water at a lower temperature at higher altitudes. A point to remember is that at higher altitudes the atmospheric pressure has a lower value than at sea level. A vacuum pump can simulate conditions at a higher altitude by mechanical means. A good vacuum pump is capable of evacuating a system to a pressure of 29.76 in. Hg (755.9 mm Hg) or better. At this pressure, water boils at 40°F (4.44°C). In other words, if the ambient temperature is 40°F (4.44°C) or higher, the water boils out of the system.

Recall that at 0 in. Hg at sea level, water boils at 212°F (100°C). To find the boiling point of water in a vacuum, use the table in figure 13-3. Note that the boiling point of water is lowered only 112° (44.45°C) to 100°F (37.8°C) as the pressure is decreased from 0 in. Hg at sea level to 28 in. Hg (711.2 mm Hg). However, the boiling point drops by 120° as the pressure decreases from 28 in. Hg (711.2 mm Hg) to 29.91 in. Hg (759.7 mm Hg).

BOILING POINT OF WATER UNDER A VACUUM	
(English System*)	
System Vacuum Inches Mercury	Temperature °F Boiling Point
24.04	140
25.39	130
26.45	120
27.32	110
27.99	100
28.50	90
28.89	80
29.18	70
29.40	60
29.66	50
29.71	40
29.76	30
29.82	20
29.86	10
29.87	5
29.88	0
29.90	-10
29.91	-20

* The student may refer to a handbook for a similar chart giving the vacuum in mm Hg versus the boiling point of water in °C.

Fig. 13-3

The degree of vacuum achieved and the amount of time the system is subjected to a vacuum determine the amount of moisture removed from the system.

The recommended minimum pumping time is thirty minutes. If time allows, however, a four-hour pumpdown achieves better results.

The removal of moisture from a system can be compared to the boiling away (vaporization) of water in a saucepan. It is not enough to cause the water to boil, time must be allowed for the water to boil away.

MOISTURE REMOVAL AT HIGHER ALTITUDES

The information just given for moisture removal by a vacuum pump is true for normal atmospheric pressures at sea level, 14.7 psig. It also holds true for higher pressures at higher altitudes if the boiling point is reduced to a point below the ambient temperature.

As indicated in unit 5, moisture (water) boils at a lower temperature at higher altitudes. However, it must be pointed out that vacuum pump efficiency is reduced at higher altitudes.

For example, the altitude of Denver, Colorado is 5,280 feet above sea level. Water boils at 206.2°F (96.78°C) at this altitude, but the maximum efficiency of a vacuum pump is reduced. A vacuum pump that can pump 29.92 in. Hg at sea level can only pump 25.44 in. Hg at this altitude. Note in figure 13-3 that water boils at about 130°F (54.44°C) at a pressure of 25.44 in. Hg.

The formula for determining the vacuum pump efficiency at a given atmospheric pressure is as follows:

$$\frac{\text{Atmospheric Pressure in your location}}{\text{Atmospheric Pressure at sea level}} \times \text{pump rated efficiency} = \text{actual efficiency (in. Hg)}$$

Assume that a vacuum pump has a rated efficiency of 29.92 in. Hg at sea level and that the atmospheric pressure at Denver is 12.5 psia. To determine the actual efficiency at this location (Denver), the formula is applied in the following manner:

$$\frac{12.5}{14.7} \times 29.92 = 25.44 \text{ in. Hg}$$

In this example, the ambient temperature must be raised above 130°F (54.44°C) if the vacuum pump is to be efficient for moisture removal. To increase the ambient temperature under the hood, the automobile engine can be operated with the air conditioner turned off. The compressor, condenser, and some of the hoses may be heated sufficiently; however, some other parts, such as the evaporator and the receiver/drier, will not be greatly affected.

Another method of moisture removal is the *sweep* or *triple evacuation* method. Although this method cannot remove all of the moisture, it should be sufficient to reduce the moisture to a safe level if the system is otherwise sound and a new drier is installed.

TRIPLE EVACUATION METHOD

The basic steps in the triple evacuation method are given here. The procedures for connecting the manifold and gauge set into the system, operating the vacuum pump, and adding and purging refrigerant, are given in the Service Procedures section of this text.

Procedure

1. Connect a manifold and gauge set to the system. Insure that all hoses and connections are tight and secure.
2. Pump a vacuum to the highest efficiency for 15-20 minutes.
3. Break the vacuum by adding Refrigerant 12. Increase the pressure to 1-2 psig.
4. Pump a vacuum to the highest efficiency for 15-20 minutes (second time).
5. Break the vacuum by adding Refrigerant 12. Increase the pressure to 1-2 psig (second time).
6. Pump a vacuum to the highest efficiency for 25-30 minutes (third time).
7. The system is now ready for charging.

REVIEW

Briefly answer each of the following questions.

1. What chemical symbol is used to denote a vacuum?
2. What tool is used to remove moisture from a system?
3. What is the vacuum level that a good vacuum pump can achieve?
4. What is the minimum length of time a vacuum pump should be used for moisture removal?
5. Why is the air-conditioner compressor not recommended as a vacuum pump for the removal of moisture?

UNIT 14 SERVICE VALVES

At times the service technician must *enter* the air-conditioning system to perform diagnostic procedures which require the recording of pressures within the system. Unit 15 is concerned with the gauges and manifold used in the actual diagnostic procedures. This unit deals with the *service valve*. This is a device that allows the service technician to enter the refrigeration system by mechanical means. The service valve is usually located on the compressor.

Air-conditioning units may have one, two, or three service valves. Although most systems have two service valves, for simplicity this unit will describe a system operating with only one valve. The system, however, can be equipped with either one of two types of service valves: the hand shutoff valve or the Schrader valve.

THE HAND SHUTOFF-TYPE VALVE

The hand shutoff valve is a three-position device that can be used for the three functions shown in figure 14-1.

A   To shut off refrigerant flow; the gauge port is not part of the system

B   Normal refrigerant operation; the gauge port is not part of the system

C   Normal refrigerant operation; the gauge port is part of the system

The following sections describe each position and define the points at which refrigerant is allowed to flow.

No Refrigerant Flow — Gauge Port Out of System

In the position shown in figure 14-1A, the service valve is said to be front seated. For this case, the refrigerant is trapped in the hose end of the service valve. The gauge port fitting is toward the atmosphere. Tracing the path through the valve shows that the gauge port connects to the compressor only. If the compressor is operated with the service valve in this

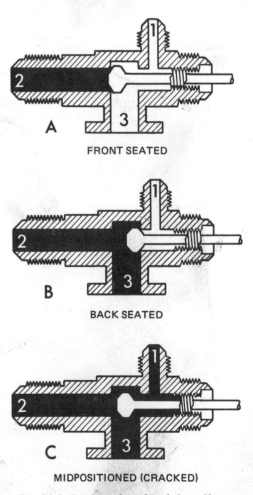

A
FRONT SEATED

B
BACK SEATED

C
MIDPOSITIONED (CRACKED)

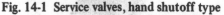

Fig. 14-1 Service valves, hand shutoff type

position and the gauge port capped, there is no area to pump refrigerant into and immediate damage may result to the compressor.

A compressor should be operated with the service valve(s) in the front-seated position only when performing necessary tests.

Normal Refrigerant Operation — Gauge Port Out of the System

As shown in figure 14-1B, a service valve in this position is said to be back seated. In this case, the compressor and hose outlet are connected and refrigerant is free to flow if the compressor is started. The gauge port is closed off and pressure readings cannot be taken when the service valve is back seated. All service valves should be in this position when the system is operating normally.

Normal Refrigerant Operation — Gauge Port in the System

When the service valve is in the position shown in figure 14-1C, it is said to be in the cracked or mid position. In this case the system can be operated while pressures are recorded through the gauge port openings.

The technician must always back seat the valves before attempting to remove the gauge hose from the service valves. Failure to do so results in a loss of refrigerant. For example, figure 14-1C shows that refrigerant is present at all outlets when the service valve is in the cracked position.

THE SCHRADER-TYPE VALVE

The Schrader-type service valve is commonly used in automotive air-conditioning units. This type of valve has only two positions: cracked or back seated, figure 14-2.

To use the Schrader valve, a special fitting is attached to the service hose.

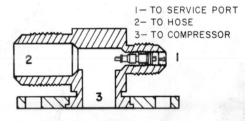

1— TO SERVICE PORT
2— TO HOSE
3— TO COMPRESSOR

Fig. 14-2 Schrader-type service valve

When this fitting is screwed onto the Schrader valve, a pin depresses the center of the valve and pressure readings are indicated on the gauges. When the fitting is removed, the valve closes and returns to the back-seated position. The service technician must not remove the hose from the fitting while it is still attached to the service valve. To do so results in a loss of refrigerant.

The Schrader-type valve cannot be front seated. When unit repair is necessary, this condition is desirable.

Service valves require little repair and maintenance. On occasion, a service valve may leak. If the leak is through the gauge port opening, a cap with a rubber insert can be used. If the leak is around the service stem or other part of the valve, it is usually recommended that the entire service valve be replaced.

As indicated previously, most automotive air-conditioning systems have two service valves. However, some systems have three valves. When three valves are used, two of them are low-side valves used for pressure or temperature control testing. Testing information is given in the section on service procedures (Section 3 of this text).

The service technician should be aware that service valves are not always installed on the compressor. The high-side service valve can be located anywhere from the outlet of the compressor to the inlet of the condenser. The low-side service valve(s) is located between the outlet of the evaporator and the inlet of the compressor.

REVIEW

Briefly answer each of the following questions.

1. How many service valves are used on the compressor? What are these valves called?
2. How many positions does the hand shutoff service valve have?
3. What position of the service valve(s) causes damage to the compressor?
4. In what position is the service valve(s) under normal operation?
5. Describe the action of the Schrader-type valve.

UNIT 15 MANIFOLD AND GAUGE SET

A basic tool for the air-conditioning service technician is the manifold and gauge set. Since system pressures accurately indicate total system performance, a means must be provided to make these measurements on any air-conditioning unit. The manifold and gauge set is essential in making these measurements. The servicing of most automotive air conditioners requires the use of a two-gauge manifold set, figure 15-1. Some systems, however, require a three-gauge set, figure 15-2, or one two-gauge set with a single gauge, figure 15-3, page 66.

For a two-gauge set, one gauge is used on the low (suction) side of the system. The other gauge is used on the high (discharge) side of the system. Systems requiring the use of a third gauge have a second low-side fitting which requires a low-pressure gauge.

MANIFOLD

The gauges are connected into the air-conditioning system through a manifold and high-pressure hoses. The manifold,

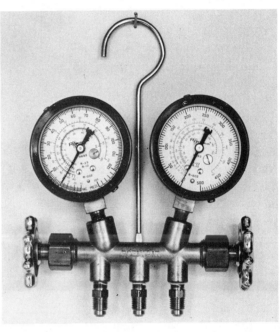

Fig. 15-1 Manifold and gauge set, side wheel

Fig. 15-2 Manifold and three-gauge set, front wheel

figure 15-4, contains provisions for fittings to which gauges and hoses can be connected. In addition, two handwheels are provided on the manifold for controlling the flow of refrigerant through the manifold.

The gauges are attached to the manifold by 1/8-in. NPT (pipe) connections. Hoses connect to the manifold with 1/8-in. NPT x 1/4-in. SAE (flare) half-unions. (Later paragraphs in this unit describe the types of hoses used with the manifold.)

The low-side hose fitting is directly below the low-side gauge and the high-side hose fitting is below the high-side gauge. The center hose fitting of the manifold is used for charging, evacuation, or any other service that is required.

Both the low and high sides of the manifold are provided with hand shutoff valves. When the hand valve is turned all the way to the right, in a clockwise (CW) direction, the manifold is closed.

Fig. 15-3 Single-gauge compound gauge used for system diagnosis

Fig. 15-4 Manifold bar and hand wheels (hand valves)

However, the gauge indicates the system pressure in the hose. Figure 15-5 shows both manifold hand valves in the closed position. For this condition, pressures can still be recorded on each gauge.

The hand valve is opened by turning it to the left or counterclockwise (CCW). When the hand valve is open, the system is opened to the center hose port of the manifold set. This condition is desirable only when refrigerant must be allowed to enter or leave the system.

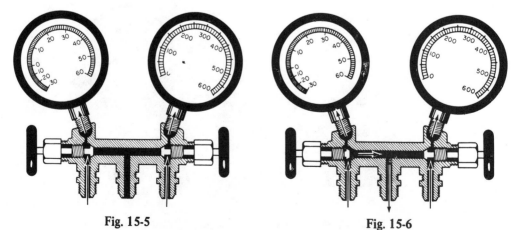

Fig. 15-5   Fig. 15-6

If the low-side manifold hand valve is opened, figure 15-6, the passage is complete between the low-side port and the center port only. The low-side gauge indicates only the low-side pressure. The high side remains closed and the high-side gauge indicates only the high-side pressure.

Similarly, when only the high-side hand valve is opened, figure 15-7, the passage is complete between the high-side port and the center port. Again, the low-side and high-side gauges indicate only the pressure in their respective sides.

If both hand valves are opened, figure 15-8, both the low-side and high-side ports are open to the center port. However, the pressures indicated on the gauges are not accurate when both hand valves are opened. Some of the high-side pressure feeds through the manifold to the low-side gauge, with the result that the high-side pressure indication is decreased and the low-side pressure indication is increased, figure 15-8.

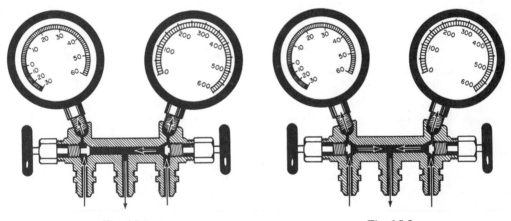

Fig. 15-7   Fig. 15-8

The manifold is used to perform nearly all of the air-conditioning system tests and diagnostic procedures. Manifolds are available in a front valve type, a side valve type, and an offset valve type.

LOW-SIDE GAUGE

The gauge used on the low side of the system is called a *compound gauge*, figure 15-9. A compound gauge is designed to give both vacuum and pressure indications. This gauge is connected through the manifold and the high-pressure hose to the low side of the air-conditioning system.

Fig. 15-9 Compound gauge

The vacuum scale of a compound gauge generally is calibrated to show pressures from thirty inches of mercury (30 in. Hg) (760 mm Hg) to zero inches of mercury (0 in. Hg) (0 mm Hg). The pressure scale is calibrated to indicate pressures from zero pounds per square inch gauge (0 kg/cm^2) to one hundred twenty pounds per square inch gauge (8.437 kg/cm^2) (0-120 psig or 0-8.437 kg/cm^2). The compound gauge is constructed so as to prevent any damage to the gauge if the pressure should reach a value as high as 250 psig (17.577 kg/cm²). The gauge described in this paragraph is designated in the following manner:

30" – 0 –120 psi, with retard to 250 psi.

Pressures above 80 psig (5.625 kg/cm²) are rarely experienced in the low side of the system. However, such pressures may result if the manifold hoses are crossed so that the manifold gauges are connected backwards to the air-conditioning system. (Even experienced service technicians can make this type of error.)

HIGH-SIDE GAUGE

The high-side gauge, figure 15-10, indicates the pressure in the high side of the system. Pressures in this area under normal conditions seldom exceed 250 psig (17.577 kg/cm²). However, as a safety factor, it is recommended that the minimum scale indication of the gauge be 300 psig (21.09 kg/cm²). A popular scale for the high-side gauge is 0-500 psig (0-35.154 kg/cm²), figure 15-10.

Fig. 15-10 Pressure gauge

The high-side gauge is not calibrated as a compound gauge. Therefore, it cannot be damaged whenever the system is pulled into a vacuum.

GAUGE CALIBRATION AND SCALES

Many gauges are provided with calibration adjustment screws. A good gauge is reasonably accurate to about two percent of the total scale reading when it is calibrated so that the needle rests on zero when there is no applied pressure.

To calibrate a gauge, it is necessary to remove the glass or plastic cover and the retaining ring (bezel). A small screwdriver can then be used to turn the adjusting screw

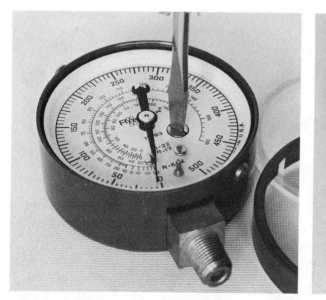

Fig. 15-11 Screwdriver used to recalibrate gauge to zero

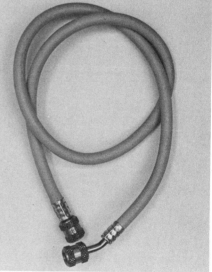

Fig. 15-12 Typical charging hose

in either direction until the pointer is lined up with the zero mark, figure 15-11. The adjusting screw must not be forced; to do so can damage the gauge.

Many gauges have inner scales which indicate the temperature-pressure relationship of three types of refrigerant: R12, R22, and R502. This relationship is outlined in Unit 7 and is considered again in Section II of this text.

HOSES

Charging hoses, figure 15-12, are constructed to withstand working pressures of 500 psi (35.154 kg/cm^2). Such hoses may have a burst pressure rating of up to 2,000 psi (140.61 kg/cm^2).

Hoses are available in several colors: white, yellow, red, and blue. A standard code can be used when connecting the hoses: blue is used on the low side, red is used on the high side, and white is used for the center port. The color-coded hoses lessen the chance of accidentally reversing the manifold connections to the air-conditioning system.

Hoses can be purchased in standard lengths and any length can be obtained by special order. Standard lengths are 12 in., 18 in., 36 in., 60 in., and 120 in. The most frequently used length is 36 in. In general, this length is sufficient for most automotive service needs.

The ends of standard charging hoses are designed to fit the 1/4-inch SAE (flare) fittings of the manifold set and compressor access ports. The hose fittings are equipped with replaceable nylon, neoprene, or rubber gasket inserts. These gaskets are always a potential source of leaks during evacuation and charging procedures and should be replaced periodically. Hoses are available with a built-in pin on one end, figure 15-13, for use on Schrader-type access ports. The hose end without the pin attaches to the manifold set. The hose end with the pin attaches to either the Schrader or hand shutoff-type service valve of the system. If the hose is not equipped with a pin, a Schrader-type adapter is available. If the pin (or adapter) is not used, gauge pressures cannot be determined and system servicing is not possible on systems equipped with Schrader valves.

Fig. 15-13 Schrader access adapter

THE THIRD GAUGE

As stated previously, some air conditioners require a third gauge for testing system pressures. This additional gauge is used on systems having some type of pressure control for the evaporator. Pressure controls are covered in Unit 21. The two low-side gauges are used to determine the pressure drop across the control device. Figure 15-14, page 70, shows the use of a three-gauge manifold. More information concerning the three-gauge manifold is given in Section 3, Service Procedures.

Fig. 15-14 Three-gauge manifold set used to check system pressures

REVIEW

Select the appropriate answer from the choices given. For questions 6 through 10, cross out the incorrect word or words to make the sentence read correctly.

1. What scale is required for the low-side (compound) gauge?

   a. 0-500 psig
   b. 30"-120/150 psig
   c. 0-300 psig
   d. 30"-120/250 psig

2. What is the recommended minimum scale of the high-side (pressure) gauge?

   a. 0-500 psig
   b. 30"-120/150 psig
   c. 0-300 psig
   d. 30"-120/250 psig

3. What is the overall purpose of the manifold?

   a. to hold gauges and hoses.
   b. to permit access to the system.
   c. to permit system service.
   d. All of these are correct.

4. When is the third gauge used?

   a. when checking pressure increase across a control
   b. when checking pressure drop across a control
   c. when checking pressure increase across the compressor
   d. when checking pressure drop across the compressor

5. When both of the manifold hand valves are closed,

   a. the low-side gauge shows the low-side pressure.
   b. the high-side gauge shows the high-side pressure.
   c. both gauges show the respective pressure of the low side and the high side of the system.
   d. both gauges indicate incorrect pressures.

6. To open a manifold hand valve, turn it (clockwise) (counterclockwise).

7. A low-side gauge indicates pressure in the (evaporator) (condenser).

8. A good gauge is reasonably accurate to about (one) (two) (three) percent of the total scale.

9. (White) (yellow) (red) (blue) are the colors generally provided when a color-coded hose set is used.

10. Charging hoses should have a rated working pressure of (300) (500) (1,000) pounds per square inch.

UNIT 16   LEAK DETECTORS

The methods of detecting leaks in an air-conditioning system range from using a soap solution to the use of an expensive self-contained electronic instrument.

The most popular detection instrument is the halide gas torch. Its popularity is due to its initial low cost, ease of handling, and simplicity of construction and operation.

HALIDE LEAK DETECTOR

The halide leak detector can detect a leak as slight as one pound in ten years; however, a great deal of practice and experience is required to be able to recognize such a slight leak.

The halide leak detector consists of two major parts: the detector unit and the gas cylinder. The gas cylinder is a nonrefillable pressure tank containing a gas such as propane. The detector unit consists of a valve (which controls the flow of gas to the burner), the burner (a chamber where the gas and air are mixed), and the search hose (a rubber tube through which air passes to the chamber).

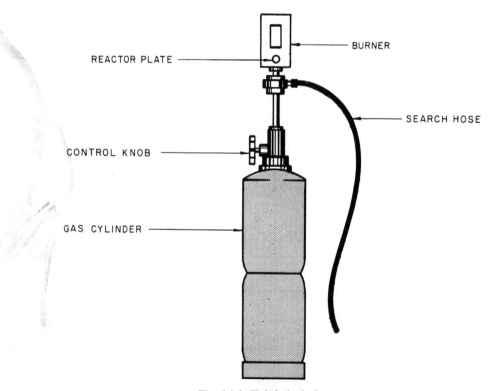

Fig. 16-1 Halide leak detector

Principle of Operation

Air is drawn through the search hose into the burner and the area of the copper reactor plate. When the gas and air mixture is ignited, the flow of gas is regulated until the flame burns about one-quarter inch above the opening in the reactor plate. This plate is heated by the flame to a red hot temperature.

When the search hose comes into contact with leaking refrigerant, the refrigerant is drawn into the search tube and is brought to the reactor plate. As a result, the flame turns violet. In some cases, if the leak is severe enough, the flame is put out.

The proper use of the halide detector is covered elsewhere in this text. However, the following precautions in the use of this device cannot be stressed too often.

CAUTION

A halide leak detector must be used in well-ventilated spaces only. It must never be used in a place where explosives, such as gases, dust, or vapors, are present. The vapors or fumes from the halide leak detector *must not be inhaled*; they may be poisonous.

Maintenance

Relatively little maintenance is required by the halide leak detector. On occasion, it may be necessary to replace the reactor plate (a part of the burner) to insure the proper operation of the unit.

Improper operation of the leak detector can result from an obstructed or collapsed search hose, or from dirt in the orifice or burner.

LEAK DETECTION USING A SOAP SOLUTION

A soap solution may be a more efficient method of locating small leaks. Since leaks often occur in areas of limited access, a halide or electronic leak detector cannot be used to locate such leaks.

To perform the soap solution leak test, mix one-half cup of soap powder with water to form a thick solution which is just light enough to make suds with a small paintbrush. When this solution is applied to the area of a suspected leak, soap bubbles reveal the leak.

In many instances, the leak in an air-conditioning system can be either a cold leak or a pressure leak. A cold leak occurs only when the unit is not at its operating temperature, such as in a car that is parked overnight. A pressure leak occurs at periods of high pressure within the system, such as when the automobile is slowly moving in heavy traffic on a very warm day.

To locate either a cold leak or a pressure leak, it may be desirable to introduce a dye solution into the system. This dye is available in either yellow or red forms. The dye is safe for air-conditioning system use and does not affect the operation of the system.

When a leak cannot be detected in the shop, a dye solution is then added. After the automobile is driven a few days, the leak can be detected by the dye trace.

Once a dye is introduced into the system, it must remain there unless the complete system is cleaned out, the oil changed, and the drier replaced. The method of introducing dye into the system is covered in Section 3, Service Procedure 21.

ELECTRONIC LEAK DETECTORS

Electronic leak detectors are the most sensitive of all leak detection devices. The initial purchase price of an electronic leak detector is higher than that of a halide leak detector. In addition, this more sophisticated device requires more maintenance than the halide leak detector.

Electronic leak detectors are also known as halogen leak detectors. Such a device can detect a Refrigerant 12 rate of loss as slow as one-half ounce per year. This value corresponds to one hundred parts of refrigerant to one million parts of air (100 ppm).

Two examples of the electronic leak detector are the General Electric Type H-10 and the Cordless Type H-11, figure 16-2. The H-10 detector operates on 120 volts, 60 hertz. The H-11 detector is a portable, cordless model that operates from a rechargeable battery. Both units are simple to operate and easy to maintain.

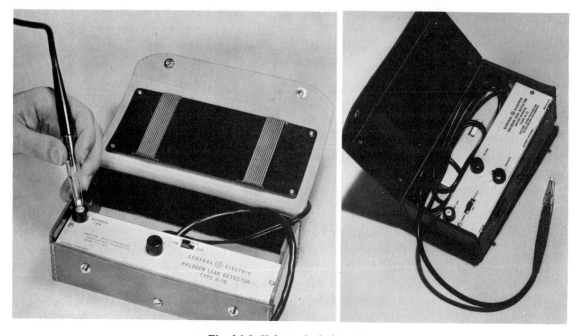

Fig. 16-2 Halogen leak detectors

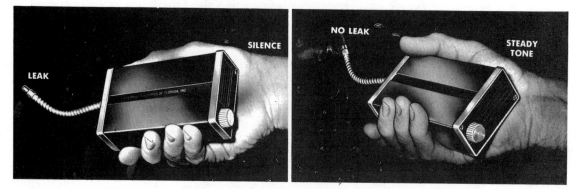

Fig. 16-3 Portable halogen leak detector

A more portable halogen leak detector is the model 508 TIF manufactured by Thermal Industries, figure 16-3. This device is powered by two ordinary flashlight batteries and weighs just 23 ounces. Because the detector uses batteries, there is no warmup period. In addition, there is no element to wear out.

Many other types of leak detectors are available. Space does not permit the description of each type of leak detector in this text. The student should contact local refrigeration suppliers for additional information on leak detectors.

REVIEW

Briefly answer each of the following questions.

1. What method of leak detection is most popular?
2. Name at least two precautions to observe when handling a leak detector.
3. What type of leak warrants the use of a dye solution?
4. How is a soap solution added to the system?
5. What is the sensitivity of an electronic leak detector?

UNIT 17
THE RECEIVER/DEHYDRATOR

The receiver/dehydrator (drier) is a very important part of an air-conditioning system. Since the load on the evaporator varies with temperature increases, increased humidity, or refrigerant losses due to small leaks, a storage area is necessary to hold extra refrigerant until it is needed by the evaporator. The receiver portion of the receiver/dehydrator unit serves as this storage area. Because of its function in storing liquid refrigerant, the use of a receiver means that it is not necessary to measure precisely the charge of refrigerant into the system. Several ounces over or under the recommended charge make little difference in system operation. In early air-conditioner units, a separate tank was often used as a receiver. In systems having a receiver tank, a separate dehydrator or drier is used. The drier is usually an in-line type and

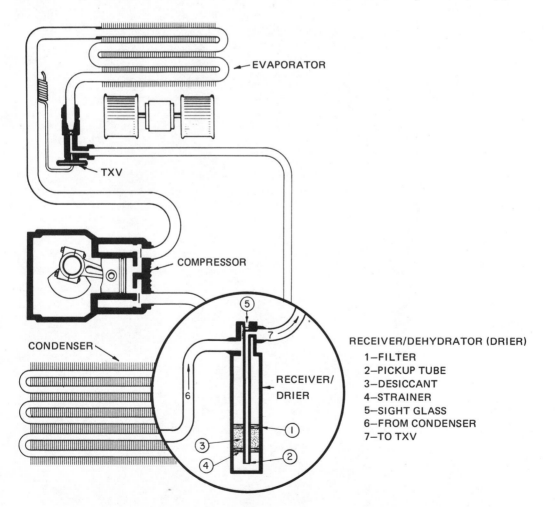

EVAPORATOR

TXV

COMPRESSOR

CONDENSER

RECEIVER/
DRIER

RECEIVER/DEHYDRATOR (DRIER)
1—FILTER
2—PICKUP TUBE
3—DESICCANT
4—STRAINER
5—SIGHT GLASS
6—FROM CONDENSER
7—TO TXV

Fig. 17-1 Location of receiver/drier in the air-conditioning system

contains a filter and desiccant or drying material. A sight glass added at the outlet of the drier gives the service technician a means of observing the refrigerant flow in the system. Figure 17-1 illustrates the location of the receiver/drier in the system and also indicates the components of the device.

RECEIVER/DRIER COMPONENTS

The Desiccant

A desiccant is a solid substance which can remove moisture from a gas, liquid, or solid. The desiccant commonly used in the drier is silica gel, molecular sieve, or Mobil-Gel®. The desiccant may be placed between two screens (which also act as strainers) within the receiver, figure 17-2, or it may be placed in a metal mesh bag and suspended from a metal spring. In some cases, the bag of desiccant is simply placed in the tank and is not held in place. It is not uncommon to shake a drier tank and hear the desiccant move. This sound does not mean that the receiver/drier is damaged (depending upon the type of receiver/drier).

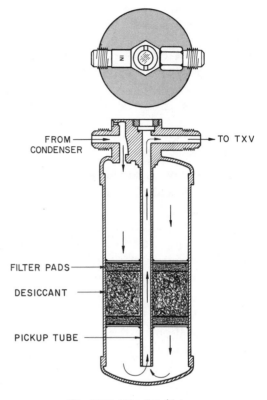

Fig. 17-2 Receiver/drier

The capacity of the desiccant for absorbing moisture depends upon the volume and type of desiccant used. For example, five cubic inches (81.94 cu. cm) of silica gel can absorb and hold about 100 drops of water at 150°F (65.56°C).

The Filter

Many driers contain filters through which the refrigerant passes before it leaves the tank. The filtering material prevents desiccant dust and other solids from being carried with the refrigerant into the air-conditioning system. Some driers have two filters, one on each side of the desiccant. The refrigerant must pass through both filters and the desiccant before leaving the receiver tank. Some driers do not have a filter and rely on the strainer to catch all foreign particles that otherwise would pass into the receiver/drier and from there into the system proper.

The Pickup Tube

The pickup tube is a device provided to insure that 100% liquid refrigerant is fed to the thermostatic expansion valve. Since the refrigerant entering the tank can be a mixture of gas and liquid, the tank also acts as a separator. The liquid refrigerant drops to the bottom of the tank and the gaseous part of the refrigerant remains at the top. The pickup tube extends to the bottom of the tank, thus insuring that a constant supply of gas-free liquid is delivered to the thermostatic expansion valve.

The Strainer

The strainer is made of fine wire mesh and is placed in the tank to aid in removing impurities (in particle form) as refrigerant passes through the receiver/drier. Some tanks have two strainers, one on each side of the desiccant. These strainers also serve to hold the desiccant in place (in a manner similar to that of filters). Although some driers may not have a filter, all driers should have one or more strainers. Refrigerant must pass through either filter(s) or strainer(s) before leaving the receiver tank.

The Sight Glass

The sight glass serves two purposes: (1) it indicates if there is enough refrigerant in the system, and (2) it indicates if the refrigerant is dry within safe limits. The sight glass is located in the liquid or outlet side of the receiver/drier. In this location, the service technician can readily observe the state of the refrigerant within the system. When the system is operating properly, a steady stream of liquid free of bubbles can be observed in the glass. The presence of bubbles or foam indicates a system malfunction or a loss of refrigerant.

OPERATION OF THE RECEIVER/DRIER

The location of the receiver/drier has a direct bearing on its ability to absorb and hold moisture. As indicated previously, five cubic inches of silica gel desiccant can hold 100 drops of moisture at 150°F (65.56°C). As the temperature increases, the ability of the desiccant to hold moisture decreases. Thus, the ability of a desiccant to hold moisture is indirectly proportional to the surrounding temperature.

One manufacturer recommends the addition of alcohol to the air-conditioning system. However, the presence of alcohol in the system also decreases the drier's capacity to hold moisture. Although the alcohol prevents any moisture in the system from freezing, the presence of alcohol is detrimental in the long run. It is extremely important to remove the moisture because it reacts with Refrigerant 12 to form hydrochloric acid. Since this acid attacks all metal parts, the thermostatic expansion valve, compressor valve plates, and service valves will be damaged if moisture is allowed to remain in the system.

When the air-conditioning system is operating in the late evening and early morning hours when the outside temperatures are lower, the drier holds the moisture and prevents it from circulating in the system. Temperature increases during the day also cause the temperature of the desiccant to increase. When the desiccant reaches its saturation point, some of its moisture is released into the system.

As little as one droplet of moisture can collect inside the thermostatic expansion valve and change to ice in the valve orifice. This ice then blocks the flow of refrigerant and the cooling action stops.

Evidence of moisture in the system is not easy to detect in the shop procedures because it takes some time for the droplets to form and turn to ice. Diagnosis of this condition is made easier if the customer has this complaint:

> "The air conditioner works fine for about fifteen minutes or so, but then it just quits. It even puts out hot air. I can turn it off for a few minutes, then turn it on, and it works fine for another ten to fifteen minutes."

This complaint is a common one and results from the addition of moisture or moisture-laden air to the air-conditioning system through careless installation or servicing procedures. In addition, this condition may be due to an improper pump-down for moisture removal before charging. To correct the condition, a new drier must be installed and the system must be pumped as long as possible to remove excess moisture before recharging.

INSTALLATION AND SERVICING

The receiver/drier is usually located under the hood of the car in front of the radiator. The drier should be placed where it can be kept as cool as possible. Late model General Motors driers are located on the engine side of the fan shroud. At least one independent manufacturer mounts the drier in the evaporator where it is always surrounded by the cool air of the evaporator.

Generally, fittings on driers are 3/8-in. male flares for both the inlet and outlet ports. Few 1/4-in. male flare fittings are used, while 3/8-in. female flare fittings are sometimes used. The majority of General Motors' driers and late model Chrysler products have 3/8-in. male or female O-ring fittings. The fitting provided depends on the year and model of the car.

Driers are also equipped with 5/16-in. barb-type fittings. The hose slips over the fitting and is then held in place with hose clamps. This type of drier is popular with independent manufacturers because it eliminates two fittings that are otherwise necessary and thus reduces the cost of the unit.

Manufacturers' recommendations should be followed when mounting a drier. For proper operation, the vertical-type drier must be mounted so that it does not incline more than 15°. The inlet of the drier must be connected to the condenser outlet.

The word IN is generally stamped on the inlet side of the drier, figure 17-2. If the inlet is not stamped, an arrow indicating the direction of refrigerant flow should be visible. The service technician must remember that the refrigerant flows from the condenser bottom toward the thermostatic expansion valve inlet. By connecting the drier in reverse, insufficient cooling can result.

As a result of improper handling or shipping, the internal parts of the drier may become dislodged and cause a partial restriction within the drier. This condition is indicated by a marked

Fig. 17-3 Recevier/driers

temperature change between the inlet and the outlet of the tank. If the restriction is great enough, frosting occurs at the drier outlet.

If the pickup tube is broken because of rough handling, abnormal flashing of the gas occurs in the liquid line. This is the same indication that is evident due to a low charge of refrigerant. In either case, a new drier must be installed.

When installing or servicing an air-conditioning system, the drier should be the last part connected to the system. Care should be exercised to prevent moisture and moisture-laden air from entering the system and the drier.

Do not uncap the drier until the unit is ready for installation. Remember: the desiccant attracts moisture from the surrounding air.

To remove moisture, it is essential to perform a complete evacuation of the system with an approved vacuum pump. This procedure is covered by Service Procedure 4, Section 3 of this text.

Whenever a refrigeration system is opened for service, foreign matter can enter the system. Dirt and moisture or other noncondensible materials cause the quality of the refrigerant to deteriorate.

The corrosion of all metal parts due to hydrochloric acid (formed from the reaction of moisture and refrigerant) causes small metal particles to slough off the affected components. These particles can stop the flow of refrigerant in the system by clogging the screens that are placed in the system to remove such impurities.

Screens are located in the inlet of the thermostatic expansion valve, the inlet of the compressor, and in the receiver/drier. All but the screen in the drier can be cleaned or replaced. If the screen in the drier becomes clogged, the entire receiver/drier unit must be replaced.

Some factory-installed systems include the receiver/drier as part of an assembly called *Valves In Receiver* (VIR), figure 17-4. (This device is covered in more detail in Unit 21). Repair and testing procedures for this assembly are given in the Service Procedures in Section 3 of this text.

ACCUMULATOR

Some air-conditioning installations contain a device that resembles a receiver/drier. This device is known as an *accumulator*, figure 17-5. The accumulator is provided to prevent liquid refrigerant from entering the compressor. The accumulator also serves as a tank to store excess liquid refrigerant and contains a desiccant.

Another name for the accumulator is the *suction accumulator* since it is located in the

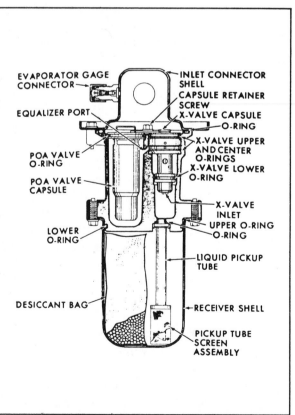

Fig. 17-4 Cutaway view of valves in receiver (VIR) showing detail of components.

Fig. 17-5 Accumulator located at the outlet of the evaporator

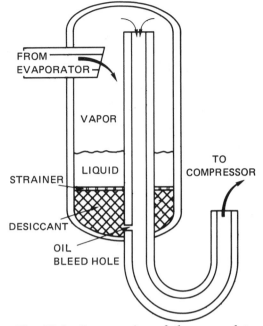

Fig. 17-6 Cutaway view of the accumulator. Note bleed hole to prevent oil from being trapped.

suction line of the system, figure 17-6. This device is used in systems that, under certain conditions, may have a flooded evaporator. The accumulator separates the liquid refrigerant from the vapor. In other words, it *accumulates* the liquid.

Refrigerant enters the top of the accumulator and liquid refrigerant falls to the bottom of the tank. Gaseous refrigerant remains at the top of the tank and is moved to the compressor through the pickup tube. At the bottom of the tank, the pickup tube contains a small hole or orifice. This orifice allows a very small amount of trapped oil or liquid refrigerant to return to the compressor.

Recall that a compressor can be damaged by an excess of liquid since it is a *positive displacement pump* and is not designed to compress liquids. Since only a controlled amount of liquid is allowed to return to the compressor through the pickup tube orifice, the compressor is not damaged.

The characteristics and composition of the desiccant in the accumulator are the same as those for the receiver/drier. The accumulator is *not* serviceable. If this device is found to be defective or *wet*, the entire unit must be replaced. Air-conditioning systems equipped with an accumulator have an expansion tube that serves as a metering device to the evaporator. If the expansion tube is clogged, it is again necessary to replace the accumulator. The expansion tube is covered in detail in Unit 18.

REVIEW

Briefly answer each of the following questions.

1. What is the purpose of silica gel in the dehydrator (drier)?
2. What is the purpose of the filter in the dehydrator (drier)?
3. What is the purpose of the pickup tube?
4. On which side of the drier is the sight glass placed?
5. When should alcohol be added to the air conditioner?

6. What effect does alcohol have on the moisture-holding capacity of the desiccant?

7. What acid forms in an air-conditioning system that contains moisture?

8. At what angle of incline can the drier be mounted?

9. At what point in the installation is the drier connected into the air-conditioning system?

10. Can the drier be installed in reverse?

UNIT 18 THE THERMOSTATIC EXPANSION VALVE

The control of the amount of refrigerant entering the evaporator core is the job of the thermostatic expansion valve (TXV). The TXV is usually found outside the evaporator case at the inlet of the evaporator. The TXV may also be found inside a device called the valves-in-receiver (VIR) in some factory-installed systems. Another type of valve known as an *expansion tube* is used in a few systems. The VIR is covered in Unit 21. The expansion tube is described at the end of this unit.

There are two types of thermostatic expansion valves in common use: the internally-equalized valve and the externally-equalized valve. Many factory-installed air conditioners use an externally-equalized valve and aftermarket manufacturers commonly use an internally-equalized valve. Figure 18-1 illustrates the typical location of the thermostatic expansion valve in the air-conditioning system.

OPERATION OF THE THERMO-STATIC EXPANSION VALVE

The diagram in figure 18-2, page 84, illustrates the construction of an expansion valve. The valve has an orifice with a needle-type valve and seat to provide variable metering. The needle is actuated by a diaphragm which is controlled by three forces:

- the evaporator pressure exerted on the bottom of the diaphragm which tends to keep the valve closed.

- the superheat spring pressure against the bottom of the needle valve which tends to keep the valve closed.

- the pressure of the inert liquid in the remote bulb

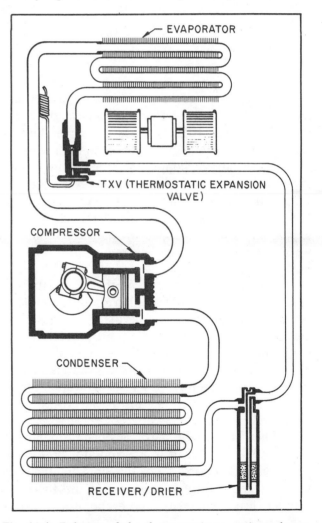

Fig. 18-1 Relation of the thermostatic expansion valve to the air-conditioning system

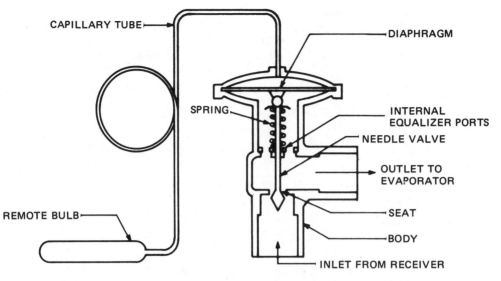

Fig. 18-2 Thermostatic expansion valve

or capillary tube against the top of the diaphragm which tends to open the valve.

Remote Bulb

Several types of inert liquid can be used in the remote bulb. However, for the moment, it is assumed that the fluid in the bulb is the same as that used in the system (Refrigerant 12). Because the same fluid or refrigerant is used, each exerts the same pressure, assuming that the temperature of each fluid is the same.

Under normal conditions, the liquid refrigerant entering the evaporator is in vapor form by the time it exits the evaporator. This suction gas is superheated. Although the superheated vapor is much warmer than the temperature at which evaporation takes place, the pressure of the vapor is unchanged. The remote bulb of the expansion valve is clamped on the suction line. In this location, the bulb senses the warmer temperature and the temperature and pressure of the inert fluid within the bulb increase.

The increased pressure of the inert fluid exerted on the top of the diaphragm is greater than the combination of the evaporator pressure and the superheat spring pressure. As a result, the needle is moved away from the seat in the orifice. The needle valve opens until the superheat spring pressure and the evaporator pressure are great enough to balance the remote bulb pressure.

For example, when the needle valve is closed, it does not allow enough refrigerant to enter the evaporator. Thus, the evaporator pressure is low and the suction vapor is warm. This condition causes a positive pressure on top of the diaphragm and the needle valve opens.

When the needle valve is open, too much refrigerant is allowed to enter the evaporator. As a result, the evaporator pressure is high and the suction vapor is cool. This condition creates a positive pressure under the diaphragm which closes the needle valve. When the three pressures of the thermostatic expansion valve balance in the manner just described, the evaporator remains fully operational under all load conditions.

The TXV has three main functions: it throttles, modulates, and controls.

Throttling Action

The expansion valve separates the high side of the air-conditioning system from the low side. Since there is a pressure drop across the valve, the flow of refrigerant is restricted, or throttled. The state of the refrigerant entering the valve is high-pressure liquid. The refrigerant leaving the valve is a low-pressure liquid. A drop in refrigerant pressure is accomplished without changing the state of the refrigerant.

Modulating Action

The TXV is designed to meter the proper amount of liquid refrigerant into the evaporator as required for the proper cooling action. The amount of refrigerant required varies with different heat loads. The TXV modulates from the wide open position, figure 18-3, to the closed position, figure 18-4. The valve seeks a point between these two positions to insure the proper metering of the refrigerant.

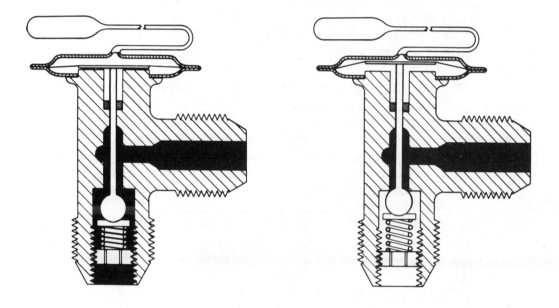

Fig. 18-3 Open thermostatic expansion valve   Fig. 18-4 Closed thermostatic expansion valve

Controlling Action

The expansion valve is designed to change the amount of liquid refrigerant metered into the evaporator in response to load or heat changes. As the load increases, more refrigerant is required by the evaporator. As the load is decreased, the valve closes and less refrigerant is delivered to the evaporator. This controlling action of the valve maintains the proper system temperature.

Superheat

The liquid refrigerant delivered to the evaporator coil usually completely vaporizes, or evaporates, before it reaches the coil outlet. Since it is known that the liquid refrigerant vaporizes at low temperature (approximately -21.6°F or -29.8°C), it can be seen that the vapor remains cold, even after all of the liquid is evaporated.

The cold vapor flowing through the remainder of the coil continues to absorb heat and becomes superheated. In other words, the temperature of the refrigerant is increased above the point at which it evaporates or vaporizes.

For example, an evaporator operating at a suction pressure of 28.5 psig (2.0 kg/cm²) has a saturated liquid temperature of 30°F (-1.11°C), according to the temperature-pressure chart in figure 18-5. As the refrigerant vaporizes (due to the absorption of heat from the evaporator), the temperature of the vapor rises until the temperature at the coil outlet, or tailpipe, reaches 35°F (1.67°C). Thus, the difference between the inlet and the outlet temperatures is 5°F (-15°C).

This difference in temperature is known as *superheat*. All expansion

TEMPERATURE-PRESSURE CHART (Evaporator temperature range)	
TEMPERATURE °F	PRESSURE psig
20	21
22	22.4
24	23.8
26	25.3
28	26.8
30	28.5
32	30
34	31.7
36	33.4
38	35.1
40	36.9

Fig. 18-5 Temperature-pressure chart, TXV range

valves are adjusted at the factory to operate under the superheat conditions present in the particular type of unit for which they are designed. When an expansion valve is being replaced, it is important to use a valve having the proper superheat range and the proper size. Although many thermostatic expansion valves look the same, they differ greatly in their applications.

THE THERMOSTATIC EXPANSION VALVE AS A CONTROL DEVICE

The thermostatic expansion valve consists of seven major parts as shown in figure 18-6:

- valve body
- valve seat
- valve diaphragm
- push rod(s)
- valve stem and needle
- superheat spring with adjuster
- capillary tube with remote bulb

As indicated previously, the remote bulb is fastened to the outlet, or tailpipe, of the evaporator. The bulb senses tailpipe temperatures and activates the diaphragm in the valve through the capillary tube. In this manner, the proper amount of refrigerant is metered into the evaporator core.

For example, a high evaporator tailpipe temperature means that the evaporator is *starved* for refrigerant. This condition is indicated by an increase in the superheated vapor leaving the evaporator. As a result, the low-side pressure gauge indicates lower than normal readings.

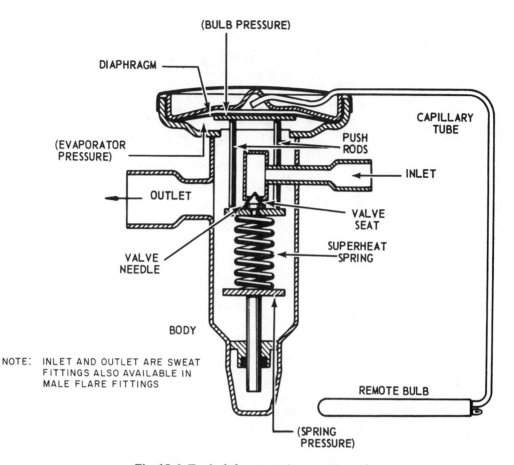

(BULB PRESSURE)

DIAPHRAGM

CAPILLARY TUBE

(EVAPORATOR PRESSURE)

PUSH RODS

INLET

OUTLET

VALVE SEAT

SUPERHEAT SPRING

VALVE NEEDLE

BODY

NOTE: INLET AND OUTLET ARE SWEAT FITTINGS ALSO AVAILABLE IN MALE FLARE FITTINGS

REMOTE BULB

(SPRING PRESSURE)

Fig. 18-6 Typical thermostatic expansion valve

The increased heat at the tailpipe causes an increase in the pressure exerted on the diaphragm by the expanding gases in the remote bulb through the capillary tube. The diaphragm, in turn, forces the push rods down against the valve stem and the needle valve, which is then pushed off its seat. In this way, more refrigerant is metered into the evaporator.

When the tailpipe temperature is low, there is less pressure on the remote bulb, capillary tube, and diaphragm, with the result that the needle valve is seated. In this case, the flow of refrigerant into the evaporator is restricted.

EQUALIZERS

It was stated previously that thermostatic expansion valves are either internally or externally equalized. The term *equalized* refers to provisions made for exerting evaporator pressure under the diaphragm. In an internally equalized valve there is a drilled passage from the evaporator side of the needle valve to the underside of the diaphragm. An externally equalized valve functions in the same manner, but can pick up the evaporator pressure at the outlet of the evaporator.

To overcome the effect of a pressure drop in larger evaporators, the externally equalized TXV is used. The external equalizer tube is connected to the tailpipe of the evaporator and runs to the underside of the diaphragm in the expansion valve. This arrangement balances the pressure of the tailpipe through the expansion valve

remote bulb. The use of an external equalizer eliminates the effect of the pressure drop across
the evaporator coil. Thus, the
superheat settings depend only on
the adjustment of the spring tension.

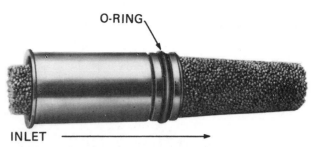

EXPANSION TUBE

The expansion tube, figure
18-7, is located at the inlet of the

Fig. 18-7 Expansion tube located at inlet of evaporator

evaporator. This tube replaces the expansion valve as a metering device in some air
conditioners. The refrigerant entering the evaporator is controlled by the expansion
tube in a manner which is based on a pressure difference and the subcooling characteristics of the refrigerant.

Unlike the thermostatic expansion valve, the expansion tube has no moving
parts. The tube is not adjustable and its *failure* is usually a result of becoming clogged.

An air-conditioning system equipped with an expansion tube does not have a
receiver/drier. The drying agent for the system is found in an *accumulator*. The
accumulator is located at the outlet of the evaporator. Accumulators were covered
in Unit 17. Testing and replacement procedures for the expansion tube are given
in the Service Procedures in Section 3 of this text.

SUMMARY

The thermostatic expansion valve is equipped with a screen in the inlet side of
the valve, figure 18-8. This screen can be cleaned if it becomes clogged. If the screen

Fig. 18-8 Screen located at the inlet of the thermostatic expansion valve

requires cleaning, the receiver/dehydrator should be replaced. If the screen is too obstructed for cleaning, a new screen (and receiver/dehydrator) should be installed. The screen *must not be omitted* from the system.

The inlet of the expansion tube does not contain a screen. If the expansion tube becomes clogged, it must be replaced. In addition, the accumulator should be replaced to prevent a recurrence of the clogged expansion tube.

If the expansion valve is removed from the air-conditioning system for cleaning or other service, it should be bench checked before it is reinstalled. Section 3 of this text, Service Procedures, covers the method of bench checking the TXV for efficiency. This procedure saves time as well as refrigerant which otherwise is lost through a defective valve.

Automotive expansion valves are provided with flare or 0-ring fittings on each side. The comparison between the fittings is shown in figure 18-9. Although the valves shown may have the same ratings, they cannot be interchanged because the two types of fittings do not mate.

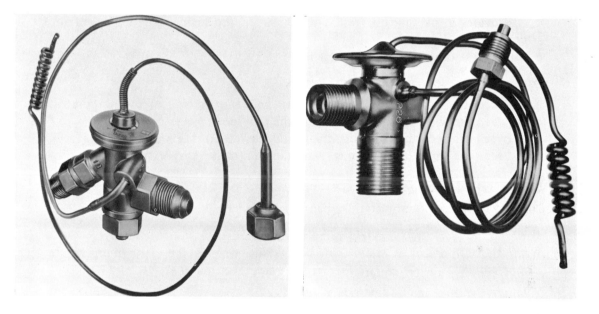

FLARE TYPE   O—RING TYPE

Fig. 18-9 **Externally equalized thermostatic expansion valve**

The previous descriptions of the thermostatic expansion valve and the expansion tube make it clear that these devices are more sensitive to foreign materials than are any other parts of the air-conditioning system. This fact makes it essential to keep the system as free of contaminants during service procedures as possible.

To prevent the vital parts of the expansion valve from sticking or becoming corroded, the air conditioner should be operated for short periods during the months that normal operation is not practical. In this manner, the internal parts of the TXV, as well as the compressor, are lubricated and are kept operating freely.

REVIEW

Select the appropriate answer from the choices given.

1. Which of the following is *not* a metering device?

    a. thermostatic expansion valve   c. expansion tube
    b. pressure modulator control   d. TXV

2. Where is the remote bulb fastened?

    a. at the evaporator inlet   c. at the tailpipe
    b. at the TXV outlet   d. in the liquid line

3. Where is the screen located?

    a. at the inlet of the TXV   c. in the center of the TXV
    b. at the outlet of the TXV   d. There is no screen in the TXV

4. Which of the following is a function of the thermostatic expansion valve?

    a. It controls the refrigerant flow into the evaporator.
    b. It controls the temperature of the refrigerant in the evaporator.
    c. It provides a dividing line restriction between the high and low sides of the system.
    d. All of these functions are performed by the TXV.

5. Where is the external equalizer tube fastened?

    a. Between the bottom of the diaphragm and the tailpipe of the evaporator.
    b. Between the top of the diaphragm and the tailpipe of the evaporator.
    c. Between the bottom of the diaphragm and the inlet of the evaporator.
    d. Between the top of the diaphragm and the inlet of the evaporator.

Briefly answer each of the following questions.

6. Name two types of thermostatic expansion valves.

7. What is meant by the term superheat with regard to a TXV?

8. When the evaporator is starved for refrigerant, what is the state (temperature and pressure) of the refrigerant leaving the evaporator tailpipe?

9. What are the three main functions of the TXV?

10. How is the expansion tube serviced?

UNIT 19 THE THERMOSTAT

An electromagnetic clutch is used on the compressors of most aftermarket units and on some factory-installed air conditioners to provide a means of temperature control. A device known as a *thermostat*, figure 19-1, controls the clutch. Located in the evaporator, the thermostat is initially set by the driver to a predetermined temperature setting. The clutch cycles at this setting to control the average in-car temperature.

The thermostat is an electrical switch which is actuated by temperature. When the interior of the car is warm, the switch closes and the air-conditioning unit operates. Similarly, when it is cold, the switch opens and the air-conditioning unit turns off. Most thermostats have a positive off position so that the clutch can be turned off regardless of the temperature. In this way, the air-conditioner fans or blower can be used without a refrigerating effect.

Two types of thermostats are available for the control of the clutch: the bellows type and the bimetallic type. Both types of thermostats are temperature actuated. Although the principle of operation is different for each type of thermostat, they serve the same purpose in that they both control the evaporator temperature by cycling the compressor on and off through the clutch.

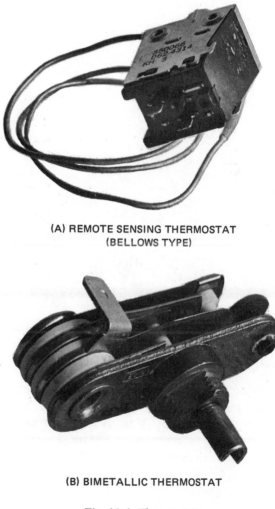

(A) REMOTE SENSING THERMOSTAT
(BELLOWS TYPE)

(B) BIMETALLIC THERMOSTAT

Fig. 19-1 Thermostats

BELLOWS-TYPE THERMOSTAT

A diagram of the construction of the bellows-type thermostat is shown in figure 19-2, page 92. A capillary tube connected to the thermostat is filled with a temperature-sensitive fluid or vapor. The capillary is attached to a bellows within the thermostat.

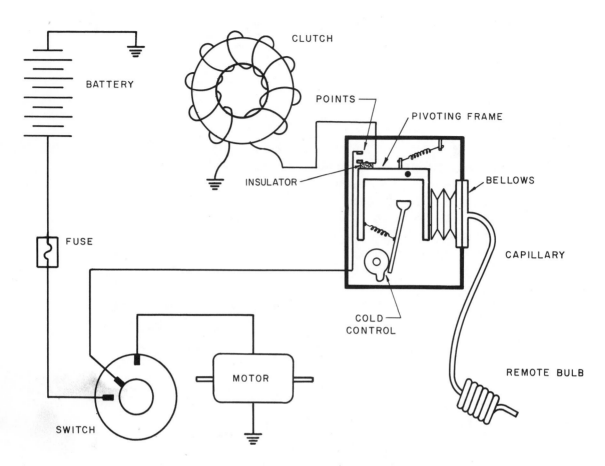

Fig. 19-2 The bellows-type thermostat

This bellows, in turn, is attached to a swinging frame assembly. Two electrical contact points are provided. One contact is fastened to the swinging frame through an insulator and the other electrical contact is fastened to the body of the unit, again through an insulator.

Operation of the Thermostat

When the gases inside the capillary tube expand, a pressure is exerted on the bellows. As a result of this pressure, the bellows closes the electrical contacts at a prescribed temperature. Manual temperature control is provided by a shaft connected to the swinging frame and an external control knob. When the knob is turned in a clockwise direction, the spring tension is increased against the bellows. More pressure is required to overcome the increased spring tension. The requirement for more pressure, of course, means that more heat is necessary. Since heat is being removed from the evaporator, this means that a lower temperature is required to *open* the points. On a temperature rise, the heat again exerts pressure on the bellows to *close* the points and allow for cooling.

Another spring within the thermostat regulates the temperature interval through which the points are open. This interval is usually a temperature rise of about 12°F (-11.11°C) and gives sufficient time for the evaporator to defrost.

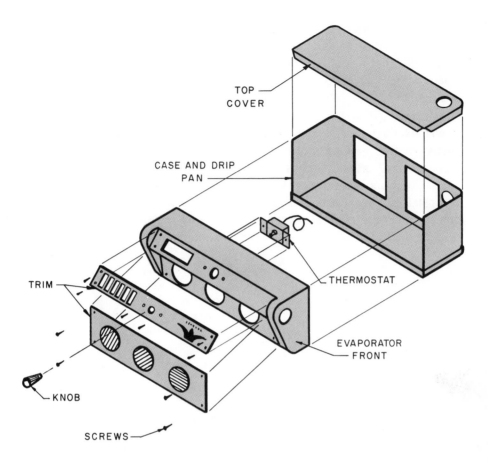

TOP COVER

CASE AND DRIP PAN

TRIM

THERMOSTAT

EVAPORATOR FRONT

KNOB

SCREWS

Fig. 19-3 Typical evaporator case showing the location of the thermostat at the front of the evaporator coil

Care must be exercised when handling a thermostat with a capillary tube. There should be no sharp bends or kinks in the capillary. When a bend must be made in the capillary, the bend is to be no sharper than one that can be formed around a finger.

For best results, the end of the capillary should be inserted into the evaporator core between the fins to a depth of about one inch. The capillary should not be inserted all the way through the fins because it will interfere with the blowers which are usually mounted behind the core.

If the capillary has lost its charge for any reason, the thermostat must be replaced. When there is no fluid in the capillary, the unit has no ON (cooling) cycle. The capillary cannot be recharged using standard tools.

BIMETALLIC-TYPE THERMOSTAT

The bimetallic-type thermostat is desirable as a replacement part because of its lower cost. This thermostat does not have a capillary tube. The thermostat depends on air passing over it to maintain the proper operation.

Manual temperature control with the bimetallic thermostat is achieved in the same manner as that described for the bellows-type thermostat. Cold air passing over the bimetallic leaf in the rear of the thermostat causes it to retract. By retracting it bows enough to open a set of points. As the temperature increases, the other leaf of the bimetallic element reacts to the heat and pulls the points back together. The off cycle range of this thermostat is also about 12°F (-11.11°C) to allow for a sufficient defrost time.

The bimetallic thermostat is limited in application because it must be mounted inside the evaporator. In many instances, the bellows-type thermostat must be used since its long capillary tube allows the thermostat to be placed some distance from the evaporator core.

Most thermostats are adjustable. In addition, a means is provided for regulating the range between the opening and closing of the points. The adjustment in some thermostats is located under the control knob in the shaft; in other thermostats, the adjustment is located under a fiber cover on the body of the unit.

A thermostat lacking a setscrew can be considered to be a nonadjustable type. Malfunction of this type of thermostat requires replacement of the complete unit.

REVIEW

Briefly answer each of the following questions.

1. What is the purpose of the thermostat?

2. What happens if the capillary tube loses its charge of inert gas?

3. Do all thermostats have a capillary tube?

4. What is the off (defrost) cycle of the thermostat if it is operating properly?

5. What is a good rule to follow when bending the capillary tube?

UNIT 20   THE MAGNETIC CLUTCH

Automotive air-conditioner manufacturers use a magnetic clutch as a means of disengaging the compressor when it is not needed. For example, the compressor is disengaged when a defrost cycle is indicated in the evaporator or when the air conditioner is not being used.

Basically, all clutches operate on the principle of magnetic attraction. There are two general types of clutches: those with a stationary field and those with a rotating field.

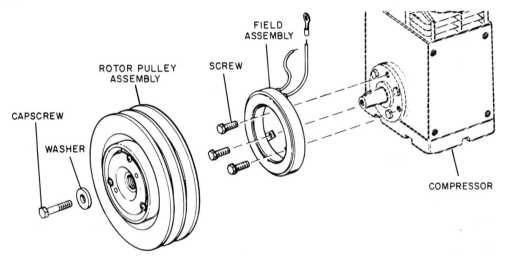

Fig. 20-1 Typical seal mounted clutch field. Three screws are removed from the seal plate and replaced with screws supplied with the field to secure it to the compressor.

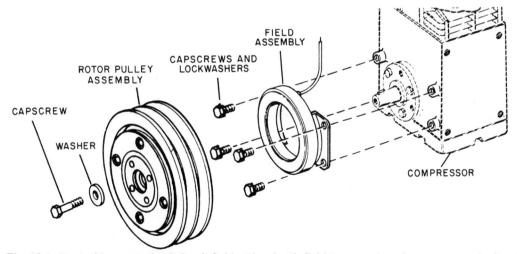

Fig. 20-2 Typical boss mounted clutch field. The clutch field is secured to the compressor body with four screws furnished with it. The seal plate is not disturbed with this type of field.

THE STATIONARY FIELD CLUTCH

The stationary field clutch is more desirable for use since it has fewer parts to wear out.

The field is mounted to the compressor by mechanical means, figure 20-2, page 95, depending on the type of field and the compressor supplied. The rotor is held on the armature by means of a bearing and snap rings. The armature is mounted on the compressor crankshaft.

When there is no current to the field, a magnetic force is not applied to the clutch. The rotor is free to turn on the armature which remains stationary on the crankshaft.

When the thermostat or switch is closed, current is applied to the field. A magnetic force is established between the field and the armature. As a result, the armature is pulled into the rotor. When the armature becomes engaged with the rotor, the complete unit turns while the field remains stationary. The compressor crankshaft then begins to turn and the refrigeration cycle starts.

When the switch or thermostat is opened, the current to the field is cut off. The armature disengages from the rotor and stops while the rotor continues to turn. The pumping action of the compressor is stopped until current is again applied to the field.

THE ROTATING FIELD CLUTCH

The rotating field-type clutch operates in the same manner as the stationary field clutch with the exception of the field placement. In this case, the field is a part of the rotor and turns with the rotor. Current is applied to the field by means of brushes which are mounted on the compressor.

Current applied to the field through the brushes sets up a magnetic field which pulls the armature into contact with the rotor. The complete unit, consisting of the armature, rotor, and field, turns and causes the compressor to turn.

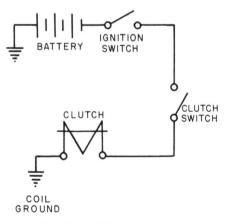

In both types of clutches, slots are machined in the armature and rotor to aid in concentrating the magnetic field and increasing the attraction between them.

Since the clutch engages and disengages at high speeds, as required for the proper

Fig. 20-3 Wiring diagram

temperature control, it is understandable that considerable scoring occurs on the armature and rotor surfaces. Such scoring is allowable and should not be a cause for concern.

It is essential that clutch coils having the proper voltage be used. A coil rated at twelve volts but used on a six-volt system does not allow the full buildup of the magnetic flux and armature slippage results. This condition leads to a shortened clutch life as well as poor cooling. Conversely, a six-volt field used on a twelve-volt system causes a short field life because the applied voltage is sufficient to cause serious

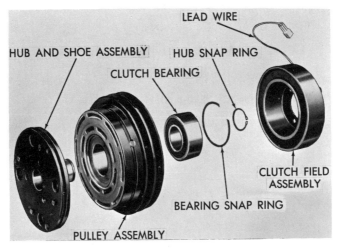

Fig. 20-4 Warner clutch plate type

damage. When six-volt equipment must be used in a car equipped with a twelve-volt system, a suitable dropping resistor must be added.

The spacing between the coil and the pulley is important. The pulley should be as close to the coil as possible to achieve better magnetic flux travel. However, the pulley should not be so close that the rotor drags on the coil housing.

The spacing between the rotor and the armature is also important. If this spacing is too close, the armature drags on the rotor when the unit is turned off. If the rotor and armature are too far apart, there will be a poor contact between the armature and rotor when the unit is turned on. Either of these situations results in serious clutch malfunctions.

The spacing of the rotor and armature should be such that when the clutch is off, there is no drag. Also, when the clutch is turned on, the proper spacing insures that no slippage will occur (except for the moment when the clutch is first engaged).

SUMMARY

The four- and six-cylinder Frigidaire compressors, as well as the Sankyo compressors, use a stationary magnetic field. However, this field is mounted on the front compressor head. The rotor also is mounted on the front head of the compressor. The armature is mounted on the crankshaft. When no current is applied, the rotor turns freely and the armature is stationary. When current is applied, the armature is pulled into the rotor and both pieces rotate together and thus turn the compressor crankshaft.

Clutch repair and service diagnosis procedures are given in the Service Procedures section of this text.

Frigidaire and Chrysler Air-Temp units do not use a magnetic clutch as a means of temperature control. Instead, these systems use a device which controls the flow of refrigerant within the system. Magnetic clutches are used only to turn on the unit when they are used and off when they are no longer wanted.

REVIEW

Briefly answer each of the following questions.

1. Name the two types of magnetic clutches.

2. What supplies current to the field for both types of clutches?

3. What type of clutch uses a brush set?

4. What type of clutch does not have a rotating field?

5. Are cycling clutches used on all air conditioners?

UNIT 21 PRESSURE CONTROLS

Within the range of 20 psig (1.41 kg/cm^2) and 80 psig (5.62 kg/cm^2), the temperature of Refrigerant 12 has a close relationship to its pressure. This relationship is illustrated further in Section 2 of this text, System Diagnosis.

Liquid refrigerant is metered into the evaporator by the thermostatic expansion valve. The amount of refrigerant required is regulated by the heat load on the evaporator. As the heat load decreases, there is a corresponding decrease in the amount of refrigerant that is metered into the evaporator by the expansion valve. In this discussion of pressure controls, the student should recall that water droplets which accumulate on the evaporator freeze when the temperature drops below 32°F (0°C).

Example

Assume that the following situation occurs. A sales representative is driving 200 miles (321.86 km) nonstop on a freeway. He is alone and driving a compact car. It rained recently and the sky is overcast.

For this example, it is assumed that the heat load is at a minimum and the humidity is as high as possible. Since the sky is overcast, the moisture from the recent rain is not being evaporated.

As the sales representative starts his trip, the TXV meters the proper amount of liquid refrigerant which evaporates properly for the heat load conditions. After driving approximately fifty miles the car interior is cool. As he continues to drive, the car interior becomes cooler and cooler. This condition requires less refrigerant and the evaporator becomes even cooler. In fact, the temperature falls well below the freezing point of water (32°F or 0°C). The accumulation of moisture on the evaporator begins to freeze and eventually all air flow through the evaporator core is blocked.

The effect is now that of no cooling. The air-conditioning system is functioning properly for the heat load, but no air can pass through the evaporator. The interior of the car gets warmer, but that does not correct the condition. The refrigerant in the evaporator prevents any melting of the ice on the fins and coils.

In this situation, the only solution is to turn the air conditioner off until the evaporator thaws. Once thawing occurs, the air conditioner can be turned on again. During the 200-mile trip, this sequence of events will be repeated several times. This practice is workable only if the driver can determine when to turn the air-conditioning system off and on; however, a driver generally cannot make this decision.

SUCTION PRESSURE REGULATORS

The condition outlined in the example cannot occur if the air conditioner is equipped with a suction pressure regulator. This device controls the pressure of the refrigerant in the evaporator by preventing the pressure from falling below a predetermined range, usually 22 psig (1.55 kg/cm^2) to 30 psig (2.11 kg/cm^2) (depending on system design). If a setting of 30 psig (2.11 kg/cm²) is assumed, the suction pressure regulator allows evaporator pressures about 30 psi (2.11 kg/cm²) to be released to the compressor. The control holds all pressures up to 30 psi (2.11 kg/cm²). In this manner, the evaporator can maintain a constant pressure of 30 psig (2.11 kg/cm²).

The operation of the evaporator in this manner is based on the assumption that the thermostatic expansion valve, suction regulator, and compressor are operating

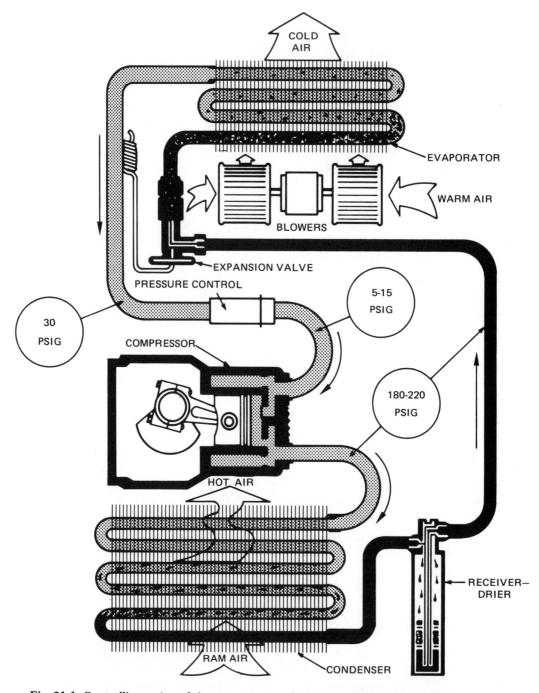

Fig. 21-1 **Controlling action of the pressure control with the proper expansion valve metering**

properly, figure 21-1. If, for example, the TXV is flooding the evaporator, the pressure in the evaporator rises above 30 psig (2.11 kg/cm²), figure 21-2. This condition can be corrected by replacing the TXV, or by correcting any other problem that may be causing the flooding condition.

Flow through any type of suction pressure regulator is never completely stopped. A bypass is included so that a small amount of refrigerant and refrigeration oil can

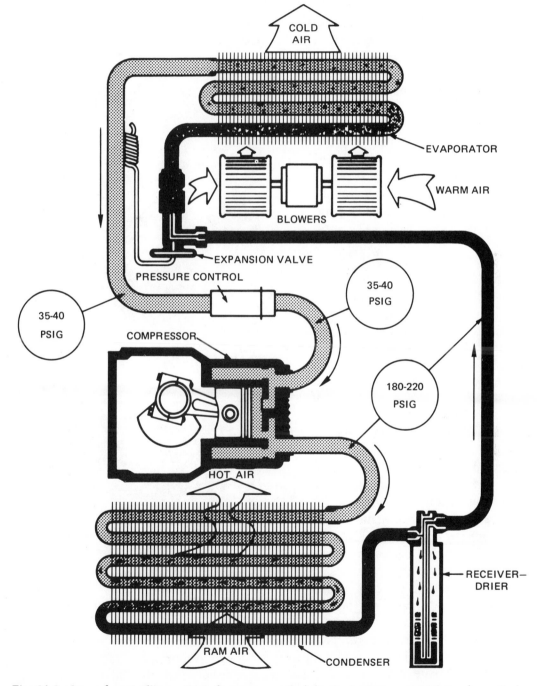

Fig. 21-2 Loss of controlling action of pressure control due to improper expansion valve metering (flooding evaporator)

circulate through the system. This provision helps to eliminate the danger of compressor damage when a malfunction in the suction regulator causes it to close.

Several types of suction pressure regulators are used in automotive air-conditioning systems. The operation of each type is covered in this unit. Procedures for testing, repairing, and replacing the different types of regulators are found in Section III.

EVAPORATOR PRESSURE REGULATOR

The evaporator pressure regulator (EPR) valve is a fully automatic suction pressure control device that is used in certain Chrysler Corporation automotive air-conditioning systems. The EPR valve is located inside the compressor and is just under the suction side service valve, figure 21-3.

OIL RETURN PASSAGE   EPR VALVE

The EPR valve, figure 21-4, maintains the evaporator pressure, and thus its temperature, at a point just above freezing. As a result, any evaporator condensate cannot freeze during the normal operation of the evaporator. The pressure in the evaporator is maintained between 22 psig (1.55 kg/cm^2) and 26 psig (1.83 kg/cm^2) by the action of the EPR valve. If the EPR valve is operating properly, the compressor inlet pressure should be about 15 psig (1.06 kg/cm^2). However, this pressure can be higher or lower, depending on the evaporator heat load.

Fig. 21-3 EPR valve and oil return passage

An EPR valve balance is maintained between the control spring pressure and the evaporator refrigerant pressure. A diaphragm seals the chamber and prevents refrigerant leaks. An increase of evaporator pressure against the diaphragm overcomes the control spring tension and moves the valve away from the seated position. As a result, there is an increase in the refrigerant flow from the evaporator to the compressor.

Fig. 21-4 EPR valve located under the low-side (suction) service valve

A decrease in evaporator pressure allows the control spring to move the valve toward the seat. The refrigerant flowing from the evaporator is restricted and the evaporator pressure increases until it reaches a value sufficient to reopen the EPR valve.

The opening and closing of the EPR valve continues until a balance is reached between the evaporator pressure and the spring tension. The valve then remains in a constant position until the evaporator heat load or the compressor speed changes and a new balance of pressures is required.

Although the EPR valve is located within the compressor on the suction side, it is not necessary to disassemble the compressor if the valve must be replaced. The EPR valve can be changed without removing the compressor from the engine compartment. Since the valve cannot be adjusted, any malfunction requires unit replacement.

An oil passage which runs inside the compressor between the suction line and the compressor crankcase also runs through the EPR valve. Since oil is carried out of the compressor in the refrigerant, the oil passage permits the oil to be returned to the crankcase, regardless of the condition of the EPR valve. In addition, the oil passage pressurizes the crankcase and prevents the crankcase pressure from dropping below the normal atmospheric pressure. If this pressure does drop into the vacuum range, atmospheric pressure can enter the system through the crankshaft seal assembly. The moisture content of the incoming air can contaminate the system. Another condition that can result from the addition of air at atmospheric pressure is higher than normal head pressures.

PILOT-OPERATED EVAPORATOR PRESSURE REGULATOR

The pilot-operated evaporator pressure regulator (POEPR) valve is an improved version of the standard EPR valve. The POEPR valve functions in the same manner as the EPR valve and differs only in that it has a built-in pilot valve which controls the main valve.

The pilot valve provides more precise control so that the evaporator can operate at lower average temperatures without the danger of icing. The POEPR valve is located under the suction valve of the compressor (as is the EPR valve) and can be serviced without disassembling the compressor. The POEPR valve is not adjustable and must be replaced if it becomes defective. The EPR and POEPR valves are interchangeable if exact replacements are not available.

EVAPORATOR TEMPERATURE REGULATOR

The evaporator temperature regulator (ETR) valve is also used on certain Chrysler Corporation systems. The ETR valve replaces the EPR valve for automatic temperature control systems.

The ETR valve operates in a manner similar to that of a solenoid valve. An ETR switch located in the rear of the evaporator case controls the valve. The switch is an electrical device and has a temperature sensing bulb that is inserted into the evaporator core. The ETR valve and ETR switch are normally open during system operation. However, if the evaporator temperature drops below 35°F (1.67°C), the ETR switch closes and a current is sent to the ETR valve. The valve also closes and stops the flow of refrigerant from the evaporator to the compressor.

The ETR and EPR valves differ in that the ETR valve is either open or closed and the EPR valve cycles between open and closed. Figure 21-5, page 104, is a graph representing the comparison of the operation of the two types of valves for a particular time period and specific conditions.

Like the EPR valve, the ETR valve is located in the suction side of the compressor and can be serviced without disassembling the compressor. The ETR valve cannot be adjusted and must be replaced if it is defective.

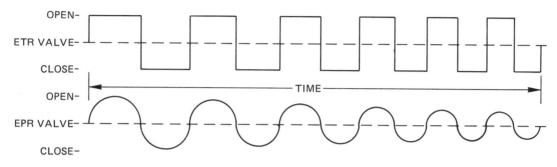

Fig. 21-5 The ETR valve is either fully open or fully closed while the EPR valve modulates from fully open-close to partially open-close.

SUCTION THROTTLING VALVE

The suction throttling valve (STV) is located at the outlet (tailpipe) of the evaporator. Certain General Motors Corporation air-conditioning systems use the STV valve as an evaporator pressure-regulating control device. The valve prevents the evaporator temperature from dropping to a value at which the condensate will freeze on the evaporator coils.

The STV maintains the evaporator pressure at a predetermined setting of 29 psig (2.04 kg/cm²) to 30 psig (2.11 kg/cm²). At this pressure, the temperature of the evaporator core surface is kept to about 32°F (0°C).

In a STV, the spring pressure and the atmospheric pressure on one side of a diaphragm oppose the evaporator pressure on the other side of the dia-

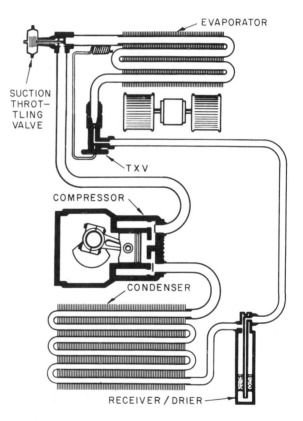

Fig. 21-6 Location of the suction throttling valve in the air-conditioning system

phragm with the result that the valve is balanced. The spring pressure is controlled in either one of two ways: by a cable or by a vacuum. The vacuum control is the most popular for the suction throttling valve.

Operation of the STV

When the evaporator pressure rises above the predetermined setting (29-30 psig) (2.04-2.11 kg/cm²), excess pressure is exerted against the valve piston. This pressure is then transmitted through the bleed holes in the piston to the underside of the diaphragm. The pressure is great enough to overcome the spring pressure and

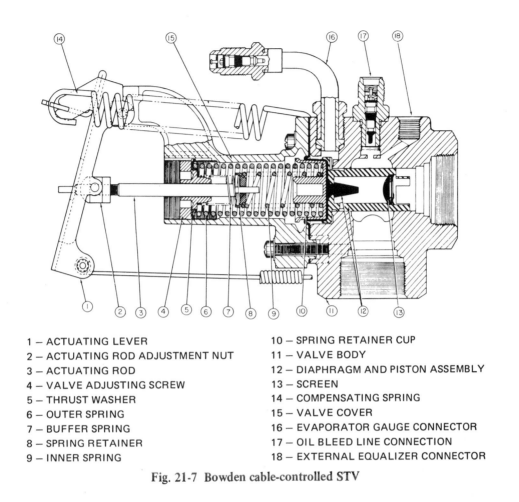

1 — ACTUATING LEVER
2 — ACTUATING ROD ADJUSTMENT NUT
3 — ACTUATING ROD
4 — VALVE ADJUSTING SCREW
5 — THRUST WASHER
6 — OUTER SPRING
7 — BUFFER SPRING
8 — SPRING RETAINER
9 — INNER SPRING

10 — SPRING RETAINER CUP
11 — VALVE BODY
12 — DIAPHRAGM AND PISTON ASSEMBLY
13 — SCREEN
14 — COMPENSATING SPRING
15 — VALVE COVER
16 — EVAPORATOR GAUGE CONNECTOR
17 — OIL BLEED LINE CONNECTION
18 — EXTERNAL EQUALIZER CONNECTOR

Fig. 21-7 Bowden cable-controlled STV

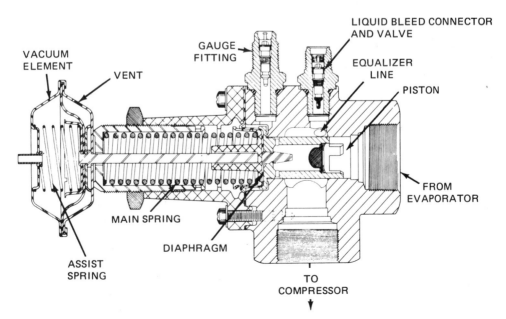

Fig. 21-8 Vacuum-controlled STV

cause the valve piston to open. As the piston opens, the excess evaporator pressure is released, the evaporator pressure decreases, and the spring pressure again moves the piston toward the closed position. This opening and closing of the piston continues until a balance is reached between the evaporator pressure and the spring pressure. The valve will stay in the position at which the two pressures are balanced until the evaporator load conditions or the compressor speed change.

The minimum pressure at which the STV operates can be preset by an adjusting screw. The maximum operating pressure is adjusted by the driver using a control on the dash panel inside the car. The preset minimum pressure value prevents the STV from being set manually to a point below that at which the valve should operate.

A diaphragm is secured firmly between the body and cover sections of the valve. The function of the diaphragm is to seal the internal valve from atmospheric pressure. An oil bypass line connects the STV to the evaporator. Under certain conditions, oil can flood the evaporator. To clear the evaporator of excess oil, a check valve is included in the fitting. A third fitting is used to attach the external equalizer of the expansion valve to the STV.

The STV has been largely replaced by the pilot-operated absolute suction throttling valve (POASTV) in recent years. The operation of the POASTV is essentially the same as that of the STV. The POASTV is a more efficient control and eliminates the possibility of leaks in the diaphragm. Such leaks are the main cause of STV failure.

PILOT-OPERATED VALVE

The pilot-operated valve, or more correctly, the pilot-operated absolute suction throttling valve (POASTV), figure 21-9, maintains the evaporator pressure at a predetermined level. This type of valve provides control with a much greater accuracy than is obtainable with many other types of controls. The POASTV holds the evaporator pressure to ± 0.5 psig (± 0.035 kg/cm^2). This means that there is at most a variation of one pound between the low pressure and the high pressure in the evaporator.

The design of the POASTV eliminates the fabric-type diaphragm that is present in the STV. The valve contains a *pilot valve* that enables it to achieve as close to absolute zero pressure as possible. The absolute pilot serves as the opposing force to the evaporator pressure. The POASTV does not rely on spring pressures or atmospheric pressure for its operation.

The inlet end of the valve has a test port to which the low-side manifold gauge is connected for testing. Two other fittings on the valve accommodate the oil bleed line and the external equalizer line of the expansion valve. If the pilot-operated valve is not adjusted properly or is defective, the entire valve assembly must be replaced, since it is a sealed unit and cannot be serviced.

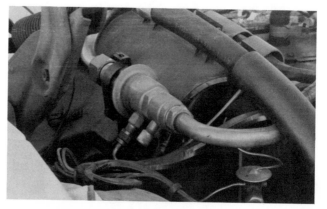

Fig. 21-9 POASTV at outlet of evaporator

Operation of the POASTV

The sequence of operation of the POASTV can be followed by examining figures 21-10 and 21-11, pages 108 and 109. Note the location of the components in figure 21-10 and study the notes associated with the six conditions of operation, figure 21-11.

A bronze bellows controls a small needle valve which, then controls a large piston. The bellows expands when the pressure surrounding it drops below 28.5 psig (2.0 kg/cm²) (the value of the pressure inside the system). The bellows contracts when the pressure exceeds 28.5 psig (2.0 kg/cm²). Each time the bellows expands, the needle valve pressure surrounding the bellows increases. When the pressure increases to a particular value, the bellows contracts and opens the needle valve. The pressure surrounding the bellows then drops. When the pressure drops sufficiently, the bellows expands.

Because of the drawing action (suction) of the compressor on the outlet side of the POASTV, a lower pressure exists at the outlet side than at the inlet side of the valve. When the bellows expands and the pressure around the bellows begins to increase, the lower pressure on the top side of the piston approaches the pressure of the underside. The closer the two pressures approach each other in value (become equal), the more the piston is closed by the spring. As the difference between the two pressures increases (the pressures are becoming more unequal), the more the bottom (higher) pressure pushes the piston open.

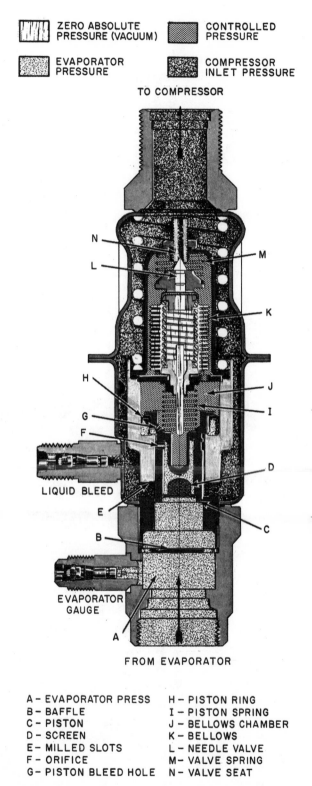

A - EVAPORATOR PRESS
B - BAFFLE
C - PISTON
D - SCREEN
E - MILLED SLOTS
F - ORIFICE
G - PISTON BLEED HOLE
H - PISTON RING
I - PISTON SPRING
J - BELLOWS CHAMBER
K - BELLOWS
L - NEEDLE VALVE
M - VALVE SPRING
N - VALVE SEAT

Fig. 21-10 Cutaway drawing of the POA suction throttling valve showing condition of refrigerant pressure within the valve as well as various parts

Ⓐ 1ST STAGE EXISTING CONDITIONS

SYSTEM IS OFF, PRESSURE EQUAL ON BOTH INLET AND OUTLET AND PRESSURE IS APPROXIMATELY 70 PSI   (NORMAL DAY OF 70 - 80° F.).

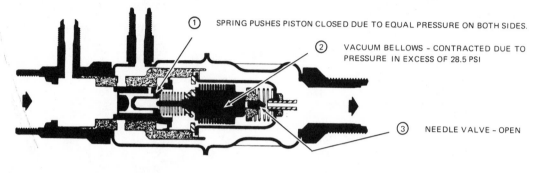

① SPRING PUSHES PISTON CLOSED DUE TO EQUAL PRESSURE ON BOTH SIDES.

② VACUUM BELLOWS - CONTRACTED DUE TO PRESSURE IN EXCESS OF 28.5 PSI

③ NEEDLE VALVE - OPEN

Ⓑ 2ND STAGE EXISTING CONDITIONS - PISTON OPENS

SYSTEM IS ON, COMPRESSOR IS PULLING DOWN PRESSURE; THEREFORE, OUTLET SIDE (COMPRESSOR SIDE) HAS LOWER PRESSURE THAN INLET SIDE.

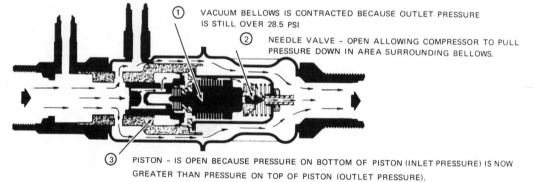

① VACUUM BELLOWS IS CONTRACTED BECAUSE OUTLET PRESSURE IS STILL OVER 28.5 PSI

② NEEDLE VALVE - OPEN ALLOWING COMPRESSOR TO PULL PRESSURE DOWN IN AREA SURROUNDING BELLOWS.

③ PISTON - IS OPEN BECAUSE PRESSURE ON BOTTOM OF PISTON (INLET PRESSURE) IS NOW GREATER THAN PRESSURE ON TOP OF PISTON (OUTLET PRESSURE).

Ⓒ 3RD STAGE EXISTING CONDITIONS - BELLOWS CLOSES

COMPRESSOR HAS PULLED OUTLET PRESSURE DOWN TO 28.5 PSI, THEREFORE:

① VACUUM BELLOWS - EXPANDS, PUSHING NEEDLE VALVE CLOSED, CAUSING —

② PRESSURE ON TOP OF PISTON TO BEGIN TO INCREASE OVER 28.5 PSI

Fig. 21-11 (Continued)

Ⓓ 4TH STAGE EXISTING CONDITIONS - PISTON CLOSES

THE PRESSURE SURROUNDING BELLOWS AND ON TOP OF PISTON HAS NOW INCREASED SUFFICIENTLY OVER 28.5 PSI   TO BECOME NEARLY EQUAL (WITHIN 1.3   PSI) OF INLET PRESSURE. SINCE –

① PRESSURE ON BOTH SIDES OF PISTON NEARLY EQUAL – SPRING TAKES OVER AND PUSHES THE PISTON CLOSED

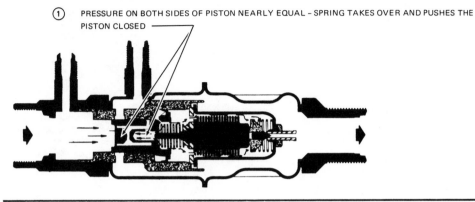

Ⓔ 5TH STAGE EXISTING CONDITIONS - BELLOWS OPENS

THE PRESSURE SURROUNDING BELLOWS AND ON TOP OF PISTON IS NOW SUFFICIENTLY OVER 28.5 P.S.I. – THE RESULT IS THAT –

① VACUUM BELLOWS - CONTRACTS DUE TO INCREASE IN PRESSURE.

② NEEDLE VALVE – OPENS AGAIN AND ALLOWS COMPRESSOR TO PULL PRESSURE DOWN IN AREA SURROUNDING BELLOWS.

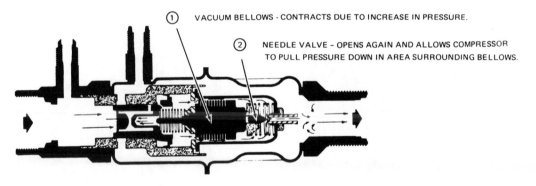

Ⓕ 6TH STAGE EXISTING CONDITIONS - PISTON OPENS

AN UNEQUAL PRESSURE OCCURS BECAUSE COMPRESSOR IS IN THE PROCESS OF PULLING OUTLET PRESSURE DOWN.

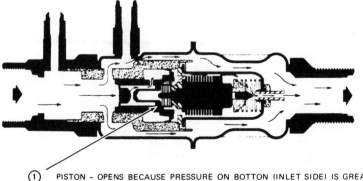

① PISTON - OPENS BECAUSE PRESSURE ON BOTTON (INLET SIDE) IS GREATER THAN PRESSURE ON TOP OF PISTON.

Fig. 21-11

When the bellows expands, the pressure on top of the piston increases until it is nearly equal to the pressure below the piston. As a result, the spring pushes the piston closed. When the bellows contracts and the pressure on top of the piston decreases, the higher pressure below the piston pushes it open.

The proper operation of the POASTV can be checked easily by the use of a manifold and gauge set. The valve operation does not depend on the atmospheric pressure; therefore, altitude compensation is not required for this type of valve.

VALVES IN RECEIVER

The valves in receiver (VIR) assembly, figure 21-12, is a combination of three different components: the thermostatic expansion valve, the pilot-operated absolute suction throttling valve, and the receiver/dehydrator (including a sight glass).

The VIR assembly is mounted near the evaporator. Both the inlet and the outlet fittings of the evaporator connect to the VIR, as well as the liquid line and the suction line. The VIR is designed to eliminate the need for the equalizer external capillary and the TXV remote bulb. The diaphragm end of the TXV is exposed directly to refrigerant vapor entering the VIR from the outlet of the evaporator. The provision for external equalizing consists of a small hole (orifice) drilled in the housing wall between the POASTV and the TXV.

The desiccant is contained in the receiver shell and is replaceable (in contrast to the desiccant in other drier models). A liquid pickup tube containing a filter screen extends to the bottom of the shell. The filter traps impurities and prevents them from circulating through the system.

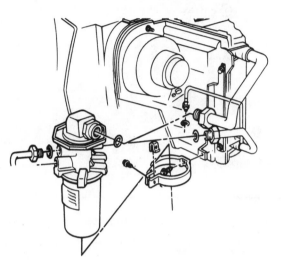

Fig. 21-12 Typical VIR installation

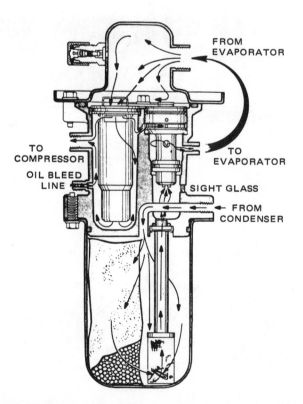

FROM EVAPORATOR

TO COMPRESSOR

OIL BLEED LINE

TO EVAPORATOR

SIGHT GLASS

FROM CONDENSER

Fig. 21-13 Cutaway section of valves in receiver (VIR) showing detail of components and direction of refrigerant flow

A replaceable sight glass is located in the VIR housing at the inlet of the TXV.

The components of the VIR function in the same manner as similar separate system components. Because the VIR components are mounted in a common housing, their appearance is somewhat different from that of the individual units covered previously.

Operation of the VIR

Liquid refrigerant from the outlet of the condenser flows to the receiver through the inlet of the VIR housing. The fluid portion of the refrigerant drops to the bottom of the receiver tank and any vapor remains at the top of the tank. The refrigerant contacts the desiccant in the receiver. Any trace amounts of moisture in the refrigerant should be removed by the desiccant.

Liquid refrigerant flows through the filter screen and the pickup tube directly into the lower inlet of the TXV. The TXV, figure 21-15, page 112,

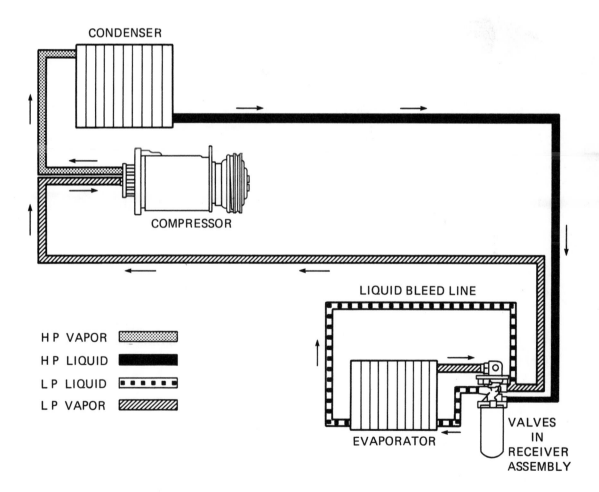

Fig. 21-14 System schematic with valves in receiver

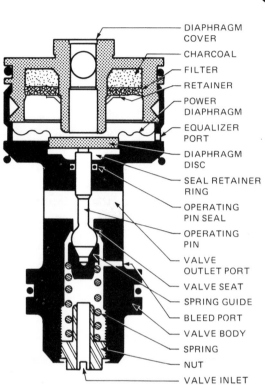

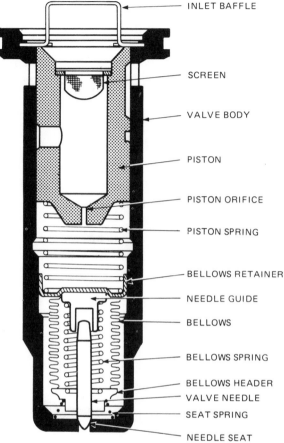

DIAPHRAGM COVER

CHARCOAL

FILTER

RETAINER

POWER DIAPHRAGM

EQUALIZER PORT

DIAPHRAGM DISC

SEAL RETAINER RING

OPERATING PIN SEAL

OPERATING PIN

VALVE OUTLET PORT

VALVE SEAT

SPRING GUIDE

BLEED PORT

VALVE BODY

SPRING

NUT

VALVE INLET

INLET BAFFLE

SCREEN

VALVE BODY

PISTON

PISTON ORIFICE

PISTON SPRING

BELLOWS RETAINER

NEEDLE GUIDE

BELLOWS

BELLOWS SPRING

BELLOWS HEADER

VALVE NEEDLE

SEAT SPRING

NEEDLE SEAT

Fig. 21-15 TXV as found in the valves in re-ceiver (VIR) assembly.

Fig. 21-16 POASTV as found in the valves in receiver (VIR) assembly.

meters liquid refrigerant into the evaporator. That is, the TXV regulates the amount of flow based on the heat load conditions of the evaporator. Once in the evaporator, the liquid refrigerant changes to a vapor by taking on heat.

Refrigerant vapor leaves the evaporator and returns to the VIR to the inlet of the POASTV. The POASTV, figure 21-16, regulates the flow of the vapor to the compressor. The amount of refrigerant vapor reaching the compressor depends on the evaporator pressure.

The outlet of the POASTV delivers low-pressure refrigerant vapor to the com-pressor where it is *compressed* to a high-pressure vapor. From the compressor, the high-pressure vapor enters the condenser. The vapor gives up its heat in the condenser and in so doing, is returned to the high-pressure liquid state. The cycle is now complete.

A Schrader-type access port is located at the top of the VIR assembly. The port is placed at the outlet of the evaporator and the inlet of the POASTV. The low-side gauge is connected to the access port as a means of checking the evaporator pressure. The VIR should hold a constant evaporator pressure of 30 psig (2.11 kg/cm^2).

This value of pressure is sufficient to maintain an evaporator coil temperature of about 32°F (0°C). A lower pressure results in lower evaporator temperatures and the formation of ice which blocks the airflow. A pressure higher than 30 psig

(2.11 kg/cm²) causes either insufficient cooling or a cooling effect that is higher than the minimum temperature possible for the system design.

The VIR assembly is serviceable. Components of the assembly are replaceable if they are found to be defective. The desiccant, and even the sight glass, can be replaced individually. It is suggested that whenever the VIR is disassembled for service, the desiccant be replaced.

REVIEW

Select the appropriate answer from the choices given.

1. Which automobile manufacturer uses a suction pressure control called an evaporator pressure regulator (EPR)?
   a. Ford Motor Company
   b. General Motors Corp.
   c. Chrysler Motors Corp.
   d. American Motors Corp.

2. The evaporator pressure range for systems with an EPR valve, if operating properly, should be:
   a. 20-25 psig (1.41-1.76 kg/cm²).
   b. 22-26 psig (1.55-1.83 kg/cm²).
   c. 29-30 psig (2.04-2.11 kg/cm²).
   d. exactly 30 psig.

3. The EPR valve is located
   a. at the compressor inlet.
   b. at the compressor outlet.
   c. at the evaporator inlet.
   d. at the evaporator outlet.

4. In a system equipped with any type of suction pressure regulator, an evaporator pressure of 36 psig (2.53 kg/cm²) probably indicates
   a. a defective pressure regulator.
   b. a defective expansion valve.
   c. the system is operating properly.
   d. the system is low in refrigerant.

5. One design feature of the VIR is the elimination of the need for
   a. a TXV equalizer tube.
   b. a sight glass.
   c. the drier desiccant.
   d. All of these are correct.

Briefly answer each of the following questions.

6. What compensation for altitude is required for the POASTV for checking system pressures?

7. What are the three major components that make up the VIR?

8. Which of the suction pressure regulators are repairable?

9. Under what condition is the compressor inlet pressure 15 psig (1.06 kg/cm²) in a system using an EPR?

10. In question 4, explain why you selected the particular answer you did.

UNIT 22 AUTOMATIC TEMPERATURE CONTROLS

The automatic heater-air conditioner system control installed in modern automobiles operates on an electropneumatic, electroservo, or electrothermo hydraulic/pneumatic principle. In other words, the temperature control is an electrical and vacuum-operated device. It is designed to provide automatic control of the automobile heater and air conditioner to hold the passenger compartment temperature to a preset level (within system capabilities), regardless of the temperature conditions outside the automobile.

The control also functions to hold the relative humidity within the car to a healthful level and to prevent window fogging.

For example, if the desired temperature is 75°F (23.89°C), the automatic control system will maintain an in-car environment of 75°F (23.89°C) at 45 to 55 percent humidity, regardless of the outside weather conditions.

In even the hottest weather, a properly operating system can rapidly cool the automobile interior to the predetermined temperature (75°F or 23.89°C). The degree of cooling then cycles to maintain the desired temperature level. In mild weather conditions, the passenger compartment can be held to this same predetermined temperature (75°F or 23.89°C) without resetting or changing the control.

During cold weather, the system rapidly heats the passenger compartment to the predetermined 75°F (23.89°C) level, and then automatically maintains this temperature level.

This unit is designed to provide the student with a basic understanding of the theory of operation of an automatic temperature control and its components. Diagnosis and repair procedures are given in the Service Procedures section of this text.

Basically, there are two types of control systems: electropneumatic (or electroservo) systems and thermo-hydraulic/pneumatic systems. The components of the electropneumatic (or electroservo) system include the sensor circuit, the amplifier, the transducer, and the servo.

The thermo-hydraulic/pneumatic unit consists of the sensors and power element assembly, the vacuum regulator and restrictor assembly, the power element lever and bracket assembly, and the temperature door actuators, levers, and control group.

ELECTROPNEUMATIC TEMPERATURE CONTROL

As indicated by the name, the electropneumatic system operates on electricity and air. That is, *electro* refers to the direct current (dc) of the automobile electrical system and *pneumatic* refers to the vacuum of the engine.

Sensors

This type of system usually has three sensors: an in-car sensor, a duct sensor, and an ambient sensor. The in-car sensor is located in the passenger compartment where it can sense the average in-car temperature. The duct sensor is located in the heater case or duct so that it can sense the average duct temperature of the air coming from the evaporator or heater core. The ambient sensor is located where it can sense the ambient temperature (temperature of the air entering the unit).

Although they may vary in physical appearance, the sensors all have the same general operating characteristics. That is, they are extremely sensitive to slight changes in temperature. The change in resistance value of each sensor is inversely proportional to a temperature change. For example, when the temperature decreases, the resistance of the sensor increases; and, when the temperature increases, the sensor resistance decreases.

The sensor is actually a resistor whose resistance value is determined by its temperature. This type of resistor is called a *thermistor*. While the theory of thermistor operation is not covered in this text, the student should be able to gain a good understanding of thermistor operation from the following description and figures 22-1A-C.

In figure 22-1A, one thermistor is installed in a duct. With air at a temperature of 60°F (15.56°C) passing through the duct, the resistance value of the thermistor is 60 ohms. Refer to the thermistor value chart given in figure 22-2, page 116. If the temperature in the duct is 90°F (32.22°C), figure 22-1B, then the resistance of the thermistor decreases to about 45 ohms. If, however, the temperature is decreased to 40°F (4.44°C), the thermistor resistance is increased to 70 ohms, figure 22-1C.

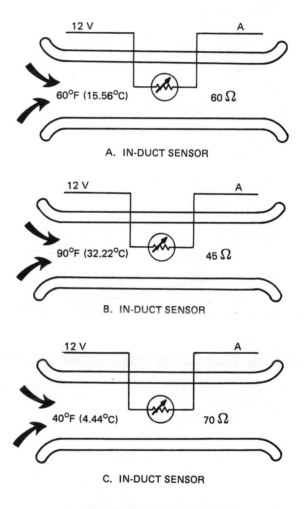

A. IN-DUCT SENSOR

B. IN-DUCT SENSOR

C. IN-DUCT SENSOR

Fig. 22-1 Thermistors

Figure 22-2 is a graph of individual sensor values at various temperatures. Compare the chart with the examples given to this point. Note that each sensor has a different value for a particular temperature.

It must be emphasized that the proper operation of the temperature control device depends on several factors, including the amount of voltage that is supplied to the amplifier after passing through the temperature control and the three sensors. Other factors in the proper operation of the control are presented later in this unit.

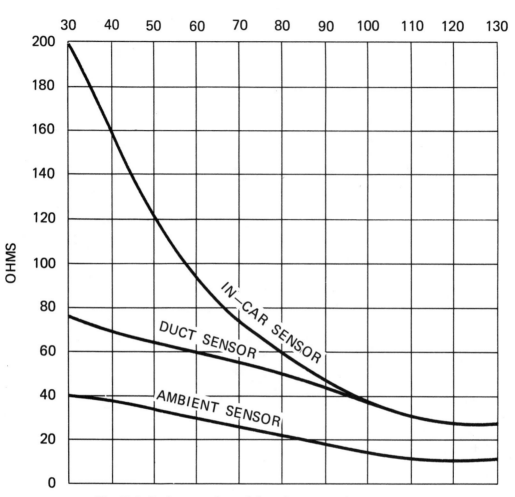

Fig. 22-2 Resistance values of thermistors at various temperatures

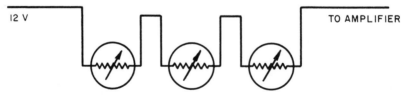

Fig. 22-3 Wiring for in-car, duct, and ambient sensors

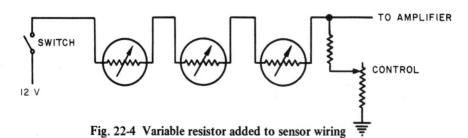

Fig. 22-4 Variable resistor added to sensor wiring

The basic sensor wiring is shown in figure 22-3. It is evident from this diagram that a temperature variation in any one or all of the sensors affects the output voltage and thus provides temperature control.

Figure 22-4 shows a 12-volt battery connected to the sensor group. As a result of the constant voltage input, the temperature control relies entirely on the sensor values. In this situation, the driver has no control over the temperature except as it is preset from the factory. To provide the driver with some control of the circuit, a variable resistor is added to the wiring as shown in figure 22-4. This resistor is connected to the temperature knob.

The arrangement shown in figure 22-4 varies the input voltage of the amplifier by adding resistance to the circuit. Thus, the sensor output (amplifier input) is varied by changing the control resistance. Several examples are shown in figures 22-5 through 22-7. The sensors have the same values in each figure. Figure 22-5 shows the maximum variable resistance; figure 22-6 shows the minimum variable resistance; and figure 22-7 shows the control set at the midpoint. These resistance settings are equivalent to temperature control settings of approximately 85°F (29.45°C), 65°F (18.34°C), and 75°F (23.89°C) respectively.

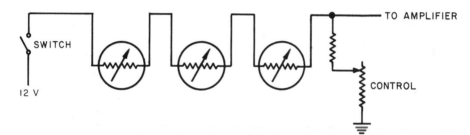

Fig. 22-5 Maximum variable resistance

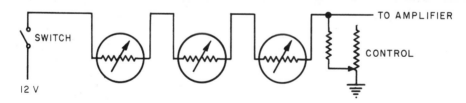

Fig. 22-6 Minimum variable resistance

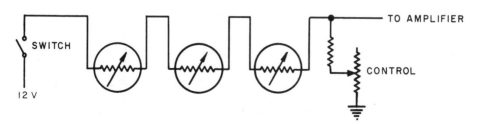

Fig. 22-7 Temperature control midway

AMPLIFIER

The amplifier provides a voltage output that is proportional to the input voltage from the sensors. The circuit diagram of the amplifier is given in figure 22-8. The amplifier is usually mounted on the rear or bottom of the control panel.

The amplifier assembly consists of a diode, transistors, a capacitor, and several fixed resistors (making up a solid-state device).

Unit repair of the amplifier assembly is not suggested for the layman. If the amplifier is found to be defective, it is to be replaced as a unit. If, however, the service technician is proficient in the repair of electrical assemblies, then, in many cases, the technician can quickly locate the cause of a malfunction and repair it. Manufacturers' shop manuals should be consulted for individual component values. Repair is not discussed in this text because a good knowledge of electrical theory is necessary. Several texts are listed in the bibliography that will aid the student in understanding electrical theory and basic direct-current fundamentals.

Figure 22-9 shows the wiring necessary to connect the sensor string and the amplifier.

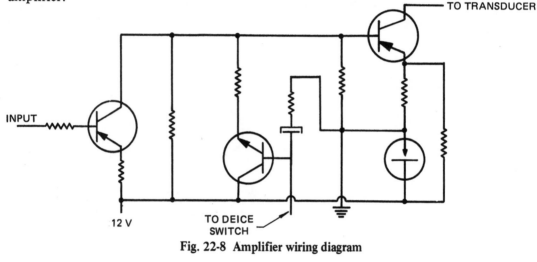

Fig. 22-8 Amplifier wiring diagram

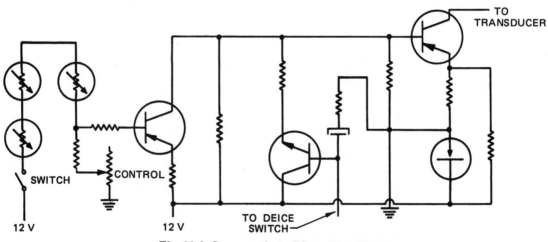

Fig. 22-9 Sensor and amplifier wiring diagram

Transducer

The transducer, figure 22-10, changes the *electrical* signal from the amplifier into a vacuum signal. This *vacuum* signal is then used to regulate the power-servo unit.

The current output of the amplifier causes the wire element of the transducer to contract and expand. This action regulates the amount of the vacuum or the vacuum signal which goes to the power servo.

The transducer cannot be repaired in the field. If the transducer does not perform correctly, it must be replaced as a complete unit.

Fig. 22-10 Transducer assembly

The vacuum at the source fitting shown in figure 22-10 is the full manifold vacuum. The vacuum at the servo fitting is inversely proportional to the power supplied

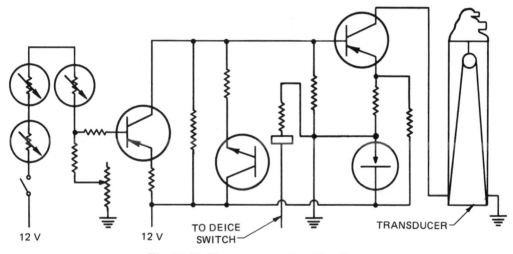

Fig. 22-11 Electropneumatic wiring diagram

to it from the amplifier. The complete electrical circuit for the electropneumatic system is shown in figure 22-11.

Power Servo

The power servo, or servo, performs most of the functions that provide control of the heating and air-conditioning components. A servo unit is shown in figure 22-12.

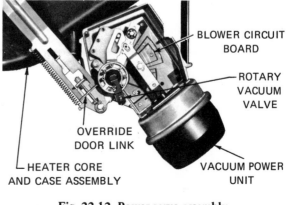

Fig. 22-12 Power servo assembly

The servo unit consists of four basic components: the vacuum power unit, the blower circuit board, the rotary vacuum valve, and the override door link that attaches to the temperature door.

The vacuum unit can be considered as a positioning device connected to a pivot arm. The device positions both the temperature door and the rotary vacuum valve. The valve, in turn, positions the other doors and the blower contacts that determine the proper blower speeds.

A vacuum schematic, figure 22-13, shows the power servo and door actuators. An electrical schematic of this unit is shown in figure 45-1 of Service Procedure 45.

ELECTROTHERMO-HYDRAULIC/PNEUMATIC TEMPERATURE CONTROL

Automatic temperature control, using thermo-hydraulic/pneumatic means, figure 22-14, operates basically the same as the electropneumatic system. This system differs, however, in control design and function.

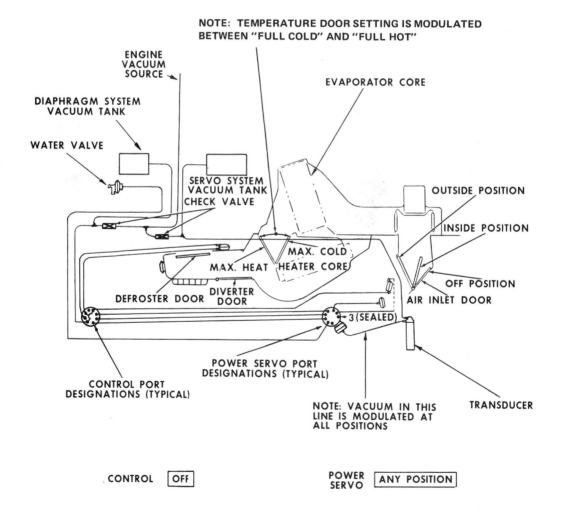

Fig. 22-13 Vacuum schematic (system off)

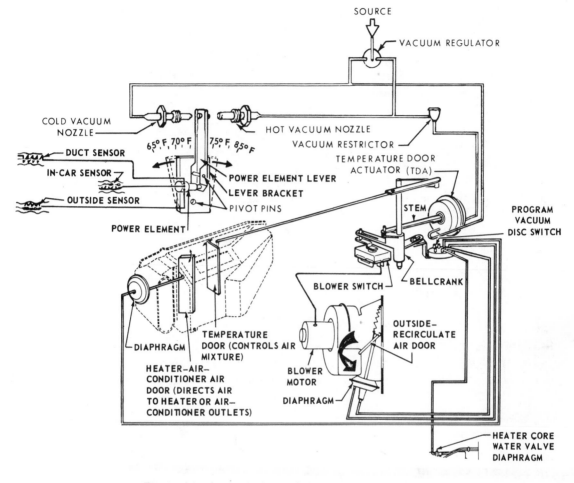

Fig. 22-14 Thermo-hydraulic/pneumatic system diagram

Note in the diagram of the system, figure 22-14, that the power element (hydraulic) assembly provides the control for this system. The temperature of the car interior can be maintained in the range from 65°F (18.34°C) to 85°F (29.45°C), depending on driver and passenger requirements.

Sensors and Power Element

Three sensors are a part of the power element assembly: an in-car sensor, a duct sensor, and an ambient sensor. The in-car sensor is located inside a duct in such a position that the air crossing it is at the average in-car temperature. The duct sensor is located in the duct of the evaporator-heater case where it can sense the average duct temperature. The ambient sensor is positioned so that it senses ambient temperatures or the temperature of the outside air as it enters the unit.

Each sensor consists of a hollow copper coil connected to a cylinder containing a piston at one end. The other end of the cylinder is sealed. The power element is filled with a liquid that expands or contracts with a temperature change.

A sensor-power element assembly is shown in figure 22-15.

Expansion or contraction of the fluid in the power element body due to a temperature change causes movement of the piston. Fluid expansion causes the piston of the power element assembly to be pushed outward. Contraction of the liquid causes the piston to move inward. Thus, the power element is a device containing a piston which transmits a signal to actuate the power element lever mechanism.

Power Element Assembly

The power lever mechanism, figure 22-16, completes the power element assembly.

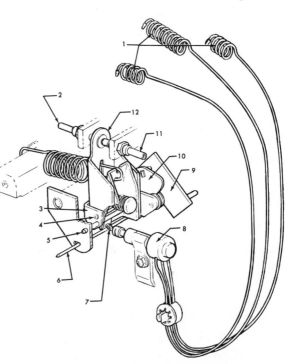

Fig. 22-15 Sensor-power element assembly

The power lever is hinged to a movable bracket. The end of the lever is located between the hot and cold nozzles and can be moved against either of the nozzles. In this manner, a vacuum is created at the temperature door

1. SENSORS
2. HOT VACUUM NOZZLE
3. POWER ELEMENT LEVER BRACKET
4. LEVER PIVOT PIN
5. BRACKET PIVOT PIN
6. POWER ELEMENT PRESSURE RELIEF PIN
7. RANGE ADJUSTING SCREW
8. POWER ELEMENT
9. TEMPERATURE RANGE
10. ECCENTRIC CAM
11. COLD VACUUM NOZZLE
12. POWER ELEMENT LEVER

Fig. 22-16 Power element lever mechanism

actuator. At the same time, the opposite end of the lever stays in contact with the piston of the power element body.

The temperature door actuator (TDA) is covered in Unit 23 under the heading of *Double Action Vacuum Motors*.

Temperature Door

The temperature door regulates the air mixture. The position of this door is determined by the power element assembly. The door regulates the duct output temperature. More information on temperature door operation is contained in unit 23 under the heading *Mode Doors*.

Program Vacuum Switch

The program vacuum switch is operated by the temperature door actuator (TDA) lever. This switch controls the coolant (water) valve, thermostatic valve, master switch diaphragm, inside-outside air diaphragm, and all other system components that are pneumatically (vacuum) operated.

In addition, the program vacuum switch activates the blower switch and the electrical selector switch, and controls the blower speeds as determined, in part, by the system operating mode. The selector switch permits the driver to choose the high or low automatic, the high or low defog, or low deice settings.

REVIEW

ELECTROPNEUMATIC TEMPERATURE CONTROL

Briefly answer each of the following questions.

1. What is the purpose of the transducer?
2. What is the purpose of the amplifier?
3. What air does the in-car sensor sense?
4. What is a thermistor?
5. How is the transducer adjusted?
6. How is the amplifier repaired?
7. What controls the output voltage of the amplifier?
8. Draw a diagram of a thermistor.
9. Draw a diagram of a resistor.
10. Where does the transducer receive its vacuum power?

ELECTROTHERMO-HYDRAULIC/PNEUMATIC TEMPERATURE CONTROL

11. Name the three sensors used in this system.
12. What is the purpose of the power element lever?
13. What is the purpose of the temperature door?

UNIT 23   ELECTRIC AND VACUUM CONTROL DEVICES

Many of the control devices used on automobiles are vacuum (pneumatic) or electrically controlled. These devices include actuators for door and trunk locks and headlight covers. However, this unit is concerned only with those control devices used in the automatic temperature control system.

HEATER CONTROL

The heater control valve may be located on the engine, on the fender well, near the heater core, or inside the heater case. In some systems, the control is actuated by a cable. However, for the automatic temperature system, the control is vacuum actuated. The operation of the control is governed by varying vacuum levels. A typical vacuum-operated hot water heater control valve is shown in figure 23-1.

The cutaway view, in figure 23-2A, of a vacuum-operated water valve shows that when no vacuum is applied, the control valve is closed and is in its normal operating position.

The combined water pressure and spring pressure help to keep the valve in the closed position. Most valves have some provision to prevent them from being installed backwards. On some installations, however, accidental reversing of the hoses can occur. Figure 23-2B shows the effect that reversing the hoses has on the water circulation.

Fig. 23-1 Water valve

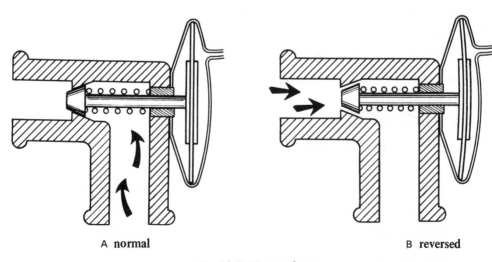

A normal   B reversed

Fig. 23-2 Water valve

If it is assumed that no vacuum is applied to the control valve in figure 23-2B, then the pressure of the water affects the spring pressure and causes the valve to open. As a result, hot water is allowed to flow in the heater core. Actually, a pulsating effect is more likely to occur at automobile speeds in excess of 50 mph (when water pressure is high). This condition has a marked effect on the operation of the temperature control.

In normal operation, the valve can be opened by varying degrees to control the water flow. Figure 23-3 shows the valve positions for no vacuum (A), a partial vacuum (B), and a full vacuum (C).

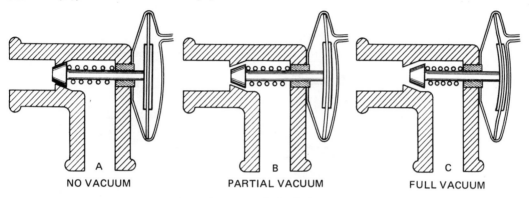

NO VACUUM   PARTIAL VACUUM   FULL VACUUM

Fig. 23-3 Water valve flow control

Since one of the functions of the control system is to provide for an in-car relative humidity of about 50 percent, the hot water valve is often *cracked* to allow a small amount of hot water to enter the system to provide heat. This hot water will provide a great deal of humidity. Thus, the hot water is mixed with the cooler air in the passenger compartment to maintain the desired humidity level.

REFRIGERANT PRESSURE CONTROLS

Most General Motors automobiles use vacuum-controlled refrigerant pressure control devices. Although some General Motors pressure control devices are still cable controlled, those used in the temperature control system are vacuum controlled. Units for large automobile models have a self-contained vacuum source. Thus, the operation of these units does not depend on the demands of the control system. The control device used in the temperature system is the pilot-operated absolute suction throttling valve (POASTV) which was covered in unit 21. Other devices used are also covered in unit 21, such as the vacuum- and cable-controlled suction throttling valve (STV), and the Chrysler evaporator pressure regulator (EPR) and evaporator temperature regulator (ETR).

MODE DOORS

Vacuum-operated mode doors include the temperature deflector, diverter, defroster, outside-inside inlet, and heater/air-conditioner outlet doors.

For various conditions, there are a number of combinations of door positions. For example, in the air-conditioning cycle alone there are six different arrangements for the mode doors. There is a different arrangement for the normal and defog settings for each of three operating conditions: full outside, full recirculate, and modulated air conditioning.

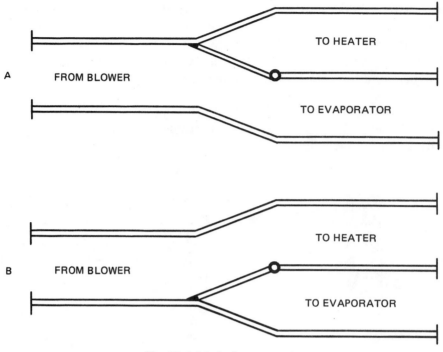

A   FROM BLOWER   TO HEATER

        TO EVAPORATOR

B   FROM BLOWER   TO HEATER

        TO EVAPORATOR

Fig. 23-4 Mode door operation

Mode doors are used to divert the movement of air from one passage to another as shown in figure 23-4. In figure 23-4A, the air is deflected into the air-conditioner core. In figure 23-4B, the air is diverted into the heater core.

Temperature Door

As indicated in the section on *Mode Doors*, the temperature door regulates the air mixture. The position of the temperature mode door determines the temperature of the duct air in an automatic temperature control system. The temperature door is regulated by a vacuum motor, a temperature door actuator, or a servo.

VACUUM MOTORS

To bring about a change in conditions, the mode doors must be operated either manually or remotely. A cable is often used to control the door. However, for automatic temperature controls, a device known as a vacuum motor is used. This device is not a motor in the usual sense. It is a motor in the sense that it imparts motion. The vacuum motor is also known as a vacuum *pot*.

Figure 23-5 shows how a vacuum motor is used to operate the mode doors. In figure 23-5A,

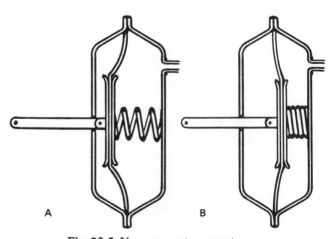

A   B

Fig. 23-5 Vacuum motor or pot

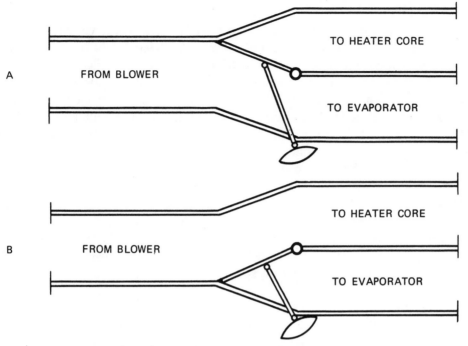

A

FROM BLOWER

TO HEATER CORE

TO EVAPORATOR

B

FROM BLOWER

TO HEATER CORE

TO EVAPORATOR

Fig. 23-6 Air diverter door with vacuum motor

the device is shown in the relaxed position. In figure 23-5B, it is in the applied position.

In the relaxed position, the spring keeps the arm extended. In the applied position, the vacuum overcomes the spring pressure and the arm is pulled to the IN position. The normal, or OFF, position of the vacuum motor is the relaxed position, figure 23-5A.

Most vacuum motors are of the type shown in figure 23-5. Some units have two vacuum hose attachments. These attachments serve as tee fittings for another vacuum motor, or they may be double action fittings, such as the ones used for temperature control on automatic temperature units. This type of control is known as a *double-action vacuum motor.* If both vacuum hose ports are on the same side of the vacuum motor, it is not a double-action vacuum motor. Fittings on both sides indicate a double-action motor.

Figure 23-6 shows the same type of duct arrangements as given in figure 23-5, but with the addition of vacuum motors.

Double-Action Vacuum Motors

This type of vacuum motor, figure 23-7, has a double-action diaphragm which allows a vacuum to be applied to either side. The vacuum causes the control arm attached to the rubber diaphragm to be extended.

Some automatic temperature control units use a double-action vacuum motor which is known as a *temperature door actuator,* or TDA.

Fig. 23-7 Double-action vacuum motor

BLOWER CONTROL

The blower control permits the driver to select a high or low volume of airflow. Although the airflow setting results in less air noise, it is less likely to maintain comfort conditions within the passenger area of the vehicle. The high airflow setting is preferred for maximum benefit. In either range, however, the airflow varies automatically with the demand placed on the system by varying weather conditions. The high blower speed is obtained only when the servo is in the maximum air-conditioning position. This part of the operation of the system is electrically controlled, not vacuum controlled. The vacuum-controlled servo has electrical contacts (which complete various circuits) as does the vacuum switch section of the servo.

TIME-DELAY RELAY

The time-delay control unit is designed to prevent the heat cycle from coming on in the automatic unit until the engine coolant has reached a temperature of 110°F (43.34°C). The unit consists of two resistors, capacitors, and transistors. Figure 23-8 shows the time-delay circuit of the wiring diagram.

AMBIENT SWITCH

The ambient switch is an electrical switch actuated by changing ambient temperature. The ambient switch is used in many custom and automatic systems.

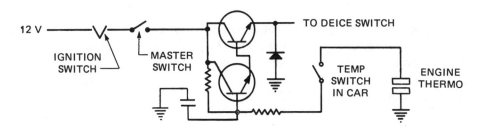

Fig. 23-8 Time-delay relay schematic

(The student should not confuse the ambient switch with the ambient sensor.)

The ambient switch is located outside the engine area where it can sense the ambient temperature only. The actual switch location depends on its design. The switch is never mounted where it is possible to sense the engine heat.

If the master switch is pressed, the ambient switch will turn the air-conditioning compressor ON at 35°F (1.67°C). The switch turns the compressor OFF if the ambient temperature falls to 25°F (-3.89°C).

Whenever the ambient temperature is in the range 64°F (17.78°C) and 55°F

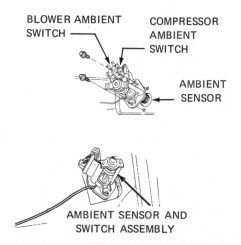

Fig. 23-9 Ambient sensor and switch assembly

(12.78°C), the ambient switch bypasses the master control and the time-delay relay and allows the blowers to run regardless of the engine coolant temperature.

When the air-conditioning compressor or blower is operated at low ambient temperatures, the humidity of the incoming air is reduced by condensing the moisture from it. In this way, window fogging is prevented when an automobile is being operated during rainy, damp, or cool weather conditions.

THERMOSTATIC VACUUM VALVE

The thermostatic vacuum valve (TVV) is a vacuum-control valve which is sensitive to temperature. The TVV is used only on late model automatic systems and is mounted where it can sense coolant temperature, such as on the side of the heater core. The TVV consists of a power element cylinder with a piston, vacuum parts, and spring. The power element is filled with a temperature-sensitive compound so that when the engine is cold and the coolant is not warm, the inlet part of the TVV is blocked and the outlet part is vented. When the coolant temperature reaches a specified range, usually 100°F to 125°F (37.78°C to 51.67°C), the compound in the cylinder expands and moves the piston until vacuum flow starts.

In the automatic temperature control system, the vacuum flow proceeds from the selector vacuum disc switch to the program vacuum disc switch, the master switch, the vacuum diaphragm, and the outside-recirculate air-cooled diaphragm. On cold days, the TVV serves only as a time delay.

SUPERHEAT SWITCH

The superheat switch is located in the rear head of some six-cylinder compressors. This device is a temperature/pressure-sensitive electrical switch which is normally in the open position, figure 23-11.

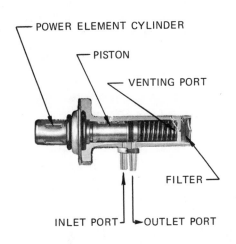

Fig. 23-10 Thermostatic vacuum valve (TVV)

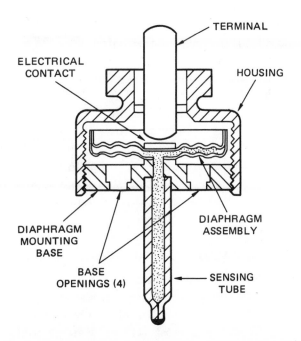

Fig. 23-11 Cutaway view of details of superheat switch

The switch remains open during system high-temperature and high-pressure conditions or low-temperature and low-pressure conditions. The switch closes when the system experiences high-temperature and low-pressure conditions.

The high-temperature and low-pressure condition of the system is usually caused by a loss of refrigerant. This loss may result in compressor or system damage if the air-conditioning system remains in operation.

The superheat switch offers a failsafe method of stopping the compressor until the problem is corrected. When the superheat switch closes, a circuit is completed through a heater of the thermal fuse. The fuse blows, opens the clutch circuit, and stops the compressor.

THERMAL FUSE

The thermal fuse protects the compressor in the event of a refrigerant loss. As described previously, the fuse works with the superheat switch. The thermal fuse consists of a temperature-sensitive fuse and a wire-wound resistor (heater) mounted as one assembly, figure 23-12.

When the superheat switch closes, a ground is created in the clutch circuit. The same current that is supplied to the compressor now feeds through the thermal fuse heater to ground. As the heater warms, the fuse link reaches its melting point. The melting of the link causes the clutch circuit to open and the clutch action stops.

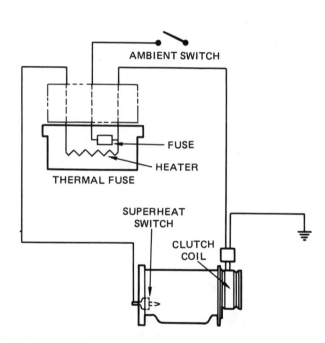

Fig. 23-12 Schematic of thermal fuse in the clutch circuit

Because of the time required to provide sufficient heat to melt the fuse link, the link is not affected during short-term high-temperature and low-pressure conditions. In some circumstances, these conditions exist without affecting the operation of the system.

CHECK VALVES AND RELAYS

Vacuum systems normally have a vacuum check valve or check relay to prevent a vacuum loss during those periods when the engine manifold vacuum is less than the value required to operate a vacuum-actuated component.

In addition, most vacuum systems contain a vacuum reserve tank (which often resembles a large fruit juice can), figure 23-13. The check valve or check relay is usually located in the vacuum line between the reserve tank and the vacuum source.

Check Valve

The check valve is opened whenever the manifold vacuum is greater than the reserve vacuum. In other words, the check valve is opened by the normal engine vacuum. In this position, the check valve connects the source to the tank. The normal engine vacuum also opens the diaphragm and allows vacuum from the control to reach the vacuum motor. Whenever the manifold vacuum drops below the value of the reserve pressure, the check valve closes. When the valve closes, the diaphragm also closes and blocks the passage from the control to the motor. As a result, the reserve vacuum is not lost because it is not allowed to bleed back through the manifold.

The manifold vacuum drops during periods of acceleration and when the engine is stopped. The vacuum

Fig. 23-13 Vacuum reserve tanks resemble fruit juice cans

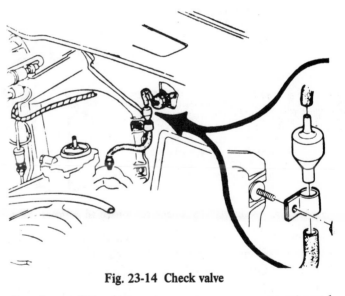

Fig. 23-14 Check valve

reserve is used both to operate the air-conditioning system vacuum components and other accessory equipment in the automobile, such as headlamp doors, door latches, and door locks.

Check Relay

The vacuum check relay serves two purposes: (1) it prevents a vacuum loss during low manifold vacuum conditions, and (2) it prevents system mode operation during these periods. Figure 23-15, page 132, is a typical vacuum schematic of a check relay.

Servicing of Check Valves and Check Relays

In general, the problems associated with check valves and check relays consist of leaking diaphragms and improper seats. Since these check valves and relays cannot

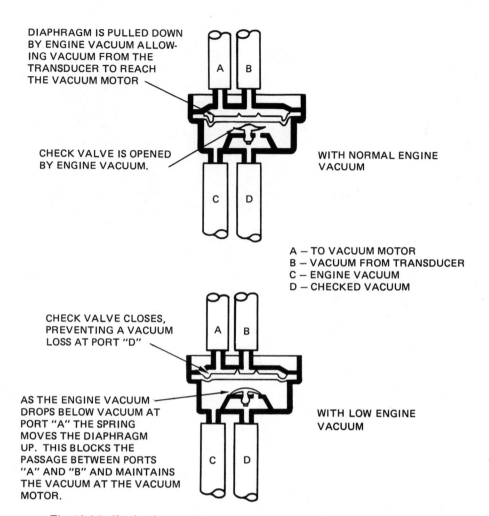

DIAPHRAGM IS PULLED DOWN
BY ENGINE VACUUM ALLOW-
ING VACUUM FROM THE
TRANSDUCER TO REACH
THE VACUUM MOTOR

A   B

CHECK VALVE IS OPENED
BY ENGINE VACUUM.

WITH NORMAL ENGINE
VACUUM

C   D

A — TO VACUUM MOTOR
B — VACUUM FROM TRANSDUCER
C — ENGINE VACUUM
D — CHECKED VACUUM

CHECK VALVE CLOSES,
PREVENTING A VACUUM
LOSS AT PORT "D"

A   B

AS THE ENGINE VACUUM
DROPS BELOW VACUUM AT
PORT "A" THE SPRING
MOVES THE DIAPHRAGM
UP. THIS BLOCKS THE
PASSAGE BETWEEN PORTS
"A" AND "B" AND MAINTAINS
THE VACUUM AT THE VACUUM
MOTOR.

WITH LOW ENGINE
VACUUM

C   D

Fig. 23-15 Check relay used to maintain vacuum at the vacuum motor

be repaired, they must be replaced as a unit assembly if they are found to be defective. Prior to replacing a check valve or a check relay, the technician must insure that a leak is not the result of a split or broken hose.

REVIEW

1. What is the most likely occurrence when the heater hose connections to the heater control valve are reversed?
2. In what position is the heater control valve when no vacuum is applied?
3. How is the operation of the POASTV controlled in General Motors units?
4. What is the purpose of the mode door?
5. What is a vacuum pot?
6. What is the position of a vacuum motor in the no vacuum condition?
7. What controls the airflow in the high range as far as blower speed is concerned?
8. What is the purpose of the time-delay switch in the heat mode?
9. How is the humidity increased in the passenger compartment?
10. Where is the heater control located?

SECTION 2
SYSTEM DIAGNOSIS

INTRODUCTION

The diagnosis of system malfunction depends largely on the technician's ability to interpret the gauge pressure readings and relate them to system problems. A system that is operating normally has a low-side gauge pressure reading that corresponds with the temperature of the refrigerant as it becomes a vapor in the evaporator (a few degrees temperature rise is allowed for the loss in the tube walls and fins). The high-side gauge pressure reading corresponds with the temperature of the gaseous refrigerant returning to a liquid in the condenser (again, a few degrees temperature drop is allowed for losses in the tube walls and fins).

Any deviation from normal readings indicates a malfunction within the system due to a faulty control device, obstruction, defective part, or improper installation.

Diagnosis of system malfunction is made easier with the knowledge that the temperature and pressure of Refrigerant 12 have a close relationship between the pressures of twenty and eighty pounds per square inch (psi). The temperature-pressure chart on page 134 shows that there is only a slight variation between the temperature and pressure of the refrigerant in the lower range.

It is correct to assume that for every pound of pressure added to the low side, a temperature increase of about one degree Fahrenheit takes place. For example, a pressure of 23.8 psi on the chart indicates a temperature of 24°F. A change of pressure of almost one pound to 24.6 psi results in a temperature increase to 25°F.

It must be pointed out that the actual temperature of the air passing over the coils of the evaporator is several degrees warmer to allow for a temperature rise caused by the loss in the fins and tubing of the evaporator.

The temperature-pressure chart can be used with the problems in this section. It may be necessary to refer to the text in Section 1, or to the Service Procedures in Section 3, to solve these problems.

Note that the various readings in this section are given in the English system units of psi and °F. For additional practice in the metric system, the student should use a temperature-pressure chart with metric values and solve the problems for the metric units of kg/cm² and °C.

TEMPERATURE-PRESSURE CHART

Evaporator Pressure Gauge Reading psi	Evaporator Temperature °F	High-pressure Gauge Reading psi	Ambient Temperature °F
0	-21	72	40
2.4	-15	86	50
4.5	-10	105	60
10.1	2	109	62
11.2	4	113	64
12.3	6	117	66
13.4	8	122	68
14.6	10	126	70
15.8	12	129	71
17.1	14	132	72
18.3	16	134	73
19.7	18	137	74
21	20	140	75
22.4	22	144	76
23.1	23	148	77
23.8	24	152	78
24.6	25	156	79
25.3	26	160	80
26.1	27	162	81
26.8	28	165	82
27.6	29	167	83
28.4	30	170	84
29.2	31	172	85
30	32	175	86
30.9	33	177	87
31.7	34	180	88
32.5	35	182	89
33.4	36	185	90
34.3	37	187	91
35.1	38	189	92
36	39	191	93
36.9	40	193	94
37.9	41	195	95
38.8	42	200	96
39.7	43	205	97
41.7	45	210	98
43.6	47	215	99
45.6	49	220	100
48.7	52	228	102
49.8	53	236	104
55.4	57	260	110
60	62	275	115
64.9	66	290	120

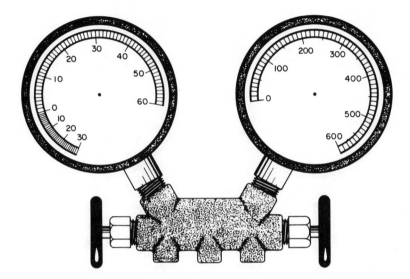

TEMPERATURE-PRESSURE RELATIONSHIP 1

Consider all conditions normal in this problem. It is designed to familiarize the student with the similarities between temperature and pressure.

1. With an ambient temperature of 95°F, what is the normal head pressure? Indicate the pressure on the gauge in the diagram.   _____ psi

2. With an evaporator temperature of 33°F, what is the normal suction pressure? Indicate the pressure on the gauge in the diagram.   _____ psi

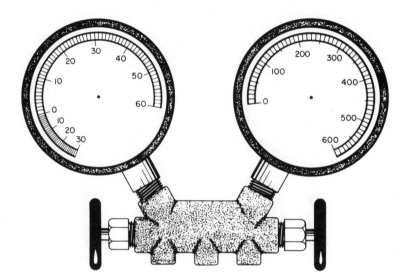

TEMPERATURE-PRESSURE RELATIONSHIP 2

Consider all conditions normal. This problem is designed to familiarize the student with the similarities of temperature and pressure.

1. A head pressure of 185 psi is normal at what ambient temperature? Show this pressure reading on the high-side gauge in the diagram.   _____ °F

2. If the evaporator temperature is 31°F, what is the low-side gauge reading? Show this pressure reading on the low-side gauge in the diagram.   _____ psi

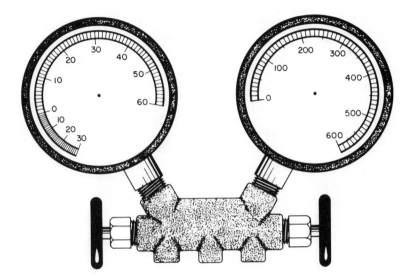

TEMPERATURE-PRESSURE RELATIONSHIP 3

Consider all conditions normal. This problem is designed to familiarize the student with the similarities of temperature and pressure.

1. The ambient temperature is 100°F. What is the normal   _____ psi
   high-side pressure? Show the pressure reading on the
   gauge in the diagram.

2. The low-side gauge reads 26 psi. What is the tempera-   _____ °F
   ture of the refrigerant in the evaporator? Show this
   temperature reading on the low-side gauge in the
   diagram.

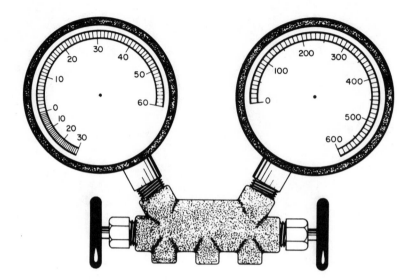

TEMPERATURE-PRESSURE RELATIONSHIP 4

Consider all conditions normal. This problem is designed to familiarize the student with the similarities of temperature and pressure.

1. The high-side gauge reads 195 psi. Show this reading on the high-side gauge. What is the ambient temperature in this problem? _____ °F

2. The low-side gauge reads 30 psi. Show this reading on the low-side gauge. What is the evaporator temperature in this problem? _____ °F

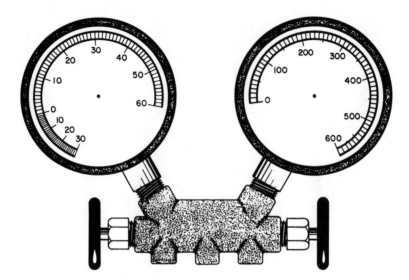

SYSTEM DIAGNOSIS 1: THE COMPRESSOR

CONDITIONS

Ambient temperature: 90°F
Low-side gauge: 50 psi
High-side gauge: 120 psi

DIAGNOSIS

1. Show the high- and low-side readings on the gauges in the diagram.

2. What should the normal high-side reading be? _____ psi

3. What is the evaporator temperature in this problem? _____ °F

4. A low-side reading of 50 psi is (high, low). _____

5. A high-side reading of 120 psi is (high, low). _____

6. This condition results in (good, poor, no) cooling from the evaporator. _____

7. An internal ___?___ of the compressor is indicated by these conditions. _____

8. To correct this condition, a new ___?___ and/or ___?___ must be installed. _____

9. This condition is generally caused by excessive ___?___ . _____

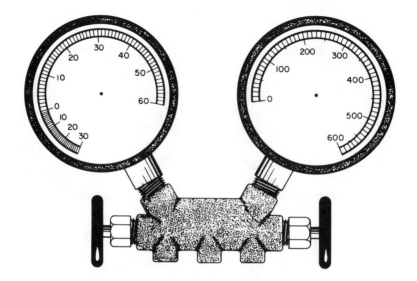

SYSTEM DIAGNOSIS 2: THE CONDENSER

CONDITIONS

Ambient Temperature: 95°F
Low-side gauge: 55 psi
High-side gauge: 300 psi

DIAGNOSIS

1. Show the high- and low-side gauge readings on the gauges in the diagram.

2. What should the normal high-side gauge reading be? _____ psi

3. What is the evaporator temperature in this problem? _____ °F

4. A low-side reading of 55 psi is (high, low). _____

5. A high-side pressure reading of 300 psi is (high, low). _____

6. This condition results in (good, poor, no) cooling from the evaporator. _____

7. Give two conditions outside the air-conditioning system that can cause this pressure.

8. Give two conditions inside the air-conditioning system that can cause this pressure.

9. Give one type of damage that can occur by operating the air conditioner with this head pressure.

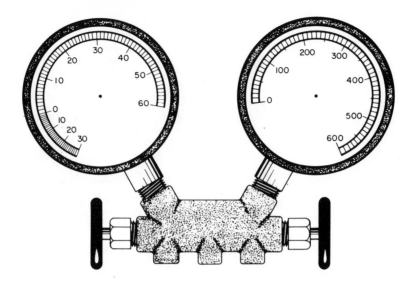

SYSTEM DIAGNOSIS 3: THE DEHYDRATOR

CONDITIONS

Ambient temperature: 100°F
Low-side gauge: 5 psi
High-side gauge: 305 psi

DIAGNOSIS

1. Show the high- and low-side gauge readings on the gauges in the diagram.

2. What should the normal high-side reading be? _____ psi

3. What is the evaporator temperature in this problem? _____ °F
   Explain.

4. A low-side reading of 5 psi is (high, low). _____

5. A high-side reading of 305 psi is (high, low). _____

6. This condition results in (good, poor, no) cooling from the evaporator. _____

7. A restriction at the __?__ is indicated by these readings. _____

8. Frosting is likely to occur at the point of __?__ . _____

9. How can this system be repaired?

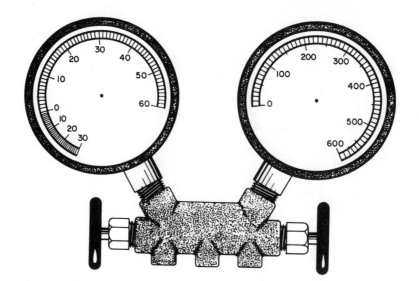

SYSTEM DIAGNOSIS 4: THERMOSTATIC EXPANSION VALVE

CONDITIONS

Ambient temperature: 95°F
Low-side gauge: 2 psi
High-side gauge: 170 psi

DIAGNOSIS

1. Show the high- and low-side manifold readings on the gauges in the diagram.

2. What should the normal high-side reading be? _____ psi

3. What is the evaporator temperature in this problem? _____ °F
   Explain?

4. A low-side reading of 2 psi is (high, normal, low). _____

5. A high-side reading of 170 psi is (high, normal, low). _____

6. This condition results in (good, poor, no) cooling from the evaporator. _____

7. This condition indicates a (starved, flooded) evaporator due to a defective __?__ . _____

8. This condition is usually accompanied by frosting at the valve __?__ . _____

9. How can this condition be corrected?

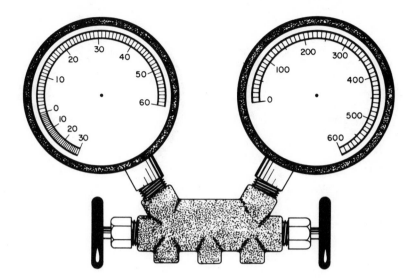

SYSTEM DIAGNOSIS 5: THERMOSTATIC EXPANSION VALVE

CONDITIONS

Ambient temperature: 95°F
Low-side gauge: 55 psi
High-side gauge: 160 psi

DIAGNOSIS

1. Show the high- and low-side manifold readings on the gauges in the diagram.

2. What should the normal high-side reading be? _____ psi

3. What is the evaporator temperature in this problem? _____ °F

4. A low-side reading of 55 psi is (high, normal, low). _____

5. A high-side reading of 160 psi is (high, normal, low). _____

6. This condition results in (good, poor, no) cooling from the evaporator. _____

7. This condition indicates a (starved, flooded) evaporator due to a malfunctioning ⎯?⎯ . _____

8. List two possible causes for this malfunctioning.

9. Can moisture in the system cause this system malfunction? Explain.

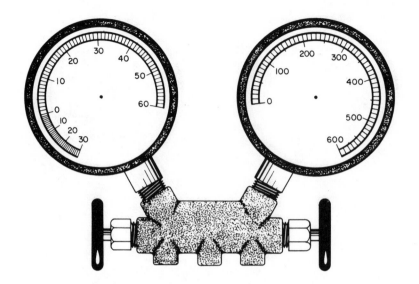

SYSTEM DIAGNOSIS 6: THE THERMOSTAT

CONDITIONS
Ambient temperature: 97°F
Low-side gauge: 10 psi
High-side gauge: 205 psi

DIAGNOSIS

1. Show the high- and low-side gauge readings on the gauges in the diagram.

2. A high-side pressure of 205 psi in this problem is (high, normal, low). _____

3. A low-side pressure of 10 psi in this problem is (high, normal, low). _____

4. What is the evaporator temperature in this problem? _____ °F

5. This condition results in (good, poor, no) cooling from the evaporator. _____

6. This condition can be accompanied by frosting of the __?__ , which blocks off airflow and results in poor __?__ . _____

7. List two possible causes of a malfunctioning thermostat that can result in this problem.

8. How can the customer unintentionally cause this problem?

9. List two types of thermostats.

10. Are all thermostats adjustable? _____

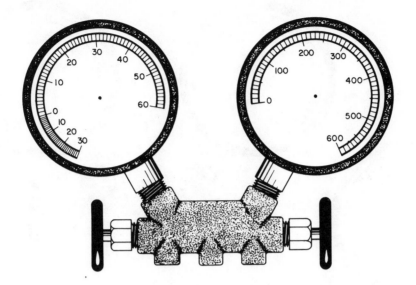

SYSTEM DIAGNOSIS 7: THE THERMOSTAT

CONDITIONS

Ambient temperature: 98°F
Low-side gauge: 60 psi
High-side gauge: 210 psi

DIAGNOSIS

1. Show the high- and low-side gauge readings on the gauges in the diagram.

2. A high-side pressure of 210 psi in this problem is (high, normal, low). _____

3. A low-side pressure of 60 psi in this problem is (high, normal, low). _____

4. What is the evaporator temperature? _____ °F

5. This condition results in (good, poor, no) cooling from the evaporator. _____

6. Give two possible causes for this malfunction.

7. How can the customer unintentionally cause this problem?

8. Can all thermostats be adjusted? Explain.

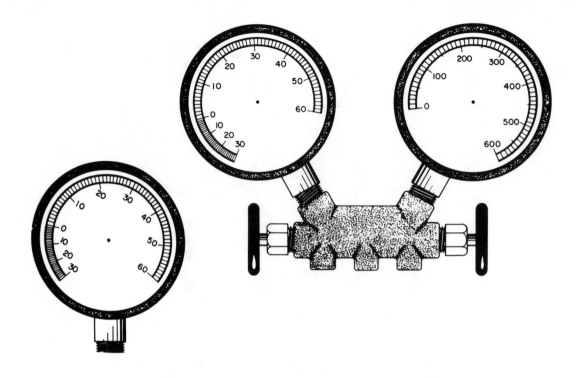

SYSTEM DIAGNOSIS 8: SUCTION CONTROL DEVICES — THE SUCTION THROTTLING VALVE

CONDITIONS

Ambient temperature: 85°F
Evaporator gauge: 5 psi

Compressor inlet: 15 in. Hg
High-side gauge: 95 psi

DIAGNOSIS

1. Show these gauge readings on the gauge set in the diagram.

2. What should the normal high-side reading be? _____ psi

3. What is the evaporator temperature in this problem? _____ °F

4. An evaporator gauge reading of 5 psi is (high, normal, low). _____

5. This system indicates an (overcharge, undercharge) of refrigerant. _____

6. A refrigerant loss from the suction throttling valve can occur at any one of three places. Name these places.
_____
_____
_____

7. All suction throttling valves cannot be repaired. State one reason for this.

8. Can the screen in the STV be removed for cleaning? Is this screen in the system before or after the screen in the thermostatic expansion valve?
_____
_____

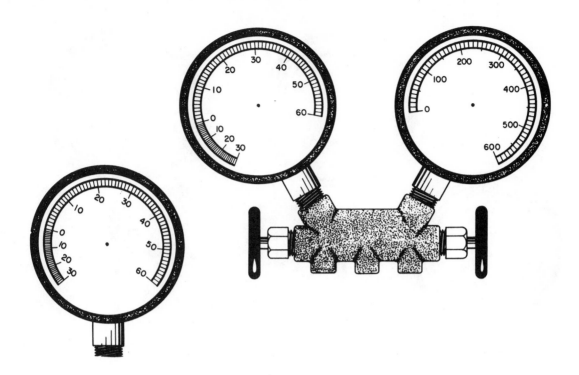

SYSTEM DIAGNOSIS 9: SUCTION CONTROL DEVICES — THE SUCTION THROTTLING VALVE

CONDITIONS

Ambient temperature: 96°F
Evaporator gauge: 38 psi

Compressor inlet: 36 psi
High-side gauge: 195 psi

DIAGNOSIS

1. Show the gauge readings on the gauge set in the diagram.

2. What should the normal high-side reading be? _____ psi

3. What is the evaporator temperature in this problem? _____ °F

4. Is the suction throttling valve causing the malfunction in this problem? Explain. _____

5. Can this system problem be corrected by an adjustment of the suction throttling valve? Explain.

6. What can be done to correct the problem in this situation?

7. What should the correct evaporator pressure be? _____ psi

8. What should the correct compressor inlet pressure be? Explain.

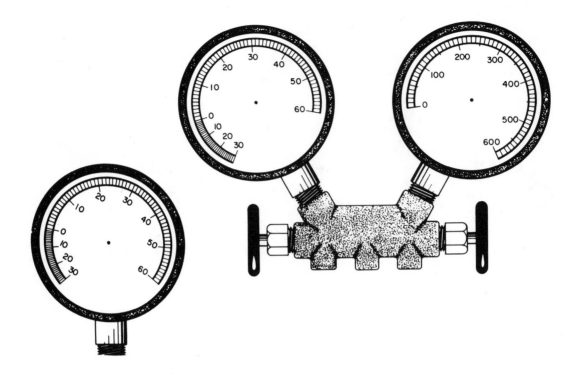

SYSTEM DIAGNOSIS 10: SUCTION CONTROL DEVICES — THE SUCTION THROTTLING VALVE

CONDITIONS

Ambient temperature: 98°F
Evaporator gauge: 38 psi

Compressor inlet: 15 psi
High-side gauge: 200 psi

DIAGNOSIS

1. Show the gauge pressures on the gauge set in the diagram.

2. What should the normal high-side pressure be? _____ psi

3. What is the evaporator temperature in this problem? _____ °F

4. This condition results in (good, poor, no) cooling from the evaporator. _____

5. Is the STV causing the malfunction in this problem? Explain.

6. Can the problem be corrected by adjusting the STV? Explain.

7. In this problem a pressure __?__ is indicated across the STV. _____

8. What can be done to correct the problem in this situation?

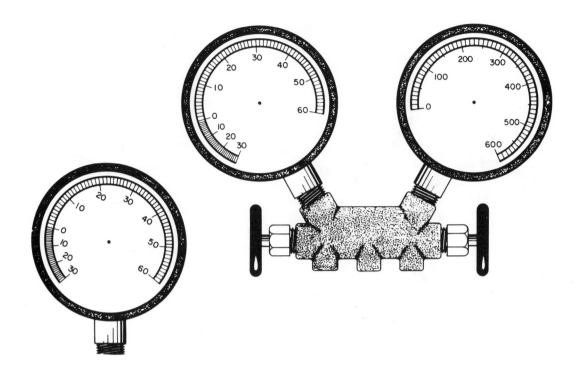

SYSTEM DIAGNOSIS 11: SUCTION CONTROL DEVICES— THE SUCTION THROTTLING VALVE

CONDITIONS

Ambient temperature: 95°F
Evaporator gauge: 15 psi

Compressor inlet: 12 psi
High-side gauge: 185 psi

DIAGNOSIS

1. Show the gauge pressures on the gauge set in the diagram.

2. The high-side pressure is (high, normal, low). _____

3. The evaporator pressure is (high, normal, low). _____

4. What is the evaporator temperature in this problem? _____

5. Is the expansion valve causing the malfunction as described here? Explain.

6. The (expansion valve, throttling valve) is causing the (starved, flooded) condition in the evaporator. _____
   _____

7. Through (normal, abnormal) operation the expansion valve is (starving, flooding) the evaporator. _____
   _____

8. The suction throttling valve (is, is not) working in this problem. _____

9. Briefly, list the steps required to correct this situation.

149

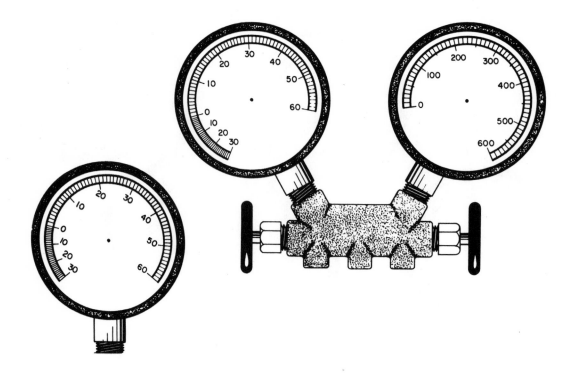

SYSTEM DIAGNOSIS 12: SUCTION CONTROL DEVICES— THE EVAPORATOR PRESSURE REGULATOR

CONDITIONS

Ambient temperature: 96°F
Evaporator gauge: 39 psi

Compressor inlet: 38 psi
High-side gauge: 190 psi

DIAGNOSIS

1. Show the pressures on the gauge set in the diagram.

2. The evaporator and compressor inlet pressures are (high, normal, low). _____

3. A malfunctioning (expansion valve, pressure regulator) is causing the (high, normal, low) low-side pressure. _____ _____

4. This condition results in (good, poor, no) cooling. _____

5. Can the EPR valve be adjusted to correct the malfunction? Explain.

6. Is the EPR valve at fault? _____

7. Briefly explain the procedures required to correct this malfunction.

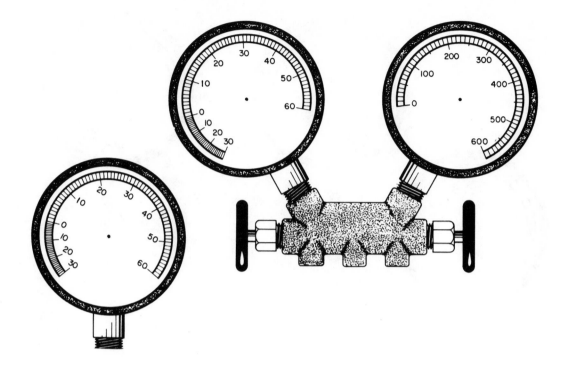

SYSTEM DIAGNOSIS 13: SUCTION CONTROL DEVICES— THE EVAPORATOR PRESSURE REGULATOR

CONDITIONS

Ambient temperature: 100°F
Evaporator gauge: 38 psi

Compressor inlet: 14 psi
High-side gauge: 212 psi

DIAGNOSIS

1. Show the gauge pressures on the gauge set in the diagram.
2. What is the evaporator temperature in this problem? _____ °F
3. The evaporator pressure is (high, normal, low). _____
4. The compressor inlet pressure is (high, low, normal). _____
5. A malfunction of the __?__ is indicated in this problem. _____
6. Give the procedure for correcting this problem.

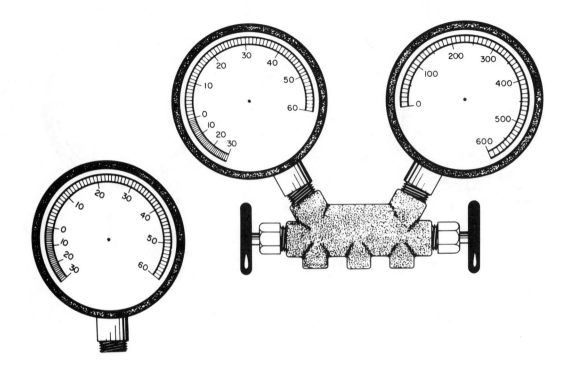

SYSTEM DIAGNOSIS 14: SUCTION CONTROL DEVICES— THE EVAPORATOR PRESSURE REGULATOR

CONDITIONS

Ambient temperature: 99°F
Evaporator gauge: 16 psi

Compressor inlet: 14 psi
High-side gauge: 207 psi

DIAGNOSIS

1. Show the gauge readings in the diagram to correspond to the conditions given.

2. What is the evaporator temperature in this problem? _____ °F

3. The EPR valve (is, is not) operating in this problem. _____

4. Can the EPR valve be adjusted for more efficient operation? Explain.

5. The expansion valve (can, cannot) be at fault in this problem. Explain. _____

6. The thermostat (can, cannot) be at fault in this problem. Explain. _____

7. What should the evaporator temperature be if the _____ °F
system is to operate properly? What is the pressure at _____ psi
this temperature?

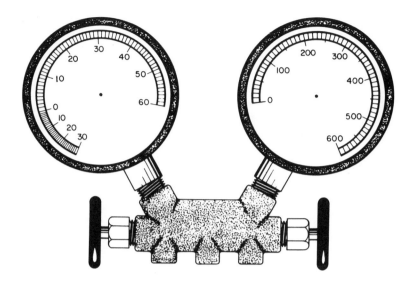

SYSTEM DIAGNOSIS 15: SUCTION CONTROL DEVICES — THE PILOT-OPERATED ABSOLUTE VALVE

CONDITIONS

Ambient temperature: 105°F
Evaporator gauge: 22 psi
High-side gauge: 222 psi

DIAGNOSIS

1. Show the gauge readings on the gauge set in the diagram.

2. An evaporator pressure of 22 psi indicates what temperature? This temperature is (too high, too low, normal) for normal system cooling. _____ °F
    _____

3. A high-side gauge pressure of 222 psi is (high, normal, low) with an ambient temperature of 105°F. _____

4. The POA valve (can, cannot) be adjusted for more efficient operation. _____

5. Give one of the advantages of the POA valve.

6. Give one of the disadvantages of the POA valve.

7. How can this condition be corrected?

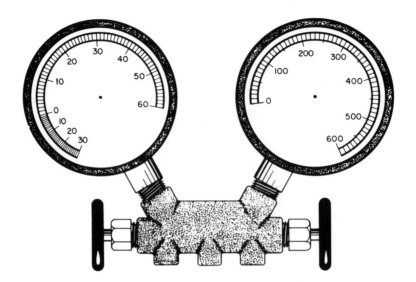

SYSTEM DIAGNOSIS 16: SUCTION CONTROL DEVICES — THE PILOT-OPERATED ABSOLUTE VALVE

CONDITIONS

Ambient temperature: 110°F
Evaporator gauge: 42 psi
High-side gauge: 240 psi

DIAGNOSIS

1. Show the gauge readings on the gauge set in the diagram.

2. An evaporator pressure of 42 psi indicates what temper-   _____
    ature?   For system cooling this temperature is con-   _____
    sidered (low, normal, high).

3. For good cooling, what should the system low-side   _____ psi
    pressure be?

4. With an ambient temperature of 110°F, what should   _____ psi
    the normal high-side pressure be?

5. In this particular problem, can the POA valve be ad-
    justed for more efficient operation? Explain.

6. Under what conditions can the POA valve be adjusted
    for more efficient operation? Explain.

7. Who uses the POA valve?

8. A leak can occur at the POA valve in one of two places.
    Name one of these places.

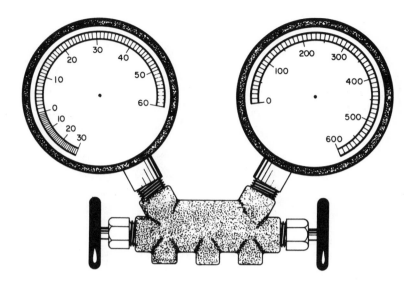

SYSTEM DIAGNOSIS 17: THE SYSTEM

CONDITIONS

Ambient temperature: 90°F
Low-side gauge: 80 psi
High-side gauge: 80 psi

DIAGNOSIS

1. Show the high- and low-side gauge readings on the gauges in the diagram.

2. What should the normal high-side reading be? _____ psi

3. The high side is (high, normal, low). _____

4. The low side is (high, normal, low). _____

5. List three possible problems with this system.

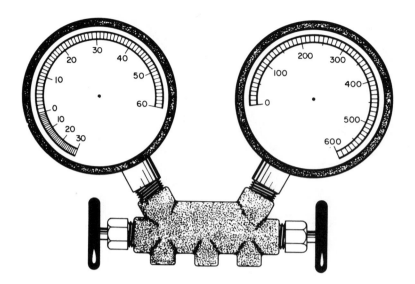

SYSTEM DIAGNOSIS 18: THE SYSTEM

CONDITIONS

Ambient temperature: 80°F
Low-side gauge: 20 psi
High-side gauge: 155 psi

DIAGNOSIS

1. Show the high- and low-side gauge readings on the gauge set in the diagram.

2. The low-side gauge is (low, normal, high). _____

3. List four possible problems with this system.

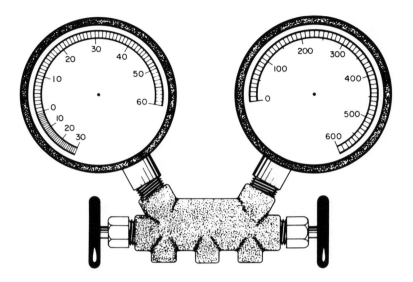

SYSTEM DIAGNOSIS 19: THE SYSTEM

CONDITIONS

Ambient temperature: 83°F
Low-side gauge: 37 psi
High-side gauge: 160 psi

DIAGNOSIS

1. Show the gauge readings on the gauge set in the diagram.

2. What is the evaporator temperature in this problem? _____ °F
   This temperature is (low, normal, high). _____

3. List four possible causes for this malfunction.

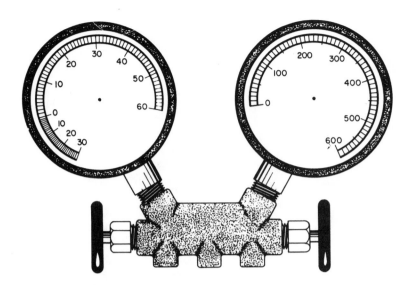

SYSTEM DIAGNOSIS 20: THE SYSTEM

CONDITIONS

Ambient temperature: 90°F
Low-side gauge: 50 psi
High-side gauge: 170 psi

DIAGNOSIS

1. Show the gauge readings on the gauge set in the diagram.

2. The high-side pressure is (high, normal, low). _____

3. List four possible causes for this malfunction.

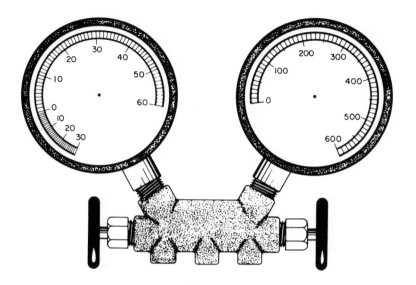

SYSTEM DIAGNOSIS 21: THE SYSTEM

CONDITIONS

Ambient temperature: 95°F
Low-side gauge: 37 psi
High-side gauge: 250 psi

DIAGNOSIS

1. Show the gauge readings on the gauge set in the diagram.

2. The low-side gauge is (high, normal, low). _____

3. The high-side gauge is (high, normal, low). _____

4. List two possible causes for this malfunction.

5. An (undercharge, overcharge) of refrigerant can cause this problem.

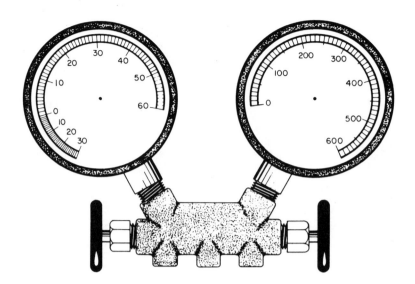

SYSTEM DIAGNOSIS 22: THE SYSTEM

CONDITIONS

Ambient temperature: 96°F
Low-side gauge: 39 psi
High-side gauge: 325 psi

DIAGNOSIS

1. Show the gauge readings on the gauge set in the diagram.

2. List six possible causes of excessive head pressure.

3. High head pressure is (always, not always) accompanied   _____
   by high suction pressure.

SECTION 3
SERVICE PROCEDURES

INTRODUCTION

The servicing of automotive air-conditioning systems becomes more complicated each year. The basic theory does not change, but different control devices are added or changed from year to year. This is true for nearly all factory-installed systems.

The service procedures given in this section are intended as *typical* procedures and are to be used only as a guide. It is impossible, for example, to state that "The low-side service valve fitting is located on the suction line near the compressor." For various reasons and from year to year, air-conditioning system manufacturers may change the locations of various system components.

The information contained in this section is given as a guide to enable the technician to perform many typical service procedures normally required. A number of service manuals are available that cover in greater detail many service procedures for specific years and models of automobiles. One such manual covers the past ten years, has little theory, and is over four inches thick.

METRICS: A WORD OF CAUTION

In 1976, automotive manufacturers began to use metric fasteners (nuts and bolts) on *some* component and accessory assemblies. This means that both metric and English fasteners are now used in the same automobile. Technicians must be extremely careful to avoid mixing English and metric fasteners.

Many metric fasteners closely resemble English fasteners in size and appearance. However, they are *not* interchangeable. For example, in some installations, a metric 6.3 x 1 bolt will replace, by design, English 1/4-20 and 1/4-28 bolts. Note in the table how close the dimensions are for these fasteners.

ENGLISH			METRIC		
SIZE	DIM		SIZE	DIM	
	DIA	THD		DIA	THD
1/4-28	0.250	28	M6.3 x 1	0.248	25.4

The diameters differ by only 0.002 inch and the threads by 2.6 threads per inch. These differences are small, but an English nut on a metric bolt will *not* hold. Mismatching of fasteners causes component damage and may result in personal injury.

SERVICE PROCEDURE 1:
CONNECTING THE MANIFOLD AND GAUGE SET INTO THE SYSTEM (HAND SHUTOFF SERVICE VALVES)

This procedure can be used when it becomes necessary to install the manifold and gauge set on the air-conditioning system to perform any one of the many operational tests.

Safety glasses should be worn while working with a refrigerant. Remember, liquid refrigerant splashed in the eyes can cause blindness.

TOOLS

Manifold and gauge set equipped with compound and pressure gauges
Three service hoses
Service valve wrench
Suitable wrenches to remove the protective caps from the service ports
Suitable eye protection
Fender covers

PROCEDURE

Prepare the System

1. Place a fender cover on the car to avoid damage to the finish of the car.
2. Use a wrench of the correct size to remove the protective caps from the service valve stems. Some caps are made of light metal and can be removed by hand.
3. Using the correct wrench, remove the protective acorn caps from the service ports. *CAUTION: Remove the caps slowly to insure that no refrigerant leaks past the service valve.*

Connect the Manifold Gauge Service Hoses to the Compressor

1. Connect the low-side manifold hose to the suction side of the compressor.

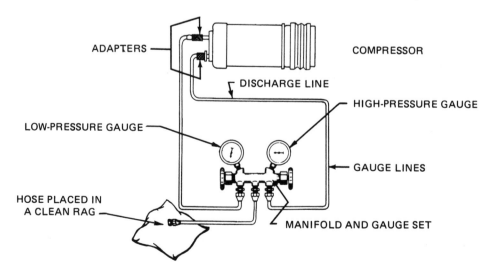

Fig. SP1-1 Typical manifold set connections

2. Connect the high-side manifold hose to the discharge side of the compressor. Both of the connections (1 and 2) are to be fingertight.

3. Make sure the hand shutoff valves are closed on the manifold set before the next step.

Purge the Service Hoses

1. Use a service valve wrench and rotate the suction-side service valve stem two or three turns clockwise.

2. Repeat the procedure in step 1 with the discharge service valve stem.

3. Purge the air from the low-side hose by cracking the low-side hand valve for a few seconds; then close the valve.

4. Repeat the procedure in step 3 with the high-side hand valve to purge the air from the high-side hose.

Prepare the System for Operational Tests

1. Start the motor and adjust the speed to about 1,250 rpm by adjusting the idle speed screw or the setting on the high cam.

2. Turn on the air conditioner and adjust all controls for maximum cold (with the blower on high speed).

3. If the motor is cold, allow sufficient time for the engine to warm up, between five and ten minutes.

4. Perform operational tests as required.

REVIEW

Briefly answer each of the following questions.

1. If refrigerant is leaking past the service valve because of a poor seat, where does it leak out of the system?

2. How is the suction side of the compressor valve identified?

3. How tight should the manifold hoses be fastened to the service valve ports?

4. How are the service valves midpositioned?

5. How is the manifold hand valve cracked?

SERVICE PROCEDURE 2:
CONNECTING THE MANIFOLD AND GAUGE SET INTO THE SYSTEM (SCHRADER VALVE FITTINGS)

This procedure is recommended when it becomes necessary to install the manifold and gauge set on the air-conditioning system equipped with Schrader-type service valves to perform any one of the many operational tests.

Safety glasses should be worn while working with a refrigerant. Remember, liquid refrigerant splashed in the eyes can result in blindness.

TOOLS

Manifold and gauge set equipped with compound and pressure gauges
Three service hoses, each equipped with a Schrader adapter
Service valve wrench
Suitable eye protection
Suitable wrench to remove the port caps
Fender covers

PROCEDURE

Prepare the System

1. Place a fender cover on the car to avoid damage to the finish of the car.
2. Using a wrench of the correct size to avoid damage, remove the protective acorn caps from the compressor high- and low-side service ports. *CAUTION: Remove the caps slowly to insure that no refrigerant is leaking past a defective Schrader valve.*

Connect the Manifold Gauge Service Hoses to the Compressor

1. Service hoses must be equipped with a Schrader valve depressing pin. If the hoses are not so equipped, a suitable adapter must be used.

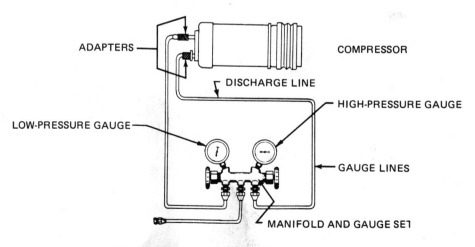

Fig. SP2-1 Typical manifold set connections

2. Make sure that the manifold hand shutoff valves are closed before the next step.

3. Connect the low-side manifold hose to the suction side of the compressor.

4. Connect the high-side manifold hose to the discharge side of the compressor. The connections in steps 3 and 4 are to be fingertight.

Purge the Service Hoses

1. Purge the air from the low-side hose by cracking the low-side service valve on the manifold for a few seconds; then close the valve.

2. Repeat step 1 with the high-side manifold valve to purge the air from the high-side hose.

Prepare the System for Operational Tests

1. Start the engine and adjust the speed to about 1,250 rpm by adjusting the idle speed screw or the setting on the high cam.

2. Turn on the air conditioner and adjust all controls for maximum cooling (with the blower on high speed).

3. If the engine is cold, allow sufficient time for the engine to warm up, between five and ten minutes.

4. Perform operational tests as necessary.

REVIEW

Briefly answer each of the following questions.

1. Why is it important to wear safety glasses?

2. Describe a compound gauge.

3. What is meant by purging air?

4. Are the Schrader-type fittings equipped with service valves?

5. Is it necessary to have manifold hand shutoff valves with the Schrader-type fittings?

SERVICE PROCEDURE 3:
PURGING THE AIR-CONDITIONING SYSTEM

The air-conditioning system is purged when all of the refrigerant in the system is removed. This procedure is necessary to replace component parts that have failed during normal operation.

Adequate ventilation should be maintained during this operation. Do not discharge Refrigerant 12 near an open flame as toxic phosgene gas is formed.

TOOLS

Complete manifold and gauge set   Suitable hand wrenches
Service valve wrench   Eye goggles
Protective covers

Fig. SP3-1 Manifold hookup to purge system

PROCEDURE

Prepare System

1. Connect the manifold and gauge set into the system. Set all controls to the maximum cold position.
2. Set the engine speed to 1,000-1,200 rpm and operate for 10-15 minutes.
3. This procedure should be followed whenever possible to stabilize the system. However, certain system malfunctions can make this procedure impossible.

Purge Refrigerant from the System

1. Return the engine speed to normal to prevent dieseling. Shut off the engine.
2. Open the low- and high-side manifold valves slowly to allow refrigerant to bleed off through the center hose.
3. Open the hand valves only enough to bleed off the refrigerant. Rapid purging draws excessive oil from the system.

4. The center hose can be placed on a clean rag. If any refrigeration oil is pulled out of the system, it shows on the rag.

System Purged of Refrigerant

1. Both manifold gauges read zero when the system is purged.
2. Close the hand manifold valves when the refrigerant ceases to bleed off.
3. The system is now purged of refrigerant and can be opened for service as required.
4. Cap all openings and hoses to avoid the possibility of dirt or foreign matter entering the system.

REVIEW

Briefly answer each of the following questions.

1. What is meant by purging the air-conditioning system?
2. What happens if Refrigerant 12 is discharged near an open flame?
3. After stabilizing the system, why is the engine speed returned to normal before the engine is shut off?
4. What is the result if a hand valve is opened all the way while purging?
5. How does one know when the system is purged of refrigerant?

SERVICE PROCEDURE 4:
LEAK TESTING THE SYSTEM USING A HALIDE LEAK DETECTOR

The halide leak detector is essentially a propane torch. This device, figure SP4-1, is the most popular form of leak detector as far as the service technician is concerned because of its low initial cost and its low upkeep. Other than propellant replacement, the only maintenance required is an occasional reactor plate replacement.

To check the sensitivity of the reactor plate, the pickup hose is passed over a recently opened (but empty) can of refrigerant. Alternatively, a service valve can be cracked open. The flame of the torch should be violet in color. If little or no color change occurs, the reactor plate must be replaced.

When leak testing, all joints and fittings should be free of oil. This

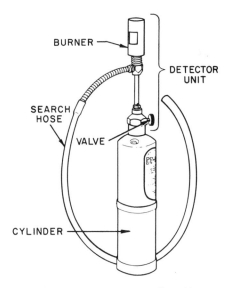

Fig. SP4-1 Leak detector (torch)

precaution eliminates the possibility of a false reading caused by refrigerant absorbed in the oil. Cigarette smoke, purging of another unit nearby, and refrigerant vapors in the surrounding air can also give false readings on the detector.

A halide leak detector must only be used in a well-ventilated area. It must never be used in spaces where explosive gases are present. When refrigerant comes into contact with an open flame, phosgene gas is formed. Never inhale the vapors or fumes from the halide leak detector — they can be poisonous.

TOOLS

Service valve wrench
Suitable hand wrenches
Eye protection
Fender covers
Manifold and gauge set
Halide leak detector

PROCEDURE

Prepare the System

1. Connect the manifold and gauge set to the system.

2. Place the high- and low-side compressor service valves in the cracked position.

3. Place the high- and low-side manifold hand valves in the closed position.

4. Determine the presence of refrigerant in the system. A minimum value of 50 psig is needed for leak detection.

5. If there is an insufficient charge of refrigerant in the system, continue with the next step, *Add Refrigerant for Leak Test Pressure*. If the charge is sufficient, omit the next step and proceed with the step, *Prepare the Leak Detector*.

Add Refrigerant for Leak Test Pressure

1. Open the high- and low-side hand valves to purge the hoses of air. Then close the valves.

2. Attach the center manifold hose to the refrigerant container.

3. Open the refrigerant container service valve.

4. Open the high-side manifold hand valve until a pressure of 50 psi is reached on the low-side gauge. Then close the high-side hand valve.

5. Close the refrigerant container service valve and remove the hose.

Prepare the Leak Detector

1. Open the valve and light the gas. Adjust for a low flame; that is, one which burns about 1/2 in. above the reactor plate.

2. Allow the flame to burn until the copper reactor plate becomes cherry red in color.

3. Lower the flame until it is about 1/4 in. above or just even with the reactor plate.

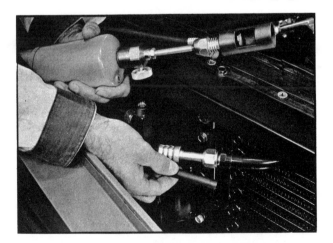

Fig. SP4-2 Leak testing the condenser

Check for Leaks in the Air-conditioning System

1. Move the search hose under all of the joints and connections in the system. Check all seals and control devices.

2. Disconnect any vacuum hoses connected to the system. Check the vacuum hose ports for refrigerant vapors.

Reaction of Halide Leak Detector in the Presence of Refrigerant

In the presence of refrigerant, a color change will occur in the flame above the reactor plate:

- Pale blue: no refrigerant loss
- Pale yellow at the edges of the flame: very small refrigerant loss
- Yellow: small amount of refrigerant loss
- Purplish-blue: large amount of refrigerant loss
- Violet: heavy amount of refrigerant loss; the volume may be great enough to extinguish the flame

Repair System

1. After the leak is located, purge the system of refrigerant.
2. Make repairs as indicated. Check the compressor oil as outlined in Service Procedures 19, 20, or 21.
3. Add oil if required. Add refrigerant and recheck for leaks.
4. If no leaks are found, the system can be evacuated and charged.
5. Perform other service procedures as necessary.

REVIEW

Briefly answer each of the following questions.

1. What gas is formed when Refrigerant 12 comes into contact with an open flame?
2. What pressure is normally required to detect a leak?
3. How high should the flame burn in the leak detector?
4. What color is the flame in the presence of a small refrigerant loss?
5. What part of the leak detector is used to search for leaks?

SERVICE PROCEDURE 5:
LEAK TESTING THE SYSTEM
USING AN ELECTRONIC LEAK DETECTOR

The electronic leak detector is the most sensitive of all types of leak detectors. Some of these electronic detectors can sense a refrigerant leak as small as one-half ounce per year. The initial cost and upkeep are the controlling economic factors to be considered in purchasing electronic leak detectors. If a shop does a great deal of air-conditioner service, this type of leak detector can be of great value in detecting *impossible* leaks.

An electronic leak detector must be used in a well-ventilated area only. It must never be used in spaces where explosive gases are present.

Fig. SP5-1 Leak detector

TOOLS

    Service valve wrench
    Hand tools
    Fender covers
    Manifold and gauge set
    Electronic leak detector

PROCEDURE

Prepare System

1. Follow the procedure as outlined in Service Procedure 4.

Add Refrigerant for the Leak Test Pressure

1. Follow the procedure as outlined in Service Procedure 4.

Prepare the Leak Detector

    NOTE: Follow the procedure as outlined in the manufacturer's instructions provided with the leak detector. Although the procedures may vary considerably for different leak detectors, the following steps can be used as a guide.

1. Turn the controls and the sensitivity knobs to off or zero.

2. Plug the leak detector into an approved voltage source and turn the switch on. Allow a warmup period of about five minutes.

3. After the warmup period, place the probe at the reference leak and adjust the controls and sensitivity knob until the detector reacts. Remove the probe — the reaction should stop. If the reaction continues, the sensitivity adjustment is too high. If the reaction stops, the adjustment is adequate.

Check the System for Leaks

1. Move the search hose under all of the joints and connections. Check all seals and control devices.

2. Disconnect any vacuum hoses connected to the system. Check the vacuum hose ports for refrigerant vapor (indicating a control leak).

3. When a leak is located, the detector reacts as it does when placed by the reference leak.

4. Do not keep the probe in contact with refrigerant any longer than is necessary to locate the leak.

   Never place the probe in a stream of refrigerant or where a severe leak is known to exist. The sensitive components of the leak detector can be damaged in this situation.

Repair System

1. After the leak is located, purge the system of refrigerant.

2. Repair the leak as indicated. Check the compressor oil as outlined in Service Procedures 19, 20, or 21.

3. Add oil and refrigerant. Recheck for leaks.

4. If no leaks are found, purge the system, evacuate, and charge the system as outlined in Service Procedures 3, 6, and 7.

5. Perform other service procedures as necessary.

REVIEW

Briefly answer each of the following questions.

1. What is the sensitivity of the electronic leak detector?

2. What is the greatest advantage of the electronic leak detector?

3. What disadvantage may there be in the use of an electronic leak detector?

SERVICE PROCEDURE 6:
EVACUATING THE SYSTEM
USING A VACUUM PUMP OR CHARGING STATION

The air-conditioning system must be evacuated whenever the system is serviced to the extent that it is purged of refrigerant. Evacuation rids the system of all air and moisture that was allowed to enter the unit. At or near sea level, a good vacuum pump is one that can achieve a value of 29 in. Hg or better. For each 1,000 feet of elevation, the reading is about 1 inch higher. For example, at 5,000 ft., the vacuum reading is about 24 in. Hg.

As the pressure in the air-conditioning system is lowered, the boiling temperature of the water (moisture) that is present in the system is also lowered. The water vapor can then be pulled out of the system. The table in figure SP6-1 illustrates the effectiveness of moisture removal for a given vacuum.

System Vacuum, psi	Temperature, °F
27.99	100
28.89	80
29.40	60
29.71	40
29.82	20
29.88	0

Fig. SP6-1 Boiling point of water in a vacuum

TOOLS

Service valve wrench
Hand wrenches
Fender covers
Manifold and gauge set
Vacuum pump or charging station

PROCEDURE

Prepare the System

1. Connect the manifold and gauge set to the system.

2. Place the high- and low-side compressor service valves in the cracked position.

3. Place the high- and low-side manifold hand valves in the closed position.

4. Remove the protective caps from the inlet and exhaust of the vacuum pump. Make sure the port cap is removed from the exhaust port to avoid damage to the vacuum pump.

5. Connect the center manifold hose to the inlet of the vacuum pump.

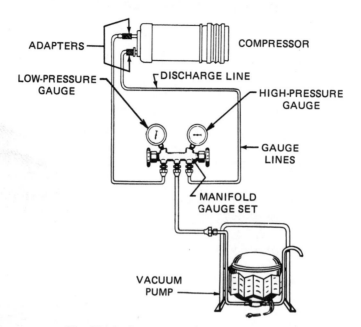

ADAPTERS

COMPRESSOR

LOW-PRESSURE GAUGE

DISCHARGE LINE

HIGH-PRESSURE GAUGE

GAUGE LINES

MANIFOLD GAUGE SET

VACUUM PUMP

Fig. SP6-2 Connections for evacuation of system

Evacuate the System

1. Start the vacuum pump.
2. Open the low-side manifold hand valve and observe the compound gauge needle. The needle should be pulled down to indicate a slight vacuum.
3. After about five minutes, the compound gauge should indicate below 20 in. Hg and the high-side gauge needle should be slightly below the zero index of the gauge.
4. If the high-side needle does not drop below zero (unless restricted by a stop), system blockage is indicated.
5. If the system is blocked, discontinue the evacuation. Repair or remove the obstruction. If the system is clear, continue the evacuation.
6. Operate the pump for 15 minutes and observe the gauges. The system should be at a vacuum of 24-26 in. Hg minimum if there is no leak.
7. If the system is not down to 24-26 in. Hg, close the low-side hand valve and observe the compound gauge.
8. If the compound gauge needle rises, indicating a loss of vacuum, there is a leak which must be repaired before the evacuation is continued. Leak check the system as outlined in Service Procedure 4 or 5.
9. If no leak is evident, continue with the pumpdown.

Complete the Evacuation

1. Pump for a minimum of 30 minutes, longer if time permits.
2. After pumpdown, close the high- and low-side manifold hand valves. (The high-side valve can be opened after the system is checked for blockage.)
3. Shut off the vacuum pump, disconnect the manifold hose, and replace the protective caps.

Check the System for Irregularities

1. Note the compound gauge reading; it should be about 29 in. Hg.

2. The compound gauge needle should not rise at a rate faster than 1 in. in five minutes.

3. If the system fails to meet this requirement, although not indicated previously, a partial charge must be installed and the system must be leak checked as outlined in Service Procedure 4 or 5.

4. After the leak is detected and repaired, the system must be purged of refrigerant and completely evacuated.

5. If the system holds the vacuum as specified, continue with the charging procedure (or other procedures as required).

REVIEW

Briefly answer each of the following questions.

1. What is the recommended minimum pumping requirement for a vacuum pump at sea level?

2. How is moisture removed from the system when the system is under a vacuum?

3. Can moisture normally be removed from a system under a vacuum of 27 in. Hg?

4. What action is indicated if the system cannot be pumped down to a vacuum in 15 minutes?

5. What is the recommended minimum pumpdown time?

6. If the system is leakfree, the vacuum rise after pumpdown should be no greater than 1 in. Hg per ___?___ minutes.

SERVICE PROCEDURE 7:
CHARGING THE SYSTEM
USING POUND CANS OF REFRIGERANT (SYSTEM OFF)

Containers of refrigerant are commonly called *pound cans*, but actually hold 14 ounces of refrigerant. Pound cans are popular and are used in many shops, including shops with a large volume of business and those operating on a smaller scale.

The service technician must insure that only Refrigerant 12 is introduced into the air-conditioning system. To assist in identifying Refrigerant 12, the containers generally are painted white. For positive identification, however, the technician should check that the chemical name on the container is dichlorodifluoromethane (the symbol is CCl_2F_2).

CAUTION

Above 130°F, liquid refrigerant completely fills a container and hydrostatic pressure builds up rapidly with each degree of temperature added.

- Never heat a refrigerant container above 125°F. (it should never be necessary to heat a refrigerant container at all)
- Never apply a direct flame to a refrigerant container or place an electric resistance heater close to the container.
- Do not abuse a refrigerant container.
- Use only approved wrenches to open and close the valves.
- Store the container in an upright position.
- Do not handle refrigerant without suitable eye protection and do not discharge refrigerant into an enclosed area having an open flame.

TOOLS

Service valve wrench   Fender covers
Suitable hand wrenches   Manifold gauge set
Eye protection   Can tap

MATERIAL

Refrigerant 12

PROCEDURE

Prepare the System

1. With both manifold hand valves in the closed position, connect the manifold and gauge set into the system.
2. Place the high- and low-side compressor service valves in the cracked position, if the unit is so equipped.
3. Place the system under a vacuum after an adequate pumpdown.

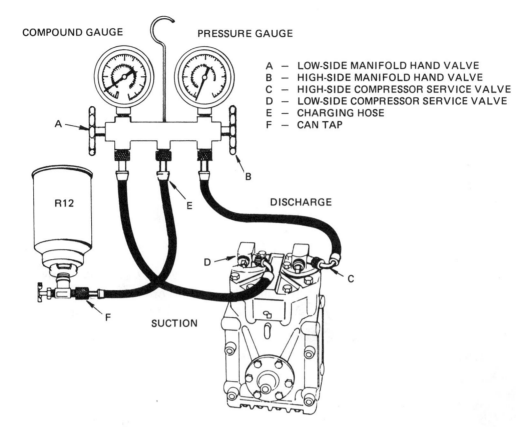

COMPOUND GAUGE   PRESSURE GAUGE

A — LOW-SIDE MANIFOLD HAND VALVE
B — HIGH-SIDE MANIFOLD HAND VALVE
C — HIGH-SIDE COMPRESSOR SERVICE VALVE
D — LOW-SIDE COMPRESSOR SERVICE VALVE
E — CHARGING HOSE
F — CAN TAP

A

R12

E

B

DISCHARGE

D

C

F

SUCTION

Fig. SP7-1 Charging the system with liquid

Install the Can Tap Valve on the Container of Refrigerant

1. The valve stem should be in the out, or counterclockwise, position.

2. Attach the valve to the can. Secure the locking nut if the valve is so equipped.

3. Connect the center manifold hose to the can tap port.

4. Pierce the can by closing the can tap shutoff valve. Turn the valve stem all the way in the clockwise direction.

Purge the Line of Air

1. Once the can is pierced, back the can tap valve out as far as possible (turn in a counterclockwise direction).

2. The center hose is now charged with refrigerant. *Do not crack* the high- or low-side hand valves.

3. Loosen the center hose connection at the manifold set (E in figure SP7-1) until a hiss can be heard. Allow gases to escape for a few seconds, then retighten the connection.

4. The system is now purged and under a vacuum.

Charge the System

1. Open the high-side gauge manifold hand valve.

2. Observe the low-side gauge pressure. If the gauge indication does not move from the vacuum range into the pressure range, system blockage is indicated.

3. If the system is blocked, correct the condition, evacuate, and continue with the procedure.

4. Invert the container and allow the liquid refrigerant to enter the system.

5. Tap the refrigerant container on the bottom. The can is empty if it gives a hollow ring.

6. Repeat this procedure with additional cans of refrigerant as required to charge the air conditioner completely. Refer to the manufacturer's specifications regarding the system capacity.

Complete the System Charge

1. Close the high-side manifold hand valve.

2. Remove the can tap from the center hose.

3. Rotate the compressor clutch by hand through two or three revolutions to insure that liquid refrigerant has not entered the low side of the compressor.

4. Start the engine and set it to fast idle.

5. Engage the clutch to start the compressor. Set all controls to maximum cooling.

6. Conduct a performance test if indicated.

7. Back seat the compressor service valves. Remove the manifold gauge set from the system.

8. Replace all protective caps and covers.

REVIEW

Briefly answer each of the following questions.

1. What is the net weight of the contents of a pound can?

2. What is the proper name for Refrigerant 12? Underline one of the following:
   a. dichlorodifluoromethane   b. monochlordifluoromethane

3. What is the chemical symbol for Refrigerant 12? Underline one of the following:
   a. $CHClF_2$ b. CCl_2F_2 c. CH_2Cl_2

4. Why is it important to be able to recognize the chemical name and symbol for Refrigerant 12?

5. Which side of the compressor is used to charge the system with liquid when the system is off?

SERVICE PROCEDURE 8:
CHARGING THE SYSTEM
USING POUND CANS (SYSTEM RUNNING)

Refer again to the introduction and caution outlined in Service Procedure 7, *Charging the System Using Pound Cans of Refrigerant (System Off)*.

CAUTION

With the refrigerant can or tank inverted, vapor rises to the top of the container and liquid refrigerant is forced into the charging hoses. *Do not* invert the refrigerant container with low-side pressures in excess of 40 psig. Regulating the valve on the container or the manifold hand valve insures a pressure of 40 psig or below. Liquid refrigerant entering the compressor low side can cause serious damage to internal parts such as pistons, reed valves, head, and head gaskets.

If the ambient temperature is lower than 80°F do not invert the refrigerant container. The car engine and air-conditioning system should be at operating temperature.

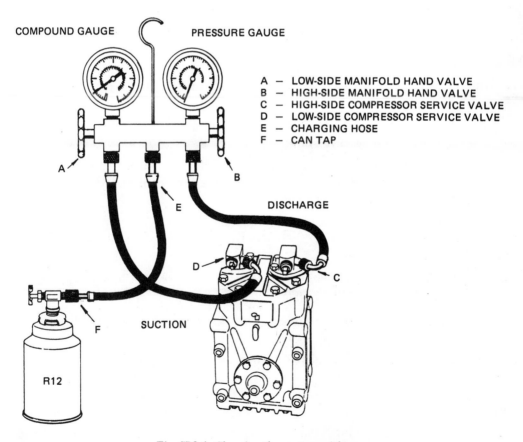

COMPOUND GAUGE   PRESSURE GAUGE

A — LOW-SIDE MANIFOLD HAND VALVE
B — HIGH-SIDE MANIFOLD HAND VALVE
C — HIGH-SIDE COMPRESSOR SERVICE VALVE
D — LOW-SIDE COMPRESSOR SERVICE VALVE
E — CHARGING HOSE
F — CAN TAP

DISCHARGE

SUCTION

R12

Fig. SP8-1 Charging the system with gas

TOOLS

Service valve wrench
Hand wrenches
Eye protection

Fender covers
Manifold and gauge set
Can tap

MATERIAL

Refrigerant 12

PROCEDURE

Prepare the System

1. Connect the manifold and gauge set into the system. Set both hand valves in the closed position.

2. Set the compressor high- and low-side service valves in the cracked position.

3. Place the system under a vacuum after an adequate pumpdown.

Install the Can Tap on the Can of Refrigerant

1. Set the can tap in the counterclockwise position.

2. Attach the valve to the refrigerant container. Secure the locking nut if so equipped.

3. Connect the center manifold hose to the can tap port.

4. Pierce the can by turning the shutoff valve in the clockwise position.

Purge the Line of Air

1. With the can pierced, back the can tap valve out (turn in a counterclockwise direction).

2. The center hose is now charged with refrigerant and air. Do not crack the high- or low-side manifold hand valves.

3. Loosen the center hose connection at the manifold set (E in figure SP8-1) until a hiss can be heard. Allow gas to escape for a few seconds and then retighten the connection until it is fingertight.

4. The system is now purged and under a vacuum.

Check the System for Blockage

1. Open the high-side gauge manifold hand valve. Observe the low-side gauge pressure. Close the high-side hand valve.

2. If the low-side gauge does not move from the vacuum range into the pressure range, system blockage is indicated.

3. Correct the blockage, if indicated. Then evacuate and continue with the next operation.

Charge the System

1. Start the engine and adjust the speed to about 1,250 rpm by turning the idle screw or the setting on the high cam.

2. Insure that both of the manifold hand valves are closed.

3. Adjust the controls for maximum cooling with the blower on high speed.

4. Open the low-side gauge manifold hand valve to allow gaseous refrigerant to enter the system.

5. After the pressure on the low side drops below 40 psig, the can should be inverted to allow more rapid removal of the refrigerant.

6. Tap the can on the bottom to determine if it is empty. An empty can will give a hollow ring.

7. Repeat this procedure with additional cans of refrigerant as required to charge the system completely. Refer to the manufacturer's specifications regarding the capacity of the system.

   NOTE: If the system capacity is not known, charge the unit until the sight glass is clear, then add another 1/4 pound of refrigerant.

Complete the System Charge

1. Close the low-side manifold hand valve.

2. Remove the can tap from the center hose.

3. Conduct the performance test if indicated.

4. Back seat the compressor service valves and remove the manifold and gauge set.

5. Replace all protective caps and covers.

REVIEW

Briefly answer each of the following questions.

1. What rule is followed in inverting the refrigerant container?

2. When the system is running, through which side is refrigerant fed?

3. What is the result if the refrigerant is fed into the system through the other side?

4. How can it be determined if the refrigerant can is empty?

5. Are both of the compressor service valves in the midposition for system charging?

SERVICE PROCEDURE 9:
CHARGING THE SYSTEM
FROM A BULK SOURCE

Shops that perform a large volume of air-conditioner service can obtain bulk refrigerant containers in 25- and 145-pound cylinders. The use of the bulk containers requires a set of scales, or other approved measuring device, to determine when the proper system charge is obtained.

Read the service caution given in Service Procedure 7. The importance of the careful handling of refrigerant and refrigerant containers cannot be overemphasized. All cases of injury stem from carelessness and improper handling.

Remember, accidents are caused — by an act of carelessness.

TOOLS

Service valve wrench
Hand wrenches
Eye protection

Fender covers
Manifold and gauge set
Scales

PROCEDURE

Prepare the System

1. With both manifold hand valves in the closed position, connect the manifold and gauge set to the system.

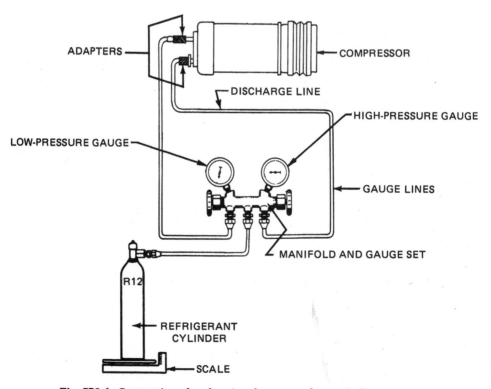

Fig. SP9-1 Connections for charging the system from a bulk source

2. Place the high- and low-side compressor service valves in the cracked position, if the unit is so equipped.

3. Place the system under a vacuum after the prescribed pumpdown.

Connect the Refrigerant Container and Purge the System

1. Connect the center manifold gauge hose to the refrigerant cylinder adapter.

2. Open the refrigerant cylinder hand valve.

3. Crack the center hose at the manifold gauge set for a few seconds to purge the hose of air.

4. The system is now purged and under a vacuum.

Check the System for Blockage

1. Do not start the engine at this time and do not turn the air conditioner on.

2. Open the high-side manifold hand valve. Observe the low-side gauge. Close the high-side hand valve.

3. System blockage is indicated if the low-side gauge needle does not move from the vacuum range into the pressure range.

4. If the system is blocked, correct the blockage, reevacuate the system, and continue with the procedure.

Charge the System

1. Insure that both the high- and low-side manifold hand valves are closed.

2. Start the engine and adjust the speed to about 1,250 rpm.

3. Adjust the air-conditioning controls for maximum cooling with the blower on high speed.

4. Keep the refrigerant cylinder in an upright position. Liquid refrigerant must not be allowed to enter the compressor since this can cause serious damage.

5. Open the low-side manifold hand valve and allow the gaseous refrigerant to enter the system.

6. Place the cylinder on a scale to insure that the refrigerant is measured properly. If the system capacity is not known, add refrigerant until it just passes the sight glass and then add four more ounces. The amount of refrigerant used can be determined by the scale reading. (Subtract the new scale reading from the original scale reading.)

Complete the System Charge

1. When the system is fully charged, close the low-side manifold hand valve.

2. Close the cylinder service valve and remove the hose from the adapter.

3. Conduct the performance tests or other tests as required.

4. Return the engine to its normal idle speed. Shut off the engine.

5. Back seat the compressor service valves and remove the manifold and gauge set.

6. Replace all protective caps and covers.

REVIEW

Briefly answer each of the following questions.

1. While charging the system with the engine running, determine the following:
   a. What is the position of the compressor low-side service valve?
   b. What is the position of the compressor high-side service valve?
   c. What is the position of the manifold hand valve on the low side?
   d. What is the position of the manifold hand valve on the high side?

2. What is the position of the refrigerant cylinder?

3. How can the proper amount of refrigerant charge be insured?

SERVICE PROCEDURE 10:
ADDING DYE OR TRACE SOLUTION TO THE AIR-CONDITIONING SYSTEM

A dye or trace solution can be introduced into an air-conditioning system to aid in pinpointing a small leak. The dye shows the exact location of a leak by depositing a colored film around the leak. Depending on the dye used, the film may be orange-red or yellow. Once the dye is introduced into the air-conditioning system, it remains until the system is cleaned. The trace solution or dye is formulated for use in air-conditioning systems and does not affect system operation in any way.

TOOLS

Manifold and gauge set
Copper tubing, 1/4″ x 1′
Flare nuts, 1/4 in.
Service valve wrench or Schrader adapter

Hand wrenches
Oil filler
Can tap

MATERIAL

Dye or trace solution as required
Refrigerant 12

PROCEDURE

Prepare the System

1. Connect the manifold and gauge set to the system. Purge all lines of air.
2. Fasten the center manifold hose to the oil filler tube which contains 8 to 12 ounces of dye or trace solution.
3. Construct a charging line using a one-foot piece of copper tubing and female flare nuts. Secure the charging line to the refrigerant can tap and oil filler tube.
4. Attach the can tap to the can of Refrigerant 12 and pierce the can.
5. Purge the copper line of air.

Add Dye to the System

1. Start the engine and operate it at idle speeds. Set the controls for maximum cooling.
2. Open the low-side manifold hand valve slowly and allow the 8 to 12 ounces of trace dye to enter the system.
3. Little or no refrigerant must be allowed to enter the system. Shut the manifold hand valve.
4. Shut off the air conditioner and the car engine.

Observe the System

1. Observe the hoses and fittings for signs of the dye solution. If no signs of a leak are evident, arrange to have the car available the following day for diagnosis and repair.

2. If one or more leaks is detected, make repairs as required. The dye solution can remain in the system without causing harm to the system.

Return the System to Normal Operation

1. Remove the manifold and gauge set.

2. Replace the protective caps.

REVIEW

Select the appropriate answer from the choices given.

1. When dye trace solution is introduced into the system,

    a. it eventually fades out.
    b. it must be flushed out.
    c. it remains until flushed out.
    d. a blue trace is visible at the point of the leak.

2. Dye trace should not be used unless absolutely necessary because

    a. it does not mix well with refrigerant.
    b. it does not mix well with refrigeration oil.
    c. it seriously affects system operation.
    d. it leaves a discolored refrigerant trace unless flushed from the system.

3. Dye trace helps pinpoint a leak by leaving a

    a. red film.   c. yellow film.
    b. orange film.   d. Any of the above.

4. Dye solution is best used to pinpoint or detect

    a. a rapid leak.   c. a slow leak.
    b. vacuum system problems.   d. excessive moisture.

5. To remove the dye solution, it is necessary to

    a. discharge and recharge the system.
    b. discharge, evacuate, and recharge the system.
    c. discharge, clean, evacuate, and recharge the system.
    d. add neutralizer to the system.

SERVICE PROCEDURE 11:
ISOLATING THE COMPRESSOR FROM THE SYSTEM

When a system has both high- and low-side compressor service valves, the compressor can be isolated from the system. The refrigerant can be retained in the system while the compressor is serviced. If a system uses a Schrader-type service port, the compressor cannot be isolated. In this situation, the compressor must be purged of refrigerant to perform any service procedures.

TOOLS

Service valve wrench
Hand wrenches
Eye protection

Fender covers
Manifold and gauge set

PROCEDURE

Prepare the System

1. With the manifold and gauge set connected into the system, set both hand valves in the closed position.

2. Set both compressor service valves in the cracked position.

3. Stabilize the system by running the car engine at about 1,200 rpm with the air-conditioner controls turned on maximum cooling for about 10 minutes.

Isolate the Compressor

1. Return the car engine to idle speed, about 500 rpm.

2. Close the low-side service valve until the low-side gauge reads 10 in. Hg.

3. Turn off the car motor. Completely close (front seat) the low-side service valve.

4. Close the high-side service valve.

5. Open the low-side manifold hand valve and allow trapped refrigerant to escape.

6. Repeat step 5 with the high-side hand valve. Close both valves when the gauges read zero.

7. The compressor is now isolated and can be removed from the car if necessary.

   Service valves must be removed from the compressor. Do not attempt to remove the hoses.

Return the Compressor to the System

1. If the compressor was removed from the car, replace the service valve gaskets with new gaskets.

2. Purge the air from the compressor as follows:

   a. Open the high-side manifold hand valve.
   b. Crack the low-side compressor service valve until it is no longer in the front-seated position.
   c. The low-side refrigerant pressure forces air out of the compressor through the high-side manifold set.
   d. After a few seconds of purging, close the high-side manifold hand valve.

3. Midposition the low-side compressor service valve.

4. Midposition the high-side compressor service valve.

Continue the Performance Test

1. With the manifold and gauge set connected, check the refrigerant charge.

2. Add refrigerant as necessary.

Return the System to Service

1. Back seat the high- and low-side compressor service valves.

2. Remove the service hoses and replace the protective caps.

REVIEW

Briefly answer each of the following questions.

1. Why is it desirable to isolate the compressor from the system?

2. Can all compressors be isolated from the air-conditioning system? Why?

3. When isolating the compressor, what is the recommended compressor speed?

4. After the compressor is isolated, what is the pressure in the compressor?

5. Is it possible to isolate a compressor equipped with Schrader valves? Explain.

SERVICE PROCEDURE 12:
PERFORMING A VOLUMETRIC TEST
OF THE AIR-CONDITIONING COMPRESSOR

The volumetric or compressor capacity test is performed to determine the condition of the discharge reed valves and the piston rings.

TOOLS

Manifold and gauge set
Test caps, 1/4 in.
Test cap, 1/2 in.

Test cap, 5/8 in. or 3/4 in. (as applicable)
Service valve wrench
Hand wrenches

MATERIAL

Refrigerant for recharging the system, if necessary

PROCEDURE

Prepare the System for Volumetric Test

1. Attach the gauge and manifold set to the compressor, figure SP12-1.

2. Start the engine and adjust the speed to 1,000-1,200 rpm.

3. Adjust the controls for maximum cooling. Operate the system for about 10-15 minutes.

4. After 10-15 minutes, shut off all of the air-conditioning controls.

5. Return the engine speed to idle to prevent dieseling. Shut off the engine.

6. If the compressor is equipped with high- and low-side service valves, the compressor can be isolated, the valves removed, and another set of valves substituted for this test. If service valves are provided, follow the procedure outlined in Service Procedure 11.

7. If the compressor is equipped with Schrader-type service valves, the system must be purged of refrigerant. Follow the procedure outlined in Service Procedure 3.

8. When the system is purged of refrigerant, disconnect the high-side hose from the compressor outlet. Cap the hose end to prevent dirt and moisture from entering while the compressor check is being made. Repeat the procedure with the low-side hose.

9. If the compressor is isolated, remove the high- and low-side service valves and substitute other valves for this test.

   Do not remove the high- and low-side compressor hoses if the compressor is isolated!

10. Seal the compressor inlet fitting with the correct size of flare cap.

11. Connect the high-side gauge hose to the high-side compressor service valve. Open the high-side manifold hand valve.

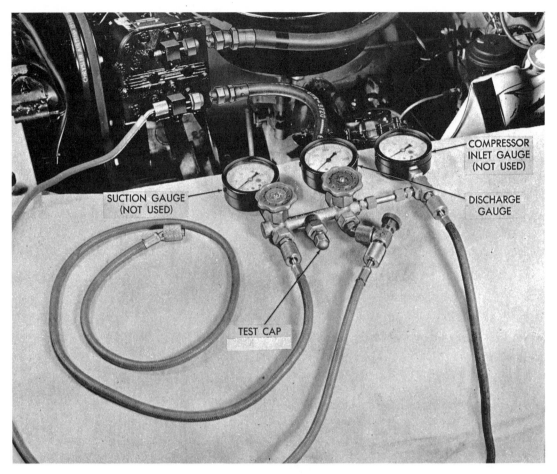

Fig. SP12-1 Volumetric test connections

12. Disconnect the low-side gauge hose from the compressor and the manifold.

13. Remove the center hose on the manifold and install a 1/4-in. test cap on the manifold fitting. The test cap is made by drilling a 1/4-in. acorn cap with a #71 drill to give an orifice of 0.026 in.

14. If a Schrader-type valve is used, install an adapter to open the low side of the compressor to the atmosphere. If service valves are used, *both sides must be cracked or front seated.* The acorn nut must be removed from the low-side valve.

Perform the Volumetric or Capacity Test

1. Start the engine and allow it to idle at exactly 500 rpm.

2. Engage the clutch and operate the compressor as an air pump.

   NOTE: Never operate the air-conditioning compressor as an air pump for more than 15 seconds at a time. To do so can seriously damage the compressor because of improper lubrication. The manufacturer's warranty is void if compressor failure is due to a lack of lubrication.

   Air is drawn in at the compressor inlet and is pressurized to the center of the gauge manifold and the high-side gauge.

3. As soon as the maximum pressure is reached, turn off the compressor.

4. Read the high-side manifold gauge. The high-side gauge should read 180-200 psi.

5. If the reading is low, a faulty reed valve or a faulty valve plate gasket is indicated.

6. Make repairs as required. Follow the procedure outlined in this text.

Recheck the System

1. If necessary repairs are made, the compressor should be rechecked. Follow the procedure outlined.

Return the Compressor to Service

1. Remove all caps and plugs. Reconnect all lines and service valves.

2. If the system was purged, evacuate the system and recharge it as outlined previously.

3. If the compressor was isolated, purge the compressor of air as follows:
   a. Open the high-side manifold hand valve.
   b. Crack the compressor low-side service valve from the front-seated position.
   c. After a few seconds of purging, close the high-side manifold hand valve.
   d. Midposition the low- and high-side compressor service valves.

Continue the Performance Test

1. With the manifold gauge set connected, check the refrigerant charge.

2. Add refrigerant if necessary.

Return the System to Service

1. Back seat the high- and low-side compressor service valves.

2. Remove the service hoses and replace the protective caps.

REVIEW

Briefly answer each of the following questions.

1. What is the purpose of the volumetric test?

2. To what specific parts of the air conditioner does the volumetric test apply?

3. At what speed should the compressor be run to hold the test?

4. What is the proper high-side gauge reading for the test?

5. If the high-side gauge reading is low, what malfunction is indicated?

SERVICE PROCEDURE 13:
PERFORMANCE TESTING THE AIR CONDITIONER

Humidity is an important factor in the temperature of the air delivered to the interior of the car. The service technician must understand the effect that humidity has on the performance of the system. When the humidity is high, the evaporator has a double function to perform. The evaporator must lower the air temperature as well as the temperature of the moisture carried in the air. The process of condensing the moisture in the air transfers a great deal of heat energy into the evaporator. As a result, the amount of heat that the evaporator can absorb from the air is reduced.

The evaporator capacity used to reduce the amount of moisture in the air is not wasted, however. Lowering the moisture content of the air entering the vehicle adds to the comfort of the passengers.

This procedure serves as a guide to the service procedures related to performance testing of the automobile air conditioner. The technician should refer to the manufacturer's service manuals for specific data.

TOOLS

Service valve wrench
Hand wrenches
Eye protection

Fender covers
Manifold and gauge set
Thermometer

PROCEDURE

Prepare the System

1. With the manifold and gauge set connected into the system, set both hand valves in the closed position.

2. Set the compressor high- and low-side service valves in the cracked position.

3. Run the engine at the high cam setting or adjust the idle screw to about 1,500-1,700 rpm.

4. Place the fan in front of the radiator to assist the ram airflow.

5. Turn on the air conditioner. Set all controls to maximum cooling.

6. Insert a thermometer in the air-conditioning duct as close as possible to the evaporator core. Set the blower on medium or low speed.

Visual Check of the Air Conditioner

1. The low-pressure gauge should be indicating within the range 20-30 psig.

2. The high-side gauge should be within the specified range of 160-220 psig.

3. The discharge air temperature should be within the specified range of 40°F-50°F.

Inspect the High Side and Low Side of the System for Even Temperatures

1. Feel the hoses and components in the high side of the system to determine if the components are evenly heated.

   CAUTION: Certain system malfunctions cause the high-side components to become superheated to the point that a serious burn can result if care is not taken when handling these components.

2. Note the inlet and outlet temperatures of the drier assembly. Any change in the temperature indicates a clogged or defective drier.

3. All lines and components on the high side should be warm to the touch.

4. All lines and components on the low side of the system should be cool to the touch.

5. Note the condition of the thermostatic expansion valve. If the valve is frosted or cold on the inlet side, the valve may be defective.

Test the Thermostats and Control Devices

1. Refer to the service manual for the performance testing of the particular type of control device used.

2. Determine that the thermostat engages and disengages the clutch. There should be about a 12°F temperature rise between the cutout and cut-in point of the thermostat.

3. Figure SP13-1 is a guide for determining the proper gauge readings and temperatures.

Ambient Air Temperature, °F	70	80	90	100	110
Average Compressor Head Pressure, psig	150-190	170-220	190-250	220-300	270-370
Average Evaporator Temperature, °F	38-45	39-47	40-50	42-55	45-60

Fig. SP13-1

4. The relative humidity at a particular temperature is a factor in the quality of the air as indicated by figure SP13-2. (This figure should be regarded as a guide only.)

Ambient Temperature, °F	70	80	90	100
Relative Humidity, %	50 60 90	50 60 90	40 50 60	20 40 50
Discharge Air Temperature, °F	40 41 42	42 43 47	41 44 49	43 49 55

Fig. SP13-2

5. Complete the performance test as outlined in the manufacturer's service manual.

Return the System to Service

1. Return the engine speed to normal idle.
2. Back seat the high- and low-side compressor service valves.
3. Remove the service hoses and replace the protective caps.

REVIEW

Briefly answer each of the following questions.

1. What is the purpose of the performance test?
2. Does high humidity have an effect on the air-conditioning system? Explain.
3. At what speed should the engine run during the air-conditioning performance test?
4. What does a temperature change at the inlet and outlet of the drier indicate?
5. What does a temperature change from the inlet to the outlet of the expansion valve indicate?

SERVICE PROCEDURE 14:
REPLACING THE COMPRESSOR SHAFT OIL SEAL
(YORK AND TECUMSEH COMPRESSORS)

This procedure can be followed when it is necessary to replace the compressor shaft oil seal. If the seal area can be serviced on the car, it is not necessary to remove the compressor from its mountings. If the engine fan or radiator clearance makes it impossible to remove the clutch for seal service, the compressor must be removed from the car.

TOOLS

Drive handle, 1/4 in. with 3/8-in., 7/16-in., and 1/2-in. sockets
Open end wrench, 3/4 in.
NC bolt, 5/8" x 2"
Screwdriver
Razor blade

MATERIALS

Ample supply of clean refrigeration oil
Seal assembly, including the seal plate, seal nose, and gasket(s)

Fig. SP14-1 Typical shaft seal set

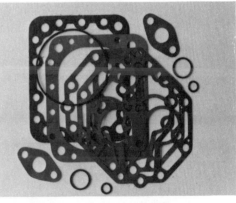

Fig. SP14-2 York overhaul gasket set

Fig. SP14-3 York valve plate assembly

Fig. SP14-4 York Roto Lock head

PROCEDURE

Prepare the Compressor for Service

1. Isolate the compressor. Follow the procedure as outlined in Service Procedure 11.
2. If the seal cannot be serviced properly with the compressor mounted in the car, remove the compressor.
3. Using a 1/2-in. socket, remove the 7/16-in. Nyloc bolt from the compressor crankshaft at the clutch hub.
4. Using a 5/8-in. NC bolt, remove the clutch rotor. This bolt is inserted into the clutch hub at the point where the 7/16-in. Nyloc bolt was removed.
5. If the fields of a stationary field clutch are mounted on the seal plate, remove the three retaining bolts and remove the fields.
6. If the rotating fields and brushes are mounted on the seal plate, remove the brushes. Take care not to break the soft carbon brushes.
7. Clean the seal plate and all adjoining surfaces.

Remove the Seal Assembly

1. Remove the six (or remaining three) capscrews from the seal plate.
2. Gently pry the seal plate loose. Be careful not to nick or mar the crankcase mating surface or the compressor crankshaft.
3. Remove the seal nose assembly from the crankshaft by prying behind the seal. Be careful not to nick or mar the crankshaft.
4. With a razor blade, remove all gasket material from the crankcase mating surface.
5. Clean all foreign matter from the crankcase, crankshaft and all adjacent surfaces.

Install the New Seal Assembly

1. The Woodruff key must be removed from the crankshaft before attempting to install the new seal.
2. Soak the new seal and all gaskets in clean refrigeration oil for a few minutes. Apply ample oil to the crankshaft and mating parts.
3. Remove the carbon nose end from the shaft seal and slide the shaft seal on the crankshaft. If drive pins are located in the shaft shoulder, line up the notches in the shaft seal spring holder to engage. *If the new seal does not have notches, remove the drive pins.*
4. Install the seal nose. Flush the assembly with clean refrigeration oil.

Install the New Seal Plate

1. Use clean refrigeration oil to flush the seal plate and seal nose to remove any foreign particles.
2. *York Compressor:* Place the new seal plate and gasket(s) over the crankshaft; then move the seal back to the final operating position. Insert the original three (or six) capscrews and adjust them until they are fingertight.
Tecumseh Compressor: Place the new seal plate and 0-ring over the crankshaft and move the seal back to the final operating position. Insert the original three (or six) capscrews and tighten them until they are fingertight.

3. Rotate the compressor crankshaft to insure that there is no binding due to misalignment.
4. Check that there is an even clearance between the crankshaft and the seal plate all around.
5. Tighten all capscrews evenly to a torque of 10-12 ft.-lb. Tighten the capscrews in a diagonally opposite sequence.

Return the Compressor to Service
1. Replace the clutch field or brush assembly.
2. Replace the Woodruff key in the crankshaft.
3. Replace the clutch rotor and 5/16-in. Nyloc bolt.
4. If the compressor was removed from the car, replace the compressor, and provide new gaskets for the service valves.
5. Purge the air from the compressor as follows:
   a. Open the high-side manifold hand valve.
   b. Crack the low-side compressor service valve from the front-seated position.
   c. Low-side refrigerant pressure forces air out of the compressor through the high-side manifold hose.
   d. After a few seconds of purging, close the high-side manifold hand valve.
6. Midposition the high- and low-side compressor service valves.

Continue the Performance Test
1. Check the refrigerant charge. Add refrigerant if necessary.
2. Check the manifold gauge readings. Correct abnormal conditions if indicated.

Return the System to Service
1. Back seat the high- and low-side compressor service valves.
2. Remove the service hoses and replace the protective caps.

REVIEW
Briefly answer each of the following questions.
1. Why is it necessary to isolate the compressor when servicing the compressor shaft seal?
2. What tool is used to remove the clutch rotor?
3. Why is the Woodruff key removed before replacing the new seal?
4. Which seal assembly used the 0-ring only?
5. What is the torque of the seal plate?

SERVICE PROCEDURE 15:
REPLACING THE COMPRESSOR SHAFT OIL SEAL
(SANKYO SD-5 COMPRESSOR)

In general, when replacing the Sankyo compressor shaft oil seal, it is advisable to remove the compressor from the car. However, if there is sufficient room to permit access to the front of the compressor, the compressor shaft oil seal can be serviced on the car. This procedure includes the removal of the compressor from the engine.

TOOLS

NOTE: The tool part numbers given are Sanyko part numbers for special tools. These tools are also manufactured by Draft Tool Company and Robinair Manufacturing Company (under different part numbers, however).

Snap ring plier (32407) (for compressors manufactured prior to November 1974)
Seal seat retainer tool (32419) (for compressors manufactured after November 1974)
Spanner wrench (32409)
Clutch face puller (32416)
Seal seat remover (32405)
Seal remover and installer (32425)

O-ring remover (32406)
Seal protector (32426)
Clutch front plate installer (32436)
Air gap gauge (32437)
Socket wrench set
Small hammer
Screwdriver
Manifold and gauge set
Safety glasses
Torque wrench

MATERIALS

Seal kit, as required
Refrigeration oil

Clean shop rag
Refrigerant 12, as required

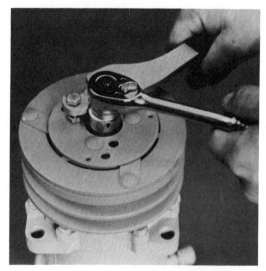

Fig. SP15-1 Removing the crankshaft hex nut

Fig. SP15-2 Removing the front clutch plate

PROCEDURE

Prepare the Compressor for Service

1. Purge the system of refrigerant as outlined in Service Procedure 3.

2. Remove the high- and low-side hoses from the compressor fittings. Plug the hoses and compressor fittings to prevent contaminants from entering the system or the compressor.

3. Loosen the compressor and/or idler pulley and remove the belt(s).

4. Remove the mounting hardware and lift the compressor from the engine compartment. Omit this step if there is sufficient clearance to service the seal without removing the compressor.

Remove the Shaft Seal

1. Using a 3/4-in. hex socket and spanner wrench, figure SP15-1, remove the crankshaft hex nut.

2. Remove the clutch front plate, figure SP15-2, using the clutch front plate puller.

3. Remove the shaft key and spacer shims and set aside.

4. Follow step a. for compressors manufactured prior to November 1974. Follow step b. for compressors manufactured after November 1974.

   a. Using the seal seat retainer tool, figure SP15-3, remove the seal seat retainer.

   b. Using the snap ring pliers, figure SP15-4, remove the seal seat retaining snap ring.

Fig. SP15-3 Removing the seal seat retainer (models prior to 11-74)

Fig. SP15-4   Removing the seal seat retainer snap ring (models after 11-74)

5. Remove the seal seat, using the seal seat remover and installer, figure SP15-5, page 200.

6. Remove the seal, figure SP15-6, page 200, using the seal remover tool.

7. Remove the shaft seal seat 0-ring, figure SP15-7, page 200, using the 0-ring remover.

8. Discard all parts removed in steps 5, 6, and 7.

Fig. SP15-5 Removing the seal seat

Fig. SP15-6 Removing the seal

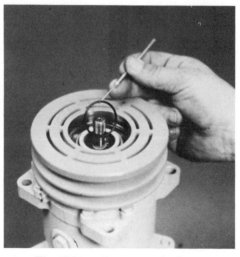

Fig. SP15-7 Removing the 0-ring

Install the Shaft Seal

1. Clean the inner bore of the seal cavity by flushing it with clean refrigeration oil.

2. Coat the new seal parts with clean refrigeration oil. *Do not touch* the carbon ring face with the fingers. Normal body acids will etch the seal and cause early failure.

3. Install the new shaft seal seat 0-ring. Make sure it is properly seated in the internal groove. Use the remover tool to position the 0-ring properly.

4. Install the seal protector on the compressor crankshaft. Lubricate the part liberally with clean refrigeration oil.

5. Place the new shaft seal in the seal installer tool and carefully slide the shaft seal into place in the inner bore. Rotate the shaft seal clockwise (CW) until it seats on the compressor shaft flats.

6. Rotate the tool counterclockwise (CCW) to remove the seal installer tool.

7. Remove the shaft seal protector.

8. Place the shaft seal seat on the remover/installer tool and carefully reinstall it in the compressor seal cavity.

9. Depending on the date of compressor manufacture, replace the snap ring or the seal seat retainer.

10. Reinstall the spacer shims and shaft key.

11. Position the clutch front plate on the compressor crankshaft.

12. Using the clutch front plate installer tool, a small hammer, and an air gap gauge, reinstall the front plate.

13. Draw down the front plate with the shaft nut. Use the air gap gauge for *go* at 0.016 in. and *no-go* at 0.031 in., figure SP15-8.

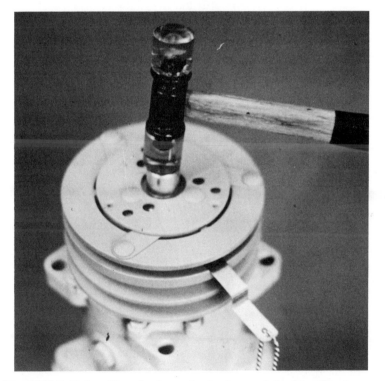

Fig. SP15-8 Reinstalling the front clutch plate and checking the air gap

14. Using the torque wrench, tighten the shaft nut to a torque of 25-30 ft.-lb.

Return the Compressor to Service

1. If the compressor was removed from the car, reinstall the compressor. Replace all bolts and braces. Tighten the bolts securely.

2. Replace the belt(s) and tighten to 90-110 ft.-lb.

3. Remove the protective covers and reconnect the hoses to the compressor low- and high-side fittings. If these fittings are of the 0-ring type, new 0-rings must be installed.

4. Check the compressor oil level as outlined in Service Procedure 20.

5. Evacuate the system as outlined in Service Procedure 6.

6. Charge the system as outlined in Service Procedure 7, 8, or 9.

7. Operate the system for 10 to 15 minutes to *run-in* the new seal. Leak check the system as outlined in Service Procedure 4 or 5.

REVIEW

Select the appropriate answer from the choices given.

1. A new shaft seal is seated on the compressor shaft flats by
   a. rotating the seal counterclockwise (CCW).
   b. rotating the seal clockwise (CW).
   c. rotating the seal back and forth.
   d. All of the above answers are correct.

2. The inner bore of the seal cavity is cleaned
   a. with a clean shop rag.   c. with mineral spirits.
   b. with clean refrigeration oil.   d. with compressed air.

3. The compressor shaft nut should be tightened to
   a. 15-20 ft.-lb.   c. 25-30 ft.-lb.
   b. 20-25 ft.-lb.   d. 30-35 ft.-lb.

4. The seal seat is secured by a snap ring on
   a. models before November 1974.   c. on all models.
   b. models after November 1974.   d. There is no snap ring.

5. The compressor drive belt should be tensioned to
   a. 80-90 ft.-lb.   c. 100-110 ft.-lb.
   b. 90-100 ft.-lb.   d. 110-120 ft.-lb.

SERVICE PROCEDURE 16:
SERVICING THE CLUTCH ROTOR AND THE CLUTCH COIL (SANKYO SD-5 COMPRESSORS)

If ample clearance is provided in front of the compressor for clutch service, the compressor need not be removed from the car for this procedure. Additional tools and materials are required if the compressor is to be removed from the car (see Service Procedure 15). Service Procedure 16 is to be used if the clutch can be serviced with the compressor in place.

TOOLS

NOTE: The tool part numbers are Sankyo part numbers.

Spanner wrench (32409)   Air gap gauge set (32437)
Front plate puller (32416)   Torque wrench
Snap ring pliers (32407 and 32417)   Socket wrench set
Pulley puller (32418)   Screwdriver
Rotor installer (32435)   Soft hammer
Front plate installer (32436)

MATERIALS

Front plate   Bearing or field coil, as required
Pulley

PROCEDURE

Removing the Clutch

1. Loosen the compressor and/or idler pulley and remove the belt(s).
2. Use a 3/4-in. hex socket and spanner wrench to remove the crankshaft hex nut (see figure SP15-1).
3. Remove the clutch front plate, using the clutch front plate puller (see figure SP15-2).
4. Using the snap ring pliers, remove the internal and external snap rings, figure SP16-1.

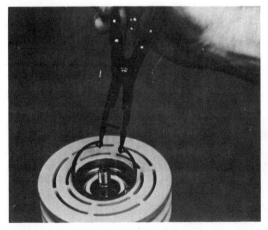

Fig. SP16-1A Removing the internal snap ring

Fig. SP16-1B Removing external snap ring

Fig. SP16-2 Removing the rotor assembly

5. Using the pulley puller, figure SP16-2, remove the rotor assembly.
6. If the clutch coil is to be replaced, remove the three retaining screws and the clutch field coil. Omit this step if the coil is not to be replaced.

Replace the Rotor Bearing

1. Using the snap ring pliers, remove the bearing retainer snap ring.
2. From the back (compressor) side of the rotor, knock out the bearing using the bearing remover tool and a soft hammer.
3. From the front (clutch face) side of the rotor, install the new bearing using the bearing installer tool and a soft hammer. Take care not to damage the bearing with hard blows of the hammer.
4. Reinstall the bearing retainer snap ring.

Replace the Clutch

1. Reinstall the field coil (or install a new field coil, if necessary) using the three retaining screws.
2. Align the rotor assembly squarely with the front compressor housing.
3. Using the rotor two-piece installer tools and a soft hammer, carefully drive the rotor into position until it seats on the bottom of the housing, figure SP16-3.

Fig. SP16-3 Installing the rotor assembly

4. Reinstall the internal and external snap rings using the snap ring pliers.

5. Align the slot in the hub of the front plate squarely with the shaft key.

6. Drive the front plate on the shaft using the installer tool and a soft hammer. *Do not use unnecessary hard blows.*

7. Check the air gap with *go* and *no-go* gauges (see figure SP15-8).

8. Replace the shaft nut and tighten it to a torque of 25-30 ft.-lb. using the torque wrench.

9. Replace the belt(s) and tighten to 90-110-lb. tension.

REVIEW

Select the appropriate answer from the choices given.

1. The compressor shaft nut is removed by using a spanner wrench and
   a. a 3/4-in. hex socket.
   b. a 3/4-in. open end wrench.
   c. an adjustable wrench.
   d. a pair of pliers.

2. The clutch field coil is secured with
   a. a snap ring.
   b. three screws.
   c. a locking nut.
   d. a retaining clamp.

3. The bearing is installed by using the bearing installer tool and
   a. a ball peen hammer.
   b. an arbor press.
   c. a soft hammer.
   d. snap ring pliers.

4. During reassembly, which part should seat on the bottom of the compressor housing?
   a. The rotor
   b. The seal
   c. The clutch field coil
   d. The clutch bearing

5. Under which condition is it *necessary* to remove the compressor from the car for service?
   a. When there is time to do the job correctly.
   b. When the customer is watching.
   c. When there is ample clearance in front of the compressor for service.
   d. When there is not enough clearance in front of the compressor for service.

SERVICE PROCEDURE 17:
REPLACING THE COMPRESSOR SHAFT OIL SEAL
(CHRYSLER AIR-TEMP)

This procedure can be used when it is necessary to replace the compressor shaft oil seal on a Chrysler Air-Temp unit. In general, the seal can be replaced without removing the compressor. The MoPar unit, using the York or Tecumseh compressor, is covered in Service Procedure 14.

TOOLS

Drive handle, 1/4 in. with 7/16-in.   NC or NF bolt, 5/8" x 2"
    and 1/2-in. sockets   Screwdriver
Open end wrench, 3/4 in.

MATERIALS

Ample supply of clean refrigeration oil
Seal assembly, including an O-ring gasket for the bearing housing
Stationary seat and gasket assembly
Rotating seal assembly

PROCEDURE

Prepare the Compressor for Service

1. If the compressor is equipped with both high- and low-side service valves, the compressor can be isolated. Follow the procedure outlined in Service Procedure 11.

2. If the compressor is not equipped with high- and low-side service valves, the system must be purged of refrigerant. Follow the procedure outlined in Service Procedure 3.

3. Using a 1/2-in. socket, remove the 7/16-in. bolt from the crankshaft. The bolt is located at the clutch hub.

4. Using a 5/8-in. NF or NC bolt, remove the clutch rotor. This bolt is inserted into the clutch hub at the point where the 7/16-in. bolt was removed.

5. If the clutch is equipped with stationary fields, locate the

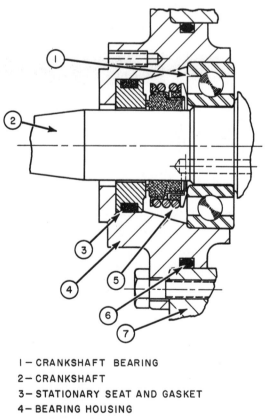

1 — CRANKSHAFT BEARING
2 — CRANKSHAFT
3 — STATIONARY SEAT AND GASKET
4 — BEARING HOUSING
5 — ROTATING SEAL ASSEMBLY
6 — O-RING GASKET
7 — CRANKCASE

Fig. SP17-1 Cutaway view of the Chrysler shaft oil seal

three screws holding it to the seal housing. Remove the screws and the fields. If the unit is equipped with rotating fields, carefully remove the brush set by removing the two screws holding the set to the seal housing.

6. Clean the seal plate and all adjacent surfaces.

Remove the Old Seal Assembly

1. Remove the Woodruff key from the crankshaft.

2. Remove the bearing housing bolts.

3. Remove the bearing housing by inserting two screwdrivers in the slots provided and prying the housing from the crankcase, figure SP17-2.

4. Remove the bearing housing 0-ring gasket and discard it.

5. Remove the stationary seat and gasket assembly from the bearing housing and discard it.

6. Remove the gas or shaft seal assembly from the crankshaft, using a small screwdriver. Discard this assembly. Take care not to nick or scratch the crankshaft. Either one of two types of interchangeable gas seals (cartridge or unitized) can be used. As a means of identifying the seals, the unitized type has a coil spring and the cartridge type has a wave spring, figure SP17-3.

7. Clean all foreign material from the bearing housing and crankshaft.

8. It may be necessary to polish these surfaces liberally with clean refrigeration oil.

Install New Seal Assembly

1. Lubricate the crankshaft, the bearing housing and all adjacent parts with clean refrigeration oil.

2. Dip the stationary seat and gasket assembly into clean refrigeration oil for a few minutes.

Fig. SP17-2 Removing the crankshaft bearing housing

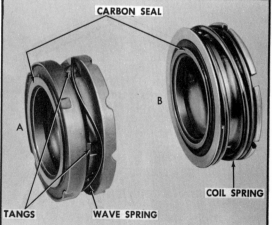

Fig. SP17-3 Gas seal identification (A) cartridge type (B) unitized type

3. Install the stationary seat and gasket assembly into the bearing housing. Insure that it is fully seated. Do not damage the seal surface.

4. Place the bearing housing 0-ring in the groove provided.

5. Dip the gas seal assembly into clean refrigeration oil for a few minutes.

6. Slide the gas seal assembly on the compressor crankshaft. Insure that the carbon nose of the seal assembly is facing outward.

7. Install the crankshaft bearing housing with the seal and 0-ring in place, on the crankcase body. Replace the capscrews and draw them in uniformly.

8. Tighten the bearing housing capscrews to a torque of 10-13 ft.-lb.

Return the Compressor to Service

1. Replace the Woodruff key. Replace the brush or field assembly.

2. Replace the clutch assembly and the 5/16-in. retaining bolt.

3. If equipped with service valves, purge the air from the compressor as follows:
   a. Open the high-side manifold hand valve.
   b. Crack the low-side compressor service valve from the front-seated position.
   c. The low-side refrigerant pressure forces air out of the compressor through the high-side manifold hose.
   d. After a few seconds of purging, close the high-side manifold hand valve.
   e. Midposition the high- and low-side compressor service valves.

4. If the unit is equipped with Schrader-type service valves, the unit must be evacuated. Follow the procedure outlined in Service Procedure 6.

Continue the Performance Test

1. If the system is equipped with compressor service valves, check for the proper refrigerant charge. Add refrigerant if necessary.

2. Check the manifold gauge readings. Correct any abnormal conditions indicated.

Return the System to Service

1. Back seat the high- and low-side compressor service valves.

2. Remove the service hoses and replace the protective caps.

REVIEW

Briefly answer each of the following questions.

1. What compressor does a Chrysler MoPar unit use?

2. What size wrench is used to remove the center bolt from the crankshaft?

3. Name the two types of fields which can be provided on the unit.

4. Which type of field does not use brushes?

5. What is the recommended torque of the bearing housing?

SERVICE PROCEDURE 18:
REPLACING THE SEAL ON GENERAL MOTORS' (FRIGIDAIRE) COMPRESSORS (SIX-AND FOUR-CYLINDER)

Seal replacement on the General Motors' (Frigidaire) six- and four-cylinder compressors is accomplished using a different procedure than is required for other types of compressors. Note that the replacement procedures for the Sankyo compressor are similar, however.

Careful handling of all seal parts is important. The carbon seal face and the steel seal seat must not be touched with the fingers because of the etching effect of the acid normally found on the fingers.

All six- and four-cylinder compressors are equipped with Schrader-type service valves. Therefore, it is necessary to purge the system of refrigerant before servicing the seal assembly. This statement is true even if the procedure can be accomplished with the compressor mounted in the car.

Seal replacement procedures are basically the same for six- and four-cylinder compressors. In this procedure, the figure numbers followed by an "A" indicate six-cylinder compressors; figure numbers followed by a "B" illustrate four-cylinder compressors. For example, figure SP18-2A, page 210, illustrates the removal of the shaft nut of a six-cylinder compressor and figure SP18-2B, page 210, illustrates the same procedure for a four-cylinder compressor.

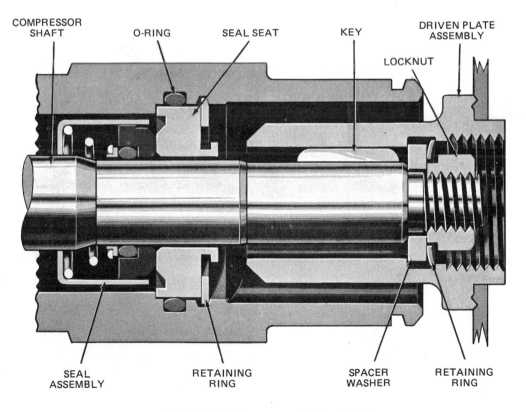

Fig. SP18-1 Compressor shaft and seal

TOOLS

Manifold and gauge set
Test fitting
Clutch hub holder
Set of hand wrenches
Internal snap ring plier
Seal seat remover/installer

0-ring installer
0-ring remover
Seal protector
Shaft seal seat remover/installer
Hub and drive plate remover/installer
Thinwall 9/16-in. socket with handle

MATERIALS

Clean refrigeration oil
Refrigerant 12

Service valve 0-rings (2)
Compressor shaft seal kit*

*NOTE: The compressor shaft seal kit consists of the following parts:

Shaft seal seat retaining ring
Shaft seal seat 0-ring

Shaft seal seat
Shaft seal

PROCEDURE

Prepare the Compressor for Service

1. The compressor and system must be purged of all refrigerant. Use the procedure outlined in Service Procedure 3.

2. If access to the compressor shaft seal is obstructed, remove the compressor from the car. The service valve should be removed from the rear of the compressor as a unit. Plug all hoses and service valve openings when removed. Attach the test fitting to the rear of the compressor.

Remove the Old Seal

1. Using a 9/16-in. thinwall socket wrench and clutch hub holding tool, remove the shaft nut, figure SP18-2A or SP18-2B.

   NOTE: Proceed with step 2 for a six-cylinder compressor. Proceed with step 4 for the four-cylinder compressor.

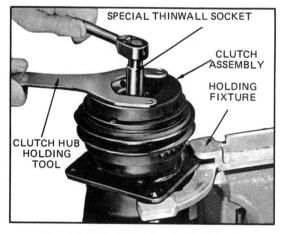

Fig. SP18-2A Removing the shaft locknut

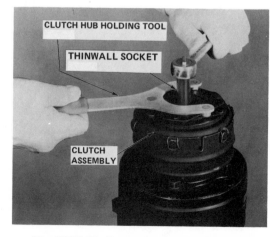

Fig. SP18-2B Removing the shaft locknut

2. Using snap ring pliers, remove the clutch hub retainer ring.

3. Remove the spacer under the retainer ring.

4. Using a clutch hub and drive plate puller, remove this part, figure SP18-3A or SP18-3B.

5. Remove the shaft seal seat retainer ring using the snap ring pliers, figure SP18-4A.

6. Remove the seal seat using a shaft seal seat remover, figure SP18-5A.

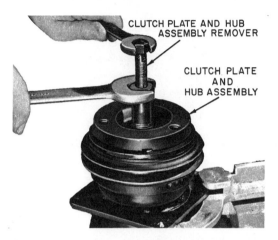

Fig. SP18-3A Removing the hub and drive plate assembly

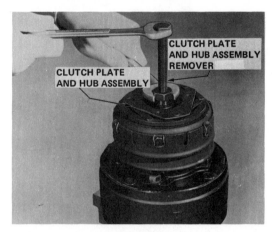

Fig. SP18-3B Removing the hub and drive plate assembly

Fig. SP18-4A Removing the shaft seal retainer

Fig. SP18-5A Removing the seal seat

7. Using the shaft seal remover, remove the shaft seal, figure SP18-6A or SP18-6B, page 212.

8. Using an O-ring remover (a wire with a hook on the end), remove the shaft seal seat O-ring, figure SP18-7A, page 212. *Take care not to scratch the mating surfaces.*

Fig. SP18-6A Removing the shaft seal assembly

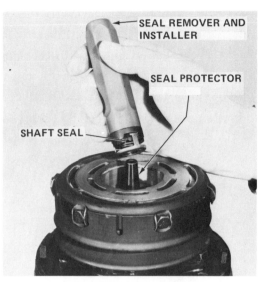

Fig. SP18-6B Removing the shaft seal assembly

Fig. SP18-7A Removing the seal seat 0-ring

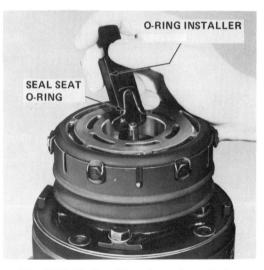

Fig. SP18-8B Installing the seal seat 0-ring

Install the New Seal

NOTE: This procedure should be followed as given to avoid damage to the new seal assembly. For example, if the seal seat is installed backwards, it is almost impossible to remove it again to reinstall it properly.

1. Insure that the inner bore of the compressor is free of all foreign matter. Flush the area with clean refrigeration oil.

2. Place the seal seat 0-ring on the installer tool and slide the 0-ring into place, figure SP18-8B. Remove the tool.

3. Coat the shaft seal liberally with refrigeration oil and place it on the shaft seal installer tool, figure SP18-9A. Slide the shaft seal into place in the bore. Rotate the seal clockwise until it seats on the flats provided. Rotate the tool counter-clockwise and remove it.

Fig. SP18-9A Installing the seal seat O-ring and
the shaft seal

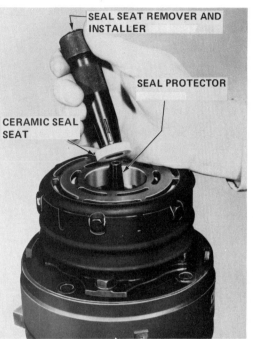

Fig. SP18-10B Installing the shaft seal seat

4. Place the shaft seal seat on the remover/installer tool, figure SP18-10B. Slide the shaft seal seat into position and remove the tool.

5. Install the shaft seal seat snap ring. Note that the beveled edge of the snap ring must face the outside of the compressor.

6. Before replacing the clutch hub and drive plate, the seal should be checked for leaks.

Leak Test the Shaft Seal

1. With the test fitting in place, connect the manifold and gauge set to the test ports.

2. Tap a can of refrigerant and purge the lines of air. Open the high- and low-side manifold hand valves to allow the refrigerant pressure to enter the compressor.

3. With a leak detector, check the shaft seal area for escaping refrigerant. Refer to Service Procedure 4 or 5.

4. If a small leak is detected, rotate the crankshaft a few turns to seat the seal; then recheck the seal area for leaks. If the leak is heavy, or if it persists, the seal must be removed and checked for defects.

Replace the Clutch Hub and Drive Plate Assembly

1. Place the drive key into the crankshaft keyway (for six-cylinder compressors), figure SP18-11A, page 214, or into the clutch plate keyway (for four-cylinder compressors), figure SP18-11B, page 214. About 3/16 in. of the key should be allowed to protrude over the end of the keyway.

Fig. SP18-11A Drive plate key installed in keyway

Fig. SP18-11B Drive plate key installed

SPECIAL TOOLS

Fig. SP18-12A Installing the driven plate

CLEARANCE .030"

Fig. SP18-13A Checking the air gap

2. Align the key with the keyways of the drive plate and compressor crankshaft. Then slide the drive plate into position.

   NOTE: Take care not to force the drive key into the shaft seal. Occasional rotation of the drive plate during assembly insures that it is seated properly.

3. Using a hub and drive plate installer, press this part on the crankshaft, figure SP18-12A. (Refer to the note following step 2 of this procedure.)

4. A clearance of 0.030 in. (± 0.010 in.) should exist between the drive plate and the rotor, figure SP18-13A.

   NOTE: Omit step 5 for a four-cylinder compressor.

5. Replace the spacer and clutch hub retainer ring. The retainer ring is installed using the snap ring plier.

6. Replace the shaft nut.

Return the Compressor to Service

1. If the compressor was removed, return it to the car. Remove the test fittings and replace the service valves using new 0-rings coated with clean refrigeration oil.

2. Evacuate the system as outlined in Service Procedure 6.

3. Charge the system as outlined in Service Procedure 7, 8, or 9.

4. Return the compressor to service or continue the performance testing as necessary.

REVIEW

Briefly answer the following questions.

1. In sequence, list the removal order of the following:

    a. Seal assembly.   c. Retaining ring.
    b. Seal seat.   ·   d. Seal seat 0-ring.

2. What wrench is used to remove the crankshaft nut from the compressor?

3. What part, if installed backwards, is almost impossible to remove?

4. What tool is used to remove the 0-ring?

5. What part(s) are not removed (not found) on the four-cylinder compressor that are removed from the six-cylinder compressor?

SERVICE PROCEDURE 19:
CHECKING THE COMPRESSOR OIL LEVEL
(AIR-TEMP, TECUMSEH, YORK COMPRESSORS)

This procedure is used when it is necessary to check the oil level in those Air-Temp, Tecumseh, and York compressors with high- and low-side compressor service valves. Compressors equipped with Schrader-type valves require that the refrigerant be purged from the system to check the oil level.

TOOLS

Service valve wrench
Hand wrenches
Eye protection

Fender covers
Manifold and gauge set
Oil dipstick

MATERIAL

Refrigeration oil

PROCEDURE

Prepare the System

1. The compressor must be isolated from the system. Follow the procedure outlined in this text.

Check the Oil Level

1. Remove the plug from the compressor body to gain access to the compressor crankcase.

2. Use the correct dipstick and measure the oil.

3. Compare the measurements with the chart, figure SP19-1, to determine the proper oil level.

	York	Tecumseh	Air-Temp
Vertical	1 1/4 in.	7/8 in.	
Inclined	2 in.	1 1/4 in.	
Horizontal	7/8 in.	1 1/8 in.	
R.H. Mount			2 3/4 in.
L.C. Mount			3 1/8 in.

Fig. SP19-1

4. Add refrigeration oil as necessary to bring the oil level to the proper height.

Return the Compressor to the System

1. Replace the oil check plug.

2. If the oil check plug was removed from the compressor for more than five minutes, purge the air from the compressor as follows:

   a. Open the high-side manifold hand valve.

   b. Crack the low-side compressor service valve from the front-seated position.

   c. The low-side refrigerant pressure forces air out of the compressor through the high-side manifold set.

   d. After five seconds of purging, close the high-side manifold hand valve.

3. Midposition the low- and high-side compressor service valves.

Continue the Performance Test

1. With the manifold gauge set connected, check the refrigerant charge.

2. Add refrigerant if necessary.

3. Continue the performance testing as required, or return the unit to service.

Return the System to Service

1. Back seat the high- and low-side compressor service valves.

2. Remove the service hoses and replace the protective caps.

   NOTE: An oil dipstick, such as the one shown in figure SP19-2, can be made from a piece of medium soft wire (such as a black coat hanger). A black wire should be used so that the oil level is readily visible on the dipstick.

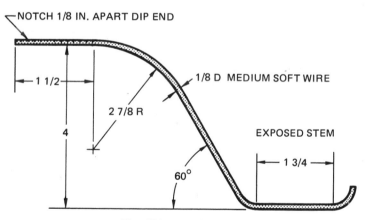

Fig. SP19-2 Oil dipstick

REVIEW

Briefly answer each of the following questions.

1. Why must the compressor be isolated from the system?

2. What tool is used to measure the oil level?

3. Should air be purged from the compressor after the oil is checked?

4. Which compressor cannot be mounted in an inclined or horizontal position?

5. Can any good, clean refrigeration oil be used in compressors?

SERVICE PROCEDURE 20:
CHECKING THE COMPRESSOR OIL LEVEL
(SANKYO SD-5 COMPRESSOR)

The compressor oil level should be checked at the time of installation and after repairs are made when it is evident that there has been a loss of oil. The Sankyo compressor is factory charged with seven fluid ounces of Suniso 5GS oil. Only this oil, or equivalent, should be added to the system.

The system must be purged of refrigerant before the oil level is checked. A special angle gauge and dipstick are used to check the oil level. The oil level chart, figure SP20-3, compares the oil level with the inclination angle of the compressor.

TOOLS

NOTE: The tool numbers given are Sankyo numbers.

Angle gauge (32448)   Adjustable wrench
Dipstick (32447)   Torque wrench
Manifold and gauge set

MATERIALS

Refrigeration oil, as required
Oil filler plug 0-ring, as required

PROCEDURE

Prepare the System

1. Start the engine and run the air conditioner so that the compressor operates at idle speed for ten minutes.

2. Turn off the air conditioner and stop the engine.

3. Purge the system of refrigerant, as outlined in Service Procedure 3. *Purge the system slowly to prevent a loss of oil.*

4. Position the angle gauge tool across the top flat surfaces of the two mounting ears.

5. Center the bubble and read the inclination angle.

6. Remove the oil filler plug. Rotate the clutch front plate to position the rotor at the top dead center (TDC), figure SP20-1.

7. Face the front of the compressor. If the compressor angle is to the right, rotate the clutch front plate counterclockwise (CCW) by 110°. If the compressor angle is to the left, rotate the plate clockwise (CW) by 110°, figure SP20-2.

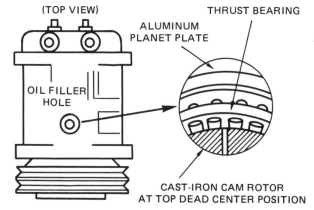

Fig. SP20-1 Position the rotor to top dead center (TDC).

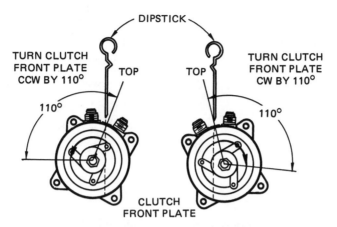

Fig. SP20-2 Rotate the clutch front plate

Check the Oil Level

1. Insert the dipstick until it reaches the stop position marked on the dipstick.
2. Remove the dipstick and count the number of increments of oil.
3. Compare the compressor angle and the number of increments with the table in figure SP20-3.
4. If necessary, add oil to bring the oil to the proper level. *Do not overfill.* Use only clean refrigeration oil of the proper grade.

Inclination Angle In Degrees	Acceptable Oil Level In Increments
0	6-10
10	7-11
20	8-12
30	9-13
40	10-14
50	11-16
60	12-17

Fig. SP20-3 Dipstick reading versus inclination angle

Return the System to Service

1. Check that the rubber 0-ring is in place. Reinstall the oil filler plug. Tighten the plug to a torque of 8-9 ft.-lb. (see step 3).
2. Leak test the system as outlined in Service Procedure 4 or 5.
3. If the oil filler plug leaks, *do not overtighten the plug.* Remove the plug and replace the 0-ring (see step 1).
4. Evacuate the system as outlined in Service Procedure 6.
5. Remove the angle gauge tool from the compressor.
6. Charge the system as outlined in Service Procedure 7, 8, or 9.
7. Return the system to service or conduct performance tests as required.

REVIEW

Select the appropriate answer from the choices given.

1. What type of oil is recommended by the manufacturer for Sankyo compressors?
   a. Suniso 5GS
   b. Capella D
   c. Any good motor oil
   d. Any good refrigeration oil

2. If the oil filler plug leaks

    a. it must be replaced.   c. it must be retightened.
    b. the 0-ring must be replaced.   d. it must be torqued to 8-9 ft.-lb.

3. The factory charge of oil in a new Sankyo compressor is

    a. 5 fluid ounces.   c. 7 fluid ounces.
    b. 6 fluid ounces.   d. 8 fluid ounces.

4. Which of the following need *not* be removed to check the oil level?

    a. Idler pulley or belt
    b. Clutch front plate
    c. Rotor
    d. None of the above components need be removed.

5. Before checking the oil level, the rotor should be positioned to

    a. top dead center (TDC).   c. 110° counterclockwise (CCW).
    b. bottom dead center (BDC).   d. 110° clockwise (CW).

SERVICE PROCEDURE 21:
CHECKING AND ADDING OIL, GENERAL MOTORS' (FRIGIDAIRE) SIX-AND FOUR-CYLINDER COMPRESSORS

The design of six- and four-cylinder compressors requires a different oil checking procedure than the one used for other types of compressors. Six-cylinder compressors are fully charged at the factory with 10.50 ounces of 525 viscosity refrigeration oil. Four-cylinder compressors are factory charged with 5.50 to 6.50 ounces of the same type of oil.

In the six- and four-cylinder compressor, it is not recommended that the oil level be checked as a matter of course. Generally, the compressor oil level should be checked only where there is evidence of a major loss, such as that caused by a broken refrigeration line, a serious leak, or damage from a collision. The oil should also be checked if the compressor is to be repaired or replaced.

To check the compressor oil charge, the compressor must be removed from the car and drained. The oil is then measured. Whenever the oil is checked, the amount of oil drained from the compressor is noted. The old oil is then discarded.

In this procedure, it is assumed that the compressor is isolated or purged of refrigerant, and is removed from the car. This procedure is given in two parts: Part I deals with the six-cylinder compressor and Part II deals with the four-cylinder compressor.

TOOLS

Set of hand tools   Graduated container(s)

MATERIALS

Refrigeration oil, as required   0-ring gaskets, as required

PROCEDURE

PART I

Drain the Compressor

1. Clean the external surfaces of the compressor so that it is free of oil and grease.

2. Remove the oil drain plug located in the compressor oil pump.

3. Place the compressor in a horizontal position with the drain hole facing downward over a graduated container.

4. Drain the compressor. Measure and note the amount of oil removed. Discard the old oil.

Add New Oil (System Stabilized)

NOTE: If the system is not stabilized before the compressor is removed from the car, as in the case of an inoperative compressor, omit this section. Instead, use the following procedure, *Add New Oil (System Not Stabilized)*.

1. If the quantity of oil drained from the compressor is four ounces or more, add the same amount of new oil to the compressor.

2. If the quantity of oil drained from the compressor is less than four ounces, add six ounces of new oil to the compressor.

3. If a major component of the system is also replaced, see *Service Notes* for the addition of oil for the component.

Add New Oil (System Not Stabilized)

NOTE: If the system is stabilized before the compressor is removed from the car, omit this section. Use the previous procedure, *Add New Oil (System Stabilized)*.

1. If the quantity of oil removed is less than 1.50 ounces and the system shows signs of a greater loss, add six ounces of new oil.

2. If the quantity of oil removed is greater than 1.50 ounces and the system shows no signs of a greater loss, add the same amount of oil.

3. If the compressor is replaced with a new unit, drain and discard the oil. Add new oil in the amount indicated in steps 1 or 2.

4. If the compressor is replaced with a rebuilt unit, replace the oil in the amount as indicated in steps 1 or 2 and then add one more ounce.

5. If a major component of the system is also replaced, see *Service Notes* for the addition of oil for the component.

PROCEDURE

PART II

NOTE: The oil should be checked whenever a four-cylinder compressor is replaced, a major component of the system is replaced, or there is evidence of a slow leak over a long period of time.

1. Clean the external surfaces of the compressor so that it is free of oil and grease.

2. Position the compressor with the shaft end up over a graduated container.

3. Drain the compressor. Allow it to drain for at least ten minutes. Measure and note the amount of oil removed, then discard the old oil.

4. Add new oil in the same amount as the oil drained.

   NOTE: If the replacement compressor is new, drain it as outlined in steps 2 and 3, then add new oil in the amount drained from the old compressor.

5. If a major component is also replaced, see the *Service Notes* for the addition of oil for the component.

6. If the loss of refrigerant occurs over an extended period of time, add three ounces of new oil. *Do not exceed a total of 6.5 ounces of oil.*

Service Notes

When the compressor is removed and drained, if it shows signs that foreign matter is present or that the oil contains chips or metallic particles, the system should be flushed. The receiver/dehydrator, desiccant, or accumulator (as applicable) should be replaced after the system is flushed. The compressor inlet and/or TXV inlet screens should be cleaned as well.

If the system is flushed, add a full ten ounces of clean refrigeration oil to the six-cylinder compressor system or six ounces to the four-cylinder compressor system.

With the exception of a system that is flushed, add oil as shown to any system that has had the following major components replaced.

COMPONENT	Six-cylinder System	Four-cylinder System
Evaporator.............	2 fluid ounces..........	3 fluid ounces
Condenser	1 fluid ounce	1 fluid ounce
Receiver/dehydrator	1 fluid ounce	1 fluid ounce
Desiccant (VIR or accumulator)	1 fluid ounce	1 fluid ounce

Disregard any loss of oil due to the changing of a line, hose, or muffler (unless the component contains a measurable amount of oil). If this is the case, add the same amount of clean refrigeration oil as measured in the component.

REVIEW

Briefly answer each of the following questions.

1. What is the normal charge and grade of oil used in the General Motors' six-cylinder compressor?

2. What is the normal charge and grade of oil used in the General Motors' four-cylinder compressor?

3. How much oil must be added for the replacement of the following parts:

   a. condenser   b. desiccant   c. receiver/dehydrator

4. If it is impossible to stabilize a six-cylinder compressor system and less than 1.50 ounces of oil are removed from the compressor, how much oil should be replaced?

5. If the system is stabilized and four ounces of oil are removed, how much oil should be replaced:

   a. in a six-cylinder compressor system?
   b. in a four-cylinder compressor system?

SERVICE PROCEDURE 22:
ADJUSTING THE THERMOSTAT (CYCLING CLUTCH UNITS)

The thermostat controls the evaporator temperature by cycling the clutch. The thermostat is preset at the factory. Different altitudes and humidity conditions can require that the thermostat be checked and occasionally adjusted to local conditions. This procedure deals with the thermostat adjustment. It should be noted that some thermostats have no provisions for adjustment.

TOOLS

Service thermometer
Manifold and gauge set
Hand wrenches

Service valve wrench
Small screwdriver

PROCEDURE

Prepare the System for Service

1. Connect the manifold and gauge set into the system.

2. Start the engine and set it to run at 1,200-1,500 rpm. Set the air-conditioning controls for maximum cooling.

3. Operate the system for 5-10 minutes with the core thermometer inserted into the evaporator at or near the thermostatic expansion valve.

   Insure that the evaporator does not have blowers mounted in the front of the unit.

4. Check the sight glass to insure that there is a full charge of refrigerant.

Check the Thermostat Operation

1. Turn the thermostat to the full on, or clockwise, position.

2. Turn the blowers to low or medium speeds.

3. Observe the manifold compound gauge: the reading should be in the 14-psig to 26-psig range after the system is operated for 5-10 minutes.

4. Observe the manifold pressure or the high-side gauge. The high-side pressure should compare approximately with the temperature-pressure chart, figure SP22-1.

5. Compare the low-pressure gauge readings with the core thermometer readings against the temperature-pressure relationship chart. The thermometer should read from 15°F to 35°F, allowing for a temperature rise due to wall loss in the evaporator coil tubing.

Check the Thermostat Cutout and Cut-in Points

NOTE: For the proper thermostat operation, a dealer service manual should be consulted. However, the following steps can be used as a guide.

1. The thermostat should cut out when the thermometer indicates 24°F to 26°F.

224

Temperature-Pressure Relationship Chart			
Low Side		High Side	
Evaporator Temperature, °F	Evaporator Pressure, psi	Condenser Pressure, psi	Ambient Temperature, °F
5	11.8	72	40
10	14.7	86	50
15	17.1	105	60
20	21.1	126	70
22	22.5	140	75
24	23.9	160	80
26	25.4	185	90
28	26.9	195	95
30	28.4	220	100
32	30.0	240	105
34	31.7	260	110
36	33.4	275	115
38	35.1	290	120
40	36.9	305	125

Fig. SP22-1

2. The thermostat should cut back in when the thermometer indicates 36°F to 38°F.

3. The manifold compound gauge should show a pressure rise of about 26-32 psig between the cutout and cut-in points.

4. Check the thermostat operation three or four times to insure consistent operation.

ADJUST THE THERMOSTAT

1. Remove the evaporator front (exit) outlets as necessary to provide access to the thermostat.

2. Find the adjustment screw (located behind an access door on some models).

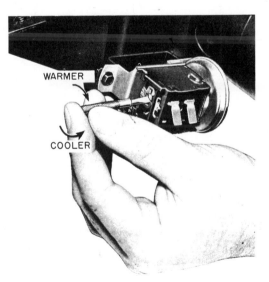

Fig. SP22-2 Thermostatic switch adjustment

NOTE: The design of some evaporators requires the thermostat to be removed from the case before access is gained to the adjusting screw.

3. Rotate the adjusting screw in a counterclockwise direction to lower the temperature by delaying the point opening. Conversely, a clockwise rotation of the screw increases the temperature.

4. Check the operation of the thermostat for the newly-adjusted cycle of operation. If the operation is determined to be correct, check the thermostat three or four times to insure consistent operation.

5. If the cycle of operation is inconsistent or cannot be adjusted, the thermostat must be replaced.

Return the System to Service

1. Return the engine to the normal idle speed. Turn off the engine.

2. Replace the thermostat access door and replace the thermostat in the evaporator case. Replace other parts that were removed to permit access to the thermostat.

3. *Remove the thermometer.*

4. Back seat the compressor service valves and remove the manifold and gauge set. Replace the protective covers and caps.

REVIEW

Select the appropriate answer from the choices given.

1. The thermostat should be adjusted to cut out when the evaporator thermometer indicates
   a. 24°F – 26°F (–4.44°C to –3.33°C).
   b. 36°F – 38°F (2.22°C to 3.33°C).
   c. 26°F – 32°F (–3.33°C to 0°C).
   d. 34°F – 36°F (1.11°C to 2.22°C).

2. What temperature rise range (cutout to cut-in) allows the proper defrost?
   a. 6°F (3.33°C)
   b. 9°F (5°C)
   c. 12°F (6.67°C)
   d. 15°F (8.33°C)

3. What precaution should be observed before inserting the thermometer into the evaporator core?
   a. Air-conditioning controls should be at maximum cooling.
   b. Engine should be running 5-10 minutes at fast idle.
   c. Insure that the evaporator does not have blowers mounted in front of the unit.
   d. all of the above are precautions to be taken.

4. What is the head pressure (refer to figure SP22-1) at an ambient temperature of 95°F (35°C) if the system is operating properly?
   a. 185 psig   c. 220 psig
   b. 195 psig   d. 240 psig

5. Between cutout and cut-in of the thermostat, what pressure increase should be noted on the low-side manifold gauge?
   a. 16-22 psig   c. 26-32 psig
   b. 22-26 psig   d. 32-36 psig

SERVICE PROCEDURE 23:
SERVICING THE MAGNETIC CLUTCH

Regardless of the type of field provided for the clutch, clutch bearings and brushes can be replaced, and brush races can be cleaned. In most cases, however, only the stationary field assembly can be replaced if it proves to be defective.

This procedure is a brief outline which deals with all clutches in general and can be used as a guide in servicing clutches.

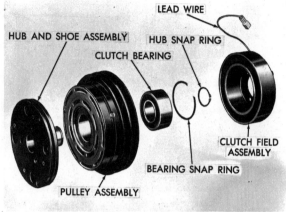

Fig. SP23-1 Magnetic clutch — stationary field type

TOOLS

Snap ring pliers
Screwdriver
NC bolt, 5/8 in.
NF bolt, 5/8 in.

Hand wrenches
Small arbor press
Ammeter

MATERIAL

Field, bearing, or brush set as required

PROCEDURE

Test the Clutch Field Coil

1. Disconnect the field coil wire from the body wiring.
2. Connect an ammeter to the positive side of the battery.
3. Connect the other side of the ammeter to the clutch coil field lead.
4. Check the field draw. At twelve volts, the field draw should be about 2.5 to 3.5 amperes.
   a. A reading of zero indicates an open field coil or bad brushes.
   b. A reading of less than 2.5 amperes indicates defective brushes or additional resistance due to the accumulation of dirt and foreign material. These conditions may cause a poor ground.
   c. The reading in excess of 3.5 amperes indicates shorted field coil windings or a shorted field coil.
   d. If the coil reading does not fall to within the 2.5- to 3.5-ampere specifications, it must be replaced or corrected as required.

Remove the Clutch Assembly

1. Loosen and remove the belts from the compressor.

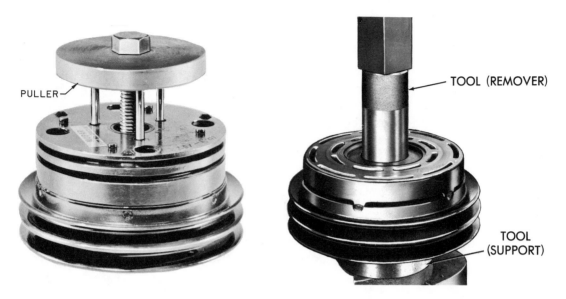

PULLER

TOOL (REMOVER)

TOOL (SUPPORT)

Fig. SP23-2   Removing the hub and shoe assembly

Fig. SP23-3 Removing the bearing from the pulley assembly

2. Remove the capscrew from the center of the compressor crankshaft.

3. Insert a 5/8-in. NC or NF (as indicated) capscrew into the threaded portion of the clutch rotor.

4. Tighten the capscrew against the crankshaft of the compressor until the rotor slips from the shaft.

5. Remove the field coil attaching screws. Lift the coil from the compressor (or, remove the screws holding the brush set in place and remove the brushes). Take care not to break the brushes.

Disassemble the Clutch Pulley Assembly

1. Remove the snap ring from the rear of the clutch hub.

2. Using the proper puller or arbor press, press the hub from the clutch rotor.

3. Remove the bearing snap ring from the rotor.

4. Place the rotor in an arbor and press the bearing from the rotor.

    NOTE: Remove the bearing only if it is to be replaced since pressing the bearing on the inner race damages it.

Assemble the Clutch Pulley

1. Inspect all parts. The clutch hub and rotor may show normal scoring. Excessive scoring, however, indicates that the clutch may require replacement.

2. Replace all parts that are defective.

3. To assemble the clutch, reverse the order of the disassembly procedure.

    NOTE: Remove the 5/8-in. bolt before the rotor is replaced. Take care not to damage the brush set when replacing the rotor.

REVIEW

Select the appropriate answer from the choices given.

1. When using an ammeter to check the clutch field draw, a reading of zero amperes indicates.

   a. an open field coil or defective brushes.
   b. excessive resistance.
   c. shorted field coil windings.
   d. Any of the conditions above.

2. A reading in excess of 35 amperes when checking the clutch field draw indicates

   a. an open field coil or defective brushes.
   b. excessive resistance.
   c. shorted field coil windings.
   d. disconnected ground wire.

3. The clutch rotor is removed from the compressor crankshaft using a

   a. hammer and center punch.
   b. pulley puller.
   c. spanner wrench.
   d. capscrew and wrench.

4. How is the ammeter connected to the clutch coil wire to make the field draw test?

   a. Disconnect the clutch field wire and connect the ammeter between the clutch field wire and ground.
   b. With the clutch field wire connected, connect the ammeter between the clutch field wire and ground.
   c. Disconnect the clutch field wire and connect the ammeter, in series between the disconnected wires.
   d. Disconnect the clutch field wire and connect the ammeter to the thermostat wire and ground.

5. From the information given in this service procedure and the test of unit 20, which of the following may not be repaired?

   a. Inboard mounted clutch coil.
   b. Outboard mounted clutch coil.
   c. Stationary clutch coil.
   d. Rotating clutch coil.

SERVICE PROCEDURE 24:
TESTING THE OPERATION OF THE EVAPORATOR PRESSURE REGULATOR VALVE (CHRYSLER)

The evaporator pressure regulator valve (EPR) is calibrated to produce maximum cooling without the formation of frost or ice on the evaporator fins. If the factory calibration is disturbed, the EPR valve does not function properly. A restriction of the EPR valve results in high evaporator temperatures and poor cooling. When the EPR valve does not restrict properly, the evaporator runs too cold and freezes.

The following evaporator pressure regulator test determines if the valve is functioning properly or not.

Fig. SP24-1 Service valve removed to show EPR valve

TOOLS

Manifold and gauge set, consisting of two compound gauges and one pressure gauge
Service valve wrench
Hand tools

MATERIALS

EPR valve, if required
Service valve gasket, if required

PROCEDURE

Prepare the System for Test

1. Connect the compound manifold gauge to the suction service port at the rear of the compressor.

2. Connect the second compound manifold gauge to the compressor inlet port located on the right head of the compressor.

3. Connect the high-side gauge hose to the discharge service valve located at the front of the compressor.

4. Purge the air from the manifold gauge hoses by cracking the hoses at the manifold for a few seconds each.

5. Adjust the engine speed to about 1,250 rpm.

6. Insure that the hoses are clear of belts and pulleys. Close the car hood. Open all windows.

7. Set the air-conditioning controls for maximum cooling. Operate the system for 10 to 15 minutes to stabilize the system.

Read Both Compound Gauges

1. With the EPR valve operating properly, the evaporator pressure gauge and the compressor inlet gauge should read within 1 or 2 pounds of each other. Both gauges should read 26-28 psig.

Force the Operation of the EPR Valve

1. Set the blower switch to the lowest position. Depress the FRESH COOL button or lever.

2. Check the evaporator outlet for increased cooling with the windows closed.

3. The evaporator pressure should stabilize at about 22-26 psig.

4. The compressor inlet pressure should drop to about 15-17 psig. If the inlet pressure does not drop to this point, increase the engine speed to approximately 2,000 rpm.

5. Repeat steps 1-4 to insure the constant operation of the EPR valve.

6. Replace the EPR valve if the pressures obtained are not within the prescribed limits.

Return the System to Service

1. Return the engine to the normal idle speed to prevent dieseling.

2. Turn off the air conditioner. Shut off the engine.

3. Remove the manifold and gauge set and replace the protective caps.

REVIEW

Select the appropriate answer from the choices given.

1. The EPR valve test is made with the engine operating at
   a. 650 rpm
   b. 950 rpm
   c. 1,250 rpm
   d. 1,500 rpm

2. The EPR valve maintains the evaporator temperature by controlling
   a. the pressure
   b. the blower speed.
   c. the humidity.
   d. the heater bypass.

3. The EPR valve test is made by comparing pressures
   a. across the EPR valve only.
   b. across the compressor (suction to discharge).
   c. between the evaporator outlet and the compressor outlet.
   d. between the compressor outlet and the evaporator inlet.

4. Which of the following are *not* found on a system having an EPR valve?
   a. TXV.
   b. Electric clutch.
   c. Receiver drier.
   d. Suction line accumulator.

SERVICE PROCEDURE 25:
TESTING THE OPERATION OF THE EVAPORATOR TEMPERATURE REGULATOR (CHRYSLER)

The evaporator temperature regulator (ETR) valve replaces the standard evaporator pressure regulator (EPR) valve in automatic temperature control systems.

The ETR valve, which prevents icing on the fins of the evaporator, is an electrical device operated by an ETR switch. A sensing tube of the switch is inserted into the evaporator fins. The switch closes if the evaporator temperature falls below 38°F. When this switch closes, a current is sent to the EPR valve in the compressor. The ETR valve shuts off the refrigerant flow until the evaporator warms up. Both the EPR and ETR valves accomplish the same function, but the ETR valve controls refrigerant flow electrically and the EPR valve controls the flow by a pressure differential.

The ETR and EPR valves are located under the suction service valve, as shown in figure SP24-1.

TOOLS

Manifold and gauge set   Hand tools

MATERIALS

ETR valve and gasket, if required   ETR switch, if required

PROCEDURE

Prepare the System for Test

1. Connect the compound manifold gauge to the suction service port at the rear of the compressor.
2. Connect the second compound manifold gauge to the compressor inlet port (located on the right head of the compressor).
3. Connect the high-side gauge hose to the discharge service valve.
4. Purge the air from the manifold gauge hoses by cracking the hoses at the manifold for a few seconds.
5. Start the engine and adjust the speed to 1,000 rpm.
6. Depress the AUTO button and set the control dial at 65. Then close all windows and doors.
7. Connect the test light to the ETR valve lead.

Conduct the Test

1. Observe the compressor inlet pressure (the pressure should be normal).
2. Observe the test light (the light should be off).
3. Watch for the test light to come on, indicating that the ETR switch is sending current to the ETR valve.
   NOTE: If the ETR switch is defective, the light may not be off as indicated in step 2, or it may not come on as indicated in step 3.

4. When the test light comes on, observe the compressor inlet pressure. The pressure should drop to a zero indication. If the reading is not zero, a defective ETR valve is indicated.

   NOTE: The head pressure varies from 25 to 35 pounds as the ETR valve opens and closes.

Return the System to Service

1. Return the engine speed to normal idle to prevent dieseling.
2. Turn off the air conditioner. Shut off the engine.
3. Remove the manifold and gauge set and replace the protective covers.
4. Remove the test light.

REVIEW

Briefly answer each of the following questions.

1. What is the purpose of the ETR valve?
2. How is the ETR valve different from the EPR valve?
3. What is the normal compressor inlet reading for the ETR/EPR system?

SERVICE PROCEDURE 26:
CHECKING AND ADJUSTING THE SUCTION THROTTLING VALVE

The suction throttling valve (STV) regulates the evaporator pressure so that it does not fall below 29-31 psig. Below 29 psig, the evaporator is too cold. In this condition, it freezes by allowing condensate to form ice on the evaporator fins and coils. If the pressure is higher than 31 psig, the discharge air temperature is warmer than normal.

This procedure is used to check STV operation. Adjustments to the valve can be made, if necessary. If at any time during the test, the head pressure exceeds 375 psig, discontinue the test and check for these problems:

- engine cooling system leak or system blocked
- restricted liquid line or receiver
- air in the refrigeration system
- overcharge of refrigerant or oil
- insufficient ram air

This procedure is in two parts: Part I deals with the Bowden cable-controlled STV; Part II deals with the vacuum-controlled STV.

TOOLS

Manifold and gauge set
Service valve wrench or Schrader adapters
Hand tools

Screwdriver
STV adjustment tool

PROCEDURE

PART I

Prepare the System for Test and/or Adjustment

1. Attach the gauge manifold set to the compressor and the STV. Use a third gauge if the system contains three fittings.

2. Start the engine and adjust the speed to 1,000-1,200 rpm. Adjust the air-conditioning controls for maximum cooling.

3. Move the temperature control back and forth 10 to 15 times to normalize the diaphragm in the STV.

4. Visually check the Bowden cable and control as well as the control lever to insure that there is free movement through the full range of operation.

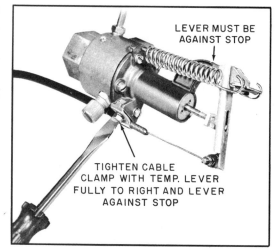

LEVER MUST BE AGAINST STOP

TIGHTEN CABLE CLAMP WITH TEMP. LEVER FULLY TO RIGHT AND LEVER AGAINST STOP

Fig. SP26-1 Adjusting the Bowden cable

Adjust the Cable

1. Position the temperature lever at the cold position and loosen the cable clamp on the valve, figure SP26-1.

2. Position the cable in the clamp to force the valve lever to seat against the stop.

3. Tighten the cable clamp screw. Check the unit for free operation.

Valve Adjustment

1. Insure that the Bowden cable is properly adjusted before making STV adjustments.

2. Increase the engine speed to about 1,600 rpm. Depress the high blower button or lever. Operate the system 5-10 minutes.

3. The evaporator pressure should read 29-31 psig.

4. Adjust the STV until the evaporator pressure is within the limits given in step 3, figure SP26-2.

   a. Engage the pins of the adjusting tool in the holes in the valve adjusting screw.
   b. Turn the screw to adjust the STV. A clockwise rotation increases the spring tension and raises the evaporator pressure.

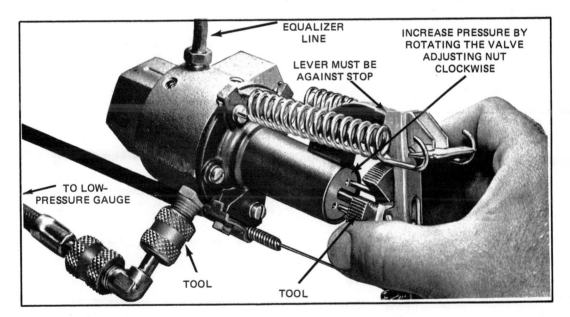

Fig. SP26-2 Adjusting the suction throttling valve

5. After obtaining a pressure of 29-31 psig, operate the control lever a few times to insure consistent operation.

Return the System to Service

1. Decrease the engine speed to normal idle to prevent dieseling. Shut off the engine and then shut off the air conditioner.

2. Remove the manifold and gauge set and replace all protective caps and covers.

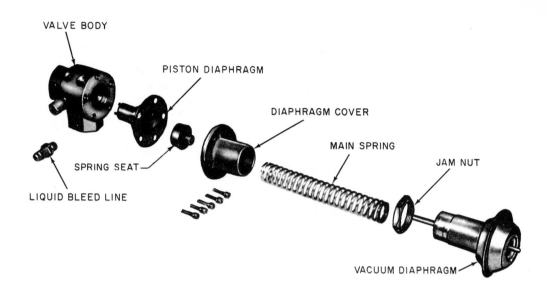

VALVE BODY

PISTON DIAPHRAGM

DIAPHRAGM COVER

MAIN SPRING

JAM NUT

SPRING SEAT

LIQUID BLEED LINE

VACUUM DIAPHRAGM

Fig. SP26-3 Exploded view of a vacuum-operated suction throttling valve

PART II

Prepare the System for Test and/or Adjustment

1. Follow the procedure as outlined in Part I.

   NOTE: The vacuum-controlled STV does not use a Bowden cable. Therefore, no cable check is required.

Valve Adjustment

1. Increase the engine speed to 1,500-1,600 rpm.

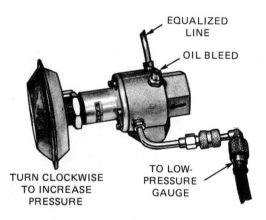

EQUALIZED LINE

OIL BLEED

TURN CLOCKWISE TO INCREASE PRESSURE

TO LOW-PRESSURE GAUGE

Fig. SP26-4 Suction throttling valve adjustment

2. Turn the blower on high and set the controls for maximum cooling. Operate the system for 5-10 minutes.

3. The evaporator pressure should now read 29-31 psig.

4. Adjust the STV until the evaporator pressure is within the stated limits.
   a. Disconnect the vacuum hose from the vacuum valve on the STV.
   b. Loosen the locknut on the vacuum control.
   c. Rotate the vacuum control clockwise to increase the spring tension and raise the evaporator pressure.

5. After obtaining a pressure of 29-30 psig, tighten the locknut and reconnect the vacuum hose.

6. Operate the control lever a few times to insure consistent operation.

Return the System to Service

1. Follow the procedure as outlined in Part I.

REVIEW

Briefly answer each of the following questions.

1. The STV maintains the evaporator pressure between __?__ and __?__ psig.

2. If the head pressure exceeds __?__ psig, this may be an indication of air in the system.

3. How can the STV be normalized?

4. What is the recommended engine speed for the STV test?

5. Can an improperly adjusted Bowden cable cause poor cooling?

6. What is the recommended engine speed for the STV adjustment?

7. Evaporator pressure is read at the __?__ .

8. Pressure below __?__ psig allows the evaporator to freeze.

9. Evaporator pressure can be increased by adjusting the STV adjustment __?__ .

10. Increased evaporator pressure means higher __?__ .

SERVICE PROCEDURE 27:
TESTING THE PERFORMANCE OF THE PILOT-OPERATED ABSOLUTE VALVE

The pilot-operated absolute value (POA) is an evaporator pressure regulator used to control the pressure and temperature of the evaporator. This valve is sealed and repair is not possible. If the following test shows that the POA valve is defective, the valve must be replaced.

TOOLS

Manifold and gauge set with Schrader-type adapters
Hand tools
Can tap

MATERIALS

POA valve, if required   Refrigerant, if required

PROCEDURE

Prepare the System for Test

1. Attach the gauge manifold set to the system. The low-side manifold is connected to the POA valve.
2. Start the engine and adjust the speed to 1,000-1,200 rpm.
3. Adjust all of the air-conditioning controls for maximum cooling.
4. Operate the system for 10-15 minutes.

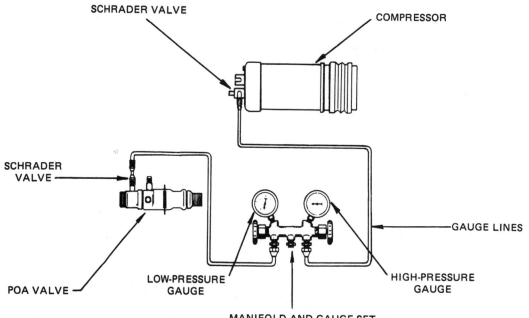

Fig. SP27-1 Gauge connection to system with POA valve

POA Valve Pressure Chart		
Altitude, ft. (Elevation)	Gauge Pressure, psig (Minimum)	Gauge Pressure, psig (Maximum)
0	27.5	29.5
1,000	28.0	30:0
2,000	28.5	30.5
3,000	29.0	31.0
4,000	29.5	31.5
5,000	30.0	32.0
6,000	30.4	32.4
7,000	30.8	32.8
8,000	31.3	33.3
9,000	31.7	33.7
10,000	32.2	34.2

Fig. SP27-2

Check the POA Valve

1. Read the compound gauge pressure. The pressure should be 27.5-29.5 psig at sea level. Refer to the chart in figure SP27-2 for the proper reading at various altitudes.
2. If the valve does not pass this test, replace the valve.

Replace the POA Valve

1. Purge the system of refrigerant, Service Procedure 3.
2. Remove the oil bleed line from the POA valve.
3. Remove the thermostatic valve external equalizer line from the POA valve.
4. Remove the inlet and outlet fittings from the POA valve. Remove the clamp which holds the assembly in place. Lift the assembly from the car.
5. Install a new valve and new 0-rings by reversing the procedure in steps 1-4.
6. Evacuate and charge the air-conditioning system as outlined in Service Procedure 6.
7. Resume the performance test if required.

Return the System to Service

1. Decrease the engine speed to normal idle to prevent dieseling.
2. Turn off the air conditioner. Stop the engine.
3. Remove the manifold and gauge set.
4. Replace the protective caps and covers.

REVIEW

Briefly answer each of the following questions.

1. What is the main difference between the pilot-operated absolute valve and the suction throttling valve?

2. What is the pressure of the POA valve if it is operating properly at sea level?

3. What is the pressure of the POA valve if it is operating properly at 10,000 feet?

4. Is the POA valve itself affected by altitude?

5. If the POA valve does not check out to specifications, can it be adjusted?

SERVICE PROCEDURE 28:
TESTING THE PERFORMANCE OF
THE VALVES-IN-RECEIVER (VIR)

The valves-in-receiver (VIR) replaces the receiver/drier, the thermostatic expansion valve, and the POA valve by combining these components in one assembly. Each component, however, functions in the same manner as in other systems. This procedure can be used to determine which part of the VIR is defective, if any.

TOOLS

Manifold and gauge set   Thermometer

PROCEDURE

Prepare the System for Test

1. Connect the compound manifold gauge to the service port of the VIR.
2. Connect the high-side manifold gauge to the high-side service port.
3. Start the engine and adjust the engine speed to 2,000 rpm.
4. With the hood open, fully open all of the windows.
5. Set the controls for maximum cooling with the blower on high.

Conduct the Test

1. Note the delivery air temperature by placing the thermometer in the right air duct.
2. Note the evaporator pressure as observed on the compound gauge.
3. If the head pressure is not normal, check for conditions which can cause an abnormal pressure reading.
4. Note the condition of the refrigerant in the sight glass.
5. Compare the observations with the chart given in figure SP28-1.

EVAPORATOR PRESSURE	SIGHT GLASS	AIR DELIVERY	PROBABLE SYSTEM DEFECT	NOTE
28-30 psig	CLEAR	40-50°F	NORMAL	
LOW	CLEAR	WARMER	TXV	1 & 2
HIGH	CLEAR	WARMER	POA	
NORMAL-LOW	CLEAR	COLDER	POA	1,3 & 4
HIGH	CLOUDY	WARMER	POA	1
NORMAL-LOW	CLOUDY	WARMER	LOW CHARGE	1
NORMAL-LOW	CLOUDY	WARMER	DRIER RESTRICTED	1

1. Can cause the superheat switch to close and blow the thermal fuse link in the compressor clutch circuit.
2. Turn the system off to warm up and equalize the system. Repeat the test. If the system performs properly on the second test, the system probably contains excess moisture. Replace the desiccant (Service Procedure 48).
3. The evaporator can become clogged with ice; thus restricting the airflow.
4. The system can go into a low pressure (or vacuum) when the blower is disconnected.

Fig. SP28-1

Return the System to Service

1. Decrease the engine speed to normal idle to prevent dieseling.
2. Turn off all of the air-conditioning controls.
3. Stop the engine.
4. Remove the manifold and gauge set and replace the protective covers.

REVIEW

Select the appropriate answer from the choices given.

1. The valves-in-receiver replaces
   - a. the TXV.
   - b. the receiver.
   - c. the POA valve.
   - d. all of these devices.

2. According to the chart in figure SP28-1, an evaporator pressure of 35 psig and a cloudy sight glass can indicate a defective
   - a. TXV.
   - b. receiver pickup tube.
   - c. POA valve.
   - d. all of these.

3. The normal air delivery temperature should be
   - a. 30°-40°F.
   - b. 35°-45°F.
   - c. 40°-50°F.
   - d. 45°-55°F.

4. The thermometer is used to check the
   - a. evaporator core temperature.
   - b. condenser temperature.
   - c. air delivery temperature.
   - d. ambient air temperature.

5. Excess moisture in the system causes the
   - a. expansion valve to freeze.
   - b. receiver pickup tube screen to freeze.
   - c. POA valve to freeze.
   - d. condenser to freeze.

SERVICE PROCEDURE 29:
TESTING THE GENERAL MOTORS'
AUTOMATIC TEMPERATURE CONTROL[*]

The automatic temperature control system used by General Motors is known as the Comfort Control or Comfortron system. This system requires special testing tools and procedures. One such tool is the Kent Moore J-22368 tester which can isolate an electrical malfunction in the control system. The tester serves as a substitute for the various component parts of the air-conditioning system.

This procedure is an outline of the steps recommended for testing the automatic temperature control. It is advised that the equipment manufacturer's service manual be consulted for specific procedures for particular air-conditioner models.

TOOLS

Testing tool, such as the Kent Moore J-22368 or J-21512 or equivalent
Ohmmeter
Hand tools
Screwdriver

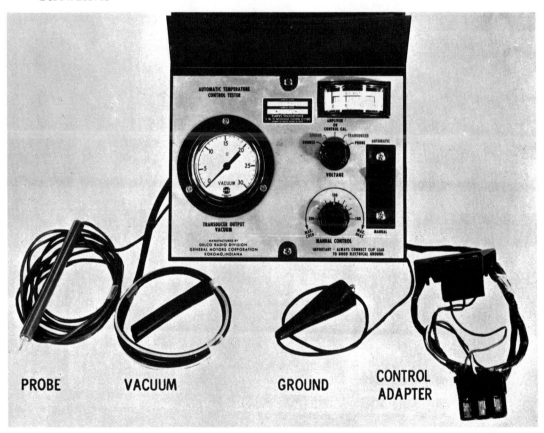

Fig. 29-1 Automatic temperature control tester

---

[*] Parts of this material are used by permission of Cadillac Motor Car Division and Oldsmobile Division of General Motors Corporation.

PROCEDURE

The Sensor String Test

1. Place the control system lever in the automatic position and set the temperature dial to 75°F.

2. Start the engine and set it to fast idle.

3. Place the amplifier switch on the tester in the SENSOR position.

4. Place the sensor switch in the AC position. The system and the tester meter should go to the full air-conditioning mode.

5. Place the sensor switch in the HTR position. The system and the tester meter should go to the full heater mode.

6. If steps 4 and 5 do not result in the correct operation, continue with the amplifier check. If steps 4 and 5 are correct, proceed.

7. Check for loose connectors at each sensor.

8. With an ohmmeter, measure the resistance values of the in-car sensor, ambient sensor, and duct sensor. The sensor resistance values are given in the shop manual of the particular vehicle that is being serviced.

9. Replace any sensor that is found to be defective.

10. If no sensors are found to be defective, carefully check all wiring and correct as necessary.

Amplifier Check

1. Place the amplifier switch on the tester in the AMPLIFIER position.

2. Turn the amplifier control counterclockwise to the stop position. The system and the tester meter should go to the full air-conditioning mode.

3. Turn the amplifier control to the stop in the full clockwise position. The system and the meter should go to the full heater position.

4. If the test meter indication does not change with variations in the amplifier control, replace the transducer.

5. If steps 2 and 3 do not indicate the correct system operation, proceed to the vacuum test. If steps 2 and 3 show the correct system operation, proceed.

6. Disconnect the lead from the temperature dial rheostat. Connect an ohmmeter to the rheostat and to the control panel ground.

7. Measure the resistance of the rheostat. It should be in the range of 1,350-1,650 ohms at the 75°F setting.

8. If the rheostat value is correct, replace the amplifier circuit board.

9. If the rheostat value is incorrect, replace the rheostat.

Vacuum Test

1. Locate and gain access to the transducer.

2. Place the amplifier switch in the AMPLIFIER position.

3. Turn the amplifier control counterclockwise to the stop. The power servo unit should go to the full air-conditioning position.

4. Turn the amplifier control clockwise to the stop position. The power servo should go to the full heater position.

5. Connect the vacuum gauge to the transducer unit. The gauge should read about 13 in. Hg.

6. Connect the vacuum gauge to the output of the transducer. Rotate the tester amplifier control from stop to stop. The output of the transducer should vary.

7. If the vacuum output does not vary, replace the transducer.

8. If the output does vary, check the power servo unit for mechanical interference.

9. If the system still does not operate properly, replace the power servo unit.

REVIEW

Briefly answer each of the following questions.

1. What is the purpose of the automatic temperature control?

2. At what setting should the dial temperature be placed for most tests?

3. What reading should the dial rheostat register on the ohmmeter during the amplifier check?

4. When performing the vacuum test, what level of vacuum is to be expected at the transducer input?

5. When making checks of the automatic temperature control units, what is the recommended engine speed?

SERVICE PROCEDURE 30:
PERFORMING THE TEMPERATURE DIAL TEST OF
THE GENERAL MOTORS' AUTOMATIC TEMPERATURE CONTROL*

The procedure for the temperature dial test is in two parts. Part I deals with the dial test using the special testing tool; Part II deals with the dial test using two thermometers. While test II is less efficient, it allows the system to be tailored to meet the individual requirements of the owner.

TOOLS

PART I

Control tester

PART II

Auxiliary electric fan   Masking tape
Two thermometers

PROCEDURE

PART I

Temperature Dial Test with the Testing Tool

1. Insure that the system is operating properly. If the operation is not correct, follow the steps of Service Procedure 29. Connect the tester into the system.
2. Place the amplifier switch in the SENSOR position.
3. Place the sensor switch in the MID position.
4. Adjust the temperature dial until the tester meter indicator is on the centerline. The temperature dial should read 75°F.
5. If the temperature dial does not read 75°F, make adjustments as outlined in Service Procedure 31.
6. If the system is operating properly, shut off the engine, remove the tester from the system, and reconnect the car wiring harness to the amplifier.

PART II

Temperature Dial Test without the Testing Tool

1. Insure that the system is operating properly. If not, correct as outlined in Service Procedure 29.
2. Using masking tape, suspend a thermometer from the headliner so that the bulb hangs at breath level over the driver's seat.
3. With masking tape, suspend the second thermometer over the front passenger's seat.
4. Close all windows and doors.

---

*This material is used by permission of Cadillac Motor Car Division, General Motors Corporation.

5. Place the temperature control lever to the AUTOMATIC position. Set the temperature dial to 75°F.

6. Start the engine and operate it at 900 rpm.

7. Make certain that all of the air-conditioning outlets are open. Adjust all outlets so that none are directed toward the thermometers.

8. Operate the system for 25-30 minutes to stabilize the system. Then record the readings from the two suspended thermometers.

9. If the thermometer readings vary from 75°F, adjust the temperature control as outlined in Service Procedure 31.

10. If the system is operating properly, return the car to the normal idle to prevent dieseling and shut off the engine. Remove the thermometers.

REVIEW

Briefly answer each of the following questions.

1. Why are two thermometers used in this test?

2. At what setting should the dial be set for comfort?

3. At what speed should the engine be running for this test?

4. How long should the system be operated before the thermometers are checked?

5. What temperature is desired on the thermometers?

SERVICE PROCEDURE 31:
ADJUSTING THE TEMPERATURE DIAL, GENERAL MOTORS' AUTOMATIC TEMPERATURE CONTROL*

The procedure in this unit is divided into two parts: Part I covers the situation when the temperature dial is operating properly and Part II covers the situation when the temperature dial is operating improperly. In some cases, it is necessary to change the temperature dial setting for customer satisfaction on a properly operating dial. If this is the case, the owner should indicate the temperature dial setting at which he is most comfortable.

TOOLS

Automatic temperature control tester
Temperature dial adjuster

PROCEDURE

PART I

Adjusting the Temperature Dial for Customer Satisfaction

1. Set the temperature dial to the setting indicated by the owner as being most comfortable.
2. Insert the temperature dial adjuster between the temperature dial and the casting.
3. Turn the dial to the 75°F setting.

PART II

Temperature Control Dial Adjustment

1. Connect the tester to the control amplifier.

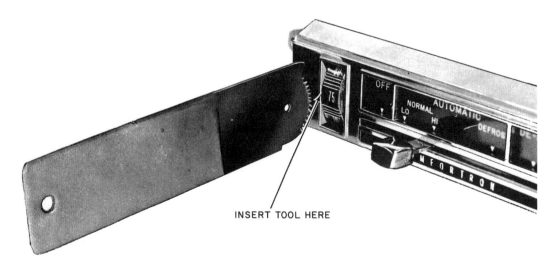

INSERT TOOL HERE

Fig. SP31-1 Adjusting the control dial

*Parts of this material are used by permission of the Cadillac Motor Car Division and Oldsmobile Division, General Motors Corporation.

2. Set the manual control on the tester as outlined in the car manufacturer's service manual.

3. Insert the dial adjusting tool between the temperature dial and the casting, figure SP31-1.

4. While holding the temperature dial on 75°F, rotate the adjusting tool until the voltmeter on the tester reads 6.5 volts.

   NOTE: Check the manufacturer's service manual for the correct reading for individual cars.

5. Disconnect the tester and reconnect the wiring harness to the amplifier.

REVIEW

Briefly answer each of the following questions.

1. When is it necessary to change the temperature dial on a unit which is operating properly?

2. What voltage should the tester read at 75°F?

SERVICE PROCEDURE 32:
BENCH TESTING THE THERMOSTATIC EXPANSION VALVE FOR EFFICIENCY

This test must be made with the expansion valve removed from the unit. Insure that the strainer screen at the inlet of the valve is clean. A partially clogged screen gives incorrect readings.

TOOLS

Manifold and gauge set

Can tap

Female flare adapter, 1/4 in.

Male flare tee, 1/4 in.

Test cap, 1/4 in. (drilled to 0.026 in.)

Adapter, 1/2″ F x 1/4″ M

Adapter, 3/8″ F x 1/4″ M

MATERIALS

Refrigerant 12

Pan of ice water and ice

Salt

Pan of hot water at 125°F

NOTE: A constant source of pressure at 70 psig or higher is required to perform this test. This pressure can be obtained from any suitable material such as dry air, carbon dioxide, dry nitrogen, Refrigerant 22, or Refrigerant 12. A cylinder of high-pressure material such as nitrogen must have a suitable pressure regulating valve.

PROCEDURE

Prepare the Thermostatic Expansion Valve for Test

1. Close the high- and low-side manifold hand valves.

2. Remove the low-side service hose at the manifold.

3. Install a 1/4-in. female flare coupler to the low-side manifold.

4. Install a 1/4-in. male flare tee to the flare coupler at the low side.

5. Reinstall the low-side manifold hose to the 1/4-in. flare tee.

6. Install a 1/4-in. test cap (drilled to 0.026) to the 1/4-in. tee.

7. Install a 3/8″ F x 1/4″ M fitting to the inlet of the expansion valve.

8. Install a 1/2″ F x 1/4″ M fitting to the outlet of the expansion valve.

9. Fasten the low-side manifold hose to the expansion valve outlet.

10. Fasten the high-side manifold hose to the expansion valve inlet.

11. Install a can tap on the can of R12.

12. Pierce the can and back the piercing tap out to release the pressure to the manifold.

13. Fill an insulated container with cracked ice and add water. Use a thermometer to indicate exactly when the temperature is 32°F. If necessary, add salt and stir the mixture.

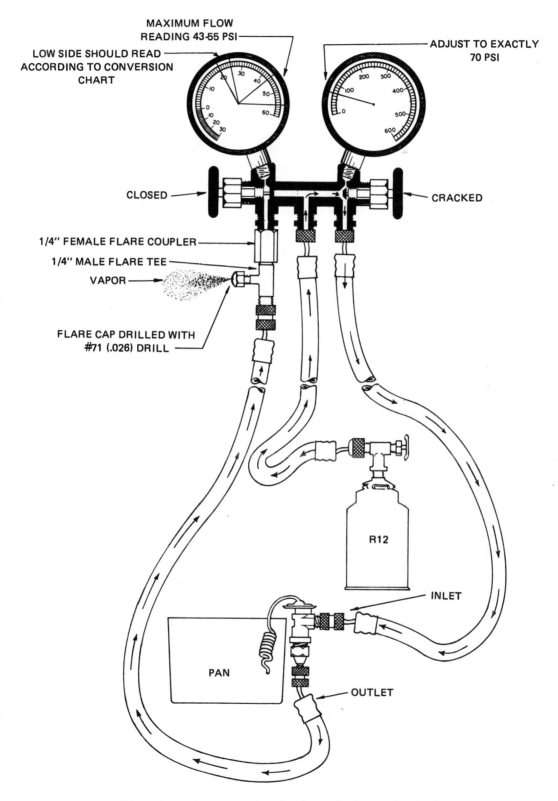

MAXIMUM FLOW
READING 43-55 PSI

LOW SIDE SHOULD READ
ACCORDING TO CONVERSION
CHART

ADJUST TO EXACTLY
70 PSI

CLOSED

CRACKED

1/4" FEMALE FLARE COUPLER

1/4" MALE FLARE TEE

VAPOR

FLARE CAP DRILLED WITH
#71 (.026) DRILL

R12

INLET

PAN

OUTLET

Fig. SP32-1 Test connections for the internally equalized valve

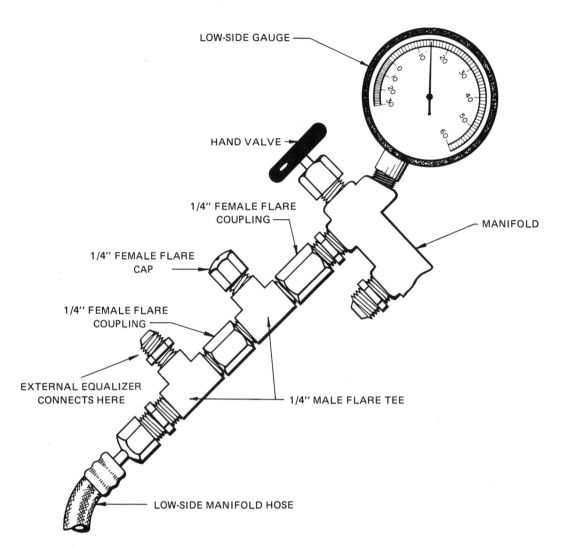

LOW-SIDE GAUGE

HAND VALVE

1/4" FEMALE FLARE COUPLING

1/4" FEMALE FLARE CAP

1/4" FEMALE FLARE COUPLING

EXTERNAL EQUALIZER CONNECTS HERE

MANIFOLD

1/4" MALE FLARE TEE

LOW-SIDE MANIFOLD HOSE

Fig. SP32-2 Modified version of Fig. SP32-1 for use with externally equalized valves

14. Heat the water in a second container until it reaches 125°F.

NOTE: The diagram for the thermostatic expansion valve test connections, figure SP32-1, is for an internally equalized thermostatic expansion valve only. If an externally equalized expansion valve is to be tested, another fitting must be added *before* the test cap, figure SP32-2. The external equalizer is connected to this fitting.

If an externally equalized expansion valve is to be tested, the following tools are required: one 1/4-in. female flare coupler and one 1/4-in. male flare tee.

Test the Expansion Valve for Maximum Flow

1. Invert the refrigerant container.

2. Place the remote bulb of the thermostatic expansion valve into a container of water heated to 125°F.

3. Open the high-side gauge manifold hand valve and adjust it to exactly 70 psig.

4. Read the low-side gauge. The maximum flow test should be 43-55 psig. Readings over 55 psig indicate a flooding valve. A reading under 43 psig indicates a starving valve.

Test the Expansion Valve for Minimum Flow

1. Place the thermal bulb into a container of liquid at 32°F.

2. Open the high-side gauge manifold hand valve and adjust it to exactly 70 psig.

3. Read the low-side gauge. Refer to the conversion chart in figure SP32-3 for the proper low-side reading. The low-side gauge must be within the limits as specified in the conversion chart if the valve is to pass the minimum flow test.

NOTE: The valve superheat settings corresponding to the valve outlet pressure readings are for Refrigerant 12 expansion valves only. Another set of pressure readings for the various superheat values is required for systems charged with a refrigerant other than Refrigerant 12.

Conversion Chart	
Superheat Setting °F.	Pounds per Square Inch Gauge Refrigerant 12 Pressure
5	23 lb. to 26 lb.
6	22 1/4 lb. to 25 1/4 lb.
7	21 1/2 lb. to 24 1/2 lb.
8	21 lb. to 24 lb.
9	20 1/4 lb. to 23 1/4 lb.
10	19 1/2 lb. to 22 1/2 lb.
11	19 lb. to 22 lb.
12	18 lb. to 21 lb.
13	17 1/2 lb. to 20 1/2 lb.
14	17 lb. to 20 lb.
15	15 1/2 lb. to 18 1/2 lb.

Fig. SP32-3 Conversion chart for TXV testing

Cleaning the Expansion Valve

NOTE: If the expansion valve fails to pass either or both of the tests on pages 252 and 253, valve cleaning can be attempted. Otherwise, a new valve must be used. Although each valve is different in structure, the following steps can be used as a guide.

1. Remove the diaphragm, the capillary, and the remote bulb assembly.

2. Remove the superheat adjusting screw. Count the number of turns required to remove the screw. Knowing the number of turns aids in relocating the proper position when reassembling the valve.

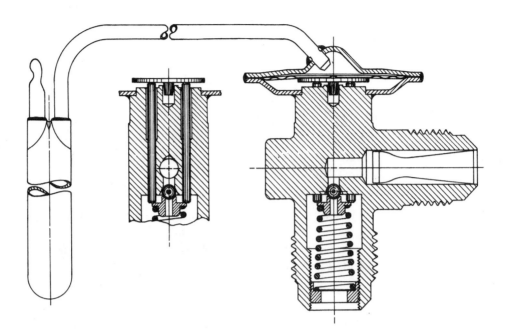

Fig. SP32-4 Cross section of the thermostatic expansion valve

3. Remove the superheat spring and the valve seat. Remove the valve and push rod(s).

4. Clean the valve and all parts in *clean* mineral spirits. Let the parts drain and then blow them dry.

5. Reverse steps 1-4 and reassemble the valve.

6. Check the expansion valve for maximum and minimum flow as outlined in this unit.

7. If the valve fails to pass the maximum/minimum flow test, attempt to adjust the superheat spring setting.

8. If the valve fails the test repeatedly, a new valve must be installed. No further repair is possible.

REVIEW

Briefly answer each of the following questions.

1. What pressure source must be available for this test?

2. Why is a minimum flow test conducted?

3. Why is a maximum flow test conducted?

4. What should the minimum flow be?

5. What should the maximum flow be?

6. Can all expansion valves be cleaned?

7. Name two types of thermostatic expansion valves.

8. What cleaning agent is recommended?

9. What size of test cap is used in this test?

10. How is an externally equalized valve tested?

11. In figure SP32-5, name as many of the component parts of the thermostatic expansion valve as possible.

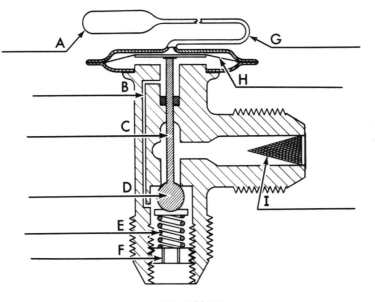

Fig. SP32-5

SERVICE PROCEDURE 33:
TESTING THE MANIFOLD GAUGE AND THERMOMETER

The various tests of the refrigeration system depend on accurate pressure and temperature readings. If the gauges are inaccurate by even a few pounds per square inch, components such as expansion valves and suction regulators are likely to be replaced when there is nothing wrong with them.

An inaccurate thermometer means that it is not possible to set thermostats properly. Because of improper settings, units can either freeze or fail to get cold enough.

The accuracy of all gauges and thermometers can be checked by testing them regularly. Special equipment is not required to test them. All that is required is a can of refrigerant and a place to leave the components overnight where the temperature is stable.

TEMPERATURE-PRESSURE
RELATIONSHIP CHART (REFRIGERANT)

Temp. F.	Press. psi	Temp. F.	Press. psi	Temp. F.	Press. psi
65	63.7	80	84.0	95	108.1
66	64.9	81	85.5	96	109.8
67	66.2	82	87.0	97	111.5
68	67.5	83	88.5	98	113.3
69	68.8	84	90.1	99	115.1
70	70.1	85	91.7	100	116.9
71	71.4	86	93.2	101	118.8
72	72.8	87	94.8	102	120.6
73	74.2	88	96.4	103	122.4
74	75.5	89	98.0	104	124.3
75	76.9	90	99.6	105	126.2
76	78.3	91	101.3	106	128.1
77	79.2	92	103.0	107	130.0
78	81.1	93	104.6	108	132.1
79	82.5	94	106.3	109	135.1

Fig. SP33-1

There is a definite temperature-pressure relationship for liquid refrigerant. The gauge set to be tested is connected to a can of Refrigerant 12 — a full can should be used. A thermometer is taped to the side of the can so that the sensing element is below the liquid level in the can.

This assembly is placed where the temperature will be fairly constant overnight, such as in a corner or under a bench. The next morning, the thermometer and the pressure gauges are read. These readings are compared to the temperature-pressure chart in figure SP33-1 to determine if the gauges and/or thermometer are correct.

It should be pointed out that if the low-side gauge is to be checked, the low-side hose must be fastened to the can tap. Conversely, if the high-side hose is connected to the can tap, the high-side gauge can be checked.

If the manifold gauge set includes a hose hanger (a device for hanging up the hose ends), both gauges can be checked according to the following procedure:

1. Connect the center hose to the can tap.

2. Crack the can tap.

3. Hang the high-side and the low-side manifold hoses on the hose hangers.

4. Open the high- and low-side manifold hand valves.

5. Check the entire assembly for leaks. If there are no leaks, the assembly can be left overnight to determine if the gauges and thermometer are correct.

REVIEW

Indicate whether each of the following statements is true or false.

_____ 1. The thermometer and gauge can be checked against each other to determine their accuracy.

_____ 2. A defective gauge can cause the unnecessary replacement of parts.

_____ 3. A defective thermometer can cause a thermostat adjustment that results in evaporator freezeup.

Briefly answer each of the following questions.

4. Refer to the temperature-pressure chart in figure SP33-1. If the thermometer reads 78°F, the low-side gauge reads 81 psig, and the high-side gauge reads 84 psig, what problem is indicated?

5. Refer to the chart in figure SP33-1. Both the high- and low-side gauges read 77 psig; the thermometer reads 80°F. What problem is indicated?

6. If the thermometer reads 74°F, what is the correct low-side manifold gauge reading?

7. Explain the answer given in question 2.

8. Explain the answer given in question 3.

SERVICE PROCEDURE 34:
PERFORMING A FUNCTIONAL TEST OF
THE AUTOMATIC TEMPERATURE CONTROL
(GENERAL MOTORS' ELECTROPNEUMATIC SYSTEM)

This procedure is typical and can be followed to perform the functional test on the electropneumatic automatic control systems used by General Motors. The manufacturer's wiring and/or vacuum diagrams should be consulted to determine the color coding if this is different from that given in figure SP45-1. Figure SP34-1 applies only to this service procedure.

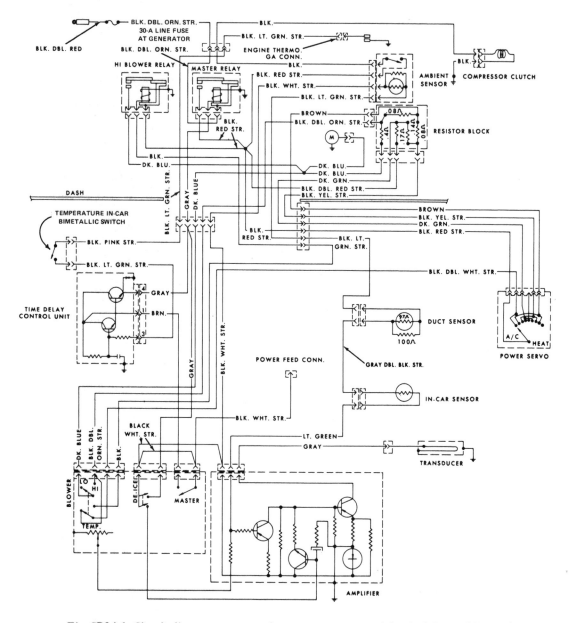

Fig. SP34-1 Circuit diagram – automatic temperature control (typical General Motors)

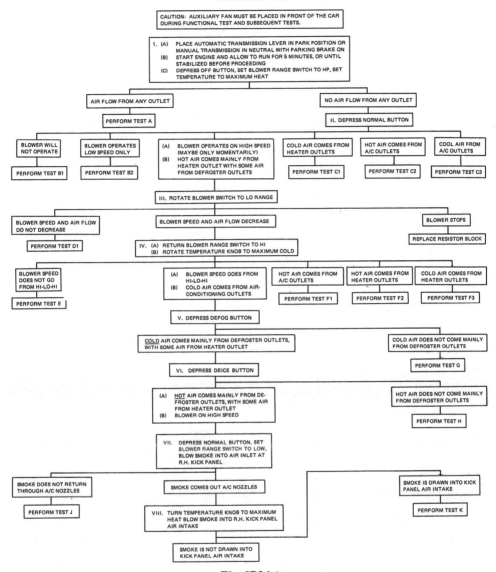

Fig. SP34-2

Before conducting this test, place an auxiliary fan in front of the automobile to direct air across the condenser. Place the automatic transmission in PARK (or for a manual, in *neutral*) with the emergency brake set. Study figure SP34-2 carefully to determine how the various parts of the test relate to each other. To perform this test, proceed according to the instructions given in the charts for tests A through K, pages 260 to 264.

TOOLS

Voltmeter
Ammeter

Test Light
Jumper lead

MATERIAL

As required

Test A

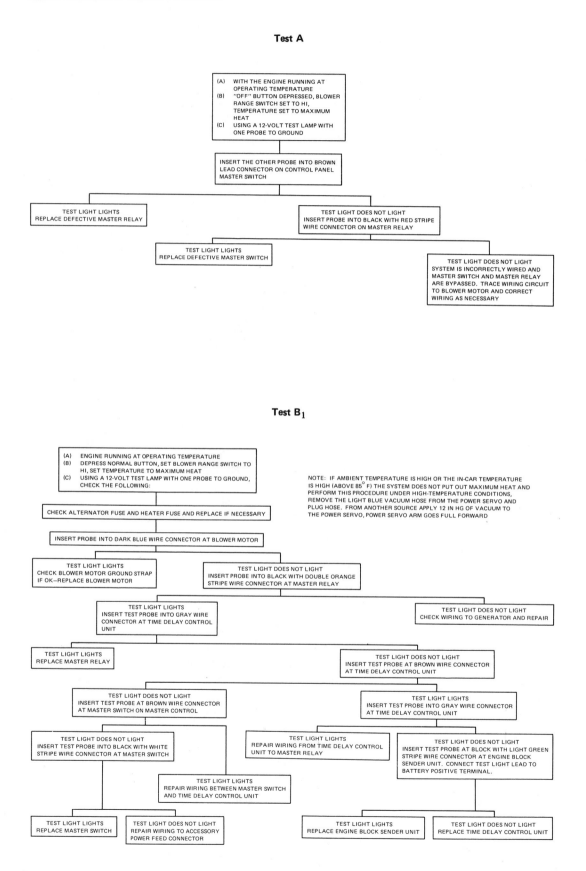

(A) WITH THE ENGINE RUNNING AT OPERATING TEMPERATURE
(B) "OFF" BUTTON DEPRESSED, BLOWER RANGE SWITCH SET TO HI, TEMPERATURE SET TO MAXIMUM HEAT
(C) USING A 12-VOLT TEST LAMP WITH ONE PROBE TO GROUND

INSERT THE OTHER PROBE INTO BROWN LEAD CONNECTOR ON CONTROL PANEL MASTER SWITCH

TEST LIGHT LIGHTS
REPLACE DEFECTIVE MASTER RELAY

TEST LIGHT DOES NOT LIGHT
INSERT PROBE INTO BLACK WITH RED STRIPE WIRE CONNECTOR ON MASTER RELAY

TEST LIGHT LIGHTS
REPLACE DEFECTIVE MASTER SWITCH

TEST LIGHT DOES NOT LIGHT
SYSTEM IS INCORRECTLY WIRED AND MASTER SWITCH AND MASTER RELAY ARE BYPASSED. TRACE WIRING CIRCUIT TO BLOWER MOTOR AND CORRECT WIRING AS NECESSARY

Test B₁

(A) ENGINE RUNNING AT OPERATING TEMPERATURE
(B) DEPRESS NORMAL BUTTON, SET BLOWER RANGE SWITCH TO HI, SET TEMPERATURE TO MAXIMUM HEAT
(C) USING A 12-VOLT TEST LAMP WITH ONE PROBE TO GROUND, CHECK THE FOLLOWING:

NOTE: IF AMBIENT TEMPERATURE IS HIGH OR THE IN-CAR TEMPERATURE IS HIGH (ABOVE 85° F) THE SYSTEM DOES NOT PUT OUT MAXIMUM HEAT AND PERFORM THIS PROCEDURE UNDER HIGH-TEMPERATURE CONDITIONS, REMOVE THE LIGHT BLUE VACUUM HOSE FROM THE POWER SERVO AND PLUG HOSE. FROM ANOTHER SOURCE APPLY 12 IN HG OF VACUUM TO THE POWER SERVO, POWER SERVO ARM GOES FULL FORWARD

CHECK ALTERNATOR FUSE AND HEATER FUSE AND REPLACE IF NECESSARY

INSERT PROBE INTO DARK BLUE WIRE CONNECTOR AT BLOWER MOTOR

TEST LIGHT LIGHTS
CHECK BLOWER MOTOR GROUND STRAP IF OK—REPLACE BLOWER MOTOR

TEST LIGHT DOES NOT LIGHT
INSERT PROBE INTO BLACK WITH DOUBLE ORANGE STRIPE WIRE CONNECTOR AT MASTER RELAY

TEST LIGHT LIGHTS
INSERT TEST PROBE INTO GRAY WIRE CONNECTOR AT TIME DELAY CONTROL UNIT

TEST LIGHT DOES NOT LIGHT
CHECK WIRING TO GENERATOR AND REPAIR

TEST LIGHT LIGHTS
REPLACE MASTER RELAY

TEST LIGHT DOES NOT LIGHT
INSERT TEST PROBE AT BROWN WIRE CONNECTOR AT TIME DELAY CONTROL UNIT

TEST LIGHT DOES NOT LIGHT
INSERT TEST PROBE AT BROWN WIRE CONNECTOR AT MASTER SWITCH ON MASTER CONTROL

TEST LIGHT LIGHTS
INSERT TEST PROBE INTO GRAY WIRE CONNECTOR AT TIME DELAY CONTROL UNIT

TEST LIGHT DOES NOT LIGHT
INSERT TEST PROBE INTO BLACK WITH WHITE STRIPE WIRE CONNECTOR AT MASTER SWITCH

TEST LIGHT LIGHTS
REPAIR WIRING FROM TIME DELAY CONTROL UNIT TO MASTER RELAY

TEST LIGHT DOES NOT LIGHT
INSERT TEST PROBE AT BLOCK WITH LIGHT GREEN STRIPE WIRE CONNECTOR AT ENGINE BLOCK SENDER UNIT. CONNECT TEST LIGHT LEAD TO BATTERY POSITIVE TERMINAL.

TEST LIGHT LIGHTS
REPAIR WIRING BETWEEN MASTER SWITCH AND TIME DELAY CONTROL UNIT

TEST LIGHT LIGHTS
REPLACE MASTER SWITCH

TEST LIGHT DOES NOT LIGHT
REPAIR WIRING TO ACCESSORY POWER FEED CONNECTOR

TEST LIGHT LIGHTS
REPLACE ENGINE BLOCK SENDER UNIT

TEST LIGHT DOES NOT LIGHT
REPLACE TIME DELAY CONTROL UNIT

Test B₂

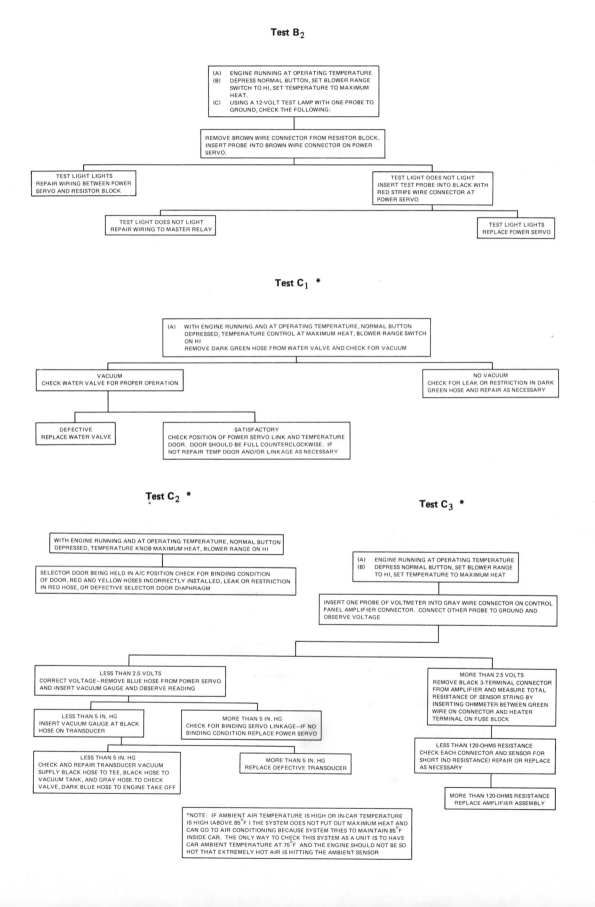

(A) ENGINE RUNNING AT OPERATING TEMPERATURE
(B) DEPRESS NORMAL BUTTON, SET BLOWER RANGE SWITCH TO HI, SET TEMPERATURE TO MAXIMUM HEAT.
(C) USING A 12-VOLT TEST LAMP WITH ONE PROBE TO GROUND, CHECK THE FOLLOWING:

REMOVE BROWN WIRE CONNECTOR FROM RESISTOR BLOCK. INSERT PROBE INTO BROWN WIRE CONNECTOR ON POWER SERVO.

TEST LIGHT LIGHTS
REPAIR WIRING BETWEEN POWER SERVO AND RESISTOR BLOCK

TEST LIGHT DOES NOT LIGHT
INSERT TEST PROBE INTO BLACK WITH RED STRIPE WIRE CONNECTOR AT POWER SERVO

TEST LIGHT DOES NOT LIGHT
REPAIR WIRING TO MASTER RELAY

TEST LIGHT LIGHTS
REPLACE POWER SERVO

Test C₁ *

(A) WITH ENGINE RUNNING AND AT OPERATING TEMPERATURE, NORMAL BUTTON DEPRESSED, TEMPERATURE CONTROL AT MAXIMUM HEAT, BLOWER RANGE SWITCH ON HI
REMOVE DARK GREEN HOSE FROM WATER VALVE AND CHECK FOR VACUUM

VACUUM
CHECK WATER VALVE FOR PROPER OPERATION

NO VACUUM
CHECK FOR LEAK OR RESTRICTION IN DARK GREEN HOSE AND REPAIR AS NECESSARY

DEFECTIVE
REPLACE WATER VALVE

SATISFACTORY
CHECK POSITION OF POWER SERVO LINK AND TEMPERATURE DOOR. DOOR SHOULD BE FULL COUNTERCLOCKWISE. IF NOT REPAIR TEMP DOOR AND/OR LINKAGE AS NECESSARY

Test C₂ *

WITH ENGINE RUNNING AND AT OPERATING TEMPERATURE, NORMAL BUTTON DEPRESSED, TEMPERATURE KNOB MAXIMUM HEAT, BLOWER RANGE ON HI

SELECTOR DOOR BEING HELD IN A/C POSITION CHECK FOR BINDING CONDITION OF DOOR, RED AND YELLOW HOSES INCORRECTLY INSTALLED, LEAK OR RESTRICTION IN RED HOSE, OR DEFECTIVE SELECTOR DOOR DIAPHRAGM

LESS THAN 2.5 VOLTS
CORRECT VOLTAGE—REMOVE BLUE HOSE FROM POWER SERVO AND INSERT VACUUM GAUGE AND OBSERVE READING

LESS THAN 5 IN. HG
INSERT VACUUM GAUGE AT BLACK HOSE ON TRANSDUCER

MORE THAN 5 IN. HG
CHECK FOR BINDING SERVO LINKAGE—IF NO BINDING CONDITION REPLACE POWER SERVO

LESS THAN 5 IN. HG
CHECK AND REPAIR TRANSDUCER VACUUM SUPPLY BLACK HOSE TO TEE, BLACK HOSE TO VACUUM TANK, AND GRAY HOSE TO CHECK VALVE, DARK BLUE HOSE TO ENGINE TAKE OFF

MORE THAN 5 IN. HG
REPLACE DEFECTIVE TRANSDUCER

Test C₃ *

(A) ENGINE RUNNING AT OPERATING TEMPERATURE
(B) DEPRESS NORMAL BUTTON, SET BLOWER RANGE TO HI, SET TEMPERATURE TO MAXIMUM HEAT

INSERT ONE PROBE OF VOLTMETER INTO GRAY WIRE CONNECTOR ON CONTROL PANEL AMPLIFIER CONNECTOR. CONNECT OTHER PROBE TO GROUND AND OBSERVE VOLTAGE

MORE THAN 2.5 VOLTS
REMOVE BLACK 3-TERMINAL CONNECTOR FROM AMPLIFIER AND MEASURE TOTAL RESISTANCE OF SENSOR STRING BY INSERTING OHMMETER BETWEEN GREEN WIRE ON CONNECTOR AND HEATER TERMINAL ON FUSE BLOCK

LESS THAN 120-OHMS RESISTANCE
CHECK EACH CONNECTOR AND SENSOR FOR SHORT (NO RESISTANCE) REPAIR OR REPLACE AS NECESSARY

MORE THAN 120-OHMS RESISTANCE
REPLACE AMPLIFIER ASSEMBLY

*NOTE: IF AMBIENT AIR TEMPERATURE IS HIGH OR IN-CAR TEMPERATURE IS HIGH (ABOVE 85°F) THE SYSTEM DOES NOT PUT OUT MAXIMUM HEAT AND CAN GO TO AIR CONDITIONING BECAUSE SYSTEM TRIES TO MAINTAIN 85°F INSIDE CAR. THE ONLY WAY TO CHECK THIS SYSTEM AS A UNIT IS TO HAVE CAR AMBIENT TEMPERATURE AT 75°F AND THE ENGINE SHOULD NOT BE SO HOT THAT EXTREMELY HOT AIR IS HITTING THE AMBIENT SENSOR

Test D

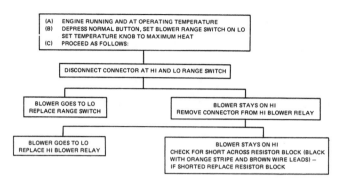

Test E

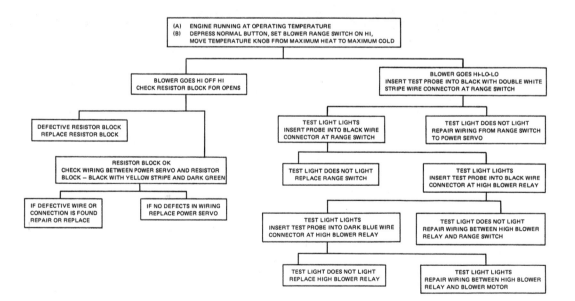

Test F₁ *

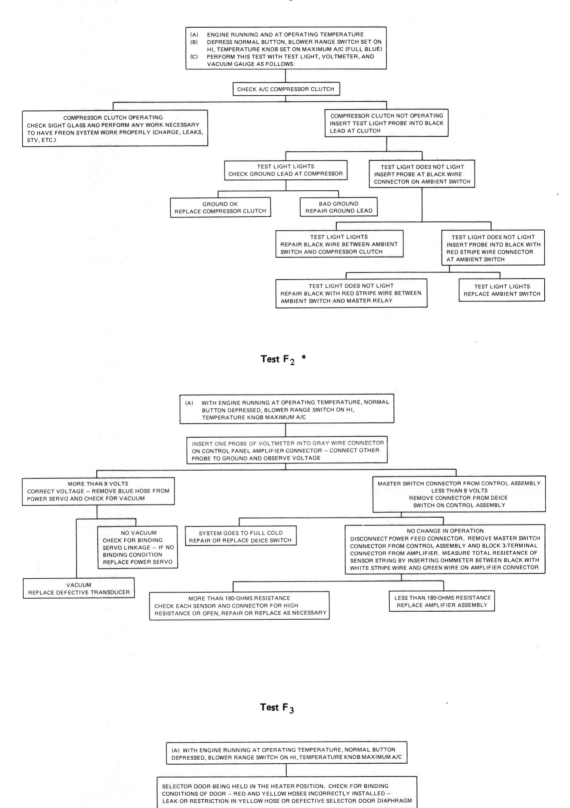

(A) ENGINE RUNNING AND AT OPERATING TEMPERATURE
(B) DEPRESS NORMAL BUTTON, BLOWER RANGE SWITCH SET ON HI, TEMPERATURE KNOB SET ON MAXIMUM A/C (FULL BLUE)
(C) PERFORM THIS TEST WITH TEST LIGHT, VOLTMETER, AND VACUUM GAUGE AS FOLLOWS:

CHECK A/C COMPRESSOR CLUTCH

COMPRESSOR CLUTCH OPERATING
CHECK SIGHT GLASS AND PERFORM ANY WORK NECESSARY TO HAVE FREON SYSTEM WORK PROPERLY (CHARGE, LEAKS, STV, ETC.)

COMPRESSOR CLUTCH NOT OPERATING
INSERT TEST LIGHT PROBE INTO BLACK LEAD AT CLUTCH

TEST LIGHT LIGHTS
CHECK GROUND LEAD AT COMPRESSOR

TEST LIGHT DOES NOT LIGHT
INSERT PROBE AT BLACK WIRE CONNECTOR ON AMBIENT SWITCH

GROUND OK
REPLACE COMPRESSOR CLUTCH

BAD GROUND
REPAIR GROUND LEAD

TEST LIGHT LIGHTS
REPAIR BLACK WIRE BETWEEN AMBIENT SWITCH AND COMPRESSOR CLUTCH

TEST LIGHT DOES NOT LIGHT
INSERT PROBE INTO BLACK WITH RED STRIPE WIRE CONNECTOR AT AMBIENT SWITCH

TEST LIGHT DOES NOT LIGHT
REPAIR BLACK WITH RED STRIPE WIRE BETWEEN AMBIENT SWITCH AND MASTER RELAY

TEST LIGHT LIGHTS
REPLACE AMBIENT SWITCH

Test F₂ *

(A) WITH ENGINE RUNNING AT OPERATING TEMPERATURE, NORMAL BUTTON DEPRESSED, BLOWER RANGE SWITCH ON HI, TEMPERATURE KNOB MAXIMUM A/C

INSERT ONE PROBE OF VOLTMETER INTO GRAY WIRE CONNECTOR ON CONTROL PANEL AMPLIFIER CONNECTOR – CONNECT OTHER PROBE TO GROUND AND OBSERVE VOLTAGE

MORE THAN 9 VOLTS
CORRECT VOLTAGE – REMOVE BLUE HOSE FROM POWER SERVO AND CHECK FOR VACUUM

MASTER SWITCH CONNECTOR FROM CONTROL ASSEMBLY LESS THAN 9 VOLTS
REMOVE CONNECTOR FROM DEICE SWITCH ON CONTROL ASSEMBLY

NO VACUUM
CHECK FOR BINDING SERVO LINKAGE – IF NO BINDING CONDITION REPLACE POWER SERVO

SYSTEM GOES TO FULL COLD
REPAIR OR REPLACE DEICE SWITCH

NO CHANGE IN OPERATION
DISCONNECT POWER FEED CONNECTOR. REMOVE MASTER SWITCH CONNECTOR FROM CONTROL ASSEMBLY AND BLOCK 3-TERMINAL CONNECTOR FROM AMPLIFIER. MEASURE TOTAL RESISTANCE OF SENSOR STRING BY INSERTING OHMMETER BETWEEN BLACK WITH WHITE STRIPE WIRE AND GREEN WIRE ON AMPLIFIER CONNECTOR

VACUUM
REPLACE DEFECTIVE TRANSDUCER

MORE THAN 180-OHMS RESISTANCE
CHECK EACH SENSOR AND CONNECTOR FOR HIGH RESISTANCE OR OPEN, REPAIR OR REPLACE AS NECESSARY

LESS THAN 180-OHMS RESISTANCE
REPLACE AMPLIFIER ASSEMBLY

Test F₃

(A) WITH ENGINE RUNNING AT OPERATING TEMPERATURE, NORMAL BUTTON DEPRESSED, BLOWER RANGE SWITCH ON HI, TEMPERATURE KNOB MAXIMUM A/C

SELECTOR DOOR BEING HELD IN THE HEATER POSITION. CHECK FOR BINDING CONDITIONS OF DOOR – RED AND YELLOW HOSES INCORRECTLY INSTALLED – LEAK OR RESTRICTION IN YELLOW HOSE OR DEFECTIVE SELECTOR DOOR DIAPHRAGM

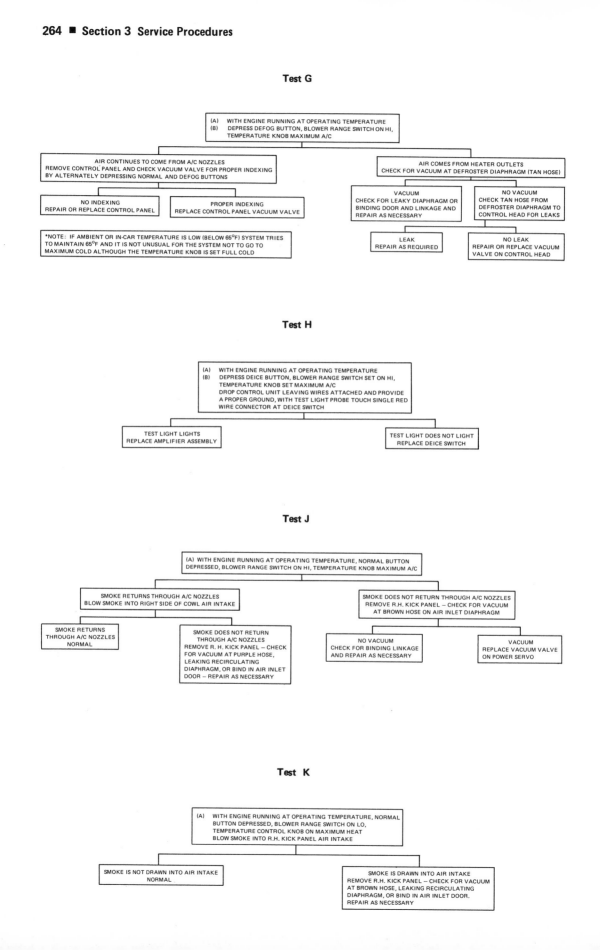

REVIEW

Briefly answer each of the following questions.

1. What does the term *electropneumatic* mean?

2. What tools are required to conduct the tests given in this unit?

3. What precautions are to be taken before conducting these tests?

4. Why are such precautions necessary?

SERVICE PROCEDURE 35:
PERFORMING A FUNCTIONAL TEST OF THE AUTOMATIC TEMPERATURE CONTROL (CHRYSLER MOTORS' ELECTROPNEUMATIC SYSTEM)

This procedure is typical and can be used to perform the functional test on the Chrysler automatic temperature control system. The manufacturer's wiring and/or vacuum diagrams should be consulted to determine the color coding or arrangements if these are different from the ones given in figures SP35-1 and SP35-2. Figures SP35-1 and SP35-2 apply only to Service Procedure 35. Before beginning this test, place an auxiliary fan in front of the automobile to direct air across the condenser. Place the automatic transmission in PARK (or, for a manual transmission, in *neutral*) with the emergency brake set.

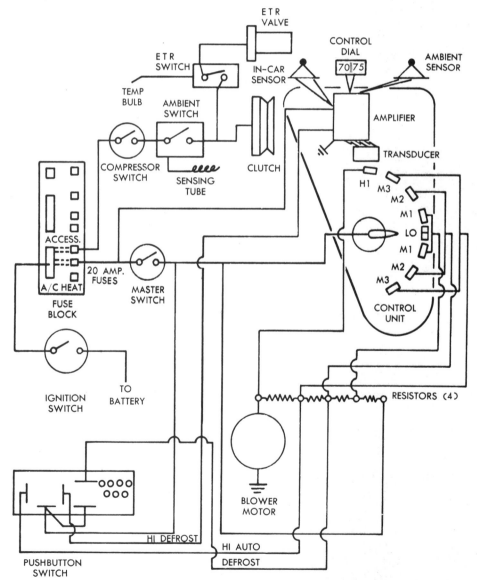

Fig. SP35-1 Typical Chrysler automatic temperature control wiring diagram

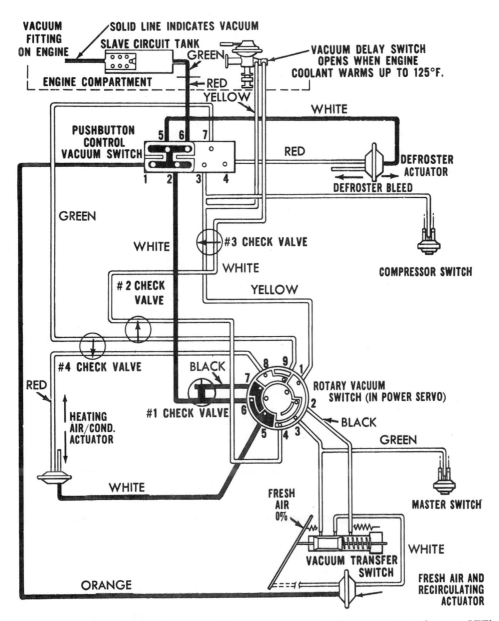

Fig. SP35-2 Typical Chrysler automatic temperature control vacuum system (system OFF)

TOOLS

Kelsey-Hayes tester (Chrysler No. C-4064)

MATERIAL

As required

PROCEDURE

Connect the Tester

1. Insert the tester connectors in series with the system harness and the control unit harness.

2. Attach the tester ground lead (white) to achieve a good body ground.

3. Attach the tester hot lead (black) to the tan wire at the three-terminal connector on the blower motor resistor block.

4. Use a tee to connect the vacuum line of the tester to the right-hand port of the water valve thermostat.

Calibrate the Tester

1. Start the engine and set the speed to 1,000 rpm.

2. Set the voltmeter knob to the OFF position.

3. Set the vacuum control knob to minimum.

4. Depress the AUTO pushbutton.

5. Slowly rotate the tester vacuum knob to the CALIBRATE position.

   NOTE: The vacuum gauge should read between 4 and 6 in. Hg. This reading indicates if the amplifier and transducer are reducing the manifold vacuum to the correct control vacuum for a given electrical signal.

   If the correct reading is not indicated, check that the manifold vacuum is being delivered to the control unit assembly. (Check for kinked or damaged vacuum hoses.) If the full manifold vacuum is being received, the control unit assembly is defective and should be replaced.

Test the Ambient Sensor

1. Move the voltmeter knob to the ambient sensor position.

2. Note the position of the voltmeter needle: it should be in the center green area.

   NOTE: If the needle is in the red area to the right of center, the sensor is open; if the needle is to the left of center, the sensor is shorted.

   CAUTION: Do not allow the voltmeter knob to remain in any of the sensor positions for more than 30 seconds to prevent damage to the sensors.

Test the Temperature Control Dial

1. Set the instrument panel dial at 75°F.

2. Set the tester voltmeter knob to the TEMP. CONTROL position.

3. Note the position of the voltmeter needle: it should be in the green area.

   NOTE: If the needle is in either red area, the temperature control is open or shorted. In some cases, the needle is out of calibration.

4. An ohmmeter can be used to check the calibration of the temperature control dial. The meter should read 300 ohms with the dial set at 75.

Test the In-car Sensor

1. Set the voltmeter knob to the IN-CAR position.

2. Note the position of the voltmeter needle: it should be in the green area.

   NOTE: If the needle is in the red area, the sensor is either open or shorted. Do not allow the voltmeter knob to remain in this position for more than 30 seconds to prevent damage to the sensor.

AUTO TEMPERATURE SEQUENCE CHART

Pushbutton Position	Control Vacuum	Fresh Air Door Position	AC/Heat Door Position	Defrost Door Position	Blower Motor Speed
OFF	Below 8 inches Hg. Above 8 inches Hg.	0% F/A 0% F/A	A/C (open) Heater (closed)	Closed Bleed	Off Off
AUTO SLOWLY ROTATE VACUUM CONTROL KNOB FROM MINIMUM TO MAXIMUM	MINIMUM (0 IN. HG) ↓ 3.5	20% 20% 100%	A/C A/C A/C	CLOSED CLOSED CLOSED	HI HI to M3 M3
		100%	A/C	CLOSED	M3 to M2
		100% 100%	A/C A/C	CLOSED CLOSED	M2 to M1 M1 to LO
	8.0	100% 100%	HEAT HEAT	BLEED BLEED	LO LO to M1
		100%	HEAT	BLEED	M1 to M2
	12.0	100%	HEAT	BLEED	M2 to M3
	↓	100% 100%	HEAT HEAT	BLEED BLEED	M3 M3
SLOWLY ROTATE VACUUM CONTROL KNOB FROM MAXIMUM TO MINIMUM	12.0 ↓ 7.0 ↓ 2.5 ↓ 0 ↓	100% 100% 20% 20%	HEAT A/C A/C A/C	BLEED CLOSED CLOSED CLOSED	M3 LO M3 HI
HI-AUTO SLOWLY ROTATE VACUUM CONTROL KNOB FROM MINIMUM TO MAXIMUM	MINIMUM (0 IN. HG) ↓ 3.5 ↓ 8.0 ↓ 12.0	20% 20% 100% 100% 100% 100% 100% 100% 100%	A/C A/C A/C A/C HEAT HEAT HEAT HEAT HEAT	CLOSED CLOSED CLOSED CLOSED BLEED BLEED BLEED BLEED BLEED	HI HI to M3 M3 M3 M3 M3 M3 M3 M3
SLOWLY ROTATE VACUUM CONTROL KNOB FROM MAXIMUM TO MINIMUM	12.0 ↓ 7.0 ↓ 2.5 ↓ 0	100% 100% 20% 20%	HEAT A/C A/C A/C	BLEED CLOSED CLOSED CLOSED	M3 M3 M3 HI
DEFROST SLOWLY ROTATE VACUUM CONTROL KNOB FROM MINIMUM TO MAXIMUM	MINIMUM (0 IN. HG) ↓ 3.5	20% 20% 100%	HEAT BLEED HEAT BLEED HEAT BLEED	OPEN OPEN OPEN	HI HI to M3 M3
		100%	HEAT BLEED	OPEN	M3 to M2
		100%	HEAT BLEED	OPEN	M2
		100%	HEAT BLEED	OPEN	M2
SLOWLY ROTATE VACUUM CONTROL KNOB FROM MAXIMUM TO MINIMUM	8.0	100% 100%	HEAT BLEED HEAT BLEED	OPEN OPEN	M2 M2
		100%	HEAT BLEED	OPEN	M2
	12.0	100%	HEAT BLEED	OPEN	M2 to M3
	↓	100%	HEAT BLEED	OPEN	M3
HI-DEFROST (TEMP. CONTROL DIAL HAS NO EFFECT)	12.0 IN. HG OR ABOVE	100%	HEAT BLEED	OPEN	M3

Fig. SP35-3 Auto-temp sequence chart

Sequence Test

NOTE: This test puts the system through all of its operating modes from air conditioning with a high blower setting to heating with a high blower setting.

1. Set the voltmeter knob to the voltage position.

2. Set the vacuum knob to the minimum position.

3. Refer to figure SP35-3, page 269, Auto Temp Sequence Chart, to determine the position of the doors and the changes in blower speed as the vacuum control knob is rotated.

REVIEW

Briefly answer each of the following questions.

1. What is the precaution taken when conducting the sensor tests?

2. How is the calibration of the temperature control dial checked?

3. What prevents a vacuum signal from reaching the control unit?

4. What tool(s) are used to conduct this test?

5. What is the purpose of the auto-temp sequence test?

SERVICE PROCEDURE 36:
PERFORMING A FUNCTIONAL TEST OF THE AUTOMATIC TEMPERATURE CONTROL
(FORD MOTORS' AUTOMATIC CLIMATE CONTROL SYSTEM)

This procedure is typical and can be used to perform the functional test on Ford automatic climate control systems. The testing sequence is given for performing seven tests on system components. Figures SP36-1 and SP36-2 show the vacuum and electrical diagrams for this system. However, the manufacturer's service manuals should be consulted to determine the color coding and arrangement of a system if it differs from the diagrams.

Before conducting either test, a check should be made that there are no vacuum or wiring problems outside of the units being tested. Place an auxiliary fan in front of the condenser. Place the transmission in PARK (or, for a manual transmission, in *neutral*) with the emergency brake set.

The tools and materials required are listed in each of the following test procedures:

A. Instrument Panel ACC Functional Control Switch Test
B. Automatic Climate Control Box Test
C. High-range Relay Test
D. Power-servo Assembly Test
E. Temperature Sensors and Control Rheostat Test
F. Heater Water Control Valve Test
G. Water Valve Solenoid Test

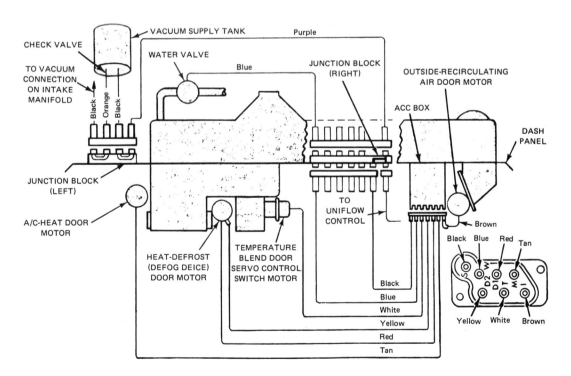

Fig. SP36-1 Automatic climate control vacuum system

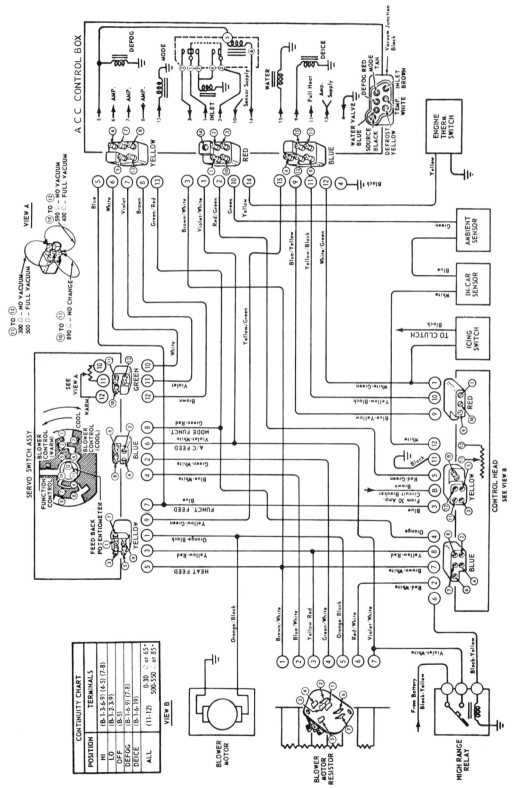

Fig. SP36-2 Automatic climate control electrical system schematic

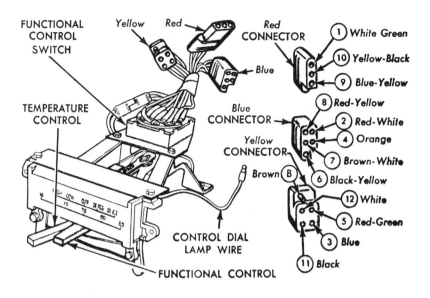

Fig. SP36-3 Functional control switch

TEST A: INSTRUMENT PANEL ACC FUNCTIONAL CONTROL SWITCH TEST

To test the switch and connecting wiring for continuity and the proper resistance, it is necessary to remove the control assembly from the instrument panel. Refer to the wiring diagram for the location of the test points for this procedure.

NOTE: When testing for continuity, there should be continuity only between those points given. If the procedure indicates that there should be continuity between terminals 4 and 5, there should be *no* continuity between points B and 5, for example.

TOOL

Ohmmeter

MATERIAL

As required

PROCEDURE

Test the High Position

1. Check for continuity between terminals B, 1, 3, 6, and 9.
2. Check for continuity between terminals 4 and 5.
3. Check for continuity between terminals 7 and 8.
4. If there is no continuity in steps 1-3, repair or replace the switch. If there is continuity, proceed with the next test.

Test the Low Position

1. Check for continuity between terminals B, 1, 2, 3, and 9.

2. If there is no continuity between any of these terminals, repair or replace the switch. If there is continuity, proceed with the next test.

Test the OFF Position

1. Check for continuity between terminals B and 5.
2. If there is continuity, proceed with the next step. If there is no continuity, repair or replace the switch.

Test the Defog Position

1. Check for continuity between terminals B, 1, 6, and 9.
2. Check for continuity between terminals 7 and 8.
3. Proceed with the next test if there is continuity. If there is no continuity, repair or replace the switch.

Test All Positions

1. Test for continuity between terminals 11 and 12 (0-30 ohms) with the temperature control set at 65°F.
2. Test for continuity between terminals 11 and 12 (500-550 ohms), with the temperature control set at 85°F.
3. If the continuity is not as specified, repair or replace the switch as necessary.

TEST B: AUTOMATIC CLIMATE CONTROL (ACC) BOX TEST

The ACC box can be checked quickly for malfunction. If the ACC box fails to pass any one of the following tests, it must be replaced as a unit. If the ACC box passes all of the tests, the problem is elsewhere in the system.

TOOLS

One jumper wire, 6 in. long with an alligator clip on one end and a double female connector on the other
One jumper wire, 3 ft. long with an alligator clip on each end
One 12-in. jumper wire with a female connector on one end and an alligator clip on the other
Two vacuum hoses, 1/8" x 2"
One vacuum hose, 1/8" x 3"
Four vacuum connectors
One vacuum gauge

MATERIAL

ACC box, if required

PROCEDURE

Prepare the System for Test

1. Remove the glove box to permit easy access to the ACC box.

2. Ground the ACC box.

3. Disconnect the three multiple electrical connectors from the ACC box.

4. Disconnect the vacuum harness from the ACC box.

5. Connect the 1/8" x 3" jumper hose between the harness and the ACC box (S black).

6. Start the engine and operate it at 1,500 rpm.

Inlet Door Solenoid Test

1. Apply 12 volts to terminal 2 of the red connector, figure SP36-4.

2. Connect a vacuum gauge to vacuum port I on the ACC box.

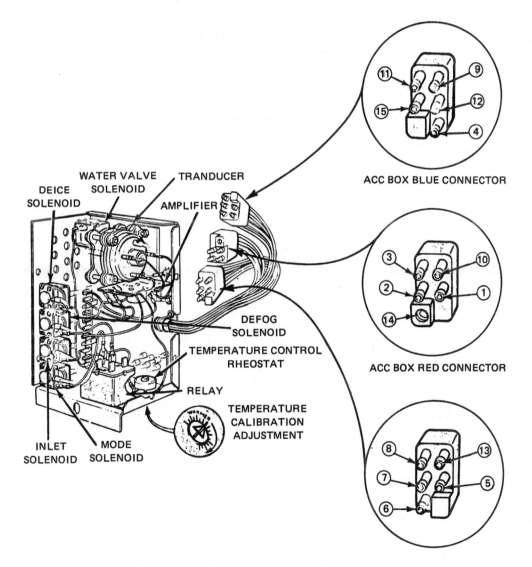

Fig. SP36-4 ACC box components

3. A solenoid click should be heard in the ACC box and a vacuum should be indicated on the gauge.

4. If no click is heard, the ACC box is defective and should be replaced. If the click is heard, proceed with the next test.

Defog Solenoid Test

1. Apply 12 volts to terminal 5 of the yellow connector.

2. Connect a vacuum gauge to port D1 of the ACC box connector.

3. A solenoid click should be heard in the ACC box and a vacuum should be indicated on the gauge.

4. If no click is heard, the ACC box is defective and should be replaced. If a click is heard, proceed with the next test.

Deice Solenoid Test

1. Apply 12 volts to terminal 9 of the blue connector.

2. Connect a vacuum gauge to port D2.

3. A solenoid click should be heard in the ACC box and a vacuum should be indicated on the gauge.

4. If no click is heard, the ACC box is defective and must be replaced. If a click is heard, proceed with the next test.

Mode Solenoid Test

1. Apply 12 volts to terminal 13 of the yellow connector.

2. Connect the vacuum gauge to port M of the ACC box.

3. A solenoid click should be heard and a vacuum should be indicated on the gauge.

4. If no click is heard, the unit is defective and should be replaced. If a click is heard, proceed with the next test.

Water Valve Solenoid Test (for units built after February 19, 1968)

1. Apply 12 volts to terminal 15 of the blue connector.

2. Connect a vacuum gauge to port W.

3. A solenoid click should be heard and a vacuum should be indicated on the gauge.

4. If no click is heard, the unit is defective and must be replaced. If a click is heard, proceed with the next test.

Cold Water Blower Cutoff Relay Test

1. Apply 12 volts to terminal 5 of the yellow connector.

2. Ground terminal 14 of the red connector.

3. A relay click should be heard in the ACC box when grounding the wire.

4. If no click is heard, the unit is defective. If a click is heard, proceed with the next test.

Transducer Test

1. Connect the power servo yellow connector to the ACC box yellow connector.
2. Connect the vacuum gauge to port T of the ACC box connector.
3. Apply 12 volts to terminal 12 of the blue connector.
   NOTE: There should be no vacuum reading on the gauge at this point.
4. Ground terminal 10 of the red connector.
   NOTE: There should now be a full vacuum reading on the gauge at this point.

Return the Unit to Service

1. If the unit is operating properly, reassemble the unit:
   a. Connect the red and blue multiple connectors of the wiring harness to the red and blue connectors of the ACC box.
   b. Remove the ground jumper lead.
   c. Remove the vacuum gauge.
   d. Reconnect the vacuum harness.
   e. Replace the glove box.

TEST C: HIGH-RANGE RELAY TEST

The high-range relay test is best accomplished by substituting relays. If the relay is not functioning properly, it should be replaced.

MATERIAL

High-range relay

PROCEDURE

Replace the High-Range Relay

1. Disconnect the relay harness, figure SP36-5.
2. Connect the new relay into the harness.
3. Ground the new relay and check for the proper operation.
4. If the new relay is good, discard the old relay and install the new relay.
   NOTE: If the new relay appears to be bad, check for wiring problems and correct them as necessary.

TEST D: POWER-SERVO ASSEMBLY TESTS

This procedure can be used to test the power-servo assembly for proper operation.

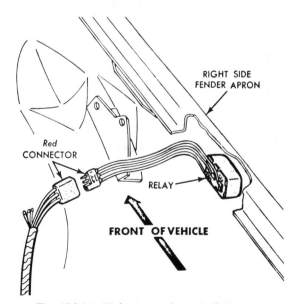

Fig. SP36-5 High-range relay installation

TOOLS

Vacuum gauge   Ohmmeter

MATERIAL

As required

PROCEDURE

Prepare the System for Test

1. Disconnect the three multiple connectors from the power-servo connectors.
2. Connect a vacuum gauge to an outside vacuum source and the power-servo vacuum actuator.
3. Place the transmission in PARK.
4. Start the engine and operate it at idle speed.

Servo Switch Potentiometer Open or Short Test

1. Using the ohmmeter, check the resistance of the following points:
   a. from 10 to 11
   b. from 11 to 12
   c. from 10 to 12
2. The resistance readings for step 1 should be as follows:
   a. from 10 to 11: 890 ohms, ±10%
   b. from 11 to 12: 300 ohms with no vacuum and 500 ohms with a full vacuum, ±60 ohms
   c. from 10 to 12: 590 ohms with no vacuum and 400 ohms with a full vacuum, ±60 ohms

Servo Switch Potentiometer Wear Test

1. Check the resistance from terminals 12 to 10 while slowly increasing the vacuum from zero to maximum.
   NOTE: The resistance readings should be smooth and continuous.
2. Check the resistance from terminals 12 to 11, while slowly increasing the vacuum from zero to maximum.
   NOTE: The resistance readings should be smooth and continuous.
3. If the readings are not as specified, the potentiometer must be replaced.

Servo Switch Open or Short Test

1. Check the resistance of the terminals 1 through 12 to ground.
   NOTE: All readings should be open (one megohm or higher).

Test of Servo Switch Warm Operation with No Vacuum

1. Check the continuity from terminal 5 to terminals 1, 2, 3, 4, and 6.
2. Terminals 1 through 4 should show continuity and terminal 6 should read open.

Test for Servo Switch Warm Operation with Increase/Decrease Vacuum

1. Check the continuity from terminal 5 to terminals 1 through 4 while slowly increasing the vacuum.
2. Circuits 5-1, 5-2, 5-3, and 5-4 should each open in sequence.
   NOTE: Circuit 5-4 should open before the crank reaches the midway position.

Test for Servo Switch Cool Operation with No Vacuum

1. Check the continuity from terminal 6 to terminals 1 through 5.
2. All five circuit checks should show open.

Test for Servo Switch Cool Operation with Increase/Decrease Vacuum

1. Check the continuity from terminal 6 to terminals 1 through 4 in sequence while the vacuum is slowly increased.
2. Circuits 6-4, 6-3, 6-2, and 6-1 should close in sequence.
3. Circuit 6-4 should close just after the crank arm reaches the midway position.

Test for Servo Switch Functional Operation at High Vacuum

1. Check that continuity exists between terminals 7 to 8, 7 to 9, and 8 to 9.
2. No continuity should exist between these three terminals and any other terminal.

Operational Test for Servo Switch High Vacuum to Zero Vacuum

NOTE: This test is given in two parts. Part I covers the ACC box with a water control valve solenoid and Part 2 covers the ACC box less a water control valve solenoid.

Part 1

1. Check the continuity from terminals 7 to 8, 7 to 9, and 8 to 9 in sequence as the vacuum is slowly decreased to zero.
2. The continuity between terminals 8 and 9 should be unbroken.
3. The continuity between terminals 7 and 8 should open at about the midway position of the crank arm movement.
4. The continuity between terminals 7 and 9 should open at about the midway position of the crank arm movement.

Part 2

1. Check the continuity as outlined in step 1 of Part 1.
2. The continuity between terminals 7 and 9 should open soon after the crank arm starts to move.
3. The continuity between terminals 7 and 8 should open at about the midway position of the crank arm.

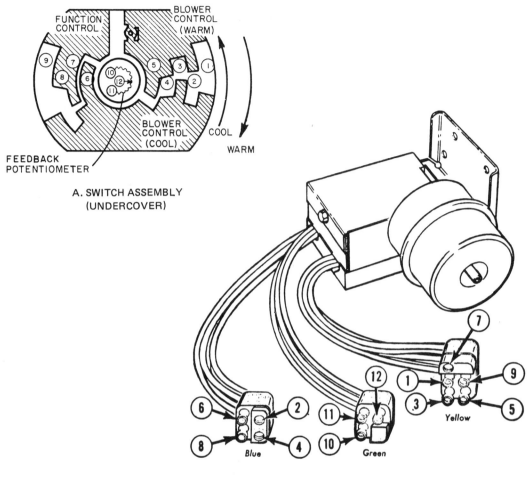

A. SWITCH ASSEMBLY
(UNDERCOVER)

B. POWER SERVO

Fig. SP36-6

TEST E: TEST OF THE TEMPERATURE SENSORS AND CONTROL RHEOSTAT

The resistance of the two sensors and the control assembly rheostat should be tested to insure the proper operation of the devices.

This procedure allows the service technician to test these devices. The automobile and sensors should be at a temperature of 70° to 80°F for accurate test results.

TOOL

Ohmmeter

MATERIAL

As required

PROCEDURE

Test the Sensors and Rheostat

1. Disconnect the battery ground cable.

2. Set the temperature control dial to 75°F.

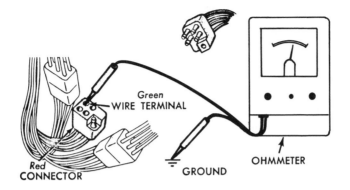

A. TEMPERATURE SENSORS AND CONTROL
RHEOSTAT RESISTANCE TEST

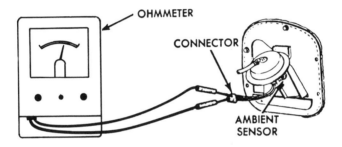

B. AMBIENT SENSOR RESISTANCE TEST

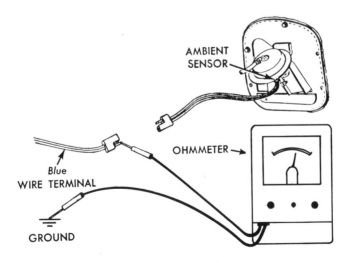

C. IN-CAR SENSOR RESISTANCE TEST

Fig. SP36-7 Testing the Rheostat and the Sensors

3. Disconnect the red wiring connector from the ACC box.

4. Connect an ohmmeter between the green wire of the electrical harness and ground.

5. Observe the resistance.

    NOTE: The resistance should be in the range of 1,200 to 1,300 ohms. If the reading is slightly higher or lower than this range, the individual sensors and the rheostat resistance should be checked.

Test the Rheostat

1. Measure the total resistance with the temperature dial set at 85°F. Note the reading.

2. Measure the total resistance with the temperature dial set at 65°F. Note the reading.

3. A resistance differential of 400 to 500 ohms indicates that the rheostat is good.

4. If the resistance difference is less than 400 ohms, check the rheostat for a loose shaft setscrew. If the screw is loose, tighten it and recheck the rheostat.

5. If the screw is tight and the resistance is less than 400 ohms or more than 500 ohms, the rheostat is defective and must be replaced.

Test the Ambient Sensor

1. Disconnect the connector at the sensor.

2. Connect the ohmmeter across the sensor. Note the reading.

3. The resistance should be about 165 to 185 ohms with an ambient temperature of 70° to 80°F.

4. If the resistance reading is not within the specified range, replace the sensor.

Test the In-Car Sensor

1. Test the rheostat to insure its proper operation.

2. Set the temperature control dial at 65°F.

3. Connect the ohmmeter between ground and the blue wire at the ambient sensor (ambient sensor disconnected).

4. Note the reading on the ohmmeter: the resistance should be 750 to 900 ohms.

5. If the resistance reading is not in this range, replace the sensor.

TEST F: HEATER WATER CONTROL VALVE TEST

Before conducting this test, the water valve solenoid must be checked for proper operation. Refer to Test G, *Water Valve Solenoid Test* for the correct testing procedure.

TOOL

Vacuum gauge

MATERIAL

As required

PROCEDURE

Prepare for the Test

1. Start the engine. Set the temperature control to 85°F.
2. Set the functional lever to LOW. Allow the engine to run until the water is warm.
3. Check the blend door vacuum motor position.

   NOTE: The position should be between mid- and full-vacuum.
4. Check the discharge air from the heater ducts.

   NOTE: The discharge air should be warm. If it is not, check the water control valve.

Test the Water Control Valve

1. Remove the 1/8-in. vacuum line from the valve.
2. Install a vacuum gauge between the line and the water control valve. Note the reading on the vacuum gauge.
3. If there is no vacuum and no heat, the water control valve is defective, or the heater core is restricted.
4. Replace the control valve or clean the heater core as necessary.

TEST G: WATER VALVE SOLENOID TEST

This procedure tests the ability of the solenoid to operate the heater water control valve.

TOOL

Vacuum gauge

MATERIAL

As required

PROCEDURE

1. Apply 12 volts to terminal 15.
2. Connect the vacuum gauge to port W.
3. Listen for a click of the solenoid and note the vacuum reading on the gauge.
4. If no click is heard and/or there is no vacuum reading on the gauge, the ACC box is defective.

REVIEW

Briefly answer each of the following questions.

1. What name does Ford Motor Company give its automatic temperature control system.
2. If the inlet door solenoid is found to be defective during the ACC box test, how is the solenoid repaired?

3. How is the high-range relay test made?

4. In the servo switch potentiometer test, the resistance from terminals 10 to 11 should be 890 ohms ± 10%. In other words, the resistance should be from ___?___ ohms to ___?___ ohms.

5. Does a one-megohm reading on an ohmmeter indicate an open or a short circuit?

SERVICE PROCEDURE 37:
INSTALLING MOUNT AND DRIVE ASSEMBLIES

The mount and drive assembly covered in this procedure is designed for several specific Chrysler automobile models, namely those with a slant six-cylinder engine, with or without power steering.

No attempt should be made to install this mount and drive kit on other automobile models. Each kit is designed for a particular engine. The installation instructions included with each kit must be followed exactly to avoid costly mistakes. Measure all bolts to insure that they are as specified. Check all hoses to insure that they do not rub against moving parts, such as pulleys and the accelerator linkage.

These installation procedures are for a typical mount and drive package.

TOOLS

Complete set of mechanic's hand tools, including pullers, screwdrivers, and hose clamp pliers

MATERIALS

Mount and drive kit, as required   Belts or hoses to replace defective parts
Permatex

PROCEDURE

1. Drain the radiator. Disconnect the water hoses and the transmission fluid cooling lines. Unfasten the radiator mounting screws and carefully remove the radiator from the engine compartment.

2. Remove the engine fan, fan spacer, and water pump pulley. Discard the original fan spacer.

3. Always clean the face of the crankshaft pulley thoroughly before installing the drive pulley. Remove the bolts retaining the crankshaft pulley, and, if the car is equipped with power steering, remove and discard the power steering pulley only. Install the drive pulley, using three 5/16″ x 1″ NC bolts with lockwashers, and one 3/4″ x 2 1/4″ NF bolt with lockwasher.

4. IMPORTANT: *The fuel filter line must be modified on some models to facilitate compressor mount/drive clearance.*

   .a. Unfasten the fuel filter line clamp from the water pump housing.
   b. Remove the original fuel line tubing and the union fitting located between the carburetor and the filter bowl.
   c. Cut the tubing so that the original union fitting can be removed and reinstalled against the flanged end of the 5/16″ x 6 1/2″ copper fuel line.
   d. Fasten the new tubing and union fitting to the carburetor.
   e. Bend the long fuel line, with the filter bowl, up and over the valve cover (as shown on the engine schematic).
   f. Bend the new copper line as required and then insert the tubing into the filter bowl hose.
   g. Use the original clamp and tighten it securely around the tubing.

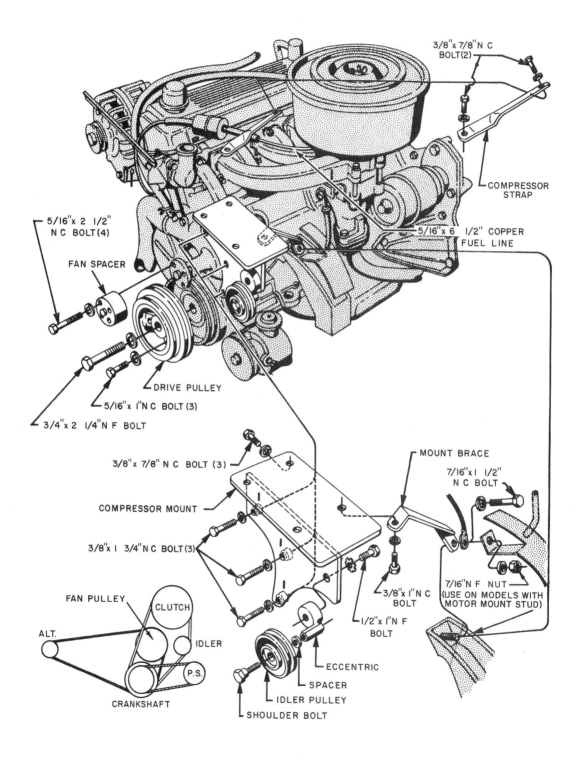

3/8"x 7/8"N C BOLT(2)

COMPRESSOR STRAP

5/16"x 6 1/2" COPPER FUEL LINE

5/16"x 2 1/2" N C BOLT(4)

FAN SPACER

DRIVE PULLEY

5/16"x I"N C BOLT (3)

3/4"x 2 1/4"N F BOLT

3/8"x 7/8" N C BOLT (3)

MOUNT BRACE

7/16"x I 1/2" N C BOLT

COMPRESSOR MOUNT

3/8"x I 3/4"N C BOLT(3)

3/8"x I"N C BOLT

7/16"N F NUT (USE ON MODELS WITH MOTOR MOUNT STUD)

1/2"x I"N F BOLT

FAN PULLEY

CLUTCH

IDLER

ALT.

P.S.

CRANKSHAFT

ECCENTRIC

SPACER

IDLER PULLEY

SHOULDER BOLT

Fig. SP37-1 Typical mount and drive assembly

5. Remove the bolts from the engine as indicated on the schematic. Hold the mount in the approximate position with relation to the engine to identify the exact bolts to be removed.

6. Loosely install the compressor mount on the engine, using three 3/8″ x 1 3/4″ NC bolts with lockwashers. Insert the bolts through the three front vertical mounting holes and welded spacers into the water pump housing.

7. Install the clutch coil and clutch on the compressor. Loosely install the compressor and clutch to the mount, using three 3/8″ x 7/8″ NC bolts with lockwashers. Install the bolts in the compressor through the two forward and one left rear top plate holes.

8. Loosely install the compressor strap and mounting brace.
   a. Compressor Strap: insert a 3/8″ x 7/8″ NC bolt with lockwasher through the flat strap end into the engine head. A second 3/8″ x 7/8″ NC bolt with lockwasher is inserted through the opposite strap end into the compressor side.
   b. Mounting Brace: insert into the engine block a 7/16″ x 1 1/2″ NC bolt with lockwasher through the battery ground wire (power steering models only), the welded ear of the brace, and the motor mount bracket. On Models equipped with a motor mount stud, fasten the brace with a 7/16-in. NF nut and lockwasher. Then insert a 3/8″ x 1″ NC bolt with lockwasher through the upper brace and remaining top plate hole into the compressor.

9. All assembly bolts and/or nuts should be uniformly tightened to prevent strain or misalignment.

10. Install the eccentric and idler assembly to the front vertical, using a 1/2″ x 1″ NF bolt with starwasher.

11. Insert a 1 5/8-in. fan spacer between the original fan and pulley. Install this assembly using four 5/16″ x 2 1/2″ NC bolts. Tighten the bolts securely.

12. Thread all drive belts as shown on the schematic. Adjust and tighten each belt as required to obtain the proper belt tension.

13. Replace the radiator, connect the water hoses, and connect the transmission fluid cooling lines. Add coolant.

    NOTE: Both the mount and the drive pulley must be furnished by the same company to guarantee alignment.

REVIEW

Briefly answer each of the following questions.

1. List three precautions to be observed when installing a mount and drive assembly.

2. Are mount and drive assemblies interchangeable?

3. Why is it necessary to remove the radiator?

4. Why is it stated that the drive pulley and compressor mount must be furnished by the same company?

5. What can happen if the idler pulley is not in line with the compressor clutch and the drive pulley?

6. What is the purpose of the fan spacer?

7. Explain the answer given for question 2.

8. How is the compressor driven from the engine?

SERVICE PROCEDURE 38:
INSTALLING THE EVAPORATOR ASSEMBLY, CONDENSER, HOSES, AND HARDWARE

After the mount and drive assembly is installed according to Service Procedure 37, the other components of the air conditioner can be installed. The components may be installed in any order — as long as the receiver/drier is installed last (to prevent the possibility of excess moisture and foreign matter from entering the system as other components are installed.)

Custom air-conditioner units are available for most year/model automobiles. Each type of unit requires a different installation procedure. For example, the installation of some units requires that parts of the fresh air or heater system ducts be removed so that the air-conditioning ducts can be connected into the system. For other units, the radio, lighter, and even the glove box are relocated to permit the installation.

Although this procedure is not intended for a particular installation, it can serve as a guide to the DOs and DON'Ts of installing an aftermarket air conditioner.

TOOLS

Complete set of mechanic's hand tools
Electric drill with drill set

Hole saw, 2 in.

MATERIALS

Automotive air conditioner
Installation package

Clean refrigeration oil

PROCEDURE

Preparation

1. Carefully unpack the air conditioner and the installation package. Check the contents against the packing slip to insure that the following major parts are included:

   - Compressor
   - Condenser
   - Receiver/drier

   - Thermostatic expansion valve
   - Liquid line hose (drier to evaporator)
   - Suction line hose (evaporator to compressor)

   - Clutch coil or brush set
   - Clutch rotor assembly
   - Evaporator case with blower assembly
   - Hardware package
   - Discharge line hose (compressor to condenser)
   - High-pressure liquid line (condenser to drier)

3. Lay out all of the parts on a workbench and check for damage.

4. Read the installation information provided with the unit.

Mount the Evaporator

1. Remove those parts designated for the evaporator installation in the installation sheet provided with the unit.

2. Hold the evaporator in position and note the location of all of the mounting hardware.

3. After insuring that there are no electrical wires, cables, or other hoses on the reverse side of the panel where the evaporator installation is to be made, drill the holes for the mounting hardware.

4. Note where the hoses are to pass through the firewall and the floorboard (for the condensate hose).

5. Again, after insuring that there are no electrical wires, cables, brake or gas lines behind the panels:
   a. Drill a 2-in. hole through the firewall for the refrigeration hoses.
   b. Drill a 1/2-in. hole through the floorboard for the condensate hose.

   NOTE: There may be two condensate hoses. As a result, two holes must be drilled. Take care not to drill into the transmission housing.

6. Install the suction hose to the evaporator outlet fitting as follows:
   a. If flare-type fittings are used on the suction hose, use refrigeration oil on the fittings. Using two wrenches, install and tighten the hose. Caution: do not overtighten the fittings.
   b. If the suction hose has a barb-type fitting, use refrigeration oil on the fittings. Then place a clamp over the hose and push the hose into the fitting. Tighten the clamp, but take care not to overtighten the clamp on the hose.

7. With the expansion valve secured to the evaporator core, install the liquid line to the TXV inlet, according to the procedures outlined in step 6.

8. Slide the condensate hose(s) to the provisions of the evaporator case.

9. Pass the hose(s) through the firewall hole drilled previously. The hose(s) must not interfere with cables, electrical wiring, or any mechanical linkages under the dash. Reroute the hoses if necessary to avoid any interference.

10. Place the evaporator assembly into position and secure it to the hardware (steps 2 and 3).

11. Pass the condensate hose(s) through the floorboard hole(s) drilled previously.

Mount the Condenser

1. Remove those parts designated for the condenser assembly in the installation sheet provided with the unit.

2. Position the condenser and note the location of the mounting hardware.

3. After insuring that there is no interference with the hood latch cables, headlamp linkage or vacuum lines (if the car is so equipped), battery box, battery, radiator, or electrical wires, drill the holes for the condenser mounting hardware.

4. Install the hot gas discharge hose to the top fitting of the condenser as follows:

   a. If the hose has a flare-type fitting, use refrigeration oil on the fittings. Using two wrenches, install and tighten the hose. Do not overtighten the hose fitting.

   b. If the hose has a barb-type fitting, use refrigeration oil on the fitting, place a clamp over the hose, and push the hose on the fitting. Tighten the clamp, but do not overtighten it on the hose.

5. Install the high-pressure hose to the bottom fitting of the condenser using the procedure outlined in step 4.

6. If necessary, drill a 2-in. diameter hole so that the hoses can be passed through the panel to the engine side of the radiator. There must be no obstructions on the other side of the panel. In many cases, holes or slots are provided and drilling is not necessary.

7. Pass both hoses through the panel. The hoses must not interfere with any of the components given in step 3. Reroute the hoses if necessary.

8. Secure the condenser to the mounting hardware installed in steps 2 and 3. The condenser must be at least one inch in front of the radiator.

Mount the Compressor

1. Mount the compressor to the mount assembly (installed in Service Procedure 37.)

2. Locate and secure the compressor mounting braces as required (see the illustration in Service Procedure 37).

3. Insure that all bolts are installed in the compressor to hold it securely to the engine. Do not cross thread any of the bolts. Tighten the bolts securely, but do not overtighten them.

4. Install the clutch coil or brush set on the compressor.

5. Install the clutch rotor (pulley) assembly on the crankshaft. Use only the Nyloc capscrew provided.

6. Spin the rotor to insure that it rotates freely. If a scraping or grinding noise is noted, remove the rotor to determine the problem. Correct and reinstall the rotor.

7. Check the alignment of the clutch rotor with the crankshaft drive pulley.

8. If the rotor is not aligned, check that the compressor and compressor mount are installed properly. Correct the mountings as necessary.

9. Install and tighten the drive belt, but do not overtighten the belt.

10. Check for belt alignment. If the belt is not aligned properly, the belt cannot stay on the pulley during operation. Correct the belt alignment as necessary.

Mount the Receiver/Drier

1. Check the length of the liquid line and high-pressure hoses to determine the approximate location of the receiver/drier.

2. After determining the location, drill holes for the receiver/drier mounting hardware. Do not drill into the receiver tank. Also, insure that the other side of the panel is unobstructed before drilling the holes.

3. Mount the drier with its hardware. Do not remove the protective covers from the drier at this time. The drier should be mounted in a position that is as close to vertical as possible.

Connect the Hoses Into the System

1. Remove the protective covers from the suction line and the inlet service valve of the compressor.

2. Using refrigeration oil on the hose fitting, connect the hoses as follows:

   a. If the hose has a flare-type fitting, use two wrenches to tighten it. Do not overtighten the fitting.

   b. If the hose has a barb-type fitting, slip the clamp over the hose and slide the hose on the fitting. Tighten the clamp, but be careful not to overtighten it.

3. Repeat steps 1 and 2 with the hot gas discharge hose (compressor to condenser).

4. Repeat steps 1 and 2 with both hoses to the receiver/drier. See notes A and B.

   Note A: Determine the direction of flow through the receiver/drier. The flow direction is generally indicated by an arrow or the word IN. The flow is toward the TXV. Do not reverse the receiver/drier.

   Note B: Work quickly. Do not allow foreign matter or airborne moisture to enter the system.

Leak Test the System

1. Follow Service Procedure 4 or 5 and leak test the system.

2. If a leak is found in one of the hose connections, retighten the connection. See step 3 following.

3. Do not overtighten the hose connection. If the leak persists, follow either step 3a or step 3b.

   a. If the hose has a flare-type fitting, remove the hose and check for a defective flare or foreign matter in the fitting. Use more refrigeration oil on the fitting. Reinstall the fitting and tighten it.

   b. If the hose is a barb-type fitting, remove the hose and cut off about an inch. Use refrigeration oil on the fitting and reinstall it. Tighten the clamp around the hose.

Evacuate the System

1. Evacuate the system according to the procedures outlined in Service Procedure 6.

2. The system can be evacuated while the electrical connections are being made.

Electrical Connections

1. Locate the accessory (ACC) terminal (either on the fuse block or in back of the ignition switch).

2. Connect a No. 10 or No. 12 wire to the accessory terminal and evaporator master switch control. Check that the circuit is protected by a fuse or circuit breaker.

3. Connect the clutch lead wire from the evaporator thermostat to the clutch coil or brush set. Make sure that the wire does not touch the manifold or any mechanical linkages. Reroute the wire if necessary.

4. For a separate assembly, connect the blower motor lead wire(s) to the evaporator blower control.

Cleanup

1. Replace the protective covers, floor mat, or any other panels removed for the installation.

2. Using tie-down clamps, secure the hoses to prevent them from interfering with:
   - any moving parts, such as cables and linkages,
   - the battery and battery box (battery fumes are harmful to the inner braid of refrigeration hoses),
   - any heat-laden components, such as the engine and manifold.

Charge the System

1. Remove the vacuum pump as outlined in Service Procedure 6.

2. Charge the system as outlined in Service Procedure 7, 8, or 9.

3. The system is now ready for use.

REVIEW

Select the appropriate answer from the choices given.

1. The receiver/drier is connected into the system
   a. first.
   b. last.
   c. at any time.
   d. before the condenser.

2. The hot gas discharge hose is connected between the
   a. compressor and the condenser.
   b. evaporator and the compressor.
   c. condenser and the receiver/drier.
   d. receiver/drier and the evaporator (TXV).

3. The drive belt can jump off the pulleys
   a. because of high head pressure.
   b. if it is improperly aligned.
   c. if it is too short.
   d. if it is broken.

4. The minimum clearance between the radiator and condenser is
   a. one inch.
   b. one and a half inches.
   c. two inches.
   d. two and a half inches.

5. The clutch lead wire is connected from the clutch coil or brush set to the
   a. master control.
   b. fan control.
   c. accessory (ACC) terminal.
   d. thermostat.

SERVICE PROCEDURE 39:
REBUILDING THE YORK COMPRESSOR, ALL MODELS

This procedure can be followed when it is necessary to completely tear down a York compressor for repair. Some compressor models will vary slightly from this procedure.

All York compressors are similar in appearance. However, the year and model of the compressor must be identified when it is necessary to replace parts. Refer to the appropriate manufacturer's instruction manuals and service data.

The procedure for rebuilding the York compressor is given in five parts:

- Shaft seal assembly servicing
- Head and valve plate servicing
- Servicing pistons and connecting rods
- Servicing crankshaft and main bearings
- Oil pump assembly

TOOLS

One set of 1/4-in. drive sockets, to 9/16 in.　　Single-edge razor blades
Hard rubber hammer　　Piston ring compressor
Small screwdriver　　Allen wrench set
Needle nose pliers　　Torque wrench (ft.-lb. and in.-lb.)
Snap ring pliers

MATERIALS

Ample supply of clean refrigeration oil
Gasket set
Seal assembly
As necessary, replacements for defective parts

OIL CHARGE

Positions		Oil Level					
(See Note)		Minimum		Normal Running		Initial Charge	
Mounts	Range	Dip Stick Depth	Fractional Pints	Dip Stick Depth	Fractional Pints	Dip Stick Depth	Fractional Pints
Vertical	90°-70°	7/8"	3/8 Pt.	1 1/4"	1/2 Pt.	1-3/8"	5/8 Pt.
Inclined	50°-15°	1-5/8"	1/3 Pt.	2"	3/8 Pt.	2-3/4"	5/8 Pt.
Horizontal	10°-0°	3/4"	1/4 Pt.	7/8"	1/4 Pt.	1-5/8"	5/8 Pt.

Oil Type: Suniso #5, Texaco Capella E, or equivalent.

NOTE: The compressor can be inclined to any angle between vertical and 90 degrees either right or left. Oil level — minimum and maximum.

Fig. SP39-1

*The text and diagrams in part, are reprinted with permission from the York Corporation.

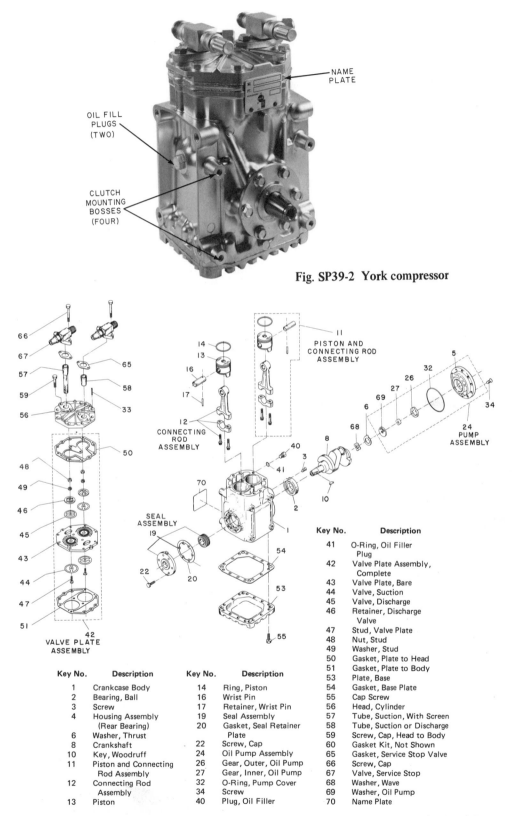

Fig. SP39-2 York compressor

Fig. SP39-3 Exploded view of typical York compressors, models A206, A209, and A210

Key No.	Description
1	Crankcase Body
2	Bearing, Ball
3	Screw
4	Housing Assembly (Rear Bearing)
6	Washer, Thrust
8	Crankshaft
10	Key, Woodruff
11	Piston and Connecting Rod Assembly
12	Connecting Rod Assembly
13	Piston

Key No.	Description
14	Ring, Piston
16	Wrist Pin
17	Retainer, Wrist Pin
19	Seal Assembly
20	Gasket, Seal Retainer Plate
22	Screw, Cap
24	Oil Pump Assembly
26	Gear, Outer, Oil Pump
27	Gear, Inner, Oil Pump
32	O-Ring, Pump Cover
34	Screw
40	Plug, Oil Filler

Key No.	Description
41	O-Ring, Oil Filler Plug
42	Valve Plate Assembly, Complete
43	Valve Plate, Bare
44	Valve, Suction
45	Valve, Discharge
46	Retainer, Discharge Valve
47	Stud, Valve Plate
48	Nut, Stud
49	Washer, Stud
50	Gasket, Plate to Head
51	Gasket, Plate to Body
53	Plate, Base
54	Gasket, Base Plate
55	Cap Screw
56	Head, Cylinder
57	Tube, Suction, With Screen
58	Tube, Suction or Discharge
59	Screw, Cap, Head to Body
60	Gasket Kit, Not Shown
65	Gasket, Service Stop Valve
66	Screw, Cap
67	Valve, Service Stop
68	Washer, Wave
69	Washer, Oil Pump
70	Name Plate

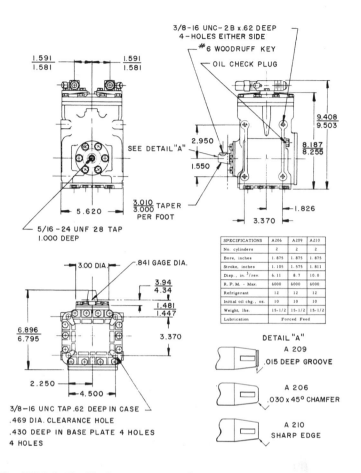

SPECIFICATIONS	A206	A209	A210
No. cylinders	2	2	2
Bore, inches	1.875	1.875	1.875
Stroke, inches	1.105	1.575	1.811
Disp., in.^{3}/rev.	6.11	8.7	10.0
R.P.M. - Max.	6000	6000	6000
Refrigerant	12	12	12
Initial oil chg., oz.	10	10	10
Weight, lbs.	15-1/2	15-1/2	15-1/2
Lubrication	Forced Feed		

Fig. SP39-4 The York compressor: dimensions and specifications

SHAFT SEAL ASSEMBLY SERVICING PROCEDURE

NOTE: A seal assembly kit is required. This kit includes the front seal plate, seal nose, spring assembly, and the gasket 0-ring for the front seal plate.

1. Remove the clutch and Woodruff key from the compressor crankshaft. Use a 5/8-in. NC bolt to remove the clutch to avoid damage.

2. Remove the clutch coil if it is seal mounted. If the clutch coil is boss mounted, it is not necessary to remove the seal for servicing.

3. Remove the seal plate capscrews and gently pry the seal plate loose. Take care not to scratch the flat sealing surfaces or the polished shaft surfaces.

4. Remove the shaft seal from the shaft by prying behind the drive ring. The drive ring is the portion of the seal assembly farthest back on the shaft. Take care not to scratch the crankshaft.

5. Clean all parts and surfaces of all foreign material and of gasket or 0-ring material.

6. Place the new seal assembly and gaskets in clean refrigeration oil.

7. Inspect all mounting surfaces for nicks and burrs. Coat all surfaces with clean refrigeration oil.

8. Place the seal plate gasket(s) or 0-ring in position on the seal housing face (it is necessary to insert the 0-ring into the compressor crankcase).

9. Push the seal assembly, less the carbon ring if it is free, over the end of the crankshaft with the carbon ring retainer facing out. Now place the carbon ring into the seal assembly with the polished surface facing out. The indentations in the outside edge of the carbon ring must engage the tangs in the retainer. Install the seal plate.

10. Insert the capscrews and tighten them until they are fingertight. There must be equal clearance between the crankshaft and the seal plate.

11. Tighten all of the capscrews in sequence so that the capscrews diagonally opposite from each other are evenly drawn to a torque of 13-17 ft.-lb.

HEAD AND VALVE PLATE SERVICING PROCEDURE

NOTE: A valve plate kit is required. This kit includes the valve plate, discharge valves, suction valves, valve retainer parts, valve plate and cylinder head gasket, and service valve gaskets.

1. Remove the capscrews from the flange-type service valves. Note that these four capscrews are longer than the remaining head capscrews. If the valves are of the Rotolock type, remove the screws by loosening the hex nuts which are a part of the Rotolock valve assembly.

2. Remove the remaining capscrews and washers in the head. Then remove the valve plate and head from the cylinder by prying or tapping under the ears which extend from the valve port. Since the head is made of aluminum, care must be taken not to damage it.

3. Remove all foreign material and gaskets from the head and compressor crankcase. Do not mar or scratch any of the mating surfaces.

4. Do not disassemble the valves. The reed valves and valve plate are an assembly and are not serviced separately.

5. Apply a thin coat of refrigeration oil to all gaskets and surfaces.

6. Place a valve plate gasket over the compressor crankcase so that the dowel pins go through the dowel pin holes in the gasket.

7. Place the valve plate assembly in position over the gasket. Check that the discharge valves face up to avoid piston damage (the smaller of the two reed valves is the discharge valve). Position the assembly over the dowel pins.

8. Place the head gasket over the valve plate so that the dowel pins pass through the holes provided in the gasket.

9. Place the head on the cylinder head gasket so the dowel pins line up with the holes in the head.

10. Insert all capscrews through the head, valve plate, and gaskets. Tighten the capscrews fingertight.

11. Insert the discharge tube and the suction screen through the head and push them into place.

12. Lay the service valve gaskets in place and install the service valves on the proper side. Insert the capscrews to hold the service valves in place. Tighten the capscrews fingertight.

13. Tighten the head and service valve capscrews to a torque of 14 to 18 ft.-lb.

14. Tighten the inside service valve capscrews first. Then tighten the outside service valve capscrews. Tighten the remaining head capscrews in a sequence so that the capscrews diagonally opposite each other are evenly drawn to the specified torque. Retorque the capscrews after two hours.

PROCEDURE FOR SERVICING PISTONS AND CONNECTING RODS

The following parts are required for this procedure:

Piston and connecting rod assembly, including the rod, cap, screws, piston, piston rings, piston pins, pin retainers, gasket kit and oil charge.

1. Remove the head and valve plate assembly according to the procedure given on page 297 (steps 1 and 2).

2. Drain the oil and remove the baseplate.

3. Remove the damaged piston assembly by removing the capscrews holding the rod cap in place.

4. If the connecting rod(s) are to be reused, match and mark the rod, cap, and crankshaft throw. Marking these parts before the connecting rod bolts are removed insures that the parts can be reinstalled properly.

5. Clean all gasket material and foreign material from the crankcase, baseplate, valve plate, and head.

6. Insert the new piston(s) assembly through the top of the compressor.
   NOTE: The wrist pin roll pin must be positioned toward the center of the compressor. If the roll pin is positioned toward the outside of the compressor, it can contact the crankshaft when the piston is at the bottom of its stroke.

7. Install the connecting rod caps. Install the connecting rod cap bolts and torque them to 90 to 100 in.-lb.

8. Replace the bottom plate and gasket. Replace the capscrews and tighten them until they are fingertight. Then continue tightening the capscrews in a sequence such that capscrews diagonally opposite each other are evenly drawn to a torque of 11 to 14 ft.-lb.

9. Replace the valve plate and head assembly. Follow the procedure as outlined in the section *Head and Valve Plate Servicing*, steps 5 through 14, page 297.

10. Replace oil as necessary to bring it to the proper level.

PROCEDURE FOR SERVICING THE CRANKSHAFT AND MAIN BEARINGS

The following parts are required for this procedure:

Crankshaft and/or main bearing or rear bearing, as required.
Gasket kit and oil charge
Seal assembly kit

The rear main bearing is a bronze-sleeve bearing with a steel outer shell. This bearing is a press fit in the bearing cavity in the rear bearing cover plate. The rear bearing and the cover plate are replaced as an assembly.

The seal end main bearing is a ball-type bearing. It is mounted in the bearing recess machined in the inside wall of the crankcase. The bearing is a shrink fit; that is, it is inserted in the recess after the crankcase is heated in an oven at 150° to 300°F.

The inner race of the bearing is a press fit on the crankshaft.

When replacing the crankshaft, the seal end main bearing should also be replaced because the existing bearing may be damaged in dismantling the assembly.

1. Remove the crankcase base and drain the oil.

2. Mark the rod caps, rods, and crankshaft throw to insure proper reinstallation. Remove the rod caps.

3. Remove the compressor shaft seal and the rear bearing housing.

4. Remove the head and valve plate assembly. Remove the piston and rod assemblies.

5. Use a clean solvent and wash the crankcase to remove all foreign matter. Blow dry.

6. Heat the *complete* crankshaft-crankcase assembly in an oven to 300°F. Avoid localized heating since this can crack the assembly.

7. At 300°F, the crankshaft and ball bearing assembly can be removed from the crankcase with little applied pressure.

8. If the crankshaft is to be reused, remove the bearing.

9. Press the new bearing on the crankshaft by exerting pressure on the inner race only.

10. Again heat the crankcase to 300°F in an oven. Slide the crankshaft and bearing assembly into place. Using the opening in the bottom of the crankcase as a point of entry, place the bearing in the recess. If necessary, apply force to the outer race to be sure that it is seated in the bottom of the recess.

    NOTE: On one side of the bearing, the faces of the inner and outer races are flush. On the other side, the face of the inner race is recessed since the races are not of the same width. Figure SP39-5 shows the proper positioning of the races in the crankcase. Allow the crankcase to cool and insert the crankshaft through the rear bearing cover plate opening. Guide the flywheel end through the inner race of the ball bearing.

11. Position the crankcase so that it is completely supported on the inner race of the bearing. Press the shaft into place until the cheek of the shaft contacts the inner bearing race.

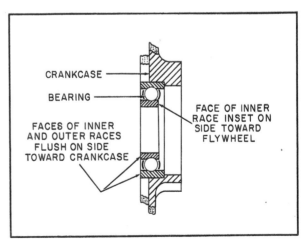

Fig. 39-5 Position of races

12. Replace the rear bearing 0-ring and assembly. Torque the mounting screws to 7-10 ft.-lb.

13. Replace the pistons in the proper position and replace the rod caps. Torque the hardware to 90-100 in.-lb.

14. Replace the seal, baseplate, valve plate, and head assembly as outlined previously.

OIL PUMP ASSEMBLY

The part required for this procedure is the oil pump assembly including the housing, gears, spacers, washers, and 0-ring.

1. Place the compressor so that it is resting on the baseplate and the front of the crankshaft. Insert the wave washer in the crankshaft cavity and then place the thrust washer on top of the wave washer. The tang of the thrust washer must be in the drive slot of the crankshaft.

2. Place the oil pump washer in the cavity with the kidney-shaped slot toward the top head of the compressor and the half-circle slot offcenter toward the left side.

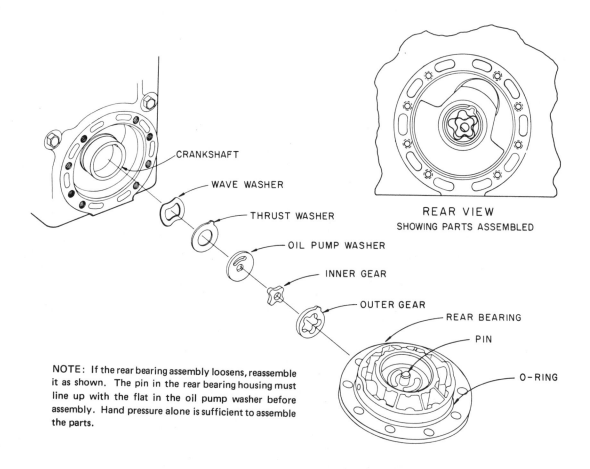

CRANKSHAFT

WAVE WASHER

THRUST WASHER

OIL PUMP WASHER

INNER GEAR

OUTER GEAR

REAR BEARING

PIN

O-RING

REAR VIEW
SHOWING PARTS ASSEMBLED

NOTE: If the rear bearing assembly loosens, reassemble it as shown. The pin in the rear bearing housing must line up with the flat in the oil pump washer before assembly. Hand pressure alone is sufficient to assemble the parts.

Fig. SP39-6 Oil pump assembly

3. Place the outer gear in the cavity with the tang of this gear in the drive slot of the crankshaft. Then place the inner gear within the outer gear. Position the inner gear so that the hole through the gear is aligned with the half circle of the oil pump washer.

4. Insert the rear bearing housing with the pin in the housing aligned with the hole in the inner gear.

5. With the bearing housing partially inserted in the compressor, rotate the housing slightly to the right and left until the parts slide into position.

6. Insert the rear bearing housing completely and rotate it slowly to the proper position. Take care not to damage the 0-ring.

7. Insert the screws and tighten them to a torque of 7-10 ft.-lb.

REVIEW

Briefly answer each of the following questions.

1. How is the rear bearing replaced?

2. How is the shrink fit front bearing removed from the crankcase?

3. Name five parts of the oil pump.

4. What parts must be removed to replace a piston assembly?

5. What parts must be removed to replace the oil pump?

SERVICE PROCEDURE 40:
REBUILDING TECUMSEH COMPRESSORS, MODELS HA-850 AND HA-1000*

This procedure can be used to tear down a Tecumseh compressor for overhaul. To aid the service technician, the procedure is given in eight parts:

- Valve Plate Replacement
- Seal Assembly Replacement
- Rear Bearing Installation
- Front Bearing Installation
- Crankshaft Installation
- Connecting Rod Installation
- Piston Assembly Installation
- Oil Pump Installation

TOOLS

Set of 1/4-in. drive sockets, to 9/16 in.
Hard rubber hammer
Small screwdriver
Needle nose pliers
Snap ring pliers

Single-edge razor blades
Piston ring compressor
Torque wrench
Allen wrench set

MATERIALS

Ample supply of refrigeration oil
Gasket set

Seal set
Any parts determined to be defective

VALVE PLATE REPLACEMENT PROCEDURE

This procedure requires a valve plate kit which includes the valve plate, discharge valves, suction valves, valve retainer parts, valve plate gasket, cylinder head gasket, and suction screen.

1. Isolate the compressor from the system.
2. Remove all bolts from the cylinder head.
3. Remove the valve plate and the cylinder head assembly from the crankcase by tapping against the side of the valve plate. Do not tap the cylinder head or crankcase body since these parts can be damaged.
4. Remove the valve plate from the cylinder head by holding the cylinder head and tapping against the side of the valve plate.
5. Remove all gasket material, dirt, and other foreign material from the surface of the cylinder head and cylinder face. Take care not to scratch or nick the mating surfaces.
6. Insert all of the mounting bolts through the cylinder head, except those for the service valves. Dip the new cylinder head gasket into clean refrigeration oil and locate it in the proper position over the mounting bolts. Locate the new valve plate assembly over the mounting bolts. Dip the valve plate gasket into clean refrigeration oil and locate it in the proper position over the mounting bolts.

*Text and diagrams used with the permission of Tecumseh Products Company.

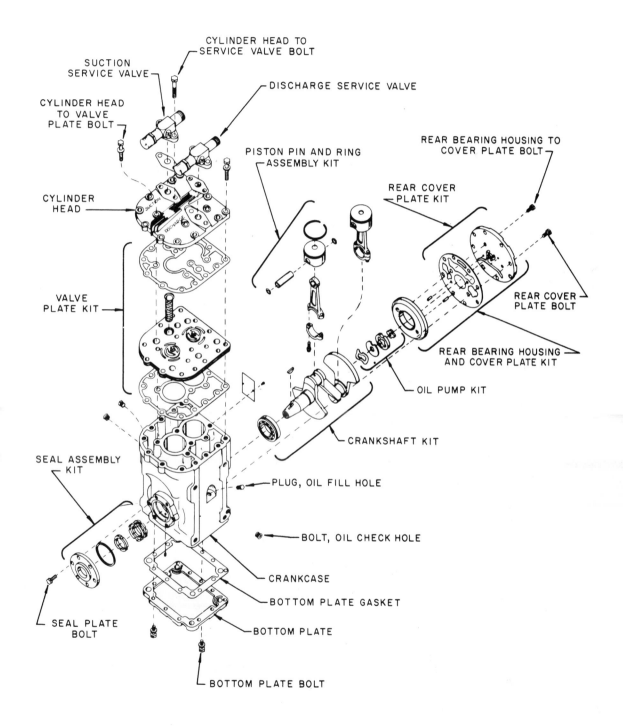

Fig. SP40-1 Exploded view of the Tecumseh compressor

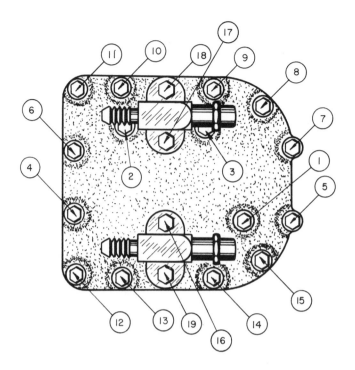

Fig. SP40-2 Tightening sequence of head bolts

7. After dipping the gaskets in refrigeration oil and assembling the plate as noted in step 6, locate the assembly on the cylinder face in the proper position. Tighten the bolts in sequence, as shown in figure SP40-2, to a torque of 15-19 ft.-lb. Retorque the bolts after a minimum elapsed period of two hours.

8. Insert the bolts through the mounting holes of the service valves. Dip the new service valve gaskets in refrigeration oil and immediately insert the valve mounting bolts through them. Locate the valves in the proper position on the cylinder head. Tighten the bolts in the sequence shown. Torque the bolts to 15-19 ft.-lb. for hex head bolts and 10-12 ft.-lb. for 12-point and Allen head bolts.

9. Two hours after the valve plate and service valves are assembled, retorque the bolts of these parts in the sequence shown to the limits specified.

SEAL ASSEMBLY REPLACEMENT PROCEDURE

A seal assembly kit is required for this procedure. This kit includes the front seal plate, seal nose and spring assembly, and the 0-ring for the front seal plate.

1. Isolate the compressor from the system.

2. Wash and clean the seal plate and the adjoining surfaces to remove dirt and foreign matter.

3. Remove the seal plate nose assembly by removing the six bolts in the plate. Gently pry the plate loose. Take care not to scratch the crankcase mating surfaces.

4. Remove the carbon nose and spring assembly from the shaft by prying behind the drive ring. The drive ring is that portion of the seal assembly farthest away

on the shaft. When prying the seal assembly from the shaft, do not scratch the crankshaft. If the rubber seal around the shaft does not come out with the carbon nose and spring assembly, remove it with long nose pliers on the edge of the grommet.

5. Remove all gasket material, dirt, and other foreign matter from the crankcase mating surfaces, the exposed crankshaft, and adjacent surfaces.

6. Remove the new shaft seal washer in the bellows seal assembly. Coat the exposed surface of the crankshaft with clean refrigeration oil. Dip the new bellows seal assembly and shaft seal washer in clean refrigeration oil. Place the bellows seal assembly over the shaft. The end which holds the shaft seal washer is to go on last. Using the hand, push the bellows seal assembly on the crankshaft to a position beyond the taper of the shaft.

7. Assemble the shaft seal washer in the bellows seal assembly. Check to insure that the bellows seal assembly and shaft are free from dirt and foreign material. Assemble the seal washer so that the raised rim is away from the bellows seal assembly. The notches in the washer are to line up with the nibs in the bellows seal assembly. Cover the exposed surface of the shaft seal washer with clean refrigeration oil.

8. Insert the new O-ring in the crankcase mating surface for the seal plate.

9. Place the new front seal plate over the shaft. Line up the mounting holes. Place the hands on each side of the front seal plate and push it against the crankcase. Insert the six capscrews and tighten them evenly. Tighten the capscrews in a circular sequence at 9-12 ft.-lb.

PROCEDURE FOR THE REAR BEARING INSTALLATION

This procedure requires the rear bearing housing and cover plate kit, an oil charge, and a gasket kit.

1. Isolate the compressor and remove it from the system.

2. Place the compressor in an upside-down position. Remove all dirt, grease, oil, and other foreign matter from the bottom plate, rear cover plate, and the surfaces next to these plates.

3. Remove the bottom baseplate by removing the twelve bolts in the base and gently tapping the side of the base. When removing the bolts, note the type of bolts removed from the various locations. The bolts must be reassembled in the same manner. Do not scratch, mar, or nick the mating surfaces.

4. Remove the rear bearing cover plate and the bearing assembly by removing all of the capscrews in the plate. Insert the edge of a thin screwdriver between the plate and the compressor crankcase. Remove the plate by prying up evenly on all edges. When removing the screws, note the type and location of each screw. All of the screws must be replaced in the same location.

5. Remove any gasket material from the bottom baseplate, the crankcase, the bottom surface, and the crankcase surface mating with the rear seal plate. Do not scratch the surfaces.

6. Flush the inner exposed parts of the compressor with solvent. Drain thoroughly.

7. Soak the new cover plate gasket in clean refrigeration oil from one to two hours. Position the oil-soaked gasket over the dowel pins in the new cover plate. Take care to align all of the holes properly. Insert the 1/4-in. diameter by 3/8 in. long capscrew through the cover plate to the housing. Tighten the screw fingertight.

8. Check to see that the oil pump parts (spring, washer, and rotor) are properly located in the crankshaft end.

9. Locate the rear bearing housing and the cover plate assembly in the proper position over the crankshaft. The oil pump shaft must be inserted in the oil pump rotor and all mounting holes must line up.

10. Insert the eight capscrews in the rear cover plate. Use new copper washers over the screws in any holes that are not blind. Tighten all of the screws in the cover plate, in the sequence shown in figure SP40-3. Tighten the screws to a torque of 12-14 ft.-lb., except for the two center bolts which should be 10-12 ft.-lb.

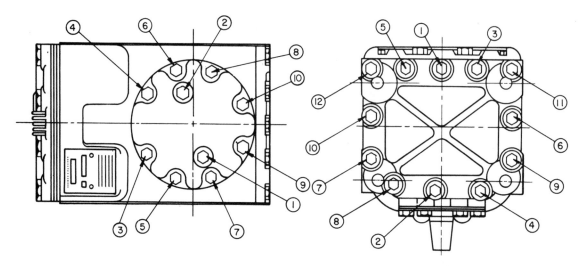

Fig. SP40-3 Rear and base tightening sequence

11. Soak the new bottom plate gasket in clean refrigeration oil for one to two hours.

12. Locate and place the bottom baseplate in the correct position on the bottom plate gasket.

13. Insert the twelve 1/4" x 11/16" bolts with washers in the bottom baseplate mounting holes. Use three new copper washers on the bolts adjacent to the rear bearing (when using kit K669-1); use one copper washer on the bolt in the center hole adjacent to the rear bearing (when using kit K669-2 or K669-3). Use steel washers on all of the remaining hex head base mounting bolts. Tighten the bolts in the sequence shown to 12-14 ft.-lb. (hex head bolts) and 9-11 ft.-lb. (button head bolts). Retorque the bolts after two hours.

14. With the compressor in the upright position, remove one of the oil fill plugs. Charge the compressor with the quality and quantity of oil specified.

PROCEDURE FOR THE FRONT BEARING INSTALLATION

The parts required for this procedure are as follows:

Front bearing (number 26546)   Gasket kit
Rear cover plate   Oil charge, as specified
Seal kit

1. Perform the *Seal Assembly Replacement Procedure*, steps 1 through 5, page 304.

2. Perform the *Rear Bearing Installation Procedure*, steps 2 through 6, page 305. Follow this with the *Valve Plate Replacement Procedure*, steps 2 through 5, page 302.

3. Remove the two caps from the connecting rods by removing the four screws that hold the caps. Mark the caps in some manner so that they can be reassembled on the same rod and in the same position as they were originally. A dot is cast on one side of each rod and cap for easy identification and to permit the correct mating of the parts. The parts should be reassembled so that the dots are on the same side.

4. With the connecting rod caps removed, push the connecting rod, piston pin, and ring assembly up and out of the crankcase.

5. Remove the front bearing retrainer setscrew by inserting a setscrew wrench for a No. 6-32 screw in the 1/4-in. untapped hole in the base on the side adjacent to the front bearing.

6. Support the crankshaft rear bearing end and gently tap the front bearing end of the crankshaft toward the compressor until the front bearing moves out of the crankcase housing.

7. Remove the crankshaft from the crankcase through the opening for the rear bearing.

8. Remove the front bearing from the crankshaft with the aid of the bearing puller. Clean the crankshaft of all oil, grease, dirt, and other foreign material.

9. Install the new front bearing by first placing the bearing in the crankcase. Insert the end nearest the retainer groove in the outer race first. Support the front end of the crankcase against a flat, smooth surface and press the bearing into the crankcase. Press on the bearing perpendicular to the crankshaft centerline and against the outer race. Position the bearing against the crankcase shoulder.

10. Insert the crankshaft into the front bearing as assembled into the crankcase.

11. Remove the dowel pins from the rear bearing housing and place the housing over the rear crankshaft journal. The side of the bearing plate which has holes for the dowel pins is placed next to the crankshaft counterweight. Using the rear bearing housing as a guide to align the crankshaft, press the crankshaft into the front bearing. Press on the rear end of the crankcase while supporting the inner race until the bearing inner race seats against the shoulder of the housing.

12. Insert the retainer setscrews to secure the front bearing (removed in step 5). Tighten the setscrews with a setscrew wrench.

13. Install the connecting rod, piston, and ring assembly according to the *Connecting Rod Installation Procedure* (step 8 and steps 12 through 18).

14. Remove the rear bearing housing used to align the crankshaft and proceed with the *Rear Bearing Installation Procedure*, steps 7 through 14, page 305.

15. Install the new seal assembly according to the *Seal Assembly Replacement Procedure*, steps 5 through 9, page 304.

CRANKSHAFT INSTALLATION PROCEDURE

The parts required for this procedure are as follows:

Crankshaft kit   Gasket kit
Rear cover plate kit   Seal kit

1. Perform the procedure given for the *Front Bearing Installation*, but omit step 9, page 307.

2. Use the new front bearing and the crankshaft included in the kits.

CONNECTING ROD INSTALLATION PROCEDURE

The parts required for this procedure are as follows:

Connecting rod and cap assembly   Oil charge
Gasket kit

1. Perform the *Rear Bearing Installation Procedure*, steps 1 through 4, page 305.

2. Remove the two screws holding the connecting rod cap and remove it from the connecting rod.

3. Position the compressor on the crankcase base after first draining the oil from the compressor.

4. Perform the *Valve Plate Replacement Procedure*, steps 2 through 5, page 302.

5. Remove the piston, pin, ring, and connecting rod assembly from the crankcase by pressing them out through the top of the crankcase assembly.

6. Remove one snap ring retaining piston pin from the side of the piston.

7. With a slight press, push the piston pin out so that it clears one side of the piston and the connecting rod bearing. Remove the connecting rod.

8. Clean the piston of all foreign matter.

9. Remove the new connecting rod cap from the rod assembly. The proper position of the cap and the connecting rod assembly with relation to each other must be maintained as described in step 3 of the *Front Bearing Installation Procedure*, page 307.

10. Locate the new connecting rod in the correct position in the piston. Push on the piston pin until it rests against the installed snap ring.

11. Reinstall the snap ring removed in step 6.

12. Insert the piston and the connecting rod assembly (less the rod caps) into the cylinder bores. The assembly is to be positioned so that the connecting rod bearings are aligned with the crankshaft journals.

13. Using a piston ring compressor, collapse the ring against the piston and complete the installation of the piston and rod assembly in the cylinder bore.

14. Dip the new valve plate gasket into refrigeration oil. Locate the gasket on top of the compressor crankcase.

15. Locate the cylinder head and valve plate assembly on the crankcase.

16. Insert the head valve plate bolts. Tighten the bolts as outlined in step 7 of the *Valve Plate Replacement Procedure*, page 302.

17. Turn the compressor over and rest it on the cylinder head.

18. Position the connecting rod bearings around the crankshaft journals. Locate the connecting rod caps in the proper positions over the journals. The parts must be mated properly. Insert the screws and torque them to 9-11 ft.-lb.

19. Rotate the crankshaft several times to insure that the connecting rod does not bind.

20. Assemble the bottom plate as outlined in the *Rear Bearing Installation Procedure*, steps 11 through 14, page 305.

PISTON ASSEMBLY INSTALLATION PROCEDURE

The parts required for this procedure are as follows:

Piston   Gasket kit
Pin   Oil charge
Ring assembly kit

1. Perform the *Connecting Rod Installation Procedure*, steps 1 through 7, page 308.

2. When removing the connecting rod caps, be sure to maintain the proper relationship of these parts with each other as they are to be reused.

3. Clean the connecting rod and caps of all foreign matter.

4. Select the correct piston, pin, and ring assembly. The assembly for a standard model HA-850 compressor is identified by the number 20520 cast on the inner top surface of the piston; for a model HA-1000 compressor, the number of the assembly is 20521. The 0.020 oversize can be identified by these figures cast on the inner surface of the piston plus the figure 0.020 stamped on the top of the piston.

5. Locate the connecting rod in the new piston assembly. Push on the piston pin until it rests against the installed snap ring.

6. Perform the *Connecting Rod Installation Procedure*, steps 11 through 18, page 308.

7. Assemble the bottom plate as outlined in the *Rear Bearing Installation Procedure*, steps 11 through 14, page 305.

OIL PUMP INSTALLATION PROCEDURE

The part required for this procedure is the specified oil pump kit.

For Compressors with Material Lists Numbered 99110, 99111, 99112, and 99113

1. An oil pump replacement for these compressors requires the installation of a new crankshaft. The oil pump kit specified contains a new crankshaft for compressors governed by the material list numbers given. Perform the procedure for *Crankshaft Installation* when changing the oil pump in these compressors.

For Compressors with Material Lists Numbered 99114 and Higher

1. Change the oil pump by performing the *Rear Bearing Installation Procedure*, steps 1 and 4, page 305.

2. Remove the used oil pump parts from the end of the crankshaft.

3. Dip the new oil pump parts in refrigeration oil and place them in the end of the crankshaft in the following order.

   a. wave washer   c. outer rotor
   b. flat washer, polished side out   d. inner rotor

4. Perform steps 8, 9, and 10 in the *Rear Bearing Installation Procedure*, page 305.

REVIEW

Briefly answer each of the following questions.

1. What component part must be removed to replace the valve plate assembly?

2. Name the parts of the seal assembly.

3. What is the recommended torque of the seal plate?

4. The compressor should be retorqued after __?__ hour(s).

SERVICE PROCEDURE 41:
REBUILDING TECUMSEH COMPRESSORS, MODELS HG-500, HG-850, AND HG-1000*

This procedure is recommended when it is necessary to tear down a Tecumseh compressor for overhaul. To aid the service technician, the procedure is given in seven parts:

- Valve Plate Replacement
- Seal Assembly Replacement
- Rear Bearing Installation
- Front Bearing Installation
- Crankshaft Installation
- Connecting Rod Installation
- Piston Assembly Installation

The compressor models covered in this procedure are made of cast iron with aluminum connecting rods and pistons (unlike the HA-850 and HA-1000 compressors which are made of cast aluminum). Ball-type main bearings are used. Lubrication is accomplished by differential pressure; thus, an oil pump is not required.

The HG series of compressors replaces the HA-850 and HA-1000 compressors. Complete interchangeability between the two series of compressors is assured by the manufacturer; the crankshaft tapers and the mounting dimensions are the same.

TOOLS

Set of 1/4-in. drive sockets, to 9/16 in.
Hard rubber hammer
Small screwdrivers
Needle nose pliers
Snap ring pliers

Single-edge razor blades
Piston ring compressor
Allen wrench set
Torque wrench

MATERIALS

Ample supply of clean refrigeration oil
Gasket set
Seal assembly
Other parts that are determined to be defective

OIL CHARGE

Compressor Position	Oil Height (inch)	Remarks
Vertical	1 5/16	Factory charge of 11 fluid oz.
Horizontal	1 9/16	Factory charge of 11 fluid oz.
Vertical	7/8	Minimum recommended height*
Vertical	1 1/16	Maximum recommended height*
Horizontal	7/8	Minimum recommended height*
Horizontal	1 1/8	Maximum recommended height*
*After connection to system and run		

*Text and diagrams reprinted with the permission of Tecumseh Products Company.

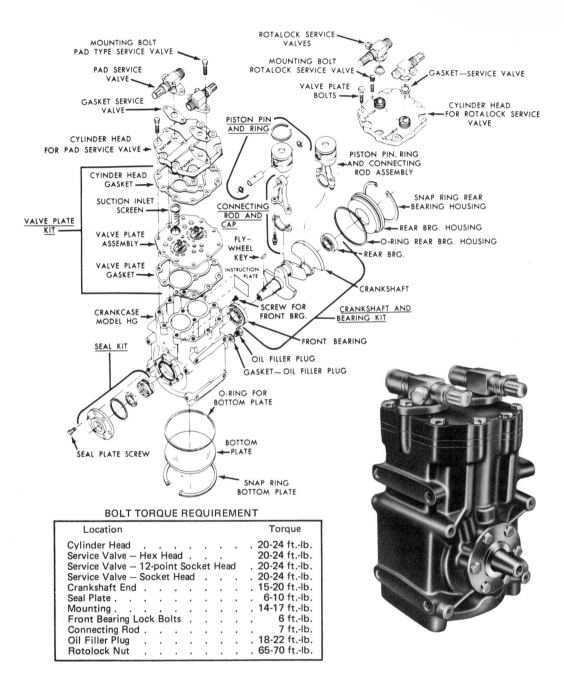

BOLT TORQUE REQUIREMENT

Location	Torque
Cylinder Head	20-24 ft.-lb.
Service Valve — Hex Head	20-24 ft.-lb.
Service Valve — 12-point Socket Head	20-24 ft.-lb.
Service Valve — Socket Head	20-24 ft.-lb.
Crankshaft End	15-20 ft.-lb.
Seal Plate	6-10 ft.-lb.
Mounting	14-17 ft.-lb.
Front Bearing Lock Bolts	6 ft.-lb.
Connecting Rod	7 ft.-lb.
Oil Filler Plug	18-22 ft.-lb.
Rotolock Nut	65-70 ft.-lb.

COMPRESSOR SPECIFICATIONS

Model	Bore	Stroke	No. Cyl.	Disp. Cu. In.	Max. rpm	Refr.	Factory Oil Charge Oz.	Suction Valve	Discharge Valve	Weight* Net	Weight* Ship.
HG500	1 7/8	1 7/8	1	5.18	6000	R-12	8	5/8	1/2	19.5 lb.	20 lb.
HG850	1 7/8	1 35/64	2	8.54	6000	R-12	11	5/8	1/2	24 lb.	24 1/2 lb.
HG1000	1 7/8	1 7/8	2	10.35	6000	R-12	11	5/8	1/2	24 lb.	24 1/2 lb.

Fig. SP41-1 **Exploded view and parts assembly kit for models HG-500, HG-850, and HG-1000 automotive compressors**

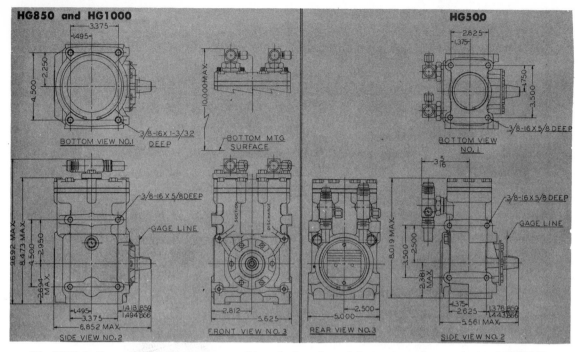

Fig. SP41-2 Comparison of compressors. Note the location of the service valves on the Model HG500 compressor.

VALVE PLATE REPLACEMENT PROCEDURE

The part required for this procedure is a valve plate kit which includes the valve plate, discharge valves, suction valves, valve retainer parts, valve plate, and cylinder head gaskets.

1. Perform steps 1 through 5 of the *Valve Plate Replacement Procedure* for compressor Models HA-850 and HA-1000 (Service Procedure 40, page 302).

2. Place the new valve plate gasket over the crankcase cylinder face. Make sure the gasket is dry.

3. Place the new valve plate assembly over the valve plate gasket so that the letter S stamped on the valve plate is visible and on the same side as the word *Suction* on the front of the crankcase. Place the valve plate assembly so that the mounting holes are aligned with those of the valve plate gasket and cylinder face.

4. Check that the suction inlet screen is clean. Insert the screen into the counterbore of the valve plate.

5. Locate the new cylinder head gasket over the valve plate so that the largest opening (circle) is over the top of the screen and the other circular holes line up with the holes in the valve plate. Keep the cylinder head gasket dry.

6. Place the cylinder head over the head gasket so that the side of the head with the word *Suction* is on the same side as the word *Suction* on the front of the crankcase.

7. Insert eight or twelve bolts as required through the cylinder head and valve plates. Tighten the bolts fingertight. Then torque the bolts in sequence so that the bolts diagonally opposite each other are evenly drawn to a torque of 20-24 ft.-lb.

8. Mount the service valves:

   a. *Rotalock type.* Connect the service valves to the correct ports and tighten the valves to a torque of 65-70 ft.-lb. Use new gaskets.

   b. *Pad base type.* Use a new service valve gasket and insert the valve mounting bolts through it. Locate the valve over the correct service valve ports. Tighten the bolts to a torque of 20-24 ft.-lb.

9. After a period of about two hours from the time of assembly, retorque the cylinder head and pad-type service valves.

SEAL ASSEMBLY REPLACEMENT PROCEDURE

The parts required for this procedure are included in the seal assembly kit: the front seal plate, seal nose, spring assembly, and 0-ring for the front seal plate.

1. Perform the complete procedure outlined in the *Seal Assembly Replacement Procedure*, page 304, for Tecumseh HA-850 and HA-1000 compressors.

PROCEDURE FOR THE REAR BEARING INSTALLATION

The parts required for this procedure are as follows:

Rear bearing   Oil charge, as specified
Gasket kit

1. Isolate the compressor and remove it from the system.

2. Remove all dirt and foreign matter from the rear and base cover plates and adjoining surfaces.

3. Remove the oil filler plug and drain the crankcase of oil.

4. With the appropriate snap ring pliers, remove the snap ring which secures the rear bearing housing in position. Remove the end plate.

5. Remove the rear 0-ring and discard.

6. Remove the rear bearing by using two offset screwdrivers with their ends inserted diametrically apart under the inner edge of the bearing outer race. Pry evenly on both sides to lift the rear bearing.

7. Remove the baseplate by turning the compressor upside down. Then, using the appropriate snap ring pliers, remove the snap ring holding the bottom cover in place. Remove the cover.

8. Remove the 0-ring and discard.

9. Clean all of the exposed parts and surfaces with solvent. Drain the parts and blow dry.

10. Support the compressor on the drive end of the shaft. Place the new bearing over the end of the crankshaft. Press on the bearing until the inner race rests against the shaft shoulder. CAUTION: *Press on the inner race of the bearing only.*

11. Insert the new 0-ring into the counterbored hole provided for the rear bearing cover plate. The 0-ring must be seated at the bottom of the bore and against its sides.

12. Check that the rear bearing housing is properly aligned and positioned on top of the bearing. Then press the bearing housing into the compressor crankcase counterbore until it is inserted to its full depth. Insert the snap ring.

13. Insert the new 0-ring into the crankcase base groove. With the bracket of the baseplate on the outside, position the baseplate in the base counterbore. Insert the snap ring. By tapping with a hammer or pressing with the hand on the base, the snap ring will enter the crankcase groove.

14. Place the compressor in the upright position. Charge the compressor with the proper amount of oil. Oil is added until the charge is 11 ounces or the oil level is 1 5/16 in. on a dipstick.

FRONT BEARING INSTALLATION PROCEDURE

The parts required for this procedure are as follows:

Front bearing   Gasket kit
Seal kit   Oil charge, as required

1. Perform the *Seal Assembly Procedure* for Tecumseh HA-850 and HA-1000 compressors, steps 1 through 5, page 304.

2. Perform the *Rear Bearing Installation Procedure*, page 305, to remove the rear bearing plate and baseplate cover.

3. Remove the cylinder head and the valve plate assembly by following the procedure outlined in the *Valve Plate Replacement Procedure* for Models HA-850 and HA-1000 compressors, steps 2 through 5, page 313.

4. Identify the rod caps and rods to insure that they can be reassembled in the same position. Remove the two rod caps by removing the four screws holding them.

5. Push the connecting rod/piston assemblies out of the crankcase.

6. Support the crankcase from the rear and gently tap the front of the crankshaft with a rubber or fiber mallet until the crankshaft moves out of the front bearing.

7. Remove the crankshaft and rear bearing from the compressor.

8. From the rear of the compressor, remove the two bolts that hold the front bearing in place. Remove the front bearing by placing a wood or metal rod against the front end of the bearing inner race and gently tapping the rod.

9. Clean all parts with solvent. Drain the parts and blow dry.

10. Install the new front bearing in the crankcase by placing the properly aligned bearing in the counterbore. Press or gently tap the outer race of the bearing until it is inserted to the full depth of the bore.

11. Install the two bolts holding the bearing in place. Torque the bolts to 6 ft.-lb.

12. Insert the crankshaft in the front bearing assembly. Align the crankshaft and press or gently tap on the rear end of the crankshaft until it moves the full length of the bearing journal and bottoms.

13. Install the connecting rod, piston, and ring assembly as outlined in the *Connecting Rod Assembly for Tecumseh Models HA-850 and HA-1000*, steps 12, 13, 18, and 19, page 308.

14. Install the rear bearing, bearing housing, and cover plate as outlined in the *Rear Bearing Installation Procedure*, steps 11 and 12, page 306.

15. Install the new seal assembly as outlined in the *Seal Assembly Replacement for Tecumseh Models HA-850 and HA-1000*, steps 5 through 9, page 304.

16. Install the baseplate by inserting the new O-ring in the counterbore. Position the baseplate (with the bracket to the outside) and press it into the counterbore. Insert the snap ring.

CRANKSHAFT INSTALLATION PROCEDURE

The parts required for this procedure are as follows:

Crankshaft kit   Seal kit
Gasket kit

1. Perform the *Front Bearing Installation Procedure*, steps 1 through 7, page 315.

2. Install the new rear bearing on the new crankshaft by pressing or tapping on the inner race of the bearing.

3. Perform the *Front Bearing Installation Procedure*, steps 12 through 16, page 315.

CONNECTING ROD INSTALLATION PROCEDURE

The parts required for this procedure are as follows:

Connecting rod and cap assembly   Oil charge
Gasket kit

1. Isolate the compressor from the system.

2. Remove all dirt and foreign material from the compressor. Pay particular attention to the area around the base and the head.

3. To remove the baseplate, first turn the compressor upside down. Then, using the appropriate snap ring pliers, remove the snap ring holding the bottom cover in place. Remove the cover.

4. Drain the oil from the compressor and discard it. Flush the exposed parts with solvent. Drain the parts and blow dry.

5. Identify the rod caps and rods to insure that they are replaced in the proper positions. Remove the two rod caps by removing the four screws holding them. If only one rod is to be replaced, remove only that rod cap.

6. Remove the valve plate and head. Follow the procedure outlined in the *Valve Plate Replacement Procedure for Tecumseh HA-850 and HA-1000 compressors*, steps 2 through 5, page 302.

7. Remove the piston and connecting rod assembly by pressing them out through the top of the crankcase.

8. Using snap ring pliers, remove the piston pin snap ring.

9. Push the piston pin out so as to clear one side of the piston and connecting rod bearing. Remove the connecting rod.

10. Clean all foreign material from the parts to be reused.

11. Remove the cap from the new connecting rod assembly to be installed. Note the relative positions of the parts so that they can be reassembled properly.

12. Place the new connecting rods in the pistons and push on the piston pin until it rests against the installed snap ring.

13. Reinstall the snap ring in the piston.

14. Perform the procedure outlined in the *Connecting Rod Installation for Tecumseh Compressors, Models HA-850 and HA-1000*, steps 12, 13, 18, and 19, page 294.

15. Insert the new O-ring in the crankcase base groove. With the bracket to the outside, position the baseplate in the groove. Insert the snap ring. Tap or press on the base so that the snap ring enters the crankcase groove.

16. Replace the valve plate and head assembly by performing the procedure outlined in the *Valve Plate Replacement Procedure*, steps 2 through 9, page 313.

PISTON ASSEMBLY INSTALLATION PROCEDURE

The parts required for this procedure are as follows:

Piston	Gasket kit
Pin and ring assembly kit	Oil charge

1. Perform the *Connecting Rod Installation Procedure*, steps 1 though 11, page 308.

2. Select the correct piston, pin, and ring assembly. A 0.020-in. oversize can be identified by a figure 2 stamped on the piston top.

3. Perform the *Connecting Rod Installation Procedure*, steps 12 through 16, page 308.

REVIEW

Briefly answer each of the following questions.

1. List three physical differences between the HG and HA series Tecumseh compressors.

2. What is the normal factory charge of oil?

3. What are two types of service valves used on the Tecumseh compressors?

4. What parts are included in the valve plate kit?

5. What is the recommended torque of the valve plate and head?

SERVICE PROCEDURE 42:
REPAIRING THE COMPRESSOR REAR HEAD AND THE VALVE PLATE (SANKYO SD-5 COMPRESSOR)

The compressor must be removed from the car for service if it is determined that the valve plate, rear head, or the valve plate gasket(s) is defective.

TOOLS

Gasket scraper
Torque wrench
Socket wrench set with a 13-mm socket

Manifold and gauge set
Soft hammer

MATERIALS

Valve plate and/or gasket set, as required
Refrigerant

Refrigeration oil
Clean shop rags

PROCEDURE

Prepare the Compressor for Service

1. Purge the system of refrigerant as outlined in Service Procedure 3.

2. Remove the low-side and high-side hoses from the compressor fittings. Plug the hoses and compressor fittings to avoid contamination.

3. Loosen the compressor and/or idler pulley and remove the belt(s).

4. Remove the mounting hardware and lift the compressor from the engine.

Remove the Valve Plate Assembly

1. Remove the five screws from the cylinder head using a 13-mm hex socket wrench.

2. Remove the head and valve plate assembly from the cylinder block by tapping lightly with a soft hammer on the gasket scraper which is placed between the valve plate and the cylinder head, figure SP42-1.

3. To remove the valve plate, insert the gasket scraper between the valve plate and the cylinder block, figure SP42-2. *Do not damage the mating surfaces.*

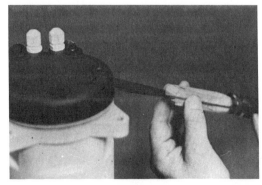

Fig. SP42-1 Removing the rear head

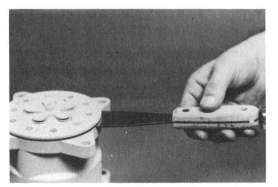

Fig. SP42-2 Removing the valve plate

4. Carefully remove all gasket material, figure SP42-3, from the mating surfaces. *Do not nick or scratch the surfaces.*

Install the Valve Plate Assembly

1. Apply a thin coat of clean refrigeration oil to all gaskets and mating surfaces.

2. Install the valve plate gasket on the cylinder block. The alignment pin insures that the gasket is installed properly.

3. Place the valve plate into position. The alignment pin must pass through the pin hole in the valve plate.

4. Install the head gasket on the valve plate. Check for the proper alignment of the gasket.

5. Reinstall the cylinder head and check for the proper alignment.

6. Install the five hex head screws and tighten them to a snug fit.

7. Tighten the five screws to a torque of 22-25 ft.-lb. Tighten the screws in the sequence shown in figure SP42-4. *Do not under or over tighten the screws.*

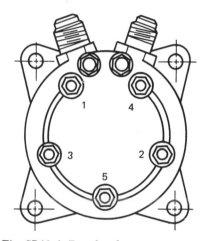

Fig. SP42-3 Removing the gasket material

Fig. SP42-4 Rear head torque sequence

8. Add 1 or 2 ounces of oil to the compressor to compensate for any loss that occurs as a result of this repair.

Return the Compressor to Service

1. Return the compressor to the car in its original position. Replace all bolts and braces. Tighten the bolts securely.

2. Replace the belt(s) and tighten them to a tension of 90-110 lb.

3. Remove the plugs and replace the compressor low-side and high-side hoses. Use new 0-rings if 0-ring type fittings are provided.

4. Check the compressor oil level as outlined in Service Procedure 20. Omit steps 1 and 2 under the heading *Prepare the System*, page 218.

5. Leak check the system as outlined in Service Procedure 4 or 5.

6. Evacuate the system as outlined in Service Procedure 6.

7. Charge the system as outlined in Service Procedure 7, 8 or 9.

8. Return the compressor to service or conduct the performance test as necessary.

REVIEW

Select the appropriate answer from the choices given.

1. The valve plate and cylinder head screws should be torqued to

   a. 20-23 ft.-lb.   c. 30-33 ft.-lb.
   b. 22-25 ft.-lb.   d. 32-35 ft.-lb.

2. How much oil should be added to compensate for any loss as a result of repairs as outlined in this procedure?

   a. 1-2 ounces.   c. No oil need be added.
   b. 3-4 ounces.   d. All of the oil should be replaced.

3. Which of the tools used in this procedure is, in your opinion, a metric tool (not a standard U.S. tool)?

   a. The torque wrench   c. The gasket scraper
   b. The soft hammer   d. The 13-mm socket

4. Gasket material should be *carefully* removed from all mating surfaces

   a. to insure that they are not nicked or scratched.
   b. to insure that all old gasket material is removed.
   c. to insure the proper sealing of the new gasket.
   d. All of the above are correct answers.

5. Which of the following gauge pressure readings best indicates a defective valve plate or gasket?

   a. High suction pressure with low head pressure.
   b. Low suction pressure with high head pressure.
   c. Low suction pressure with low head pressure.
   d. High suction pressure with high head pressure.

SERVICE PROCEDURE 43:
TROUBLESHOOTING COMPRESSOR AND RELATED NOISE

Compressor noise, or noise that seems to be caused by the compressor, is often difficult to locate. This procedure can be used as an aid in determining the possible cause and cure of the noise problem. Since the compressor is a mechanical device, however, some noise is to be expected from the compressor itself.

TOOLS

As required

MATERIAL

As required

PROCEDURE

Belt Noise

Possible Cause	To Correct
1. Belts too long (cannot be tightened).	1. Replace with belts of the proper length.
2. Frayed or damaged belt(s).	2. Replace with new belt(s).
3. Loose belt(s).	3. Tighten the belt(s).

Pulley Noise

Possible Cause	To Correct
1. Defective or worn drive pulley.	1. Replace the drive pulley.
2. Loose idler pulley.	2. Tighten the idler pulley.
3. Defective idler pulley bearing.	3. Replace the bearing.
4. Loose clutch rotor.	4. Tighten the clutch rotor.
5. Defective clutch bearing.	5. Replace the clutch bearing.

Mount Noise

Possible Cause	To Correct
1. Missing bolt(s).	1. Replace bolt(s).
2. Broken bolt(s).	2. Replace bolt(s).
3. Loose bolt(s).	3. Tighten the bolt(s).
4. Broken weld in mount.	4. Repair or replace the mount.
5. Broken mount or brace.	5. Repair or replace as necessary.

Slipping Clutch Noise

Possible Cause	To Correct
1. Defective clutch coil.	1. Replace the clutch coil.
2. Worn or defective brush set.	2. Replace the brush set.
3. Improper ground connection.	3. Insure good ground connection.
4. Loose wire connection.	4. Repair as necessary.
5. Worn rotor and/or armature.	5. Replace the assembly as necessary.
6. Improper air gap.	6. Set the air gap to the proper value.

Compressor Noise

Possible Cause	To Correct
1. Defective bearing(s).	1. Replace the bearing(s) or replace the compressor.
2. Loose connecting rod.	2. Repair or replace the connecting rod; or, replace the compressor.
3. Broken reed valve.	3. Replace the valve plate assembly.
4. Blown head or valve plate gasket.	4. Replace the gasket set.
5. Improper mounting.	5. Correct the mounting. Add braces and/or brackets if necessary.

SERVICE HINTS

Problem	Possible Cause
1. Unable to keep belts tightened.	1. a. The pulley is driven out of concentric alignment.
	1. b. Broken discharge reed valve in the valve plate.
	1. c. Steel core broken in the steel belt.
	1. d. Improper tightening of the compressor adjustment bolt(s).
2. Unable to locate the leak even though the system looses a pound of refrigerant in every two- to three-week period.	2. a. Leak in evaporator. Use the leak detector inside the car and check for leaks at the air outlets.
	2. b. The inner layer of the rubber hose is leaking. Carefully inspect the hose for fresh oil along the outer layer of the hose.
	2. c. Cold seal and leak. Introduce a trace solution. See Service Procedure 10.

Problem	Possible Cause
3. Unable to keep the valve plate gasket(s) in the compressor after repeated replacement.	3. a. Excessive head pressure under certain conditions.
	3. b. Excessive head pressure caused by defective cooling system under conditions of slow or fast driving.
	3. c. Small (pinhole) leak in the cooling system.
	3. d. Defective fan clutch on the engine cooling fan.
4. Unable to determine the system problem although the customer complains of no cooling after 10-15 minutes of highway driving.	4. a. Moisture in the system. Purge and evacuate for a minimum of four hours. Recharge.
	4. b. Moisture in the system. Purge and replace the receiver/drier. Evacuate the system for a minimum of one hour.
	4. c. Engine overheating during highway driving.

REVIEW

For each *problem* listed, there are several possible *causes* given in this procedure. For each of the problems given, indicate at least one possible cause.

Problem 1. Compressor clutch slips.

Problem 2. Unable to keep valve plate gasket(s) in compressor even after repeated replacement.

Problem 3. Compressor mount is noisy.

Problem 4. Unable to determine system problem. Customer complains of "no cooling" after 10-15 minutes of highway driving.

Problem 5. Compressor drive belt(s) noisy.

SERVICE PROCEDURE 44:
REBUILDING THE CHRYSLER AIR-TEMP V-2 COMPRESSOR*

This procedure can be used when it is necessary to rebuild the Chrysler Air-Temp compressor. According to the manufacturer, the specifications for this compressor are as follows: 9.45-cubic inch displacement with a bore of 2 5/16 in. and a stroke of 1 1/8 in. The V-type compressor has reed valves located in each head. The two-cylinder Chrysler Air-Temp compressor has an oil charge of eleven ounces.

TOOLS

Hand wrenches	Rubber hammer
EPR valve wrench	Screwdrivers
Internal and external snap ring pliers	Pilot studs
1/4-in. drive set, to 9/16 in.	Arbor press
Allen wrench set	Torque wrenches
Razor blades	Ring compressor

NOTE: Special tools can be obtained from the Kelsey-Hayes Company, Detroit, Michigan.

MATERIALS

Refrigeration oil
Compressor shaft seal kit
Gasket kit
Any parts that are determined to be defective

PROCEDURE

Prepare the Compressor for Service

1. All operations are performed with the compressor removed from the car. Perform the necessary isolation or purging procedures as outlined in this book.

2. Remove the compressor from the car.

3. Remove the 5/16-in. bolt from the crankshaft located at the center of the clutch hub.

4. Using a 5/8-in. NF (or NC) bolt, remove the clutch rotor.

5. If there is a stationary field, remove the field. For a rotating field, remove the brush set.

6. Clean the external surfaces of the compressor to prevent contamination by foreign particles.

7. Remove the oil plug and drain the oil from the compressor into a graduated beaker. Note the amount of oil removed, then discard the oil. New oil will be used to recharge the compressor.

---

* Text and diagrams are, in part, by courtesy of the Chrysler Motor Corporation.

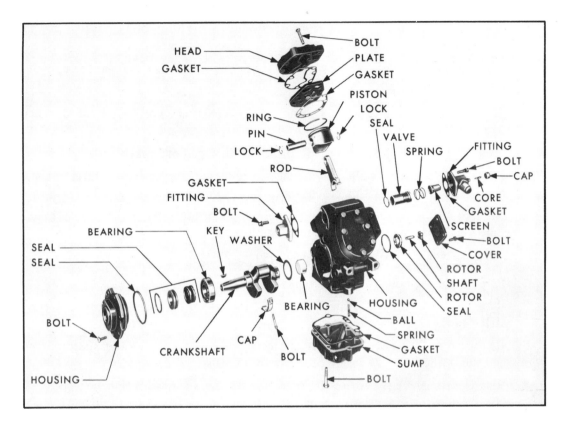

Fig. SP44-1 Exploded view of the V-2 compressor

Compressor Disassembly Procedures

A. Cylinder Head and Valve Plate

1. Remove the seven cylinder head bolts from each head. If the head and valve plate assembly does not separate easily from the crankcase, tap the assembly with a rubber hammer. *Do not* use a screwdriver to pry these components apart as scoring of the mating surfaces can result.

2. Remove all gasket material from the mating surfaces and check for scratches and burrs. Light scratches can be removed with a crocus cloth.

3. *Do not* attempt to disassemble the reed valves from the valve plate. Inspect the reed valves for bent or broken reeds. Replace the complete assembly if necessary.

   CAUTION: Do not touch or pry at the reed valves.

B. Piston and Connecting Rods

1. Remove the six bolts holding the sump on the compressor crankcase.

2. Remove the sump. If necessary, tap the sump with a rubber hammer; do not pry. Do not damage the oil pressure spring (note the location of this part in the exploded view, figure SP44-1).

3. Remove the oil pressure spring and the rubber ball from the crankcase.

4. Clean the sump cover and the compressor crankcase mating surfaces of all gasket material.

5. Note the position of the rod caps and remove the four bolts holding the two caps on the connecting rods.

6. Remove the rod caps. Remove the piston and rod assemblies from the cylinders.

7. Replace the caps on the rods in their correct position.

8. Inspect the rods and caps for scoring. If these parts are worn or damaged, replace them as an assembly.

9. Inspect the pistons for damage. Replace the damaged or broken rings.

10. Inspect the cylinder walls for damage. Slight scuffing or light scratches can be removed by rubbing with a crocus cloth.

11. After conditioning the cylinder bores, clean the surfaces of the block with mineral spirits and coat them with clean refrigeration oil.

C. Crankshaft Bearing Housing and Shaft Oil Seal

1. Remove the six bolts from the crankshaft bearing housing.

2. Remove the bearing housing from the crankcase by using two screwdrivers inserted in the slots provided, figure SP44-2.

3. Remove the 0-ring seal from the bearing housing. Remove the stationary seal and the 0-ring from the inside of the housing. Discard these parts.

4. Remove the shaft seal from the crankshaft using a screwdriver if necessary. Do not scratch the crankshaft. Small scratches and burrs can be removed from the crankshaft by rubbing with a crocus cloth.

Fig. SP44-2 Crankcase bearing housing removal   Fig. SP44-3 (A) Cartridge-type seal (B) Unitized-type seal

D. Crankshaft and Ball Bearing

1. Remove the crankshaft and the thrust washer from the crankcase. Make sure that the pistons and rods are completely removed.

2. The bearing can be removed from the crankshaft by using a small arbor press. If the bearing is not to be replaced, do not remove it from the crankshaft.

3. Locate the oil pump shaft. If it remains in the crankshaft, remove it to insure that it is not misplaced.

E.   The Oil Pump

1.   Remove the oil pump cover plate and seal by removing the four bolts holding the plate in position.

2.   Discard the seal.

3.   Remove the internal and external rotor.   Note the relationship between the components of the installation to insure that they are replaced properly.

4.   If the oil pump shaft was not removed with the crankshaft, remove it at this time to insure that it is not misplaced.

Inspection

NOTE: Reinspect all parts.   Any parts that are determined to be damaged beyond repair should be replaced.

1.   Inspect all parts for excessive wear.

2.   Inspect all parts for cracks and breaks.

3.   Inspect all parts for scoring, burrs, or scratches.   Small scratches should be removed by rubbing with a crocus cloth.   If a scratch cannot be removed, the part must be replaced.

4.   The valve plates and heads and the sump cover must not be bent or warped.

5.   Replace all damaged parts.

Compressor Reassembly Procedures

A.   Parts Prepared for Reassembly

1.   Clean and inspect all parts.   Replace defective parts.

2.   Submerse the new seal kit in clean refrigeration oil.

3.   Submerse the gasket kit in clean refrigeration oil.

4.   Coat all surfaces with a light coat of clean refrigeration oil.

B.   Install the Crankshaft and Bearing

1.   Using a small arbor press, slide the bearing on the crankshaft. Apply pressure to the inner race of the bearing only.

2.   Install a thrust washer at the rear of the crankshaft.

3.   Install the crankshaft in the rear bushing, through the front opening.

C.   Install the Shaft Seal and the Bearing Housing

1.   Place the bearing housing 0-ring into the groove provided.   Install the stationary seal and 0-ring in the housing.   Do not damage the seal surface.

2. Slide the shaft seal onto the crankshaft, figure SP44-4. Hold the seal firmly on the outside edges. *Do not touch the face of the carbon seal.*

3. Install the bearing housing. Insure that the housing is in proper alignment with the screw holes in the crankcase.

4. The seal assembly can be damaged if the bearing housing is rotated after the housing seal contacts the carbon seal.

5. Replace the six bolts and tighten them in a diagonal sequence to a torque of 10-13 ft.-lb.

Fig. SP44-4 Sliding the shaft seal into position

D. Replace the Oil Pump

1. Install the oil pump drive shaft through the rear housing and into the crankshaft. It may be necessary to rotate the drive shaft to engage the crankshaft properly.

2. Install the internal and external rotors.

3. Install the 0-ring in the groove provided. Install the oil pump cover plate.

4. Replace the four bolts holding the cover plate in position. Torque the bolts to 10-13 ft.-lb.

E. Replace the Piston and Connecting Rods

1. Remove the rod caps and install the pistons in the bores. If the original rods are used, reinstall them in the same position as they were prior to removal.

2. Using a ring compressor to prevent damage, slip the pistons into their bores.

3. Replace the rod caps and torque them to 52-56 in.-lb.

4. Rotate the crankshaft and check it for binding.

5. Check the crankshaft axial movement, figure SP44-5.

Fig. SP44-5 Checking crankshaft axial movement

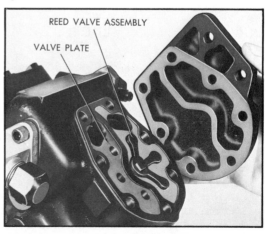

Fig. SP44-6 Valve plate in the installed position

F.   Replace the Cylinder Head and Valve Plate Assembly

1.   Install the pilot studs in the compressor crankcase.

2.   Position the valve plate gasket over the studs.

3.   Position the reed valve and the valve plate assembly over the studs.

4.   Position the head gasket over the studs.

5.   Position the head over the studs.

6.   Install the five bolts and tighten them until they are fingertight.

7.   Remove the two studs.

8.   Install the other two bolts and tighten them until they are fingertight.

9.   Repeat this procedure with the other head.

10. Tighten each bolt alternately and evenly to a torque of 23-27 ft.-lb.

11. Retorque the bolts after two hours.

G.   Install the Sump Cover

1.   Turn the compressor upside down.

2.   Drop the rubber ball into the hole drilled into the crankcase. Place the spring on top of the ball.

3.   Insert the pilot studs into two of the crankcase holes.

4.   Position the sump gasket over the studs.

5.   Position the sump cover over the studs, figure SP44-8.

6.   Install four bolts in the sump cover and tighten them until they are fingertight.

7.   Remove the pilot studs and install the other two bolts. Tighten them until they are fingertight.

8.   Alternately tighten the sump bolts to a torque of 15-19 ft.-lb.

CHARGE WITH OIL

NOTE: Recharge the compressor with the proper amount of oil.

1.   Remove the oil plug.

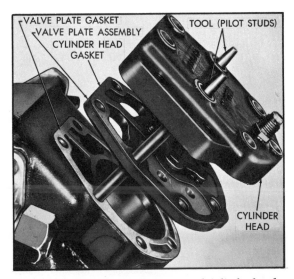

Fig. SP44-7 Installed valve plate and cylinder head

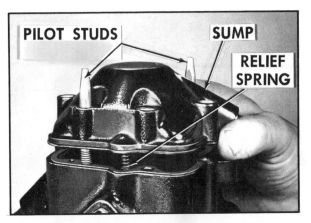

Fig. SP44-8 Installing the sump

	Foot-Pounds	Inch-Pounds
Compressor Bearing Housing Bolt.	10-13	
Compressor to Bracket Bolt.	50	
Compressor Connecting Rod Screw.		52-56
Compressor Cylinder Head Cover Bolt.	23-27	
Compressor Cylinder Head Cover (nameplate bolt)	20-24	
Compressor Discharge Adapter Bolt	14-18	
Compressor to Engine Bolt	30	
Compressor Oil Pump Cover Bolt	10-13	
Compressor Oil Sump.	15-19	
Compressor to Strut Bolt	30	
Compressor Suction Adapter Bolt.	10-14	
Magnetic Clutch to Compressor Bolt	20	

Fig. SP44-9 Torque reference

2. If the compressor is going back into service on the original vehicle, recharge with the same amount of oil that was removed (as noted).

3. If the compressor is to be placed in stock, charge the compressor with 11 ounces of oil.

4. Use only approved refrigeration oil.

REVIEW

Briefly answer each of the following questions.

1. When removing the sump, what parts should be looked for?

2. Where is the EPR valve located?

3. Name two types of shaft seals.

4. Why is it important not to touch the carbon face of the seal?

5. What is the oil charge recommended if the compressor is going into stock?

SERVICE PROCEDURE 45:
REBUILDING THE GENERAL MOTORS' (FRIGIDAIRE) SIX-AND FOUR-CYLINDER COMPRESSORS*

Rebuilding the General Motors' six- and four-cylinder compressors is considered to be a major service operation. The compressor must be removed from the car and placed on a clean workbench, preferably one that is covered with a clean piece of white paper.

When the service technician works on the internal assembly of a compressor, it is very important that cleanliness and organized work habits be observed.

An adequate service parts stock must be maintained for servicing six- and four-cylinder compressors. Some of the more important parts to be stocked are as follows:

- Piston drive balls
- Shoe discs, ten sizes
- Thrust races, fourteen sizes
- Pistons and piston rings
- Bearings: shaft, thrust, and pulley
- Oil pickup tube

- Suction reed valves
- Discharge reed valves
- Gasket set; O-ring gaskets
- Retainer rings, all sizes
- Discharge crossover tube
- Oil pump gears: drive and driven

The following procedures are based on the use of the proper service tools and on the condition that an adequate stock of service parts is at hand. Part I gives the procedure for rebuilding a six-cylinder compressor and Part II gives the procedure for a four-cylinder compressor.

The special service tools required are available from the Draf Tool Co. and Kent-Moore Tool Co., or from an air-conditioning supply house. The following list serves as a guide to the tool requirements. However, all of the tools may not be necessary for a particular operation. The list also includes all tools suggested by equipment manufacturers as being essential for proper compressor service.

TOOLS

Nonmagnetic feeler gauge set
Compressor holding fixture(s)
Pulley puller
Socket wrench set with 9/16-in. thinwall socket
Pulley bearing remover and installer
Oil pickup tube remover
Pressure test connector
Parts tray
Wrenches, pliers, screwdrivers
Torque wrench, in.-lb. and ft.-lb.
Snap ring pliers, internal and external

Compressing fixture(s)
Clutch hub holder
Hub and drive plate remover and installer
Internal assembly support block
Needle bearing installer
Suction crossover seal installer
O-ring installer
Micrometer
Dial indicator
Spring tension scale

*Some of the illustrations and charts in this procedure are used by permission of Cadillac Motor Car Division, Buick Motor Division, and Oldsmobile Division of General Motors Corporation, as well as other divisions.

MATERIALS

Overhaul gasket set   Shaft seal set

Refrigeration oil   Other parts, as required

PROCEDURE, PART I

Hub and Drive Plate Removal

1. Mount the compressor in a holding fixture and secure the fixture in a vise.
2. Using a drive plate holding tool and the 9/16-in. thinwall socket, remove the locknut from the shaft.
3. Using the snap ring pliers, remove the clutch hub retaining ring. Remove the spacer under the ring.
4. Remove the hub and drive plate with the hub and drive plate remover tool, figure SP45-2.

Pulley and Bearing Assembly Removal

1. Using the snap ring pliers, remove the pulley and bearing snap ring retainer, figure SP45-3.

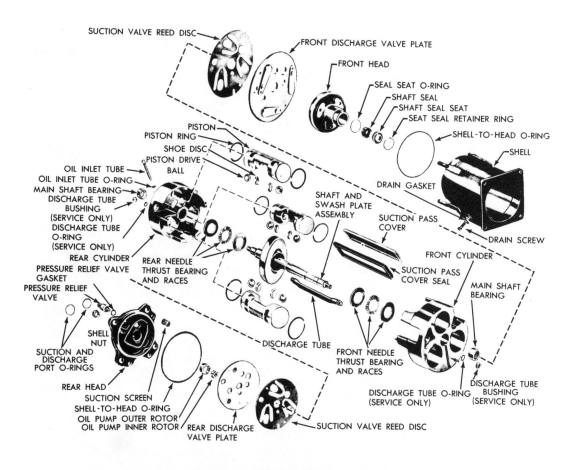

Fig. SP45-1

Fig. SP45-2 Removing the hub and drive plate assembly

Fig. SP45-3 Removing the pulley retaining ring

2. Place a puller pilot over the crank-shaft. Using a pulley puller, re-move the pulley, figure SP45-4.

   NOTE: The puller pilot must be in place. Placing the puller against the crankshaft will damage the internal assembly.

3. If the pulley bearing is to be re-placed, use a sharp tool, such as a small screwdriver, to remove the wire retaining ring.

Fig. SP45-4 Removing the pulley

4. From the rear of the pulley, press or drive the bearing out.

Coil Housing Assembly

1. Scribe the location of the coil housing with relation to the compressor body to insure proper alignment during reassembly.

2. Using snap ring pliers, remove the coil housing retainer ring, figure SP45-5, page 334.

3. Lift off the coil housing assembly.

Remove the Shaft Seal Assembly

1. Follow the procedures outlined in Service Procedure 18.

Rear Head, Oil Pump, and Valve Plate Removal

1. Remove the oil sump plug. Remove the compressor from the holding fixture and drain the oil from the compressor into a graduated container.

2. After noting the quantity of oil drained, discard the oil.

3. Return the compressor to the holding fixture with the rear head up.

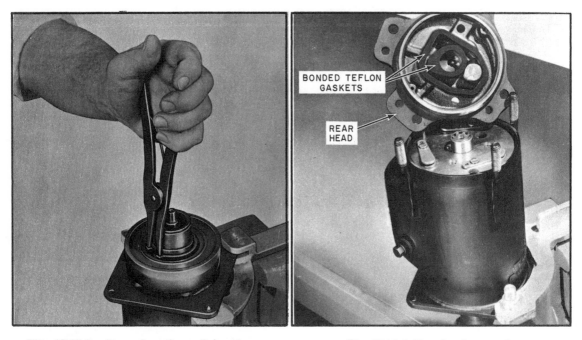

Fig. SP45-5   Removing the coil housing retainer ring

Fig. SP45-6 Rear head removal

4. Remove the four nuts from the shell
   studs. Remove the rear head,
   figure SP45-6. *Take care not to
   scratch or nick the Teflon surface.*

5. Remove the oil pump drive and
   driven gears. Set the gears aside
   in their original position to insure
   proper reassembly.

6. Remove the rear head-to-shell O-ring
   and discard.

Fig. SP45-7 Removing the rear discharge valve plate

7. Using two screwdrivers, figure
   SP45-7, carefully pry up the rear
   discharge valve plate assembly. Lift
   out the valve plate assembly.

8. Carefully lift out the suction reed
   valve.

**Remove the Internal Mechanism from
the Shell**

1. Remove the oil inlet tube and O-
   ring with the oil inlet tube remover,
   figure SP45-8. *To avoid damage
   to the tube and shell do not omit
   this step.*

Fig. SP45-8 Removing the oil inlet tube and O-ring

2. Carefully remove the compressor assembly from the holding fixture and lay it on its side.

3. Gently tap the front head casting with a soft hammer to slide the internal assembly and head out of the shell.

   Do not attempt to remove the internal assembly without removing the front head with it to avoid serious damage to the Teflon surface.

4. Place the internal assembly and the front head on the support block, figure SP45-9.

5. Carefully remove the front head. *Use extreme caution to prevent damage to the Teflon-coated surface of the front head.*

6. Remove the discharge and suction valve plates from the internal assembly.

7. Remove and discard the front O-ring gasket.

Diagnosis

Fig. SP45-9 Remove the internal assembly (held on support block) with the front head

1. If necessary, replace the six-cylinder internal assembly. Otherwise, rebuild the assembly following the procedures outlined in Service Procedure 46.

2. Examine the front and rear discharge and suction valve plates for damaged or broken valves. Replace any valves that are damaged.

3. Examine the Teflon surfaces on the front and rear heads. If damaged, nicked, or scratched, the head must be replaced.

4. Examine the suction screen in the rear head. If the screen is clogged or damaged, clean or replace it.

5. Examine the oil pump gears. If either gear shows signs of damage or wear, replace both gears.

6. Inspect the seal and seal seat for damage of any kind. If damage is noted, replace the seal assembly.

   NOTE: A new seal is suggested when the compressor is rebuilt.

7. Check the coil for loose connections or cracked insulation. If the coil is checked with an ammeter, the reading should be no more than 3.2 amperes at 12 volts.

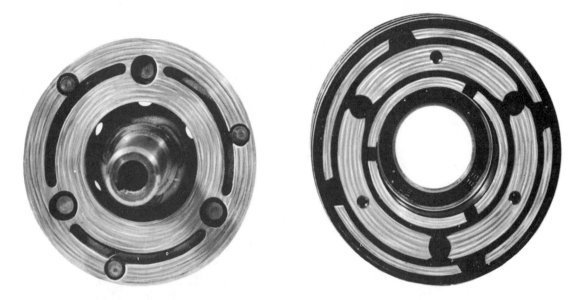

Fig. SP45-10 Scoring of the drive and driven plates is normal. Do not replace for this condition.

8. Check the pulley and bearing assembly. If the frictional surface of the pulley shows signs of warpage due to excessive heat, the pulley should be replaced. Slight scoring, figure SP45-10, is normal. If the assembly is heavily scored, it should be replaced.

9. Check the pulley bearing for signs of excessive noise or looseness. Replace if necessary.

10. Inspect the hub and drive plate. Refer to the comments of step 8.

Replace the Internal Mechanism

1. Place the internal mechanism, oil pump end down, in the support block.

2. Place the suction valve plate and then the discharge valve plate in place over the dowel pins.

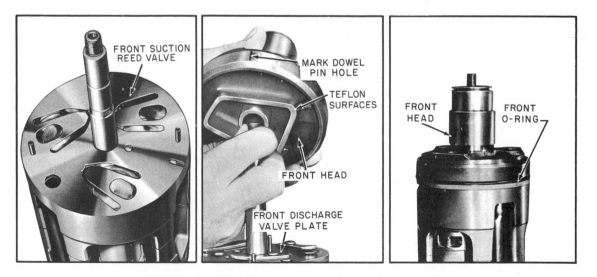

Fig. SP45-11 Installing the front reed valve, head, and O-ring

3. Carefully locate the front head in place over the dowel pins, figure SP45-11. *Take care not to damage the Teflon surface.*

4. Place the front 0-ring in position. This 0-ring is properly located between the head and discharge valve.

5. Locate the oil pickup tube hole with the center of the shell, figure SP45-12. Slide the shell over the internal assembly.

6. Gently tap the shell in place with a soft hammer. *Do not pinch or distort the 0-ring.*

Install the Rear Head Assembly

1. Hold the internal mechanism securely in the shell and invert the assembly. Place the assembly with the front end down in the holding fixture. Secure the fixture in a vise.

2. Insure that the internal mechanism is in the proper position and drop the oil pickup tube in place, figure SP45-13. Some units are equipped with an 0-ring. If so equipped, make sure the 0-ring is in place.

3. Install the suction valve plate and the discharge valve plate in their proper positions.

4. Install the oil pump gears. Install the rear 0-ring gasket.

5. Position the rear head casting so it is aligned with the dowel pins, figure SP45-14. *Note the position in which the outer oil pump gear must be placed to prevent damage to the Teflon surface of the head.*

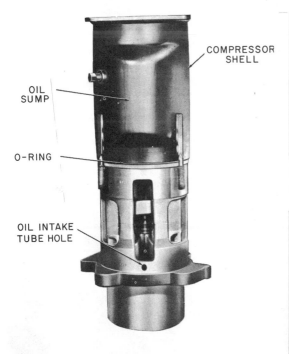

Fig. SP45-12 Replace the shell over the internal assembly

Fig. SP45-13 Installing the oil intake (pickup) tube

Fig. SP45-14 Installing the rear head

6. Position the oil pump and slide the rear head into place.

7. Install the four hex nuts and torque them to 19-23 ft.-lb.

Install the Seal Assembly

1. Follow the procedures outlined in Service Procedure 18.

Leak Test the Compressor

1. Follow the procedures outlined in Service Procedure 18.

2. If either internal 0-ring leaks, the assembly must be disassembled to find the cause and correct the leak.

3. If no leaks are found, continue with the next procedure.

Replace the Coil Housing

1. Note the original position of the coil housing by the scribe marks.

2. Slip the coil housing into place.

3. Replace the snap ring to secure the housing.

Replace the Pulley and the Bearing Assembly

1. Press the new bearing into the pulley, figure SP45-15, and replace the wire retaining ring (if bearing replacement is necessary).

2. Using the proper tool, figure SP45-16, press or drive the pulley and bearing assembly on the compressor front head.

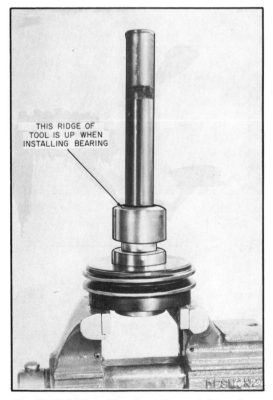

Fig. SP45-15 Installing the pulley and drive plate bearing

Fig. SP45-16 Installing the pulley and drive plate on the compressor

3. Install the retainer snap ring.

Replace the Hub and Drive Plate

1. Follow the procedures outlined in Service Procedure 18.

2. Turn the clutch hub by hand to insure that it (or the internal assembly) is not dragging or binding.

3. Spin the pulley to insure that it is not dragging or binding. It should turn freely.

Return the Compressor to Service

1. Refill the compressor with 525 viscosity refrigeration oil. If the compressor is being returned to the car, refill it with the same amount of oil that was drained and recorded earlier. If the compressor is being returned to stock, refill it with ten ounces of oil.

2. Return the compressor to stock or service as applicable.

PROCEDURE, PART II

Hub Assembly and Seal Assembly Removal

1. Follow the procedures as outlined in Service Procedure 18.

2. Mount the compressor with the front side up in a holding fixture. Secure the fixture in a vise.

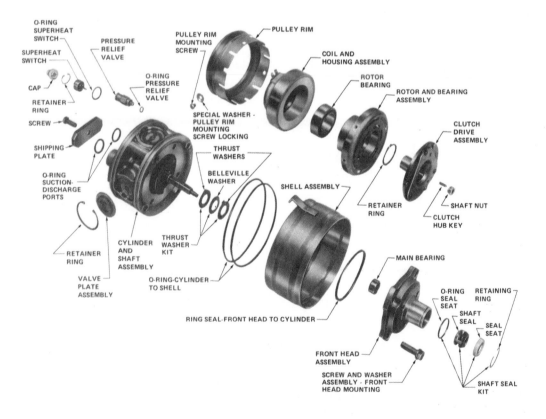

Fig. SP45-17 Exploded view of four-cylinder General Motors compressor

Clutch Rotor-Bearing and Coil-Pulley Rim Removal

1. Mark the location of the clutch coil terminals to insure proper reassembly.

2. Remove the rotor and bearing assembly retaining ring using the snap ring pliers, figure SP45-18.

3. Install the rotor bearing and puller guide over the end of the compressor shaft, figure SP45-19. *The guide should seat on the front head of the compressor.*

4. Using a puller, remove the clutch rotor and assembly parts, figure SP45-20.

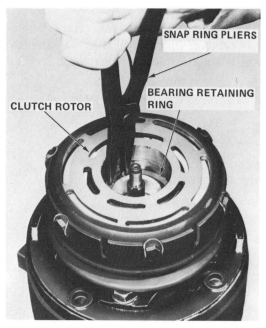

Fig. SP45-18 Removing bearing retaining ring

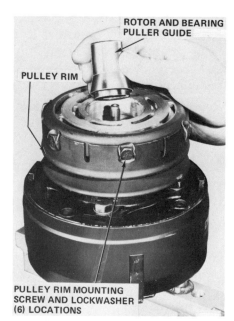

Fig. SP45-19 Positioning the rotor and bearing puller guide

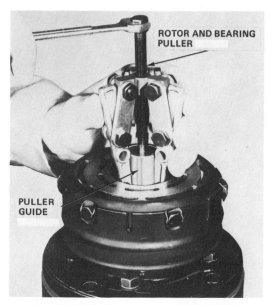

Fig. SP45-20 Removing the clutch rotor

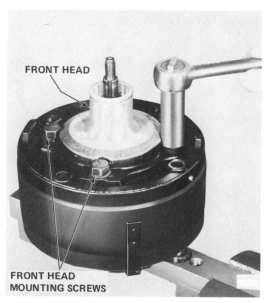

Fig. SP45-21 Removing the front head screws

Front Head and Main Bearing Removal

1. Remove the four front head mounting screws, figure SP45-21.

2. Carefully lift off the front head. Remove and discard the front head seal ring.

    NOTE: At this point the main bearing, front seal ring, Belleville washers, and thrust washers may be serviced.

Remove the Internal Assembly from the Shell

1. Pry the shell retaining strap from the cylinder, figure SP45-22. Position the strap so that it clears the cylinder as the shell is removed.

2. Reposition the holding fixture, as shown in figure SP45-23. Install the puller bolts and tighten them until they are fingertight against the compressor cylinder and the fixture protrusions contact the compressor shell. *The step protrusions must pass both sides of the cylinder to avoid damage before the procedure can be continued.*

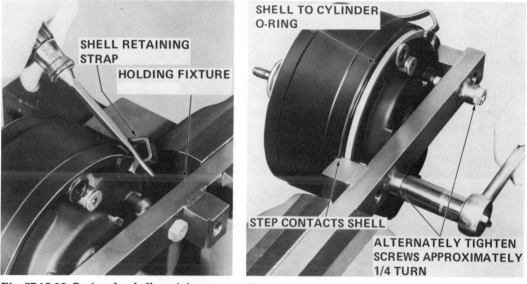

Fig. SP45-22 Prying the shell retaining strap   Fig. SP45-23 Removing internal assembly from shell

3. Alternately tighten each bolt one-quarter turn to push the shell free of the 0-rings. *The compressor must be at room temperature for this procedure.*

    NOTE: If one bolt (step 3) seems to require more force than the other, immediately turn the other to bring the screw threading sequence into step. *Do not turn the bolts any more than is necessary to remove the shell.*

4. Remove the shell. Remove and reverse the holding fixture to secure the internal assembly.

Diagnosis

1. If major damage is obvious, the compressor must be replaced. Compressor rebuilding is limited to main bearing and valve plate replacement. These procedures are outlined in Service Procedure 46.

2. Discard all 0-rings. Replace with new 0-rings.

3. Examine the Belleville washers and the thrust washers. If scored or damaged, replace the washers as a set.

4. Inspect the seal and seat for damage of any kind. A new seal is suggested whenever a compressor is rebuilt.

5. Check the pulley and bearing assembly. If the frictional surface shows signs of warpage due to excessive heat, the pulley should be replaced. Slight scoring is normal. If the assembly is heavily scored, it should be replaced.

6. Check the pulley bearing for signs of excessive noise or looseness. Replace the bearing if necessary.

7. Inspect the hub and drive plate. Refer to comments of step 5.

Replace the Internal Assembly

1. With the internal assembly in a holding fixture, dip the front and rear O-rings in refrigeration oil and slide them over the assembly into the grooves provided. Do not damage the O-rings during the assembly.

2. Place the shell on the assembly and rotate the retaining strap to its original position.

3. Attach the shell installing fixture, figure SP45-24. Align the step projections of the fixture to contact the shell evenly on both sides.

4. Push the shell as close to the O-ring as possible by hand and check for alignment. Tighten the screws fingertight.

5. Alternately tighten the screws one-quarter turn to push the shell over the O-rings and back against the stop flange.

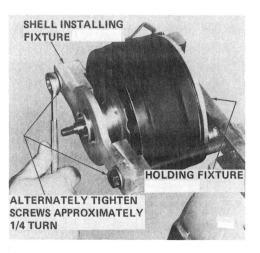

SHELL INSTALLING FIXTURE

HOLDING FIXTURE

ALTERNATELY TIGHTEN SCREWS APPROXIMATELY 1/4 TURN

Fig. SP45-24 Using the shell installing fixture for reassembly

NOTE: If one screw (step 5) seems to require more force than the other, immediately turn the other screw to bring the screw threading sequence into step. *Do not force or overtighten the screws.*

6. Bend the shell retaining strap into place by gently tapping it with a hammer.

Replace the Front Head and Main Bearing

1. Make sure that the front seal ring and the Belleville thrust washer set are in place.

2. Place the front head in position. Secure the head with four hex head mounting screws.

3. Tighten the screws to a torque of 18-22 ft.-lb.

Replace the Clutch Rotor-Bearing and Coil-Pulley Rim

1. Position the assembly on the front head of the compressor.

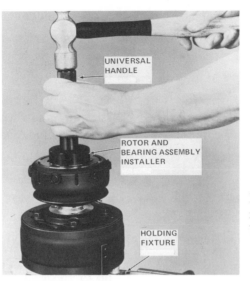

Fig. SP45-25 Using the rotor and bearing assembly installer.

2. Using the rotor assembly installer with a univeral handle, figure SP45-25, drive the assembly into place. *Before the assembly is fully seated, insure that the coil terminals are in the proper location and the three protrusions on the rear of the coil housing align with the locator holes in the front head.*

3. Install the retainer ring, using snap ring pliers.

Replace the Hub Assembly and the Seal Assembly

1. Follow the procedures outlined in Service Procedure 18.

Leak Test the Compressor

1. Follow the procedures outlined in Service Procedure 18.

2. If either internal 0-ring leaks, the assembly must be disassembled to determine the cause and correct the leak.

3. If no leaks are found, continue with the next procedure.

Return the Compressor to Service

1. Refill the compressor with 525 viscosity refrigeration oil. If the compressor is being returned to the car, refill it with the same amount of oil that was drained and recorded earlier. If the compressor is being returned to stock, refill it with six ounces of oil.

2. Return the compressor to stock or service.

REVIEW

Briefly answer each of the following questions.

1. What is considered to be an important factor in rebuilding the compressor, aside from having the proper tools?

2. What precaution should be observed when removing the internal assembly of a six-cylinder compressor?

3. What internal parts are replaceable on the four-cylinder compressor?

4. If the internal assembly of a six-cylinder compressor is damaged to the point that repair is not practical, what may be done?

5. What part is damaged if the oil pump is not properly positioned during the assembly of a six-cylinder compressor?

6. What is the clearance between the hub assembly and the rotor bearing assembly of: a. the six-cylinder compressor? b. the four-cylinder compressor?

7. The rear hex nuts of the six-cylinder compressor should be torqued to ___?___ ft.-lb.

8. The front head bolts of the four-cylinder compressor should be torqued to ___?___ ft.-lb.

9. When ready to install the internal assembly of a six-cylinder compressor in the shell, where must the oil pickup tube hole be located?

10. Describe under what condition(s) the hub or rotor should be replaced on either the six- or four-cylinder compressor.

SERVICE PROCEDURE 46:
REBUILDING THE INTERNAL ASSEMBLY OF THE GENERAL MOTORS' (FRIGIDAIRE) SIX-AND FOUR-CYLINDER COMPRESSORS

This procedure deals with the disassembly, testing, parts replacement, and reassembly of the General Motors' six- and four-cylinder compressor components. It is a continuation of Service Procedure 45. Refer to Service Procedure 45 for opening comments, service tool requirements, materials required, and acknowledgments.

PROCEDURE, PART I

NOTE: If the internal assembly has sustained major damage, due possibly to the loss of refrigerant and oil, it may be necessary to replace the complete internal assembly rather than replacing individual parts. If further disassembly is considered worthwhile, proceed as follows.

Separate the Cylinder Halves

1. To insure that the components are reassembled in their original positions, mark the pistons and the cylinder bores with a prick punch.

   Do not mark or punch mark a machined surface.

2. Remove the suction crossover cover, figure SP46-2.

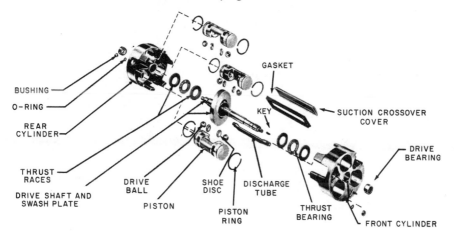

Fig. SP46-1

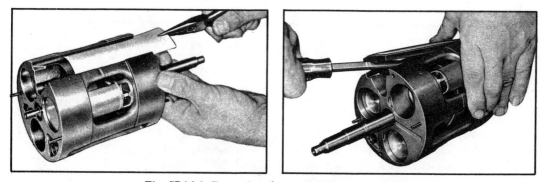

Fig. SP46-2 Removing the suction crossover cover

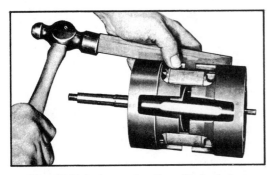

Fig. SP46-3 Separating the cylinder halves

3. Use the discharge remover tool to drive the discharge tube out of the cylinder. Drive the discharge tube toward the rear of the assembly.

4. Position the crankshaft so that the low part of the wobble plate is under the crossover tube toward the rear of the cylinder assembly.

5. Drive the cylinder halves apart and free them from the dowel pins and the discharge crossover. Use a fiber or wooden block and a hammer in this operation. Do not hit the internal assembly with a steel hammer, figure SP46-3.

6. Carefully remove the rear half of the cylinder from the pistons and set the front cylinder half (including the internal parts) into the holding fixture.

7. Push up on the shaft. One at a time, remove the pistons, balls, and shoes.

8. Remove the rings, balls, and shoes from the pistons. Note the notch at one end of the piston which identifies the front end of the piston, figure SP46-5.

9. Replace the pistons, rings, and balls into their proper positions in the parts tray, figure SP46-6.

10. Lay the ball shoes aside.

11. Remove the thrust washer and bearing combination from the rear half of the cylinder and place them in their proper positions in the parts tray.

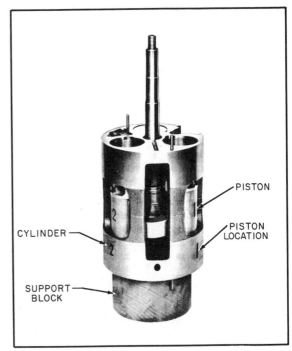

Fig. SP46-4 Piston and cylinder bores numbered

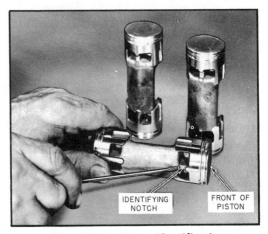

Fig. SP46-5 Piston identification

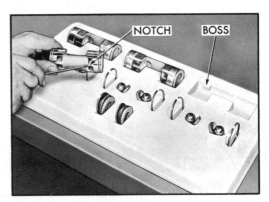

Fig. SP46-6 Parts tray

12. Remove the shaft and wobble plate from the front half of the cylinder.

13. Remove the thrust washer and bearing combination from the front half of the cylinder. Place the parts in their proper positions in the parts tray.

14. If it is determined that the front and/or rear main bearing must be replaced, use the main bearing tool to drive the bearings from the cylinder halves. If the bearings are not to be replaced, do not remove them.

Inspection and Diagnosis

1. Examine the front and rear thrust washers and bearings. Keep them in the proper position to insure that they can be reassembled correctly. If any or all of these parts show signs of wear or damage, discard all of them. Otherwise, return them to the parts tray.

2. If the thrust washers and bearings are to be replaced, place two new thrust bearings and four new *zero* thrust races in the parts tray.

3. Examine the rings. For any that are damaged or broken, place new rings in the parts tray.

4. Examine all of the balls. If any are damaged, place new balls in the parts tray.

5. Examine all pistons for chips or cracks. Examine the ball sockets for damage. For those parts found to be damaged, place new ones in the parts tray.

6. Add a zero ball shoe to each front piston ball in the parts tray. If zero ball shoes are not used, select ball shoes of 0.017 in. The method of obtaining the correct ball shoe size is covered at the end of this procedure.

7. Examine the shaft and the wobble plate. If either part shows signs of damage, both parts must be replaced as an assembly.

8. Examine both cylinder halves. Note that each half is identified with a number stamped into the casting. This identification insures that the halves can be perfectly mated and aligned. If either half is damaged, both must be replaced.

9. Wash all of the parts in a good cleaner, such as clean mineral spirits. Blow the parts dry.

Preparation for Gauging

1. Place the front half of the compression fixture in the holding fixture.

2. Place the front head in the fixture. Note that the front head is not drilled for the oil pickup tube.

3. From the parts tray, select the front thrust washers and bearing and install them on the front cylinder half.

4. Slide the long end of the shaft through the washers, bearing, and front cylinder half.

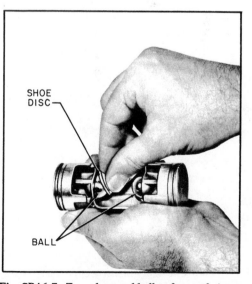

SHOE
DISC

BALL

Fig. SP46-7 Zero shoe and ball at front of piston

5. Place the rear thrust washers and bearing into place at the rear of the shaft.

6. Do not install piston rings for the gauging operation.

7. Place a ball and a zero ball shoe in the front part of the piston.

   NOTE: Zero ball shoes are usually 0.017 in. The dimension of the ball shoe can be obtained by measuring the thickness of the shoes removed from compressors.

8. Place a ball in the rear of the piston. Clean lubricant helps to hold the balls in their sockets.

9. Slide this assembly on the wobble plate and slip the front of the piston into the cylinder bore.

   NOTE: The front of the piston is identified with a notch.

10. Repeat steps 7, 8, and 9 with the other two pistons.

11. Install the four compression fixture vertical bolts and tighten them.

12. Align the rear cylinder half with the dowel pins and slide it into place.

13. Install the rear half of the compression fixture. Install the nuts and tighten them to a torque of 19-23 ft.-lb.

Gauging Procedures

   NOTE: All gauging procedures are to be performed using undamaged feeler gauges and a spring or dial scale of known calibration. Coat the feeler gauges with clean refrigeration oil.

1. Start with the number one piston. Insert a feeler gauge between the ball and wobble plate, figure SP46-8. The gauge should require a pull of 4-8 ounces for removal. If less than 4 oz. of pull are required, increase the thickness of the stock. If more than 8 oz. of pull are required, use a thinner stock.

2. Make a note of the thickness of the stock required to cause a pull of 4-8 oz.

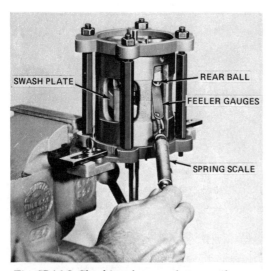

Fig. SP46-8 Checking clearance between the rear ball and the wobble plate

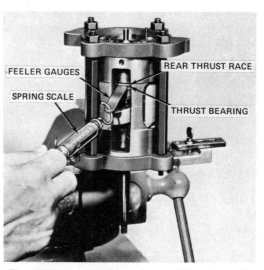

Fig. SP46-9 Checking clearance between the rear thrust bearing and the outer thrust race

3. Rotate the shaft 120 degrees and recheck the number one cylinder. Make a note of the thickness of the stock required to cause a pull of 4-8 oz. to remove the stock in this position.

4. Rotate the shaft another 120 degrees and repeat the procedure. Note the stock thickness.

5. Repeat steps 1, 2, 3, and 4 with pistons two and three.

6. If new thrust bearings and races are used, proceed with step 7. If the old bearings and races are used, go to step 8.

7. Place a feeler gauge between the thrust bearing and the upper rear thrust race, figure SP46-9. To remove the gauge, a pull of 4-8 oz. should be indicated on the scale. Note the thickness of the gauge.

8. Insure that all pistons are gauged and identified.

SHOE CHART

SERVICE *PART NUMBER	IDENTIFICATON NO. STAMPED ON SHOE
6557000	0
6556180	18
6556190	19
6556200	20
6556210	21

*The last three digits indicate the identification number on the shoes.

THRUST BEARING RACE CHART

Service *Part Number	Thickness Dimension	Identification No. Stamped on Race
6556000	0.0920	0
6556060	0.0970	6
6556070	0.0980	7
6556080	0.0990	8
6556090	0.1000	9
6556100	0.1010	10
6556110	0.1020	11
6556120	0.1030	12

*The last three digits indicate the identification number on the race.

Fig. SP46-10

Dismantle the Assembly

1. Remove the nuts and the rear ring from the compression fitting.

2. Remove the internal assembly and lay it flat on the bench.

3. Carefully drive the cylinder halves apart, using a fiber or wooden block and a hammer.

4. Place the front cylinder half (including its internal parts) in the holding fixture.

5. Carefully remove the pistons and place them in their proper positions in the parts tray. The pistons will include the balls and ball shoes.

6. It is not necessary to remove the thrust races or bearings.

7. If the original thrust races and bearings are used, disregard this step. If new zero races are used, remove the rear zero race and select a race corresponding to the feeler gauge reading. (If the feeler gauge reading was 0.0095 in., use a thrust race stamped 9 1/2; if the gauge was 0.011 in., use a race stamped 11.) Substitute this race for the zero race removed.

8. Place a rear ball shoe in the parts tray to correspond to the smallest of the three readings obtained when the clearance between the ball and plate is checked, figure SP46-11.

   EXAMPLE: If the readings on piston one are 0.019 in., 0.0195 in., and 0.019 in., use a shoe marked 19; if the readings are 0.022 in., 0.021 in., and 0.022 in., use a shoe marked 21.

9. Assemble the rings on the pistons. The scraper groove is assembled toward the center of the piston.

10. Insure that all parts are clean and free of all foreign matter. All parts must be in their proper positions in the parts tray.

Assemble the Internal Assembly

1. Rotate the wobble plate so that the high point is above the number one cylinder bore.

2. Place a ball in each end of the piston. Place the zero ball shoe at the front end of the piston and a selected ball shoe at the rear of the piston.

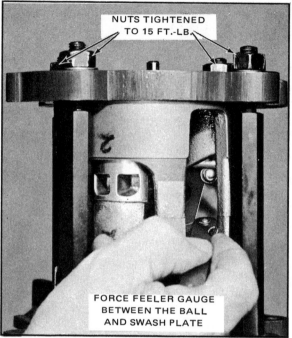

Fig. SP46-11 Checking the drive ball-to-swash plate clearance

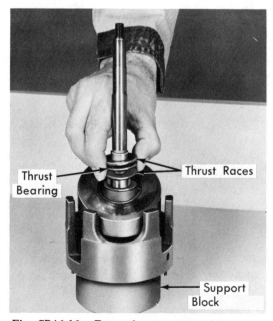

Fig. SP46-12 Front thrust races and bearing

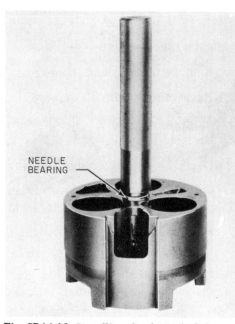

Fig. SP46-13 Installing the drive shaft bearing

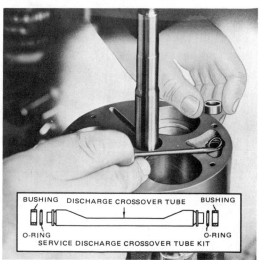

Fig. SP46-14 Installing the service discharge crossover tube

Fig. SP46-15 Installing the service discharge crossover parts

NOTE: The balls and shoes can be held in place using a thin coat of clean petroleum jelly.

3. Locate the ball shoes on the wobble plate. Carefully compress the front ring and place the piston in the front half of the cylinder.

4. Repeat steps 1, 2, and 3 with pistons two and three.

5. Place the discharge crossover tube in the front cylinder half, figure SP46-14. The flattened portion of this tube must face the inside of the compressor to allow clearance for the wobble plate.

Fig. SP46-16 Assembling the cylinder halves

6. Carefully place the rear cylinder half in position and insert the pistons into the bores one by one. Compress the rings on each piston to ease them into the bores.

7. When all of the parts are aligned properly, tap the assembly with a wooden block and hammer to seat the rear cylinder half over the dowel pins, figure SP46-16. If necessary, clamp the assembly in the compression fixture to draw the halves together completely.

8. Install the rear portion of the compression fixture and tighten the nuts to a torque of 19-23 ft.-lb.

9. Lubricate the internal mechanism generously with clean refrigeration oil.

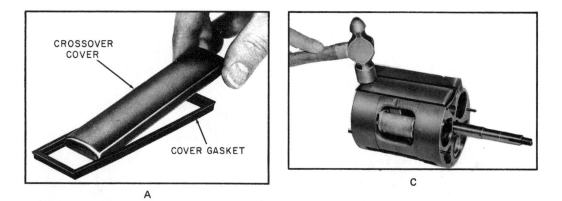

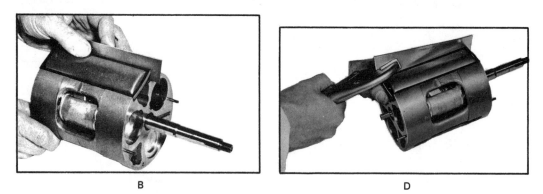

Fig. SP46-17 Installing the suction crossover and gasket assembly

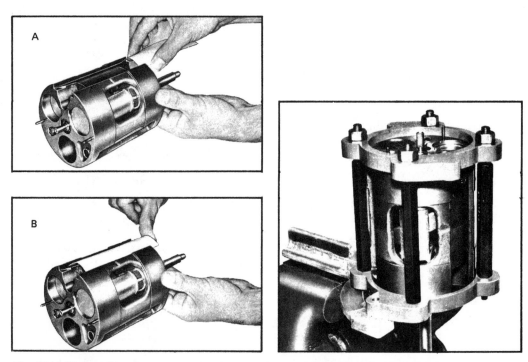

Fig. SP46-18 Installing the suction crossover cover

Fig. SP46-19 The internal mechanism

10. Check for free operation by rotating the crankshaft. If there is any binding or if tight spots are felt, these conditions must be corrected.

11. Remove the internal assembly from the compression fixture and lay it on a flat surface.

12. Install the suction crossover cover, figure SP46-17 or SP46-18. If the cover is equipped with a gasket, use a piece of flat spring steel (0.015 in. to 0.020 in. thick) as a shoehorn to press the gasket in place. This shoehorn is a part of the regular compressor tool assortment for early model compressors.

Install the Internal Assembly

1. The internal assembly, figure SP46-19, is now ready for placement in the compressor shell.

2. Follow the procedures outlined in Service Procedure 45.

PROCEDURE, PART II

NOTE: Servicing the internal assembly of the four-cylinder compressor is limited to replacement of the main bearing, thrust and Belleville washers, and the valve plates. If the internal assembly has sustained major damage, it is necessary to replace the compressor as an assembly. If repair of the internal assembly is considered worthwhile, proceed as follows.

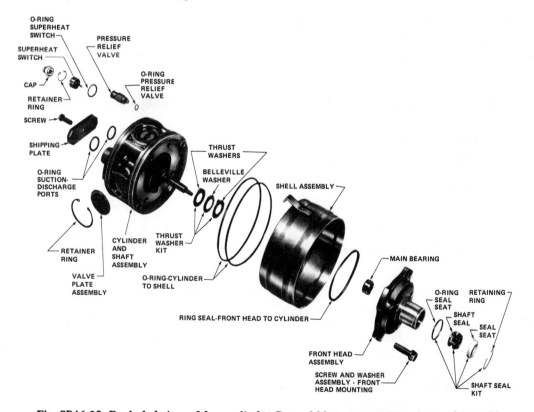

Fig. SP46-20 Exploded view of four-cylinder General Motors compressor internal assembly

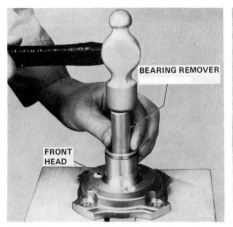

Fig. SP46-21 Removing the bearing from the front head

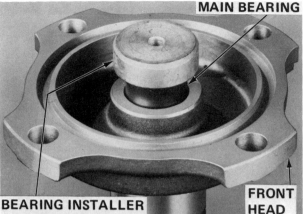

Fig. SP46-22 Installing the new bearing in the front head

Replace the Main Bearing

1. Remove the front head and main bearing assembly from the compressor as outlined in Service Procedure 45.

2. Place the front head assembly on two blocks, figure SP46-21. Using the bearing remover and the hammer, drive the bearing out of the front head.

3. Place the front head with the neck end down on a flat, solid surface of the workbench.

4. Align the new bearing using the bearing installer, figure SP46-22, squarely with the bearing bore.

5. Drive the bearing into place with a hammer. *The bearing installer must seat against the front head to insure the proper clearance depth.*

6. Reassemble the front head to the compressor as outlined in Service Procedure 45.

Replace the Thrust and Belleville Washers

1. Remove the front head and bearing assembly from the compressor as outlined in Service Procedure 45.

2. Remove the washers (two thrust washers and one Belleville washer) from the compressor shaft. Note the assembled position of the washers.

3. Install the new washer set as follows:

   a. Install the thrust washer with the tang pointing up.
   b. Install the Belleville washer with the high center of the washer pointing up.
   c. Install the second thrust washer with the tang pointing down.
   d. Lubricate the assembly liberally with clean refrigeration oil.

4. Reassemble the front head to the compressor as outlined in Service Procedure 45.

Replace the Valve Plate(s)

1. Remove the internal assembly from the shell as outlined in Service Procedure 45.

2. Using snap ring pliers, remove the valve plate retaining ring(s), as shown in figure SP46-23.

3. Lift out the valve plate(s) from the bore.

4. Inspect the top of the pistons for damage. Seriously damaged pistons mean that the compressor must be replaced. If the pistons are not damaged, proceed with step 5.

5. Replace the damaged valve plates.

6. Replace the retaining rings using the snap ring pliers.

7. Reassemble the internal assembly with the compressor shell as outlined in Service Procedure 45.

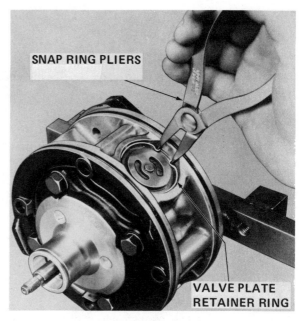

Fig. SP46-23 Removing the valve plate retaining ring

REVIEW

Briefly answer the following questions.

1. What instrument or tool is used to separate the cylinder halves of a six-cylinder compressor?

2. What is the thickness of a zero ball shoe in a six-cylinder compressor?

3. How many washers are there in a four-cylinder compressor?
   a. thrust   b. Belleville

4. What parts of a four-cylinder compressor may be replaced in the internal assembly?

5. Toward which end of the six-cylinder compressor does the notch in the piston rest?

6. If a pull of six ounces is sufficient to remove a shim of 0.018 in. on all three checks of a six-cylinder compressor, what ball shoe should be used?

7. What is the purpose of a discharge crossover tube in the six-cylinder compressor?

8. With the internal assembly removed from the shell, list the steps in the procedure for replacing a valve plate in a four-cylinder compressor.

9. Do all six-cylinder suction crossover covers require:
   a. a gasket?   b. removal/replacement?   c. new replacement?

10. What is an important point to remember when replacing the main bearing in a four-cylinder compressor?

SERVICE PROCEDURE 47:
REBUILDING THE SUCTION THROTTLING VALVE

The suction throttling valve (STV) has been used on General Motors' cars since 1962. Valves produced after 1965 cannot be serviced. This service procedure is to be followed in rebuilding the earlier model of STV only.

The following procedure is given in two parts: Part I deals with the cable-controlled STV and Part II deals with the vacuum-controlled STV.

The proper cleaning and servicing of the valve requires that it be removed from the car. Both parts of the procedure are concerned with the suction throttling valve removed from the car.

TOOLS

Pliers   Phillips No. 2 screwdriver

MATERIALS

Clean refrigeration oil
Diaphragm and/or piston assembly, as required

PROCEDURE, PART I

Dismantle the Valve

1. Clean the external surfaces of the valve with clean mineral spirits.

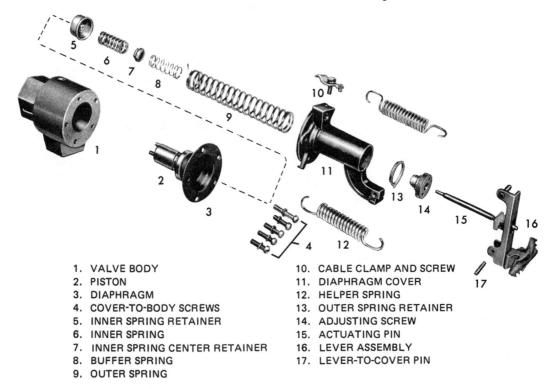

1. VALVE BODY	10. CABLE CLAMP AND SCREW
2. PISTON	11. DIAPHRAGM COVER
3. DIAPHRAGM	12. HELPER SPRING
4. COVER-TO-BODY SCREWS	13. OUTER SPRING RETAINER
5. INNER SPRING RETAINER	14. ADJUSTING SCREW
6. INNER SPRING	15. ACTUATING PIN
7. INNER SPRING CENTER RETAINER	16. LEVER ASSEMBLY
8. BUFFER SPRING	17. LEVER-TO-COVER PIN
9. OUTER SPRING	

Fig. SP47-1 Exploded view of the suction throttling valve — Bowden cable controlled

2. Remove the two helper springs located between the lever assembly and the diaphragm cover.

3. Mark the position of the diaphragm cover with relation to the valve body to insure that the parts can be aligned properly when they are reassembled.

4. Remove five cover-to-body screws.

   CAUTION: *The diaphragm cover is under a heavy spring tension.*

5. Remove the diaphragm cover, outer spring, buffer spring, inner spring center retainer, and inner spring.

6. Check the inside of the diaphragm cover barrel and remove the outer spring retainer.

7. Remove the inner spring retainer, diaphragm, and piston from the valve body. Separate the inner spring retainer from the diaphragm.

   NOTE: It is not necessary to remove the adjusting screw, lever assembly, or actuating pin.

8. Place all parts in clean mineral spirits for 10-15 minutes.

9. Remove the parts and blow them dry. Inspect all parts for damage.

10. Check the inner spring retainer for rough spots or sharp edges. Clean the retainer with a crocus cloth.

Assemble the Valve

1. Place a new diaphragm piston assembly in the bore of the valve body. Use an ample coating of clean refrigeration oil on all surfaces. The surfaces must be free of all foreign matter.

2. Place the inner spring retainer into the cavity at the center of the diaphragm.

3. Stack the inner spring, inner spring center retainer, and buffer spring on top of the inner spring retainer.

4. Carefully slide the outer spring over this assembly.

5. Replace the outer spring retainer in the diaphragm cover. Apply refrigeration oil to hold the retainer in place.

6. Slide the diaphragm cover into position and line up the holes. Make sure that the index mark made previously is aligned.

7. Press the diaphragm cover in place and insert the five screws. Tighten the screws until they are hand tight.

8. Check all five screws to insure that they are tight.

PROCEDURE, PART II

Disassemble the Valve

1. Clean all external surfaces of the valve with clean mineral spirits.

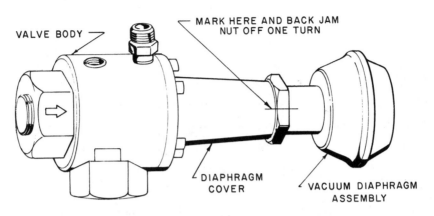

VALVE BODY

MARK HERE AND BACK JAM
NUT OFF ONE TURN

DIAPHRAGM
COVER

VACUUM DIAPHRAGM
ASSEMBLY

Fig. SP47-2 Vacuum-controlled suction throttling valve

2. Mark the jam nut. Then back off the jam nut one complete turn, figure SP47-2.

3. Remove the vacuum control diaphragm assembly.

   CAUTION: *The vacuum control assembly is under heavy spring pressure.*

4. Remove the five diaphragm-to-valve body screws and lift off the diaphragm cover.

5. Remove the spring retainer, diaphragm, and piston from the valve body. Separate the spring retainer from the diaphragm.

6. Place all parts in clean mineral spirits for 10-15 minutes.

7. Remove the parts and blow them dry. Inspect all parts for damage. Check the spring retainer for rough spots or sharp edges. Clean the parts with a crocus cloth.

Assemble the Valve

1. Place the new diaphragm/piston assembly in the bore of the valve body. Use an ample coating of clean refrigeration oil on all surfaces to insure that they are free of all foreign matter.

2. Place the spring retainer in the cavity at the center of the diaphragm.

3. With the diaphragm cover in position, replace the five screws. Tighten the screws until they are handtight. Check all five screws to be sure that they are tight.

4. Place the outer spring in the diaphragm cover and carefully replace the vacuum diaphragm assembly.

   CAUTION: *Do not cross the threads.*

5. Tighten the assembly until the diaphragm jam nut touches the diaphragm cover. Then back the jam nut off one full turn. Now tighten the jam nut against the diaphragm cover. No further adjustment in the car should be necessary.

REVIEW

Briefly answer each of the following questions.

1. Can all suction throttling valves be rebuilt? Explain.

2. What is the most common fault with the STV?

3. Name the two main parts of the STV.

4. What cleaner should be used on the STV?

5. Is it always necessary to replace the piston and diaphragm assembly? Explain.

SERVICE PROCEDURE 48:
REBUILDING THE VALVES-IN-RECEIVER (VIR)

The valves-in-receiver (VIR) should be removed from the car if it is necessary to rebuild the assembly. However, the sight glass, the liquid line valve core, and the evaporator gauge valve core can be easily replaced without removing the VIR assembly from the automobile.

The following procedure is given in three parts: Part I deals with sight glass replacement; Part II covers the replacement of either (or both) of the valve cores; and Part III covers the rebuilding of the assembly.

Kent Moore tool numbers are given in the illustrations. Only three numbered tools are required for all VIR service: the valve core remover, the pickup tube installer, and the valve capsule remover.

TOOLS

Screwdrivers
Open end wrenches
Allen wrench, 7/16 in.

Valve core remover
Pickup tube installer
Valve capsule remover

MATERIALS

Set of 0-rings
Refrigeration oil
Cleaning solvent
Any parts that are determined to be defective

PROCEDURE: SIGHT GLASS, PART I

Preparation

1. Purge the system of refrigerant as outlined in Service Procedure 3.

2. Remove the sight glass retaining nut using the 7/16-in. Allen wrench, figure SP48-1.

Remove the Sight Glass

1. Place a finger over the sight glass to hold it in place.

2. Slightly pressurize the system with refrigerant vapor.

3. Shift the finger pressure on the sight glass from side to side until the sight glass is free of the opening. The system pressure (as applied in step 2) should force the glass from the opening.

Fig. SP48-1 Location of the valves-in-receiver (VIR) sight glass

4. Discard the sight glass 0-ring, thrust washer, and nut. Inspect the sight glass. If it is damaged, discard the sight glass.

Install the Sight Glass

1. Coat the new 0-ring, nylon thrust washer, and sight glass retaining nut with refrigeration oil.

2. Install the parts in the cavity in the opposite order from that in which they were removed.

3. Tighten the retaining nut to a torque of 20-25 in.-lb.

Return the System to Service

1. Evacuate the system as outlined in Service Procedure 6.

2. Leak check the system as outlined in Service Procedure 4 or 5.

3. Charge the system as outlined in Service Procedure 7, 8, or 9.

PROCEDURE: VALVE CORE(S), PART II

Preparation

1. Purge the system of refrigerant as outlined in Service Procedure 3.

2. Determine if one or both of the valve cores must be replaced.

Remove the Valve Core

1. Remove the protective cap from the evaporator gauge valve core and/or the liquid bleed line from the bleed valve fitting of the VIR.

2. Using a numbered tool, remove either (or both) of the valve cores.

3. Discard the core(s) removed.

Install the Valve Core(s)

1. Note the different colors of the cores. The evaporator gauge core is blue and the oil bleed line valve core is gold or red.

2. Using the numbered tool, figure SP48-2, install the valve core(s).

3. When the core just begins to tighten, note the location of the tool handle and turn it an additional 180° (half turn). This provides a torque of about 24-36 in.-oz.

Return the System to Service

1. Replace the oil bleed line. Tighten the fitting but do not overtighten it.

Fig. SP48-2 Location of the valves-in-receiver (VIR) valve core

2. Evacuate the system as outlined in Service Procedure 6.

3. Leak check the system as outlined in Service Procedure 4 or 5.

4. Charge the system as outlined in Service Procedure 7, 8, or 9.

PROCEDURE: REBUILDING THE VIR ASSEMBLY, PART III

Preparation

1. Purge the system of refrigerant as outlined in Service Procedure 3.

2. While purging, clean the exterior surface of the VIR.

3. Disconnect the oil bleed line.

4. Disconnect the inlet and outlet hoses (from the compressor and the condenser).

5. Disconnect the inlet and outlet lines from the evaporator.

6. Discard all 0-rings.

7. Remove the mounting clamp(s) and lift the VIR from the car.

Disassembly of the VIR

1. Note the location of the parts shown in figure SP48-3.

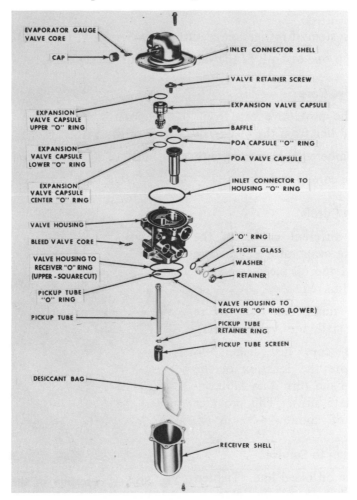

Fig. SP48-3 Exploded view of the valves-in-receiver (VIR)

2. Loosen the six receiver shell-to-valve housing retaining screws. Turn the screws approximately three turns. *Do not* completely remove the screws until instructed to do so in step 5.

3. Hold the VIR valve housing and push on the lower end of the receiver shell. This should break the seal between the shell and the housing.

4. If step 4 does not break the seal, *carefully* pry between the receiver shell mounting flange and the valve housing. Take care not to mar or scratch the mating surfaces.

5. Remove the six retaining screws (loosened in step 2).

6. Lower the receiver shell to clear the pickup tube and screen. Keep the assembly in an upright position, figure SP48-4.

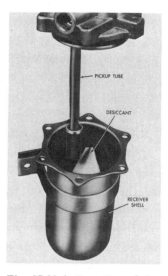

Fig. SP48-4 Location of the pickup tube and desiccant inside the receiver

7. Remove and discard the bag of desiccant.

8. Drain, measure, and discard any oil found in the receiver. Note the amount of oil drained.

9. Remove, but do not discard, the pickup tube filter screen.

10. Remove the four inlet connector shell-to-valve housing screws.

11. Carefully slip the inlet connector shell off the valve housing. Do not scratch the mating surfaces.

12. Loosen both valve capsule retaining screws about 3/16 in. *Do not* remove the screws entirely until instructed to do so in step 17.

13. Attach the valve capsule remover tool to the tapered groove projection on the expansion valve capsule as shown in figure SP48-5.

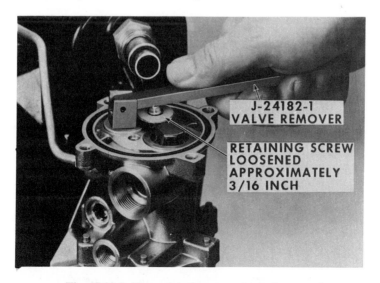

Fig. SP48-5 Removing the expansion valve capsule

14. Position the tool over one of the screws (step 12) and press down on the handle to loosen the expansion valve capsule.

15. Insert the opposite side of the valve capsule remover tool under the STV baffle. The edge of the tool must clear the edge of the capsule, figure SP48-6.

16. Taking care not to damage the valve housing 0-ring groove area, press down on the handle to loosen the STV capsule.

17. With both capsules loose, remove both retaining screws (step 12).

18. Remove the expansion valve and the STV capsules from the valve housing.

19. Remove and discard all 0-rings and/or gaskets.

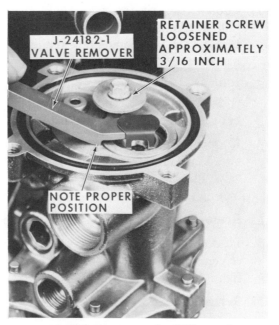

Fig. SP48-6 Removing the STV capsule

Cleaning and Inspection

1. Clean all parts in a good solvent, such as stoddard or kerosene. Trichlorethylene or naphtha, however, are the preferred solvents.

2. Carefully inspect all parts for nicks, scratches, or any other flaws.

3. Place all of the parts to be reassembled (except the desiccant bag) into a container of clean refrigeration oil.

4. Check the pickup tube filter screen to insure that it is clear of any contaminants.

Reassembly of the VIR

1. Reassemble the VIR components in the reverse order of their disassembly.

2. The capsule retaining screws should be tightened to a torque of 5-7 ft.-lb.

3. The inlet connector shell screws should be torqued to 10 ft.-lb.

4. The pickup tube screen must be in place before the receiver shell is replaced. In addition:

   a. place a new bag of desiccant into the shell, and
   b. replace the oil using the quantity noted when the old oil was removed. If less than one ounce of oil was removed, replace one ounce. If more than one ounce was removed, replace with the same amount. *Use new, clean refrigeration oil.*

5. The receiver shell screws should be torqued to 10 ft.-lb.

6. Check the work area. If there are any parts such as 0-rings on the bench, they may have been left out of the VIR assembly.

Return the System to Service

1. Place the VIR into the mounting clamp(s).

2. Using new 0-rings, connect the inlet and outlet lines (from the evaporator).

3. Using new 0-rings, connect the inlet and outlet hoses (from the compressor and the condenser).

4. Using a new 0-ring, reconnect the oil bleed line.

5. Evacuate the system as outlined in Service Procedure 6.

6. Leak check the system as outlined in Service Procedure 4 or 5.

7. Charge the system as outlined in Service Procedure 7, 8, or 9.

8. Retest the operation of the VIR as outlined in Service Procedure 28.

REVIEW

Select the appropriate answer from the choices given.

1. Special tools are required for the removal of the
   a. VIR.
   b. STV capsule.
   c. sight glass.
   d. pickup tube screen.

2. If the amount of oil removed from the receiver shell is 3/4 ounce, it should be replaced with
   a. 1/2 ounce.
   b. 3/4 ounce.
   c. 1 ounce.
   d. 1 3/4 ounces.

3. When replacing the oil bleed valve it should be
   a. snug, then turned 90°.
   b. snug, then turned 180°.
   c. snug, then turned 270°.
   d. snug, then turned 360°.

4. The evaporator gauge valve core is
   a. blue.
   b. red.
   c. gold.
   d. green.

5. The procedure for letting all of the refrigerant out of a system is called
   a. evacuation.
   b. charging.
   c. purging.
   d. leak down.

SERVICE PROCEDURE 49:
SPLICING THE REFRIGERANT HOSE AND INSERTING FITTINGS

This procedure is concerned with the proper handling of rubber refrigeration hose and insert fittings. In many cases, a break in the hose caused by rubbing or chafing against another part can be repaired using an insert splice fitting, figure SP49-1.

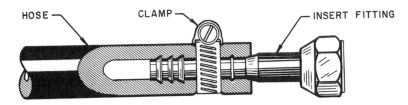

Fig. SP49-1 Insert splice fitting detail

TOOLS

Razor blade   Screwdriver

MATERIALS

Hose   Refrigeration oil, as required
Fitting(s)   Clamp(s)

PROCEDURE

Prepare the Hose

1. Locate and mark the proper length and location of the hose.

2. With a razor blade, cut the hose.

   NOTE: A single-edge razor blade should be used. Single-edge industrial blades are available at all cleaning supply houses.

3. Apply clean refrigeration oil to the inside of the hose to be used. Seal off the other hose.

Insert the Fitting

1. Insure that the fitting is free of all nicks and burrs.

2. Coat the fitting liberally with clean refrigeration oil.

3. Slip the insert fitting inside the refrigeration hose in one constant, deliberate motion.

4. Install the hose clamp and tighten it to a torque of approximately 30 ft.-lb.

   NOTE: The hose clamp should be placed at the approximate location of the fitting barb closest to the nut end of the fitting.

REVIEW

Briefly answer each of the following questions.

1. How can an insert fitting be used to repair a damaged hose?

2. What is the recommended torque for tightening the hose clamp?

3. What lubricant is used to insure an easier installation of the fitting in the hose?

SERVICE PROCEDURE 50:
REPLACING COMPONENTS

The following procedures are typical for step-by-step replacement of air-conditioning system components. For specific replacement details, refer to the shop service manual for the particular year/model of the unit.

TOOLS

Manifold and gauge set
Vacuum pump

Hand tools, as required

MATERIALS

Refrigeration oil
Gaskets and/or O-rings

Components, as required

PROCEDURE

Preparation

1. Purge the system of refrigerant. See Service Procedure 3.

2. Disconnect the battery.

3. Locate the component that is to be removed for repair or replacement.

4. Remove the necessary access panel(s) or other hardware to gain access to the component.

Remove the Component

1. For a thermostatic expansion valve:

   a. Remove the insulation tape and clamp to free the remote bulb.
   b. Disconnect the external equalizer, if the TXV is so equipped.
   c. Remove the liquid line from the inlet of the TXV.
   d. Remove the evaporator inlet fitting from the outlet of the TXV.
   e. Remove the holding clamp (if provided on the TXV) and carefully lift the TXV from the evaporator. Do not damage the remote bulb or capillary tube.

2. For an expansion tube:

   a. Remove the liquid line from the evaporator inlet.
   b. Using needle nose pliers, remove the expansion tube from the evaporator inlet line.
   c. Remove the O-ring from the inlet line.

3. For an accumulator:

   a. Remove the accumulator inlet fitting.
   b. Remove the accumulator outlet fitting.
   c. Remove the bracket attaching screw and remove the accumulator from the car.

4. For a compressor:

   a. Remove the inlet and outlet hoses or the service valves from the compressor.
   b. Remove the clutch lead wire. Loosen and remove the belt(s).
   c. Remove the mounting bolts from the compressor brackets and braces and lift the compressor from the car.

5. For a condenser:

   a. Remove the inlet and outlet hoses.
   b. Remove the mounting hardware and lift the condenser from the car.

6. For an evaporator:

   a. Aftermarket (add on) unit:
      1. Remove the inlet hose from the TXV.
      2. Remove the suction line from the evaporator.
      3. Disconnect the electrical lead wire(s).
      4. Remove the mounting hardware and lift the evaporator from the car.
   b. Factory-installed unit:
      1. Remove the inlet hose from the TXV (or VIR, if the automobile is equipped with this device).
      2. Remove the outlet hose from the evaporator, STV, POA, or VIR, as equipped.
      3. Remove the mechanical linkage or vacuum line(s) from the evaporator controls, as equipped.
      4. Remove the mounting bolts and hardware from the evaporator housing.
      5. Carefully lift the evaporator assembly from the car. Do not force the assembly.

7. For a receiver/drier:

   a. Remove the low-pressure switch wire, if the unit is so equipped.
   b. Remove the inlet and outlet hoses from the drier.
   c. Remove the mounting hardware and lift the receiver/drier from the car.
   d. Remove the low-pressure switch from the drier, if the unit is so equipped.

8. For an ETR, EPR, or POEPR valve:

   a. If an ETR valve is used, disconnect the electrical wire.
   b. Remove the two bolts holding the suction service valve to the compressor.
   c. Remove the suction service valve and gasket.
   d. Remove the valve from the compressor cavity.

9. For an STV or POA valve:

   a. Remove the TXV external equalizer from the valve assembly.
   b. Remove the oil bleed line from the valve assembly.
   c. Remove the cable- or vacuum-controlled line(s) or hose(s), if the unit is so equipped.
   d. Remove the valve inlet (evaporator outlet) line from the assembly.
   e. Remove the valve outlet (suction line) hose.
   f. Remove the mounting clamp and lift the assembly from the car.

10. For a VIR:

   a. Disconnect the oil bleed line.
   b. Disconnect the inlet and outlet hoses (from the compressor and the condenser).
   c. Disconnect the inlet and outlet lines (from the evaporator).
   d. Remove the mounting clamp and lift the assembly from the car.

11. For a superheat switch:

   a. Remove the wire from the switch.
   b. Remove the internal snap ring.
   c. Using two screwdrivers, remove the switch.
   d. Remove and discard the 0-ring.

Component Replacement

1. Use new gaskets and/or 0-rings when replacing a component.

2. Coat all components liberally with clean refrigeration oil before reassembly.

3. For reassembly, reverse the removal procedure.

Return the System to Service

1. Replace any access panels, clamps, or other hardware previously removed.

2. Connect the battery.

3. Evacuate the system as outlined in Service Procedure 6.

4. Charge the system as outlined in Service Procedure 7, 8, or 9.

REVIEW

Select the appropriate answer from the choices given.

1. Before installation, all gaskets and 0-rings should be coated with

   a. Permatex.
   b. refrigerant.
   c. form-a-gasket.
   d. refrigeration oil.

2. The hot gas discharge hose runs from the

   a. condenser to the drier.
   b. drier to the TXV.
   c. evaporator to the compressor.
   d. compressor to the condenser.

3. On which of the following is an external equalizer *not* found?

   a. Accumulator
   b. Expansion valve
   c. Suction throttling valve
   d. POA valve

4. The desiccant is found in the

   a. receiver/drier.
   b. valves-in-receiver.
   c. accumulator.
   d. All of these.

5. The expansion tube is located

   a. at the evaporator inlet.
   b. at the evaporator outlet.
   c. at the VIR inlet.
   d. at the POA outlet.

GLOSSARY

A

Absolute Pressure: pressure measured from absolute zero instead of normal atmospheric pressure.

Absolute Temperature: temperature measured on the Rankine thermometer calibrated from absolute zero. The freezing point of water on the Rankine Scale is 492°R.

Absolute Zero: the complete absence of heat, believed to be -459.67°F. This is shown as 0° on the Rankine and Kelvin temperature scales.

Accumulator: a tank located in the tailpipe to receive the refrigerant that leaves the evaporator. This device is constructed to insure that no liquid refrigerant enters the compressor.

Air Conditioner: a device used in the control of the temperature, humidity, cleanness, and movement of air.

Air Conditioning: the control of the temperature, humidity, cleanness, and movement of air.

Air Inlet Valve: a movable door in the plenum blower assembly that permits the selection of outside air or inside air for both heating and cooling systems.

Air Outlet Valve: a movable door in the plenum blower assembly that directs air flow into the heater core or into the ductwork that leads to the evaporator.

Ambient Air: air surrounding an object.

Ambient Air Temperature: see "Ambient Temperature."

Ambient Temperature: temperature of the surrounding air. In air-conditioning work, this term refers to the outside air temperature.

Ambient Sensor: a thermistor used in automatic temperature control units to sense ambient temperature. Also see "Thermistor."

Ambient Switch: a switch used to control compressor operation by turning it on or off. The switch is regulated by ambient temperature.

Amplifier: a device used in automatic temperature control units to provide an output voltage that is in proportion to the input voltage from the sensors.

Annealed Copper: copper that has been heat treated to render it workable; commonly used in refrigeration systems.

Aspirator: a device that uses suction to move air, accomplished by a differential in air pressure.

A.T.C: abbreviation for automatic temperature control.

Atmospheric Pressure: air pressure at a given altitude. At sea level, atmospheric pressure is 14.696 psi.

Atom: The smallest possible particle of matter.

Auto: abbreviation for automatic.

Automatic: a self-regulating system or device which adjusts to variables of a predetermined condition.

Automatic Temperature Control: the name of an air-conditioner control system designed to maintain an in-car temperature and humidity level automatically at a preset level or condition.

Auxiliary Seal: used on General Motors' compressors through 1960. This seal is mounted outside the seal housing and prevents refrigeration oil from entering the clutch assembly.

B

Back Idler: a pulley that tightens the drive belt; the pulley rides on the back or flat side of the belt.

Back Seat (Service Valve): turning the valve stem to the left (CCW) as far as possible back seats the valve. The valve outlet to the system is open and the service port is closed.

Bellows: an accordian-type chamber which expands or contracts with temperature changes to create a mechanical controlling action such as in a thermostatic expansion valve.

Belt: See "V-belt."

Bimetallic: two dissimilar metals fused togther; these metals expand (or contract) at different temperatures to cause a bending effect. Bimetallic elements are used in temperature sensing controls.

Bimetallic Thermostat: a thermostat that uses bimetallic strips instead of a bellows for making or breaking contact points.

Bleeding: slowly releasing pressure in the air-conditioning system by drawing off some liquid or gas.

Blower: see "Squirrel Cage Blower."

Blower Fan: see "Squirrel Cage Blower" or "Fan."

Blower Motor: see "Motor."

Blower Motor Relay: see "Blower Relay."

Blower Relay: an electrical device used to control the function or speed of a blower motor.

Blower Resistor: see "Resistor."

Boiling Point: the temperature at which a liquid changes to a vapor.

Bowden Cable: a wire cable inside a metal or rubber housing used to regulate a valve or control from a remote place.

Brazing: a high-temperature metal joining process that is satisfactory for units with relatively high internal pressures.

British Thermal Unit (Btu): the amount of heat necessary to raise one pound of water one degree Fahrenheit.

Btu: see "British Thermal Unit."

C

Calorie: the smallest measure of heat energy. One calorie is the amount of heat energy required to raise one gram of water one degree Celsius.

Can Tap: a device used to pierce, dispense, and seal small cans of refrigerant.

Can Valve: see "Can Tap."

Capillary: a small tube with a calibrated length and inside diameter used as a metering device.

Capillary Attraction: the ability of tubular bodies to draw up a fluid.

Capillary Tube: a tube with a calibrated inside diameter and length used to control the flow of refrigerant. In automotive air-conditioning systems, the tube connecting the remote bulb to the expansion valve or to the thermostat is called the capillary tube.

Capacity: refrigeration produced, measured in tons or Btu per hour.

Celsius: a temperature scale using the freezing point of water as zero. The boiling point of water is 100°C.

Change of State: rearrangement of the molecular structure of matter as it changes between any two of the three physical states: solid, liquid, or gas.

Charge: a specific amount of refrigerant or oil by volume or weight.

Charging: the act of placing a charge of refrigerant or oil into the air-conditioning system.

Charging Cylinder: a container with a visual indicator for use where a critical, or exact, amount of refrigerant must be measured.

Charging Hose: a hose with a small diameter constructed to withstand high pressures; the hose is located between the unit and the manifold set.

Charging Station: a unit containing a manifold and gauge set, charging cylinder, vacuum pump, and leak detector. This unit is used to service air conditioners.

Check Relay: see "Check Valve Relay."

Check Valve: a device located in the liquid line or inlet to the drier. The valve prevents liquid refrigerant from flowing the opposite way when the unit is shut off.

Check Valve Relay: an electrical switch to control a solenoid operated check valve.

Chemical Instability: an undesirable condition caused by the presence of contaminants in the refrigeration system.

Circuit Breaker: a bimetallic device used instead of a fuse to protect a circuit.

Clutch: a coupling device which transfers torque from a driving to a driven member when desired.

Clutch Armature: that part of the clutch that is pulled in when engaged.

Clutch Coil: see "Clutch Field."

Clutch Field: consists of many windings of wire and is fastened to the front of the compressor. Current applied to the field sets up a magnetic field that pulls the armature in to engage the clutch.

Clutch Plate: a component of General Motors' clutches prior to 1961; referred to as *ball and ramp clutch.*

Clutch Rotor: that portion of the clutch in which the belt rides. The rotor is freewheeling until the clutch is engaged. On some clutches the field is found in the rotor and the electrical connection is made by the use of brushes.

Cold: the absence of heat.

Comfortron: another name for an automatic temperature control.

Compound gauge: a gauge that registers both pressure and vacuum; used on the low-side of the systems.

Compressor: a component of the refrigeration system that pumps refrigerant and increases the pressure of the refrigerant vapor.

Compressor Discharge Pressure Switch: a pressure-operated electrical switch that opens the compressor clutch circuit during high-pressure conditions.

Compressor Displacement: a value obtained by multiplying the displacement of the compressor cylinder or cylinders by a given rpm, usually the average engine speed of 30 mph, or 1,750 rpm.

Compressor Shaft Seal: an assembly consisting of springs, snap rings, 0-rings, shaft seal, seal sets, and gasket. The shaft seal is mounted on the compressor crankshaft and permits the shaft to be turned without a loss of refrigerant or oil.

Condensate: water taken from the air; the water forms on the exterior surface of the evaporator.

Condensation: the process of changing a vapor to a liquid.

Condenser: the component of a refrigeration system in which refrigerant vapor is changed to a liquid by the removal of heat.

Condenser Comb: a comb-like device used to straighten the fins on the evaporator or condenser.

Condenser Temperature: the temperature at which compressed gas in the condenser changes from a gas to a liquid.

Condensing Pressure: head pressure as read from the gauge at the high-side service valve; the pressure from the discharge side of the compressor to the condenser.

Conduction: the transmission of heat through a solid.

Conduction of Heat: the ability of a substance to conduct heat.

Contaminants: anything other than refrigerant and refrigeration oil in the system.

Control Head: the master controls (such as temperature and fan speed) which the driver uses to select the desired system condition.

Convection: the transfer of heat by the circulation of a vapor or liquid.

Custom System: a deluxe automotive air-conditioning system that uses both inside and outside air.

Cutoff Switch: an electrical switch which is pressure or temperature operated. The switch is used to interrupt the compressor clutch circuit during certain low- or high-pressure conditions.

Cycling Clutch System: a system which uses a thermostatically controlled clutch as a means of temperature control.

Cylinder: a circular drum used to store refrigerant.

D

Declutching Fan: an engine cooling fan mounted on the water pump. A temperature sensitive device is provided to govern or limit terminal speed.

Deice Switch: a switch used to control the compressor operation to prevent evaporator freezeup.

Delay Relay: see "Time-delay relay."

Density: the weight or mass of a gas, liquid, or solid.

Desiccant: a drying agent used in refrigeration systems to remove excess moisture.

Design Working Pressure: the maximum allowable working pressure for which a specific system component is designed to work safely.

Deoxidized: a tubing or metal surface that is free of oxide formations, which are caused by the action of air or other chemicals.

Diagnosis: the procedure followed to locate the cause of a malfunction.

Diaphragm: a rubber-like piston or bellows assembly which divides the inner and outer chambers of back pressure-regulated air-conditioning control devices.

Dichlorodifluoromethane: see "Refrigerant 12."

Discharge: bleeding some or all of the refrigerant from a system by opening a valve or connection and permitting the refrigerant to escape slowly.

Discharge Air: conditioned air as it passes through the outlets and enters the passenger compartment.

Discharge Line: connects the compressor outlet to the condenser inlet.

Discharge Pressure: pressure of the refrigerant being discharged from the compressor; also known as the high-side pressure.

Discharge Pressure Switch: see "Compressor Discharge Pressure Switch."

Discharge Side: that portion of the refrigeration system under high pressure, extending from the compressor outlet to the thermostatic expansion valve inlet.

Discharge Valve: see "High-Side Service Valve."

Displacement: in automotive air conditioning, this term refers to the compressor stroke X-bore.

Distributor: a device used to divide the flow of liquid refrigerant between parallel paths in an evaporator.

Double Flare: a flare on the end of a piece of copper tubing or other soft metal; the tubing is folded over to form a double face.

Drier: a device containing dessicant; a drier is placed in the liquid line to absorb moisture in the system.

Drive Pulley: a V-pulley attached to the crankshaft of an automobile; this pulley drives the compressor clutch pulley through the use of a belt.

Drip Pan: a shallow pan, located under the evaporator core, used to catch condensation. A drain hose is fastened to the drip pan and extends to the outside to carry off the condensate.

Drying Agent: see "Desiccant."

Duct: a passageway for the transfer of air from one point to another.

E

Engine Idle Compensator: a thermostatically controlled device on the carburetor which prevents stalling during prolonged hot weather periods while the air conditioner is operated.

Engine Thermal Switch: an electrical switch designed to delay the operation of the system in cool weather to allow time for the engine coolant to warm up.

EPR: see "Evaporator Pressure Regulator."

Equalizer Line: a line or connection used specifically to obtain the required operation from certain control valves. Very little, if any, refrigerant flows through this line.

ETR: see "Evaporator Temperature Regulator."

Evacuate: to create a vacuum within a system to remove all trace of air and moisture.

Evaporation: the process of changing from a liquid to a vapor.

Evaporator: the component of an air-conditioning system that conditions the air.

Evaporator Control Valve: can refer to any of the several types of evaporator suction pressure control valves or devices that are used to regulate the evaporator temperature by controlling the evaporator pressure.

Evaporator Core: the tube and fin assembly located inside the evaporator housing. The refrigerant fluid picks up heat in the evaporator core when it changes into a vapor.

Evaporator Housing: the cabinet, or case, that contains the evaporator core. Often, the diverter doors, duct outlets, and blower mounting arrangement are found on the housing.

Evaporator Pressure Regulator: a back-pressure-regulated temperature control device used by Chrysler products.

Evaporator Temperature Regulator: a temperature regulated device used by Chrysler Air-Temp to control the evaporator pressure.

Expansion Tube: a metering device, used at the inlet of some evaporators, to control the flow of liquid refrigerant into the evaporator core.

Expansion Valve: see "Thermostatic Expansion Valve."

External Equalizer: see "Equalizer Line."

F

Fahrenheit: a thermometer scale using 32° as the freezing point of water; the boiling point of water is 212°F.

Fan: a device having two or more blades attached to the shaft of a motor. The fan is mounted in the evaporator and causes air to pass over the evaporator. A fan is also a device having four or more blades, mounted on the water pump, which causes air to pass through the radiator and condenser.

Field: a coil with many turns of wire located behind the clutch rotor. Current passing through this coil sets up a magnetic field and causes the clutch to engage.

Filter: a device used with the drier or as a separate unit to remove foreign material from the refrigerant.

Fitz-All: a can tap designed to be used on screw top and flat top refrigerant cans.

Flare: a flange or cone-shaped end applied to a piece of tubing to provide a means of fastening to a fitting.

Flash Gas: gas resulting from the instantaneous evaporation of refrigerant in a presssure-reducing device such as an expansion valve.

Flooding: a condition caused by too much liquid refrigerant being metered into the evaporator.

Fluid: a liquid, free of gas or vapor.

Flush: to remove solid particles such as metal flakes or dirt. Refrigerant passages are purged with refrigerant.

Flux: a substance used in the joining of metals when heat is applied to promote the fusion of metals.

Foaming: the formation of a froth of oil and refrigerant due to the rapid boiling out of the refrigerant dissolved in the oil when the pressure is suddenly reduced.

Foot-pound: a unit of energy required to raise one pound a distance of one foot.

Freeze Protection: controlling evaporator temperature so that moisture on its surface does not freeze and block the air flow.

Freezeup: failure of a unit to operate properly due to the formation of ice at the expansion valve.

Freezing Point: the temperature at which a given liquid solidifies. Water freezes at $32°F$; this value is its freezing point.

Freon: registered trademark of E.I. Dupont.

Freon 12: see "Refrigerant 12."

Front Idler: a V-groove pulley used in automotive air conditioning as a means of tightening the drive belt. The belt rides in the V-groove pulley.

Front Seat: closing of the compressor service valves by turning them as far as possible in the clockwise direction.

Front Seating: closing off the line leaving the compressor open to the service port fitting. This allows service to the compressor without purging the entire system. Never operate the system with the valves front seated.

Frosting Back: the appearance of frost on the tailpipe and suction line extending back as far as the compressor.

Fuse: An electrical device used to protect a circuit against accidental overload or unit malfunction.

Fusion: the act of melting.

G

Gas: a vapor having no particles or droplets of liquid.

Gauge Manifold: see "Manifold."

Gauge Set: two or more instruments attached to a manifold and used for measuring or testing pressure.

Genetron 12: registered trademark of Allied Chemicals Company (Refrigerant 12).

H

Halide Leak Detector: a device consisting of a tank of acetylene gas, a stove, chimney, and search hose used to detect leaks by visual means.

Headliner: that part of the automobile interior overhead or covering the roof inside. Some early air conditioners had ductwork in the headliner.

Head Pressure: Pressure of the refrigerant from the discharge reed valve through the lines and condenser to the expansion valve orifice.

Heat: energy; any temperature above absolute zero.

Heat Exchanger: an apparatus in which heat is transferred from one fluid to another, on the principle that heat moves to an object with less heat.

Heat Intensity: the measurement of heat concentration with a thermometer.

Heat Quantity: the amount of heat as measured on a thermometer. See "British Thermal Unit."

Heat Radiation: the transmission of heat from one substance to another while passing through, but not heating, intervening substances.

Heat of Respiration: the heat given off by ripening vegetables or fruits in the conversion of starches and sugars.

Heat Transmission: any flow of heat.

Heliarc: the act of joining two pieces of aluminum or stainless steel using a high-frequency electric weld and an inert gas, such as helium. This weld is made electrically while the inert gas is fed around the weld. This gas prevents oxidation by keeping the surrounding air away from the metals being welded.

Hg: chemical symbol for mercury (used to identify a vacuum).

High Head: a term used when the head (high-side) pressure of the system is excessive.

High-load Condition: those instances when the air conditioner must operate continuously at its maximum capacity to provide the cool air required.

High-pressure Cutout Switch: an electrical switch that is activated by a predetermined high pressure. The switch opens a circuit during high-pressure periods.

High-pressure Lines: the lines from the compressor outlet to the expansion valve inlet: these lines carry high-pressure liquid and gas.

High-pressure Relief Valve: a mechanical device designed so that it releases the extreme high pressures of the system to the atmosphere.

High Side: see "Discharge Side."

High-side Service Valve: a device located on the discharge side of the compressor; this valve permits the service technician to check the high-side pressures and perform other necessary operations.

High Suction: the low-side pressure is higher than normal due to a malfunction of the system.

High Vacuum: a vacuum below 500 microns or 0.5 mm Hg.

High-vacuum Pump: a two-stage vacuum pump that has the capability of pulling below 500 microns. Many vacuum pumps can pull to 25 microns, or 29.999 in. of mercury.

Hot Gas: the condition of the refrigerant as it leaves the compressor until it gives up its heat and condenses.

Hot Gas Bypass Line: the line that connects the hot gas bypass valve outlet to the evaporator outlet. Metered hot gas flows through this line.

Hot Gas Bypass Valve: a device used to meter hot gas back to the evaporator through the bypass line to prevent condensate from freezing on the core.

Hot Gas Defrosting: the use of high-pressure gas in the evaporator to remove frost.

Humidity: see "Moisture."

Hydrolizing Action: the corrosive action within the air-conditioning system induced by a weak solution of hydrochloric acid formed by excessive moisture chemically reacting with the refrigerant.

I

Ice Melting Capacity: refrigerant equal to the latent heat of fusion of a stated weight of ice at 144 Btu per pound.

Ideal Humidity: a relative humidity of 50%.

Ideal Temperature: temperature from 68° to 72°F.

Idler: a pulley device that keeps the belt whip out of the drive belt of an automotive air conditioner. The idler is used as a means of tightening the belt.

Idler Eccentric: a device used with the idler pulley as a means of tightening the belt.

In-car Sensor: a thermistor used in automatic temperature control units for sensing the in-car temperature. Also, see "Thermistor."

Inches of Mercury: a unit of measure when referring to a vacuum.

Inch-pound: a unit of energy required to raise one pound a distance of one inch.

In-duct Sensor: a thermistor used in automatic temperature control units for sensing the in-duct return air temperature. Also, see "Thermistor."

Insulate: to isolate or seal off with a nonconductor.

Insulation Tape: tape (either rubber or cork) that is used to wrap refrigeration hoses and lines to prevent condensate drip.

Isotron 12: a trademark of Penn Salt Company (Refrigerant 12).

K

Kinetic: referring to motion.

Kelvin: a thermometer scale using $273°K$ as the freezing point of water. Absolute zero is the beginning of this temperature scale: $0°K$ or $-459.67°F$.

L

Latent Heat: the amount of heat required to cause a change of state of a substance without changing its temperature.

Latent Heat of Condensation: the quantity of heat given off while changing a substance from vapor to a liquid.

Latent Heat of Evaporation: the quantity of heat required to change a liquid into a vapor without raising the temperature of the vapor above that of the original liquid.

Latent Heat of Fusion: the amount of heat that must be removed from a liquid to cause it to change to a solid without causing a change of temperature.

Latent Heat of Vaporization: see "Latent Heat of Evaporation."

Leak Detector: see "Halide Leak Detector."

Liquid: a column of fluid without gas pockets or solids.

Liquid Line: the line connecting the drier outlet with the expansion valve inlet. The line from the condenser outlet to the drier inlet is sometimes called a liquid line.

Load: the required rate of heat removed in a given time.

Low-head Pressure: the high-side pressure is lower than normal due to a malfunction of the system.

Low-pressure Cutout Switch: an electrical switch that is activated by a predetermined low pressure. This switch opens a circuit during certain low-pressure periods.

Low Side: see "Suction Side."

Low-side Service Valve: a device located on the suction side of the compressor which allows the service technician to check low-side pressures or perform other necessary service operations.

Low-suction Pressure: pressure lower than normal in the suction side of the system due to a malfunction of the unit.

Lubricant: a lubricating material such as grease or oil; see "Refrigeration Oil."

M

Magnetic Clutch: a coupling device used to turn the compressor on and off electrically.

Manifold: a device equipped with a hand shutoff valve. Gauges are connected to the manifold for use in system testing and servicing.

Manifold Gauge: a calibrated instrument used to measure pressures in the system.

Manifold Gauge Set: a manifold complete with gauges and charging hoses.

Mean Altitude: 900 feet is used as the mean, or average, altitude by engineers.

Melting Point: the temperature above which a material cannot exist as a solid at a given pressure.

Mercury: see "Hg."

Micron: a unit of measure; 1,000 microns = 1 mm = 0.03937 in.

Millimeter: a unit of measure; 1 millimeter = 1/1,000 meter (m).

Mobil Sorbead: a desiccant used in General Motor's driers.

Molecular Sieve: a drying agent. See "Desiccant."

Monochlorodifluoromethane: see "Refrigerant 12."

Motor: an electrical device which produces a continuous turning motion. A motor is used to propel a fan blade or a blower wheel.

Mount and Drive: pulleys, mounting plates, belts, and fittings necessary to mount a compressor and clutch assembly on an engine.

Muffler: a hollow tubular device used in the discharge line of some air conditioners to minimize the compressor noise transmitted to the inside of the car. Some units use a muffler on the low side as well.

O

Oil: an organic chemical used as a lubricant. A specially formulated oil is used in air-conditioning systems.

Oil Bleed Line: an external line that usually bypasses an expansion valve, evaporator pressure regulator, or bypass valve to insure positive oil return to the compressor at high compressor speeds and under a low charge or clogged system condition.

Oil Bleed Passage: internal orifice that bypasses an expansion valve, evaporator pressure regulator, or bypass valve to insure a positive oil return to the compressor.

Operational Test: see "Performance Test."

Overcharge: indicates that too much refrigerant or refrigeration oil is added to the system.

Oxidize: the formation of a crust on certain metals due to the reaction of the metal, heat, and oxygen.

P

Package Tray: shelf behind the rear seat in a sedan. Trunk mounted air-conditioner units use ducts through the package tray as the intake and outlets of the unit.

Performance Test: readings of the temperature and pressure under controlled conditions to determine if an air-conditioning system is operating at full efficiency.

Pickup Tube: a tube extending from the outlet of the receiver almost to the bottom of the tank to insure that 100% liquid is supplied to the liquid line or expansion valve.

Pilot-operated Evaporator Pressure Regulator: an EPR valve that is regulated by an internal pilot valve pressure.

Plenum Blower Assembly: located on the engine side of the fire wall, this assembly contains air ducts, air valves, and a blower that permits the selection of air from the outside or inside of the car and directs it to the evaporator or to the heater core if desired.

POASTV: see "Positive Absolute Suction Throttling Valve."

POA Valve: see "Positive Absolute Suction Throttling Valve."

POEPR: the abbreviation for pilot-operated evaporator pressure regulator.

Positive Absolute Suction Throttling Valve: a suction throttling valve used by Frigidaire. This valve has a bronze bellows under a nearly perfect vacuum which is not affected by atmospheric pressure.

Pounds Per Square Inch Absolute: atmospheric pressure which is not compensated for altitude or other variables.

Power Servo: a servo unit used in automatic temperature control which is operated by a vacuum or an electrical signal.

Pressure: force per unit of area; the pressure of refrigerant is measured in pounds per square inch.

Pressure Drop: the difference in pressure between any two points; a pressure drop may be caused by a restriction or friction.

Pressure Sensing Line: see "Remote Bulb."

Pressure Switch: an electrical switch that is actuated by a predetermined low or high pressure. A pressure switch is generally used for system protection.

Prestone 12: a tradename of the Union Carbon and Carbide Chemical Company (Refrigerant 12).

Primary Seal: a seal between the compressor shaft seal and the shaft to prevent the leakage of refrigerant and oil.

Programmer: that part of an automatic temperature control system that controls the blower speed, air mix doors, and vacuum diaphragms.

Propane: a flammable gas used in the halide leak detector.

Psi: abbreviation for pounds per square inch.

Psia: abbreviation for pounds per square inch, absolute.

Psig: abbreviation for pounds per square inch, gauge.

Psychrometer: see "Sling Psychrometer."

Pulley: a flat wheel with a V-groove machined around the outer edge; when attached to the drive and driven members, the pulley provides a means of driving the compressor.

Pump: the compressor. Also refers to the vacuum pump.

Pumpdown: see "Evacuate."

Purge: to remove moisture and air from a system or a component by flushing with a dry gas refrigerant.

R

Radiation: the transfer of heat without heating the medium through which it is transmitted.

Ranco Control: a tradename used when referring to a thermostat. See "Thermostat."

Rankine: a thermometer scale for which the freezing point of water is $492°R$. Absolute zero is the beginning of this thermometer scale.

Ram Air: air that is forced through the condenser coils by the movement of the vehicle or the action of the fan.

Receiver: a container for the storage of liquid refrigerant.

Receiver/Dehydrator: a combination container for the storage of liquid refrigerant and a desiccant.

Receiver/Drier: see "Receiver/Dehydrator."

Reciprocating Compressor: a positive displacement compressor with pistons that travel back and forth in a cylinder.

Reed Valves: thin leaves of screen located in the valve plate of automotive compressors; these leaves act as suction and discharge valves. The suction valve is located on the bottom of the valve plate and the discharge valve is on top.

Refrigerant: the chemical compound used in a refrigeration system to produce the desired cooling.

Refrigerant 12: the refrigerant used in automotive air conditioners. The chemical name of Refrigerant 12 is dichlorodifluoromethane. The chemical symbol is CCl_2F_2.

Refrigerant 22: a refrigerant used in some early automotive applications. Refrigerant 22 is not used today because of high pressures. The chemical name and symbol of this refrigerant are: monochlorodifluoromethane and $CHClF_2$.

Refrigeration Cycle: the complete cycle of the refrigerant back to the starting point, evidenced by temperature and pressure changes.

Refrigeration Oil: highly refined oil free from all contaminants, such as sulfur, moisture, and tars.

Relative Humidity: the actual moisture content of the air in relation to the total moisture that the air can hold at a given temperature.

Relay: an electrical switch device that is activated by a low-current source and controls a high-current device.

Remote Bulb: a sensing device connected to the expansion valve by a capillary tube. This device senses the tailpipe temperature and transmits pressure to the expansion valve for its proper operation.

Resistor: a voltage dropping device, usually wire wound, which provides a means of controlling fan speeds.

Restriction: a blockage in the air-conditioning system caused by a pinched or crimped line, foreign matter, or moisture freezeup.

Restrictor: an insert fitting or device used to control the flow of refrigerant or refrigeration oil.

Rheostat: a wire-wound variable resistor used to control blower motor speeds.

Rotor: the rotating or freewheeling portion of a clutch; the belt rides on the rotor.

S

Saddlebag: air chambers or openings in the left and right front corners of the car body between the kickpads and the exterior of the car. The General Motors' evaporator is usually located in the right saddlebag.

Saturated Vapor: saturation indicates that the space holds as much vapor as possible. No further vaporization is possible at this particular temperature.

Saturated Temperature: the boiling point of a refrigerant at a particular pressure.

Schrader Valve: a spring-loaded valve similar to a tire valve. The Schrader valve is located inside the service valve fitting and is used on some control devices to hold refrigerant in the system. Special adapters must be used with the gauge hose to allow access to the system.

Screen: a metal mesh located in the receiver, expansion valve, and compressor inlet to prevent particles of dirt from circulating through the system.

Sensible Heat: heat that causes a change in the temperature of a substance, but does not change the state of the substance.

Sensor: a temperature-sensitive unit such as a remote bulb or thermistor. See "Remote Bulb" and "Thermistor."

Service Port: a quarter-inch fitting on the service valves and some control devices; the manifold set charging hoses are connected to this fitting.

Service Valve: see "High-side (Low-side) Service Valve."

Shaft Seal: see "Compressor Shaft Seal."

Short Cycling: can be caused by poor air circulation or a maladjusted thermostat. The unit runs for very short periods.

Sight Glass: a window in the liquid line or in the top of the drier; this window is used to observe the liquid refrigerant flow.

Silica Gel: a drying agent used in many automotive air conditioners because of its ability to absorb large quantities of water.

Silver Solder: an alloy of silver containing from 35% to 45% silver. Silver solder melts at $1120°F$ and flows at $1145°F$. Ideal material for use in refrigeration service.

Sling Psychrometer: a device using mercury-filled thermometers to obtain the relative humidity reading.

Slugging: the return of liquid refrigerant or oil to the compressor.

Soft Solder 50/50: a metallic alloy of 50% tin and 50% lead; used to repair or join ferrous metal parts for temperatures up to 250°F. Not recommended for refrigeration service.

Soft Solder 95/05: a metallic alloy of 95% tin and 5% antimony; used to repair or join ferrous metal parts for temperatures below 350°F. After used for refrigeration service.

Solder: a metallic alloy used to unite metals.

Solenoid Valve: an electromagnetic valve controlled remotely by energizing and de-energizing a coil.

Solid: a state of matter that is not liquid and is not a gas or vapor.

Sorbead: a desiccant.

Specifications: information provided by the manufacturer that describes an air-conditioning system function.

Specific Heat: the quantity of heat required to change one pound of a substance by one degree Fahrenheit.

Squirrel Cage: a blower case designed for use with the squirrel cage blower.

Squirrel Cage Blower: a blower wheel designed to provide a large volume of air with a minimum of noise. The blower is more compact than the fan and air can be directed more efficiently.

Standard Ton: see "Ton."

Strainer: see "Screen."

STV: see "Suction Throttling Valve."

Subcooler: a section of liquid line used to insure that only liquid refrigerant is delivered to the expansion valve. This line may be a part of the condenser or may be placed in the drip pan of the evaporator.

Substance: any form of matter.

Suction Line: the line connecting the evaporator outlet to the compressor inlet.

Suction Line Regulator: see "Suction Throttling Valve" or "Evaporator Pressure Regulator."

Suction Service Valve: see "Low-side Service Valve."

Suction Side: that portion of the refrigeration system under low pressure; the suction side extends from the expansion valve to the compressor inlet.

Suction Throttling Valve: a back-pressure-regulated device that prevents the freezeup of the evaporator core; used by General Motors Corporation.

Suction Pressure: compressor inlet pressure. Reflects the pressure of the system on the low side.

Super Heat: adding heat intensity to a gas after the complete evaporation of a liquid.

Superheated Vapor: vapor at a temperature higher than its boiling point for a given pressure.

Superheat Switch: an electrical switch activated by an abnormal temperature-pressure condition (a superheated vapor); used for system protection.

Swaging: a means of shaping soft tubing so that two pieces of the same size of tubing can be joined without the use of a fitting. The inside diameter of one tube is increased to accept the outside diameter of the other tube.

Sweat: the use of a soft solder to join two pieces of tubing or fittings using heat.

Sweat Fitting: a fitting designed to be used in sweating.

Sweeping: see "Purge."

System: all of the components and lines that make up an air-conditioning system.

T

Tailpipe: the outlet pipe from the evaporator to the compressor. See "Suction Line."

Taps All Valve: see "Fits All Valve."

Temperature: heat intensity measured on a thermometer.

Temperature Regulated Valve: see "Hot Gas Bypass Valve."

Thermal Fuse: a temperature-sensitive fuse link designed so that it melts at a certain temperature and opens a circuit.

Thermistor: a temperature-sensing resistor that has the ability to change values with changing temperature.

Thermostat: a device used to cycle the clutch to control the rate of refrigerant flow as a means of temperature control. The driver has control over the temperature desired.

Thermostatic Expansion Valve: the component of a refrigeration system that regulates the rate of flow of refrigerant into the evaporator as governed by the action of the remote bulb sensing tail-pipe temperatures.

Thermostatic Switch: see "Thermostat."

Throttling Valve: see "Suction Throttling Valve" and "Evaporator Pressure Regulator."

Time-delay Relay: an electrical switch device that provides a time delay before closing (or opening).

Tinning: coating two surfaces to be joined with solder.

Ton of Refrigeration: the effect of melting one ton of ice in 24 hours. One ton equals cooling 12,000 Btu per hour.

Total Heat Load: in an automobile, the human heat load, plus the heat entering through the floor, glass, roof, and sides.

Torque: a turning force; for example, the force required to seal a connection; measured in foot-pounds (ft.-lb.) or inch-pounds (in.-lb.)

Trace: a colored dye (suitable for use in a refrigeration system) introduced to the system to detect leaks.

Transducer: a vacuum valve used to transfer the electrical signal from the amplifier into a vacuum signal. This vacuum signal regulates the power servo unit in automatic temperature control units.

Trunk Unit: an automotive air-conditioning evaporator that mounts in the trunk compartment and is ducted through the package tray.

U

Ucon: a tradename for refrigerant.

Undercharge: a system that is short of refrigerant; this condition results in improper cooling.

Unloading Solenoid: an electrically controlled valve for operating the throttling valve or bypass valve in some applications.

V

Vacuum: referring to a condition having less than atmospheric pressure; expressed in inches of mercury (in. Hg).

Vacuum Check Relay: a mechanical air-operated device that checks (closes off) a vacuum line to a pot whenever the manifold vacuum pressure falls below the applied vacuum pressure.

Vacuum Check Valve: an air-operated mechanical device that checks (closes) a vacuum line to the vacuum reserve tank whenever the manifold vacuum pressure falls below the reserve vacuum pressure.

Vacuum Hose: see "Vacuum Line."

Vacuum Line: a rubber tube used to transmit a vacuum reading from one point to another.

Vacuum Motor: a device designed to provide mechanical control by the use of a vacuum.

Vacuum Pot: see "Vacuum Motor."

Vacuum Power Unit: a device for operating the doors and valves of an air conditioner using a vacuum as a source of power.

Vacuum Pump: a mechanical device used to evacuate the refrigeration system to rid it of excess moisture and air.

Vacuum Reserve Tank: a metal container, resembling a large juice can, that is used to store reserve vacuum pressure.

Vacuum Tank: see "Vacuum Reserve Tank."

Valves-in-receiver (VIR): an assembly containing the expansion valve, suction throttling valve, desiccant, and receiver.

Vapor: see "Gas."

Vapor Lines: lines that are used to carry refrigerant gas or vapor.

V-belt: a rubber-like continuous loop placed between the engine crankshaft pulley and accessories to transfer rotary motion of the crankshaft to the accessory.

V-Pulley: used in automotive applications to drive the accessories, such as a water pump, generator, alternator, and power steering.

VIR: abbreviation for "valves in receiver."

Viscosity: the thickness of a liquid or its resistance to flow.

Volatile Liquid: a liquid that evaporates readily to become a vapor.

W

Water Control Valve: a mechanically or vacuum-operated shutoff valve that stops the flow of hot water to the heater.

Water Valve: see "Water Control Valve."

Woodruff Key: an index key that prevents a pulley from turning on a shaft.

...To Edward and Judith, this book is
dedicated

EDITORIAL

Marjorie A. Bruce   Source Editor
Mary V. Miller   Editorial Assistant

Particular thanks is expressed to Mr. Richard G. Herd, former Associate, Vocational-Industrial Education, State of New York for his initial assistance and encouragement; to Mr. George D. Moore, Lead Instructor of Automotive Technology, Ames College, Greeley, Colorado, and to Mr. Earl Pescatore, Automotive Specialist, Sheridan Vocational Center, Hollywood, Florida for their critical review of this revision.

This text would not have been possible without the generous cooperation of the many manufacturers of automotive air conditioners and components, whose materials are used to supplement this text.

Buick Motor Division, General Motors Corporation

Figures 22-14, 22-15, 22-16, SP18-2B, SP18-3B, SP18-6B, SP18-8B, SP18-10B, SP18-11B, SP45-17, SP45-18, SP45-19, SP45-20, SP45-21, SP45-22, SP45-23, SP45-24, SP46-20, SP46-21, SP46-22, SP46-23

Cadillac Motor Car Division, General Motors Corporation

Figures 21-10, 21-11, 21-12, 21-13, 21-14, 21-15, 21-16, 23-15, SP31-1, SP48-1, SP48-2, SP48-3, SP48-5, SP48-6

Chevrolet Motor Division, General Motors Corporation

Figures 17-4, 17-5, 17-6, 18-7, 21-7, 21-8, 22-10, 22-12, 22-13, 23-7, 23-9, 23-10, 23-11, 23-12, 23-14, SP1-1, SP2-1, SP3-1, SP4-2, SP6-2, SP9-1, SP18-1, SP18-2A, SP18-3A, SP18-4A, SP18-5A, SP18-6A, SP18-7A, SP18-9A, SP18-11A, SP18-12A, SP18-13A, SP22-2, SP26-1, SP26-2, SP26-3, SP26-4, SP27-1, SP45-1, SP45-2, SP45-3, SP45-4, SP45-5, SP45-6, SP45-7, SP45-8, SP45-9, SP45-10, SP45-11, SP45-12, SP45-13, SP45-14, SP45-15, SP45-16, SP46-1, SP46-2, SP46-3, SP46-4, SP46-5, SP46-6, SP46-7, SP46-8, SP46-9, SP46-10, SP46-11, SP46-12, SP46-13, SP46-14, SP46-15, SP46-16, SP46-17, SP46-18, SP46-19, SP47-1, SP48-4

Chrysler Motors Corporation

Figures 7-2, 9-1, 17-2, 21-3, SP12-1, SP17-1, SP17-2, SP17-3, SP24-1, SP35-1, SP35-2, SP35-3, SP44-1, SP44-2, SP44-3, SP44-4, SP44-5, SP44-6, SP44-7, SP44-8, SP44-9

Controls Company of America

Figures 9-5, 9-6, 18-2, 18-6, 18-9, SP32-4, SP32-5

Delco Radio Division, General Motors Corporation

Figure SP29-1

Everhot Products Company

Figure 23-1

Ford Motor Company

Figures SP36-1, SP36-2, SP36-3, SP36-4, SP36-5, SP36-6, SP36-7

General Electric Company

Figure 16-2

General Motors Corporation

Figures SP34-1, SP34-2

Mapco

Figure SP37-1

John E. Mitchell Company, Inc.

Figures 9-4, 9-11, 17-1, 18-1, 21-6

Murray Corporation

Figures SP47-2, SP49-1

Robinair Manufacturing Company

Figure 13-2

Sankyo

Figures SP20-1, SP20-2, SP20-3

Sears, Roebuck and Company

Figures 1-3, 1-4

Tecumseh Products Company

Figures 9-8, SP40-1, SP40-3, SP41-1, SP41-2

Thermal Industries

Figures 16-3, SP5-1

Uniweld Products, Inc.

Figures 15-9, 15-10

Warner Electric Brake and Clutch Company

Figures 20-4, SP23-1, SP23-2, SP23-3

York Corporation, Subsidiary of Borg-Warner Corporation

Figures SP14-1, SP14-2, SP14-3, SP14-4, SP19-2, SP39-2, SP39-3, SP39-4, SP39-5, SP39-6

Appreciation is expressed to the following companies for their permission to adapt material which is used in the indicated Service Procedures.

Service Procedure 29	Cadillac Motor Car Division and Oldsmobile Division, General Motors Corporation
Service Procedure 30	Cadillac Motor Car Division, General Motors Corporation
Service Procedure 31	Cadillac Motor Car Division and Oldsmobile Division, General Motors Corporation
Service Procedure 39	York Corporation
Service Procedures 40, 41	Tecumseh Products Company
Service Procedure 44	Chrysler Motor Corporation
Service Procedures 45, 46	Cadillac Motor Car Division, Buick Motor Division, and Oldsmobile Division, General Motors Corporation

INDEX

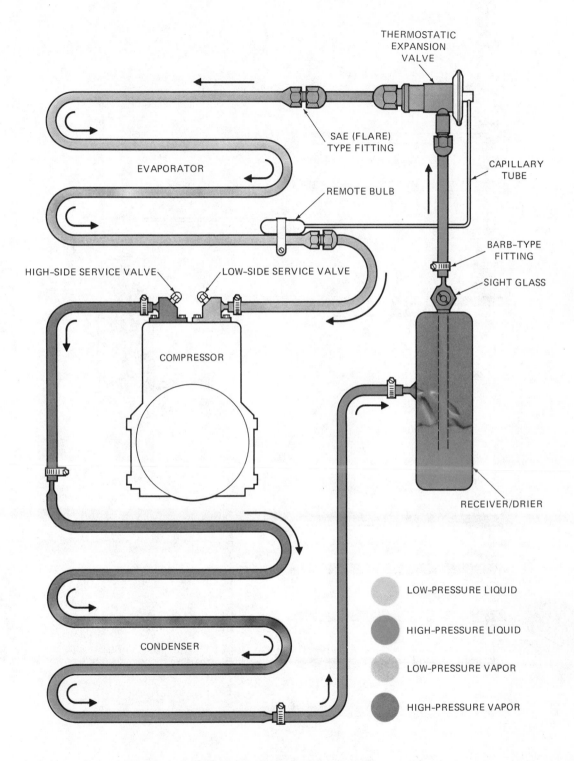

Plate 1. Normal system operation

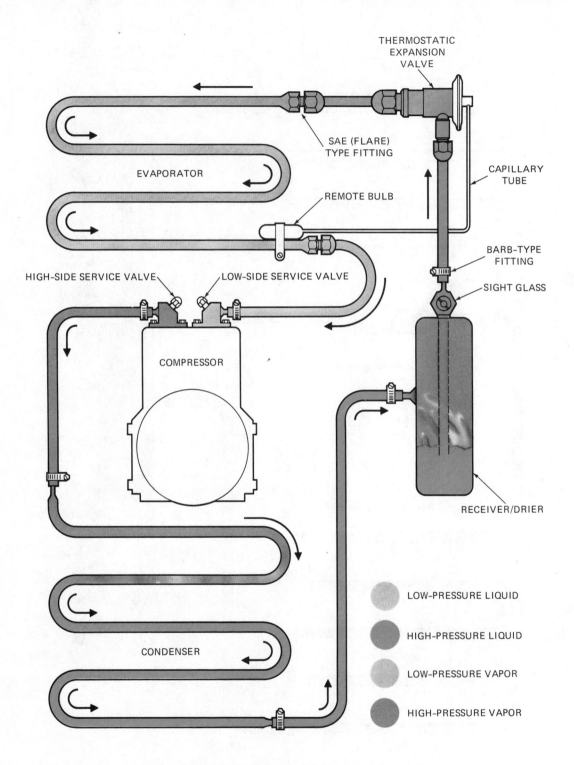

Plate 2. Evaporator flooding – defective expansion valve

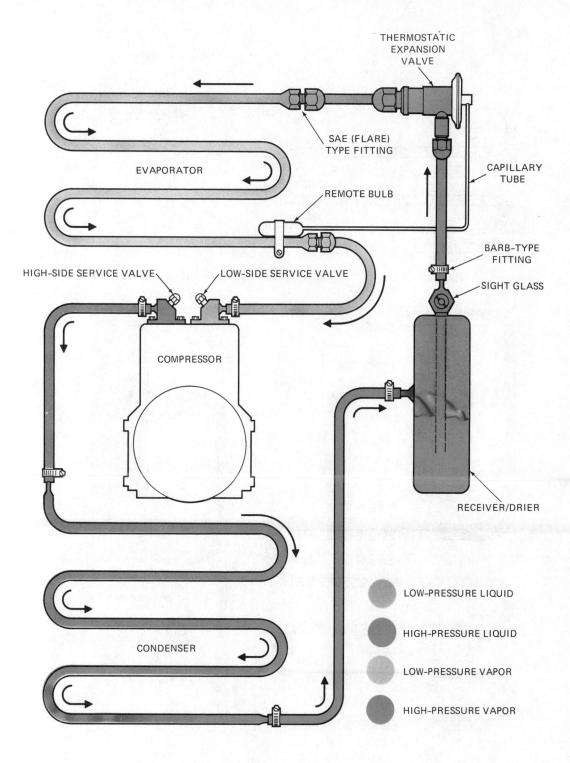

THERMOSTATIC
EXPANSION
VALVE

SAE (FLARE)
TYPE FITTING

EVAPORATOR

CAPILLARY
TUBE

REMOTE BULB

HIGH-SIDE SERVICE VALVE

LOW-SIDE SERVICE VALVE

BARB-TYPE
FITTING

SIGHT GLASS

COMPRESSOR

RECEIVER/DRIER

CONDENSER

LOW-PRESSURE LIQUID

HIGH-PRESSURE LIQUID

LOW-PRESSURE VAPOR

HIGH-PRESSURE VAPOR

Plate 3. Evaporator starving – defective expansion valve

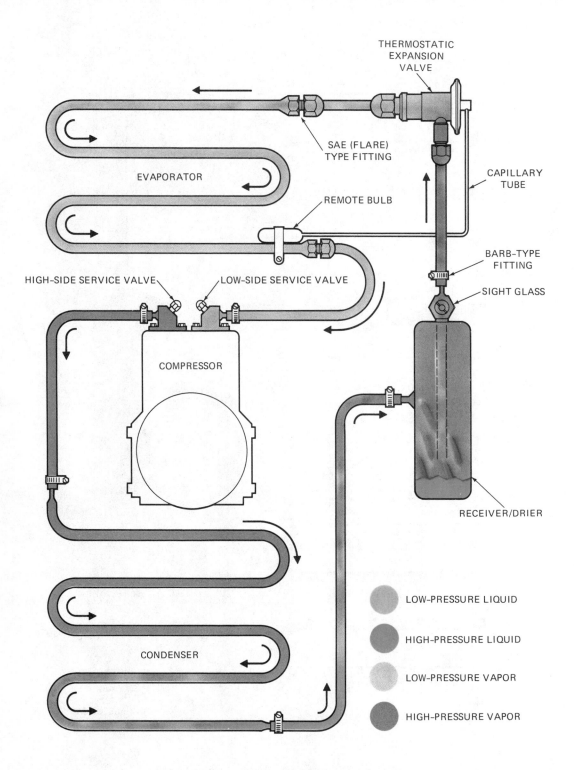

Plate 4. System undercharged with refrigerant

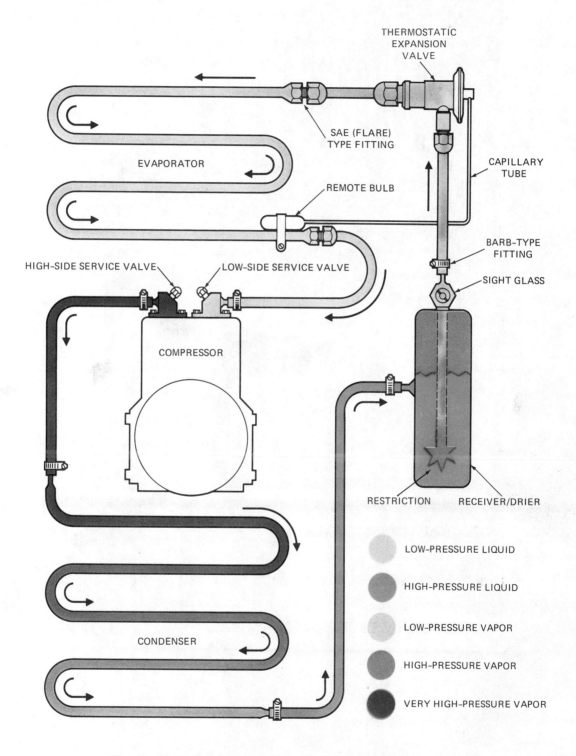

Plate 5. Restriction in receiver/drier (at pickup tube inlet strainer).

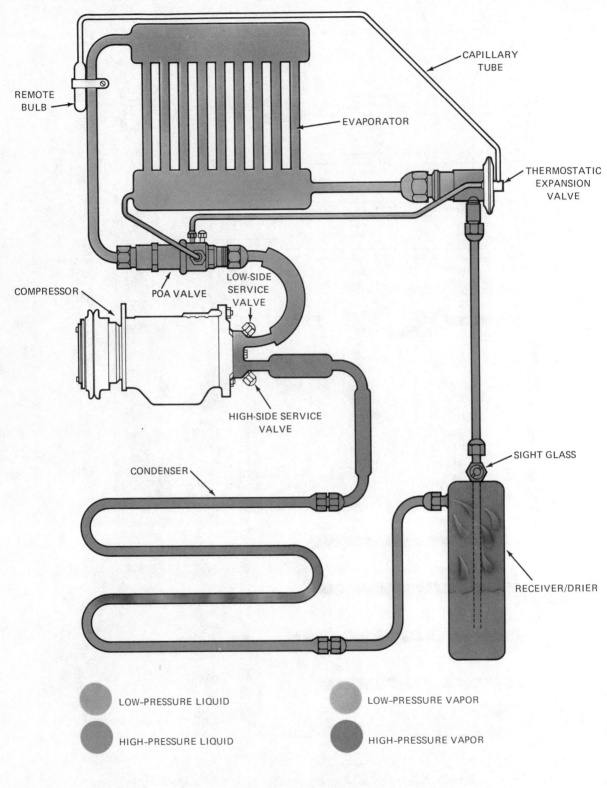

CAPILLARY TUBE

REMOTE BULB

EVAPORATOR

THERMOSTATIC EXPANSION VALVE

COMPRESSOR

POA VALVE

LOW-SIDE SERVICE VALVE

HIGH-SIDE SERVICE VALVE

SIGHT GLASS

CONDENSER

RECEIVER/DRIER

LOW-PRESSURE LIQUID

LOW-PRESSURE VAPOR

HIGH-PRESSURE LIQUID

HIGH-PRESSURE VAPOR

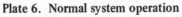

Plate 6. Normal system operation

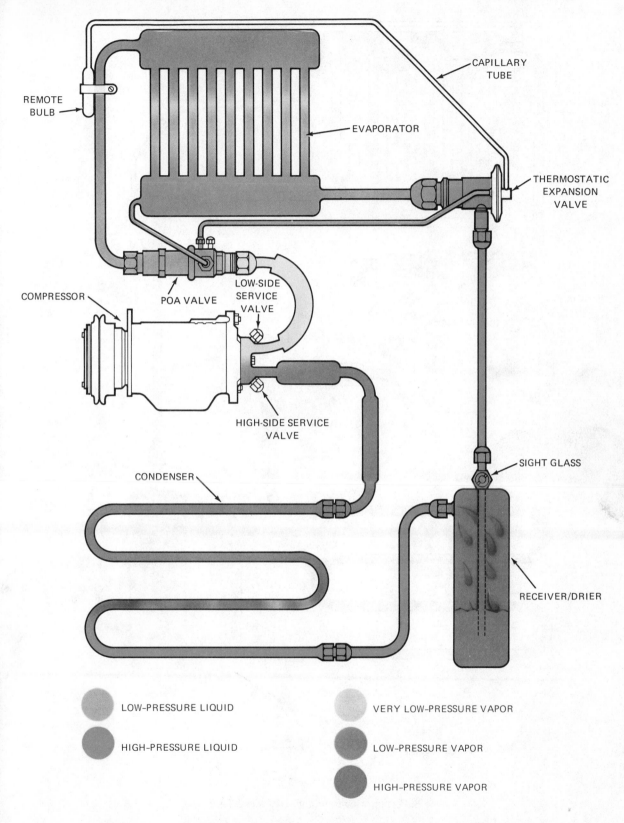

Plate 7. Evaporator flooding — defective STV

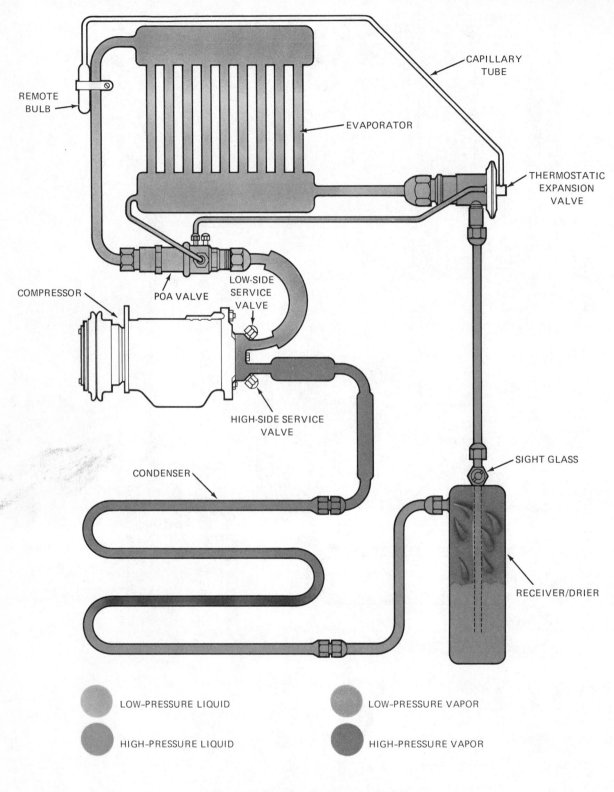

CAPILLARY TUBE

REMOTE BULB

EVAPORATOR

THERMOSTATIC EXPANSION VALVE

COMPRESSOR

POA VALVE

LOW-SIDE SERVICE VALVE

HIGH-SIDE SERVICE VALVE

CONDENSER

SIGHT GLASS

RECEIVER/DRIER

LOW-PRESSURE LIQUID

LOW-PRESSURE VAPOR

HIGH-PRESSURE LIQUID

HIGH-PRESSURE VAPOR

Plate 8. Evaporator flooding – defective TXV

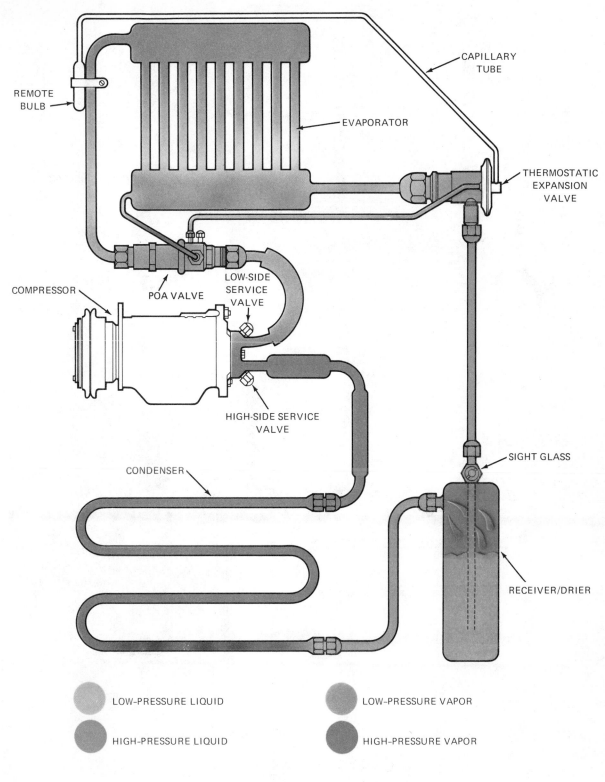

REMOTE BULB

CAPILLARY TUBE

EVAPORATOR

THERMOSTATIC EXPANSION VALVE

COMPRESSOR

POA VALVE

LOW-SIDE SERVICE VALVE

HIGH-SIDE SERVICE VALVE

CONDENSER

SIGHT GLASS

RECEIVER/DRIER

LOW-PRESSURE LIQUID

LOW-PRESSURE VAPOR

HIGH-PRESSURE LIQUID

HIGH-PRESSURE VAPOR

Plate 9. Evaporator starving – defective STV

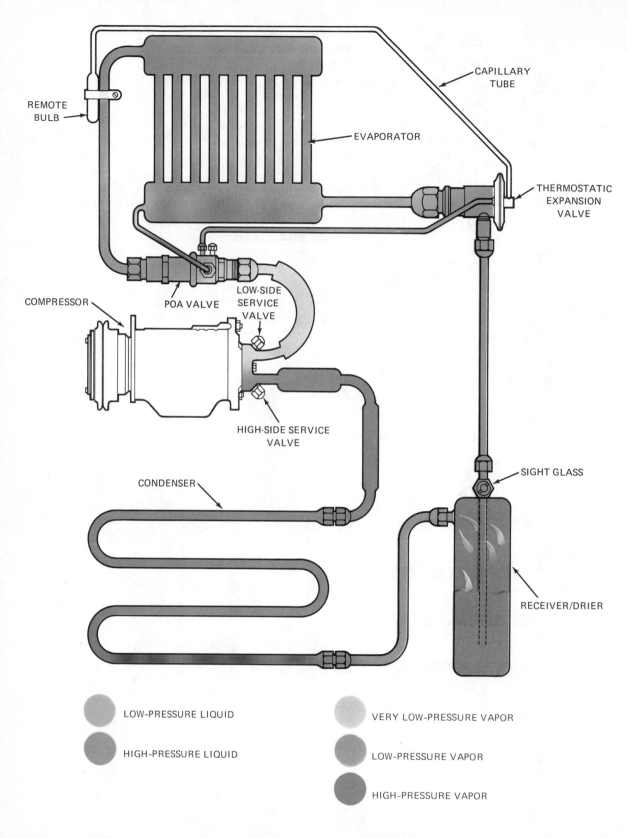

Plate 10. Evaporator starving – defective TXV

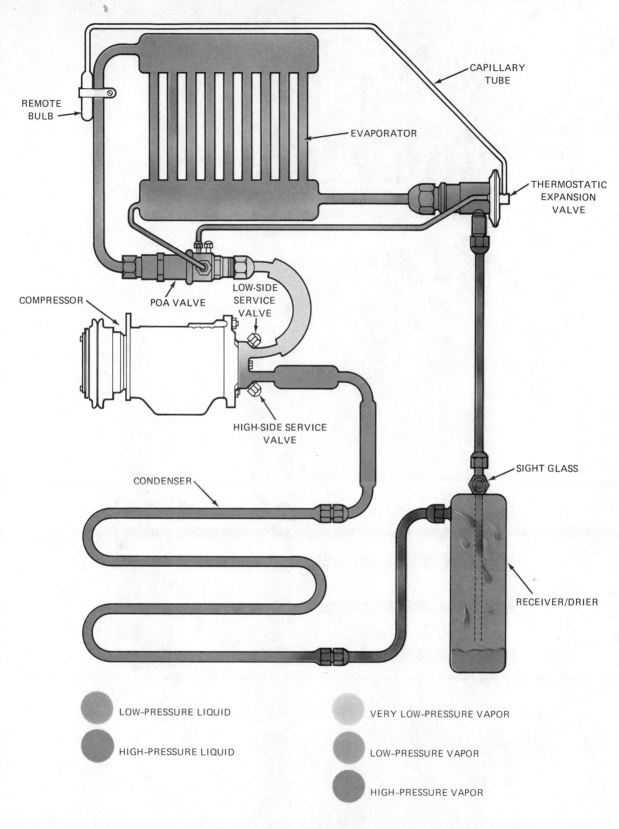

Plate 11. System undercharged

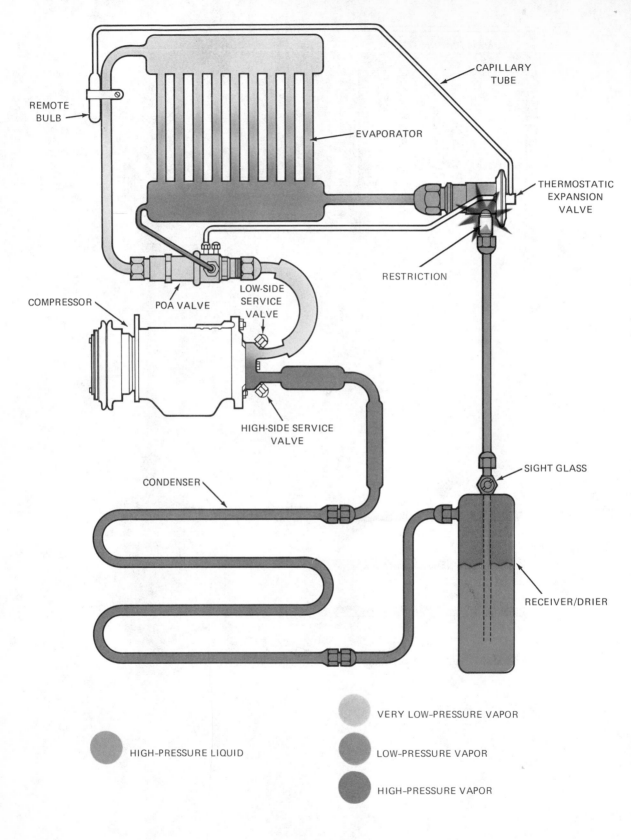

Plate 12. Restriction at TXV

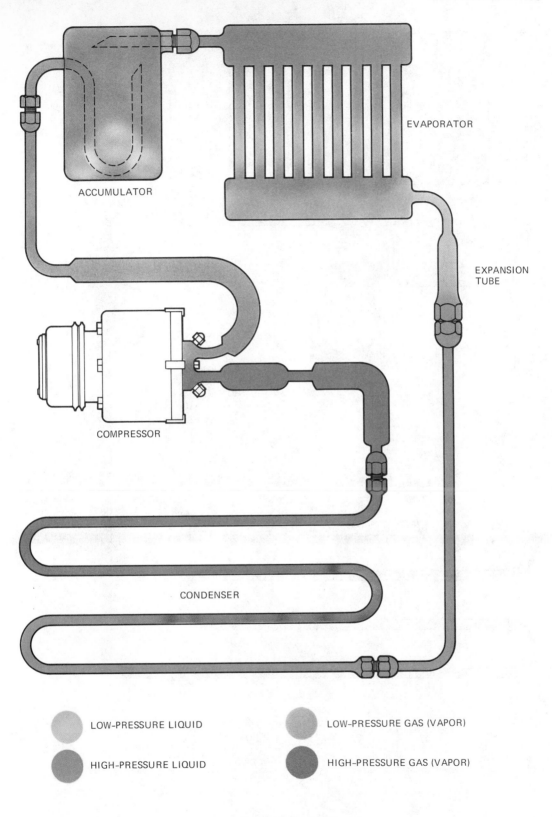

EVAPORATOR

ACCUMULATOR

EXPANSION
TUBE

COMPRESSOR

CONDENSER

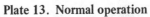

LOW-PRESSURE LIQUID

LOW-PRESSURE GAS (VAPOR)

HIGH-PRESSURE LIQUID

HIGH-PRESSURE GAS (VAPOR)

Plate 13. Normal operation

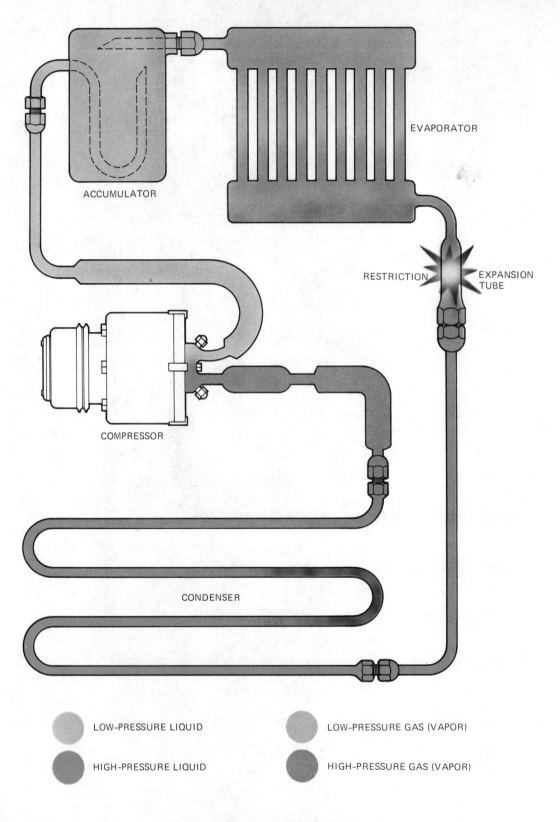

EVAPORATOR

ACCUMULATOR

RESTRICTION

EXPANSION TUBE

COMPRESSOR

CONDENSER

LOW-PRESSURE LIQUID

LOW-PRESSURE GAS (VAPOR)

HIGH-PRESSURE LIQUID

HIGH-PRESSURE GAS (VAPOR)

Plate 14. Restriction in the Expansion Tube

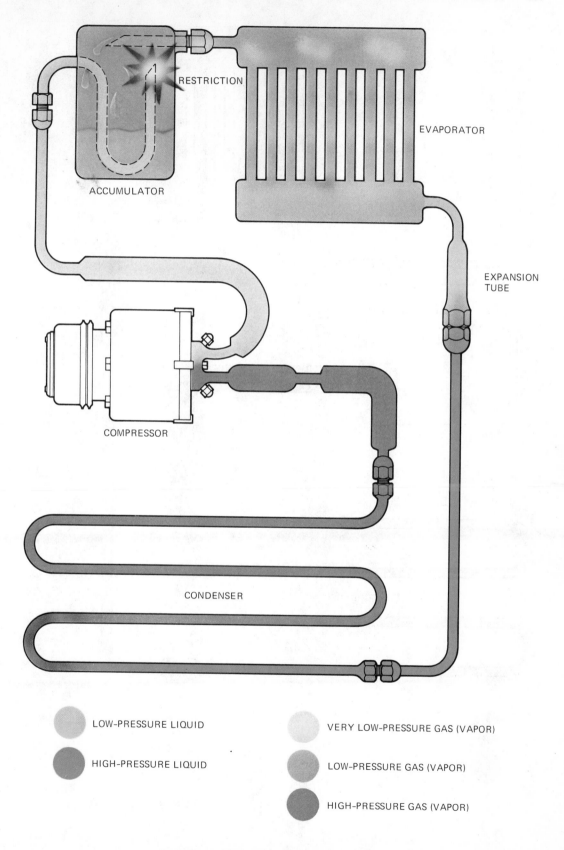

RESTRICTION

EVAPORATOR

ACCUMULATOR

EXPANSION
TUBE

COMPRESSOR

CONDENSER

LOW-PRESSURE LIQUID

HIGH-PRESSURE LIQUID

VERY LOW-PRESSURE GAS (VAPOR)

LOW-PRESSURE GAS (VAPOR)

HIGH-PRESSURE GAS (VAPOR)

Plate 15. Restriction in the Accumulator

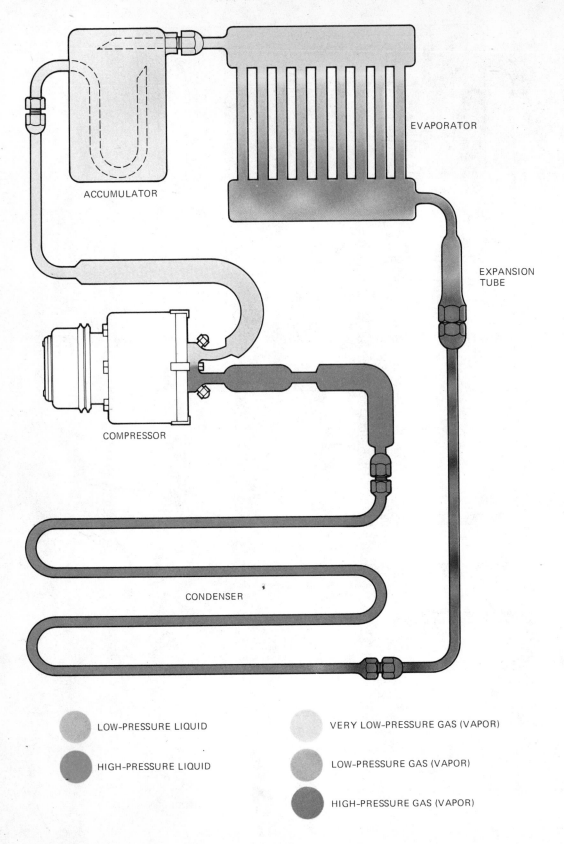

EVAPORATOR

ACCUMULATOR

EXPANSION
TUBE

COMPRESSOR

CONDENSER

LOW-PRESSURE LIQUID

HIGH-PRESSURE LIQUID

VERY LOW-PRESSURE GAS (VAPOR)

LOW-PRESSURE GAS (VAPOR)

HIGH-PRESSURE GAS (VAPOR)

Plate 16. Undercharge of refrigerant